Lecture Notes in Artificial Intelligence   7526

Subseries of Lecture Notes in Computer Science

LNAI Series Editors

Randy Goebel
   University of Alberta, Edmonton, Canada
Yuzuru Tanaka
   Hokkaido University, Sapporo, Japan
Wolfgang Wahlster
   DFKI and Saarland University, Saarbrücken, Germany

LNAI Founding Series Editor

Joerg Siekmann
   DFKI and Saarland University, Saarbrücken, Germany

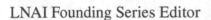

T0254719

Birte Glimm   Antonio Krüger (Eds.)

KI 2012: Advances in Artificial Intelligence

35th Annual German Conference on AI
Saarbrücken, Germany, September 24-27, 2012
Proceedings

 Springer

Series Editors

Randy Goebel, University of Alberta, Edmonton, Canada
Jörg Siekmann, University of Saarland, Saarbrücken, Germany
Wolfgang Wahlster, DFKI and University of Saarland, Saarbrücken, Germany

Volume Editors

Birte Glimm
University of Ulm, Institute of Artificial Intelligence
89069 Ulm, Germany
E-mail: birte.glimm@uni-ulm.de

Antonio Krüger
Saarland University and German Research Center for Artificial Intelligence (DFKI)
Stuhlsatzenhausweg 3, 66123 Saarbrücken, Germany
E-mail: krueger@dfki.de

ISSN 0302-9743   e-ISSN 1611-3349
ISBN 978-3-642-33346-0   e-ISBN 978-3-642-33347-7
DOI 10.1007/978-3-642-33347-7
Springer Heidelberg Dordrecht London New York

Library of Congress Control Number: 2012946346

CR Subject Classification (1998): I.2.4, I.2.6, I.2.10-11, H.3.3-4, I.6.3, H.5.2-3, H.5.5,
F.4.1, F.1.1

LNCS Sublibrary: SL 7 – Artificial Intelligence

© Springer-Verlag Berlin Heidelberg 2012
This work is subject to copyright. All rights are reserved, whether the whole or part of the material is
concerned, specifically the rights of translation, reprinting, re-use of illustrations, recitation, broadcasting,
reproduction on microfilms or in any other way, and storage in data banks. Duplication of this publication
or parts thereof is permitted only under the provisions of the German Copyright Law of September 9, 1965,
in its current version, and permission for use must always be obtained from Springer. Violations are liable
to prosecution under the German Copyright Law.
The use of general descriptive names, registered names, trademarks, etc. in this publication does not imply,
even in the absence of a specific statement, that such names are exempt from the relevant protective laws
and regulations and therefore free for general use.

Typesetting: Camera-ready by author, data conversion by Scientific Publishing Services, Chennai, India

Printed on acid-free paper

Springer is part of Springer Science+Business Media (www.springer.com)

Preface

The yearly German Conference on Artificial Intelligence is the premier forum for German research in artificial intelligence, and attracts numerous international guests, too. The KI conferences traditionally bring together academic and industrial researchers from all areas of AI and are a premier forum for exchanging news and research results on theory and applications of all aspects of AI.

KI 2012, the 35th event in this series, reflected this long-standing tradition, and continued to mirror the trends and developments of the science. KI 2012 was held on September 23–26, 2012 in Saarbrücken, Germany.

This volume contains the technical papers of KI 2012. For the technical program, we received 57 complete submissions (48 full papers, 9 short papers). From the 48 full papers, 19 were unconditionally and 2 were conditionally accepted and a further 7 were accepted as short papers. From the 9 short papers, 3 were accepted for presentation during the conference. Each submission received at least three reviews and the members of the Program Committee invested considerable effort in the discussion of the submissions.

The program of the main conference also included three invited talks: "Exploring the Potential of Social Signal Processing for Human-Machine Interaction: Synergies and Challenges" by Elisabeth André from Augsburg University, "Biosignals and Interfaces" by Tanja Schultz from the Karlsruhe Institute of Technology, and "Semantics $\sqcap$ Scalability $\models \perp$?" by Ian Horrocks from the University of Oxford.

The conference was accompanied by a doctoral consortium in which eight PhD students presented their work to the KI audience and received feedback and advice from senior researchers in the field.

The first day of the program also featured six workshops with many additional research presentations:

- Dirk Reichardt organized the 6th Workshop on "Emotion and Computing – Current Research and Future Impact"
- Sebastian Rudolph, Heiner Stuckenschmidt, and Matthias Thimm organized "AI on the Web"
- Jürgen Sauer, Stefan Edelkamp, and Bernd Schattenberg organized the 27th Workshop on "Planning and Scheduling, Configuration and Design" (PuK 2012)
- Thomas Barkowsky, Marco Ragni, and Frieder Stolzenburg organized "Human Reasoning and Automated Deduction"
- Kristina Yordanova, Sebastian Bader, and Frank Krüger organized "From Modeling to Assistance" (M2A)
- Frank Wallhoff, Bernd Schönebeck, and Stefan Goetze organized "Dialog Systems That Think Along – Do They Really Understand Me?"

In addition to the workshops, the program of the first conference day included four tutorials:

- Philippe Balbiani organized "Region-Based Theories of Space"
- Sabine Janzen and Wolfgang Maass organized "Designing Ambient Intelligence Environments"
- Marco Ragni, Rebecca Albrecht, and Stefano Bennati organized "The Cognitive Architecture ACT-R"
- Jens Haupert, Alexander Kröner, and Boris Brandherm organized "Object Memory Tools: Tailoring a Thing's Data Collection and Communication Behavior"

The organization of a conference like this one is only possible with the support of many individuals. First of all, the organizers wish to thank the authors for their contributions. We had a very strong and competent Program Committee consisting of 67 members, which ensured that each submission underwent several thorough and timely reviews. We want to thank all Program Committee members for taking the time to read, review, and discuss the submissions. Last but not least, we thank the members of the KI 2012 organizing committee:

- Local Chair: Boris Brandherm (Saarland University)
- Workshop Chair: Gabriele Kern-Isberner (TU Dortmund)
- Tutorial Chair: Wolfgang Maaß (Saarland University)
- Poster and Demo Chair: Stefan Wölfl (University of Freiburg)
- Doctorial Consortium Chair: Carsten Lutz (University of Bremen)
- Publicity Chair: Daniel Sonntag (DFKI)

We extend our thanks to all other people and institutions who helped make KI 2012 a success, especially the German Research Center for Artificial Intelligence (DFKI), Saarland University, Springer, and EasyChair.

July 2012   Birte Glimm
                                                            Program Chair

                                                          Antonio Krüger
                                                            General Chair

Organization

Program Committee

Klaus-Dieter Althoff	DFKI / University of Hildesheim
Tamim Asfour	Karlsruhe Institute of Technology (KIT)
Franz Baader	TU Dresden
Joscha Bach	Humboldt-University of Berlin
Amit Banerjee	Pennsylvania State University Harrisburg
Sven Behnke	University of Bonn
Maren Bennewitz	University of Freiburg
Ralph Bergmann	University of Trier
Marc Cavazza	Teesside University
Eliseo Clementini	University of L'Aquila
Cristóbal Curio	Max Planck Institute for Biological Cybernetics
Kerstin Dautenhahn	University of Hertfordshire
Frank Dylla	University of Bremen
Stefan Edelkamp	University of Bremen
Udo Frese	University of Bremen
Stefan Funke	University of Stuttgart
Johannes Fürnkranz	TU Darmstadt
Christopher Geib	University of Edinburgh
Birte Glimm	University of Ulm
Björn Gottfried	University of Bremen
Horst-Michael Gross	Ilmenau University of Technology
Jens-Steffen Gutmann	Evolution Robotics
Martin Günther	University of Osnabrueck
Malte Helmert	University of Basel
Joachim Hertzberg	University of Osnabrueck
Otthein Herzog	University of Bremen
Gabriele Kern-Isberner	TU Dortmund
Thomas Kirste	University of Rostock
Alexander Kleiner	Linköping University
Roman Kontchakov	Birkbeck College
Oliver Kramer	University of Oldenburg
Ralf Krestel	Leibniz University of Hanover
Torsten Kroeger	Stanford University

Kai-Uwe Kühnberger	University of Osnabrueck
Bogdan Kwolek	Rzeszow University of Technology
Gerhard Lakemeyer	RWTH Aachen University
Tobias Lang	FU Berlin
Volker Lohweg	inIT - Institute Industrial IT
Benedikt Löwe	University of Amsterdam & University of Hamburg
Robert Mattmüller	University of Freiburg
Bernd Michaelis	Otto-von-Guericke-University Magdeburg
Ralf Möller	TU Hamburg-Harburg
Justus Piater	University of Innsbruck
Felix Putze	Karlsruhe Institute of Technology (KIT)
Marco Ragni	University of Freiburg
Jochen Renz	Australian National University
Sebastian Rudolph	Karlsruhe Institute of Technology (KIT)
Benjamin Satzger	Vienna University of Technology
Juergen Sauer	University of Oldenburg
Bernd Schattenberg	University of Ulm
Malte Schilling	ICSI Berkeley
Ute Schmid	University of Bamberg
Lutz Schröder	Friedrich-Alexander-Universität Erlangen-Nürnberg
Carsten Schürmann	IT University of Copenhagen
René Schumann	University of Applied Sciences Western Switzerland Valais
Jan-Georg Smaus	Université Paul Sabatier de Toulouse
Daniel Sonntag	German Research Center for Artificial Intelligence (DFKI)
Luciano Spinello	University of Freiburg
Steffen Staab	University of Koblenz-Landau
Cyrill Stachniss	University of Freiburg
Ingo J. Timm	University of Trier
Rudolph Triebel	University of Oxford
Johanna Völker	University of Mannheim
Toby Walsh	NICTA and UNSW
Thomas Wiemann	University of Osnabrück
Diedrich Wolter	University of Bremen
Stefan Wölfl	University of Freiburg

Additional Reviewers

Bach, Kerstin	De la Rosa, Stephan
Becker, Tilman	Delhibabu, Radhakrishnan
Bercher, Pascal	Edelkamp, Stefan
Browatzki, Björn	El Haoum, Sabina

Euzenat, Jérôme
Huisman, Marieke
Knopp, Johannes
Kreutzmann, Arne
Krötzsch, Markus
Loeckelt, Markus
Minker, Wolfgang
Mossakowski, Till
Neumann, Günter

Özcep, Özgür Lütfü
Poll, Erik
Richter, Felix
Schaffernicht, Erik
Schiffer, Stefan
Schroeter, Christof
Stuckenschmidt, Heiner
Volkhardt, Michael
Wehrle, Martin

Table of Contents

Long Papers

Short Papers

Verification of Behaviour Networks
Using Finite-State Automata

Christopher Armbrust, Lisa Kiekbusch, Thorsten Ropertz, and Karsten Berns

Robotics Research Lab, Department of Computer Science,
University of Kaiserslautern, P.O. Box 3049, 67653 Kaiserslautern, Germany
{armbrust,kiekbusch,t_ropert,berns}@cs.uni-kl.de
http://rrlab.cs.uni-kl.de/

Abstract. This paper addresses the problem of verifying properties of behaviour-based systems used for controlling robots. A behaviour-based system typically consists of many interconnected components, the behaviours, which in combination realise the system's overall functionality. The connections between the behaviours are crucial for the correct operation of a system. Therefore, key properties of behaviour-based systems are verifiable based on their behaviour interconnections. In this paper, it is described how behaviour-based networks can be (automatically) modelled using finite-state machines and how model checking with the UPPAAL toolbox can then be applied for verification and analysis tasks.

Keywords: Behaviour-based System, Behaviour Network, Behaviour Modelling, Behaviour Network Verification.

1 Introduction

Behaviour-based systems (BBS) have several advantages over classic, typically monolithic robot control systems: Their distributed nature can strongly increase the fault tolerance of a system and fosters component reuse and distributed development (see [2] for more information on BBS). Unfortunately, with a higher degree of distribution comes a greater importance of the proper coordination of the single behaviours. Therefore, a concept for the development, application, and verification of behaviour networks is developed at the Robotics Research Lab (see Fig. 1). For example, principles for the design of behaviour architectures and guidelines for the development of BBS are proposed in [12]. However, the establishment of precise requirements and their formalised transfer into software usually cannot avoid all errors, which makes verification necessary. Besides, if additions are made to an existing system, the fulfilment of the requirements has to be checked again.

This paper presents a novel approach for modelling and verifying BBS by means of model checking techniques. For this purpose, networks of behaviours are represented as synchronised automata that are variations of finite-state machines (FSMs). This modelling is done automatically using partly pre-built basic

B. Glimm and A. Krüger (Eds.): KI 2012, LNCS 7526, pp. 1–12, 2012.
© Springer-Verlag Berlin Heidelberg 2012

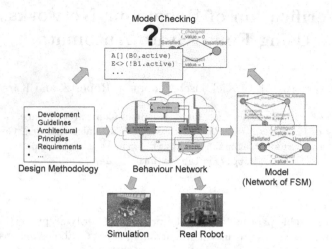

Fig. 1. A concept for the development and verification of behaviour networks

components. The UPPAAL[1] toolbox is then used to analyse the resulting networks of FSMs.

The remainder of this paper is structured as follows: Section 2 gives an overview of different approaches for verifying systems. In Section 3 the modelling of behaviour networks as well as the application of model checking techniques is explained in detail. Section 4 demonstrates how the presented concept can be used for verifying a part of the navigation system of an off-road vehicle. Finally, Section 5 concludes the paper and gives an outlook on future work.

2   Related Work

Model checking is a technique for automatically testing whether a model of a concurrent finite-state system meets a given specification (see [7] for an overview). The corresponding process consists of modelling, specification, and verification. Examples of the use of model checking are [15], which describes the use of model checking for verifying the control system of an unmanned aircraft, [11], which deals with the application and extension of model checking techniques for verifying spacecraft control software, and [10], which explains how model checking can be applied to verify a distributed coordination algorithm for robot swarms.

The authors of [8] describe the modelling of an agent's behaviour as X-machine (a computational machine resembling an FSM, but with attached memory). A main difference to the work at hand is that an agent is represented by exactly one machine (instead of several automata), which leads to very large automata when modelling complex systems. The approach in the paper at hand, by contrast, is to use several rather simple automata.

---

[1] http://www.uppaal.org/

In [13], it is described how single behaviours can be implemented in the synchronous language Quartz and how their correctness can be shown using a symbolic model checker. The author of [14] describes how model checking with UPPAAL in connection with a fault tree analysis can be used to ensure that critical events cannot occur in a system. The modelling of parts of a system as automata is necessary so that UPPAAL can be used. The work at hand could be a basis for employing the approach of [14] in BBS. Another connection of fault trees and model checking is described in [9], which explains how the correctness and completeness of fault trees can be verified using model checking. For that work, modelling a system as FSM is necessary as well. Hence, the work presented here could also be a basis for the application of that approach.

3 Behaviour Network Modelling and Verification

This section introduces the behaviour-based architecture iB2C[2] as well as the UPPAAL toolbox and explains how iB2C networks can be modelled and verified.

3.1 The Behaviour-Based Architecture iB2C

The approach for modelling behaviour networks presented in the work at hand is based on the behaviour-based architecture iB2C, which is described extensively in [12]. It has been implemented using the software framework MCA2-KL[3].

One of the main concepts of the iB2C is that all behaviours possess a common interface transferring coordination signals between them. These signals are a behaviour's *stimulation s* (used to gradually enable the behaviour), *inhibition i* (used to gradually disable it), *activity a* (the degree of influence the behaviour intends to have), and *target rating r* (the behaviour's satisfaction with the current situation). s and $i = \max\limits_{j=0,\ldots,k-1} \{i_j\}$ (with k: number of inhibiting behaviours) are combined to the *activation* $\iota = s \cdot (1 - i)$, which defines the behaviour's maximum influence within a network. To transfer only a part of its activity to the outside, a behaviour can pass so-called derived activities $\underline{a}_0, \underline{a}_1, \ldots, \underline{a}_{q-1}$ with $\underline{a}_i \leq a \; \forall i \in \{0, 1, \ldots, q-1\}$ to other behaviours. Together with its activity, they build the activity vector $\boldsymbol{a} = (a, \underline{\boldsymbol{a}})^T$. As the activation defines the upper bound of a behaviour's influence, the activity is limited to $a \leq \iota$. All behaviour signals are limited to $[0, 1]$. Apart from the standardised ports for behaviour signals, every behaviour can have an arbitrary number of additional input and output ports for transferring any kind of data. The vector of control output values $\boldsymbol{u}$ is calculated using a behaviour's transfer function F: $\boldsymbol{u} = F(\boldsymbol{e}, \iota)$ with $\boldsymbol{e}$ being the vector of its control inputs. Fig. 2 depicts the symbol of a behaviour.

iB2C behaviours can be connected in various ways. The most common types are stimulating and inhibiting connections, in which the activity output of a behaviour is connected either to the stimulation or inhibition input of another

---

[2] iB2C: integrated Behaviour-based Control.
[3] MCA2-KL: Modular Controller Architecture Version 2 - Kaiserslautern Branch.

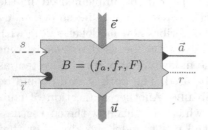

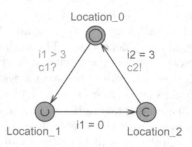

Fig. 2. The general symbol of a behaviour (s: stimulation, i: inhibition vector, $\boldsymbol{a}$: activity vector, r: target rating, $\boldsymbol{e}$: input vector, $\boldsymbol{u}$: output vector, f_a: function calculating $\boldsymbol{a}$, f_r: function calculating r, $F(\boldsymbol{e}, \iota)$: function calculating $\boldsymbol{u}$)

Fig. 3. A simple automaton with three locations (Location_0: initial, Location_1: urgent, Location_2: committed), a guard ($i1 > 3$), two updates ($i1 = 0$, $i2 = 3$), and two channel synchronisations (c1?: receiver, c2!: sender)

behaviour. Other connection types include the combination of the outputs of a number of competing behaviours using a so-called fusion behaviour (see below) or the sequencing of behaviours using a special coordination behaviour (see [4]).

The iB2C fusion behaviour combines the outputs of other behaviours connected to it according to one of three possible fusion modes (maximum, weighted average, and weighted sum). Let B_{Fusion} be a fusion behaviour to which p competing behaviours B_{Input_c} with activities a_c, target ratings r_c, and output vectors $\boldsymbol{u}_c$ are connected. In case of a maximum fusion, the outputs of B_{Fusion} are defined as follows: $\boldsymbol{u} = \boldsymbol{u}_s$, $a = \max_c(a_c)$, and $r = r_s$, where $s = \operatorname{argmax}_c(a_c)$. Fusion behaviours have the same interface as basic behaviours.

To facilitate the handling of a large number of interconnected behaviours, behavioural groups encapsulate a number of behaviours or further groups and act as new behaviours in a network.

3.2 Finite-State Automata and Uppaal

The UPPAAL toolbox (see [6]) provides an integrated environment for the modelling, simulation, and verification of real-time systems, which are represented as networks of automata (see [1]). Its modelling language extends these automata with structured data types, integer variables, and channel synchronisation. Every automaton may fire an edge separately or synchronise with another automaton.

A UPPAAL *system* consists of instantiations of several *templates*, each of which contains the definition of an automaton. The basic elements of automata are *locations*, which are connected via *edges*. Each location can be marked as *committed*. A committed state cannot delay and the next transition must involve an outgoing edge of at least one of the committed locations. Edges may have several attributes like *guards* (side-effect free Boolean expressions to determine whether an edge is enabled), *updates* (assignments), and *synchronisations* between several automata. The latter are achieved via *channels*. An edge can be labelled with a channel name followed by "!" for a sending or "?" for a receiving channel. Two types of channels exist: the binary synchronisation channel and the broadcast channel. The first provides a synchronisation between a non-deterministically chosen pair of automata, whereas the second enables a sender to synchronise with an arbitrary number of receivers (including none). In the latter case, any receiver that can synchronise in the current state must do so.

The formal language used in UPPAAL to express the requirements specification is a simplified version of TCTL[4] that consists of two types of formulae—*state formulae* (check whether an automaton is in a specific location) and *path formulae* (quantify over paths or traces). The UPPAAL toolbox features an editor for modelling systems, a simulator for running traces, and a verifier for checking properties using the above-mentioned formulae.

3.3 Modelling Behaviour Networks Using Finite-State Automata

Each behaviour B is represented by an instantiation of each of five templates, which are `StimulationInterface`, `InhibitionInterface`, `ActivationCalculation`, `ActivityCalculation`, and `TargetRatingCalculation`. The separation of a behaviour model into different automata yields a better encapsulation, which allows for reusing some of the templates for the models of different behaviours. Besides, templates dealing with more than one behaviour signal would contain much more states, which would decrease clarity and complicate adopting or enhancing the templates. A separation encapsulating single behaviour signals has been chosen as these signals are an essential part of the structure of a behaviour network. The synchronisation of the automata of B with each other as well as with the automata of other behaviours is done using synchronisation channels. The value range of the models is limited to $\{0, 1\}$ (0: "inactive"; 1: "active to some degree"). This is currently sufficient and reduces the complexity of the models. In the following, the five templates shall be explained in detail.

The `StimulationInterface` (see Fig. 4) consists of four locations, with two of them dedicated to showing whether B is stimulated or not stimulated, respectively. UPPAAL does not allow more than one synchronisation per edge. Therefore, edges that should have more than one synchronisation have been split up into several edges, one for each synchronisation. Committed locations representing intermediate states have been added between these edges. If the `StimulationInterface` is in location `Unstimulated` and receives an `s_changed` signal, it sets `s_value` to 1 and sends `s_changed_internal`. `s_value` is the stimulation of B and `s_changed_internal` is used to signal other automata of B that the stimulation has changed. Accordingly, when `s_changed` is received in location `Stimulated`, the automaton transitions through the committed location back to location `Unstimulated`, sending `s_changed_internal` and setting `s_value` to 0. The `processing` flag is used to be able to exclude intermediate states when creating queries.

---

[4] TCTL: Timed Computation Tree Logic.

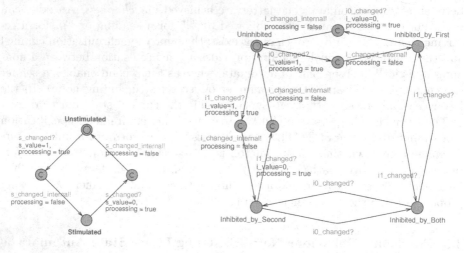

Fig. 4. `StimulationInterface` of a single behaviour

Fig. 5. `InhibitionInterface` for a behaviour that is inhibited by two others

The automaton modelling the inhibitory inputs of a behaviour is built up in a similar fashion. The most notable difference is that there can possibly be more than one inhibitory input. Hence, there is actually not one single `InhibitionInterface`, but for each number of inhibition inputs, a special template is created automatically during the modelling process. Figure 5 exemplarily shows a template for two inhibiting behaviours. The main locations are `Uninhibited`, `Inhibited_by_First`, `Inhibited_by_Second`, and `Inhibited_by_Both`. Similar to the `StimulationInterface`, the automaton updates its variables and notifies other automata of B about changes.

In an iB2C behaviour, stimulation s and inhibition i are combined to the activation ι. This is modelled by `ActivationCalculation` (see Fig. 6). The modelling of activity and target rating is done in an extremely simple form, as this is sufficient when focussing on the interaction of behaviours. Figure 7 shows the automaton of `ActivityCalculation`. It switches between `Inactive` and `Inactive_but_Activated` depending on the signal `iota_changed`. In the latter of the two states, it can switch to `Active` (and back) arbitrarily. The calculation of the target rating is modelled in a similar way by `TargetRating-Calculation` (see Fig. 8). Of course, it is possible to model the calculation of these two behaviour signals in a more realistic fashion if this is necessary for the verification process and enough information about the calculation functions is available. How this is done for a fusion behaviour will be briefly described below.

As mentioned above, the modelling approach currently limits behaviour signals to $\{0, 1\}$. Hence, instead of the real formulae for activity and target rating of a fusion behaviour (see Section 3.1), a simpler calculation is used: The activity of a fusion behaviour B_{Fusion} can only be above 0 if B_{Fusion} is activated and at least one of its input behaviours B_{Input_c} is active. Similarly,

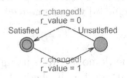

Fig. 7. ActivityCalculation
(calculating the activity)

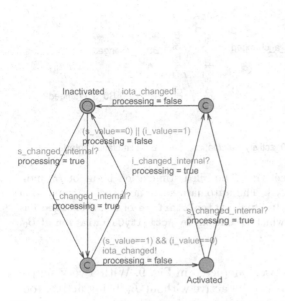

Fig. 6. ActivationCalculation (calculating the activation from the stimulation and the inhibition)

Fig. 8. TargetRatingCalculation (calculating the target rating)

it can only be unsatisfied with the situation if at least one of its input behaviours also is. These considerations lead to FBActivityCalculation with 18 and FBTargetRatingCalculation with 8 locations (in the case of two connected input behaviours). The most relevant locations are Active_01 (only B_{Input_0} active), Active_10 (only B_{Input_1} active), Active_11 (both active), and Inactive (none active). Due to the lack of space, these automata cannot be depicted here.

The creation of the UPPAAL models is done automatically from a BBS within a running MCA2-KL programme. During the model creation, the synchronisation channels between the automata are established: When a template is instantiated for behaviour B, it is provided with the correct channels depending on the connections of B with other behaviours. For example, if a behaviour B_0 stimulates a behaviour B_1 (see Fig. 9), then s_changed of the instance of StimulationInterface belonging to B_1 is set to a_changed of the instance of ActivityCalculation of B_0. Hence, when ActivityCalculation of B_0 sends a_changed, StimulationInterface of B_1 synchronises with the former.

3.4 Verification of Behaviour Network Models

As soon as a BBS has been modelled as a network of finite-state automata, UP-PAAL's verifier can be used to check certain properties of the model. By this means, it is possible to gain information about when a behaviour can get active, whether a set of behaviours can be active at the same time etc. How this is done

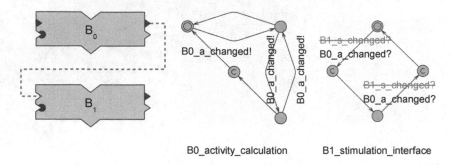

Fig. 9. B_0 stimulating B_1 with its activity. The filled stimulation input of B_0 indicates that it is permanently stimulated. The automata show how such a connection between two behaviours is modelled. In `StimulationInterface` of B_1, `s_changed` has been replaced with `a_changed` of B_0, which is sent out by `ActivityCalculation` of B_0.

shall be demonstrated using the network depicted in Fig. 9. With a very simple query it can be checked whether B_1 can be active without B_0 being active, too:

`E<> (B1_activity_calculation.Active && !B0_activity_calculation.Active)`[5]

As B_1 can only be stimulated by B_0 and $a \lesssim \iota$ (see Section 3.1) this query evaluates to false. The assertion that B_1 is always active if B_0 is active can be falsified with the following query:

`A[] (B1_activity_calculation.Active || !B0_activity_calculation.Active)`

This assertion is incorrect as B_1 can be stimulated by B_0, but still be inactive. While answering such queries for small networks is trivial, it gets much more complicated in sophisticated systems consisting of more behaviours.

4   Example

In this section, a part of the behaviour-based navigation system used to control the off-road robot RAVON[6] (see [3]) is verified against certain requirements using UPPAAL models of behaviour networks. Its purpose is to coordinate several (groups of) behaviours that realise different approaches for calculating the next target coordinates. There are two ways for driving the robot towards a goal: The first implements a direct point access, where the vehicle is guided directly to a target location. The second extends this by additionally specifying the vehicle's orientation at the target (point access with orientation).

The behaviour network called *(G) Drive Control* (see Fig. 10a) shall coordinate the following three navigation approaches:

A1)   A high-level navigation component is able to provide target coordinates (without or including a target orientation) via behaviours *(F) Nav. Direct Point Access (DPA) Interface* and *(F) Nav. Point Access with Orientation (PAO) Interface*.

---

[5] Due to the limited space, the check of the `Processing` flag is left out in the queries.
[6] RAVON: Robust Autonomous Vehicle for Off-road Navigation.

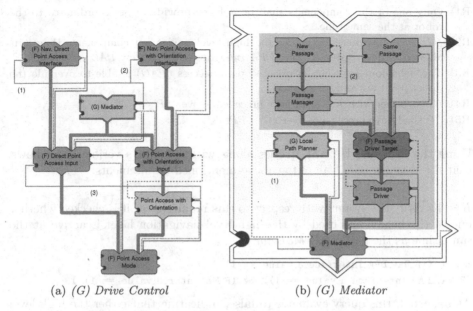

(a) *(G) Drive Control*   (b) *(G) Mediator*

Fig. 10. The two networks (grey node: simple behaviour; blue: fusion behaviour; double-bordered grey: behavioural group; dashed green edge: stimulation; red: inhibition; blue: activity transfer; dotted brown: target rating; bold grey: data)

A2) A classic A*-based local path planner (*(G) Local Path Planner, (G) LPP*) is able to provide target coordinates.

A3) A special component shall be able to provide target coordinates along with a desired orientation based on the detection of so-called "passages" (see below).

Passages are paths leading through obstacle formations in the robot's environment (see [5]). The passage components are marked with a shaded area in Fig. 10b. *New Passage (NP)* shall get active if a new passage is detected and send its coordinates to the *Passage Manager (PM)*. This in turn shall get active if it decides that the robot should enter the passage. *Same Passage (SP)* shall get active if a previously detected passage is seen again. The behaviour's intention is then to guide the robot to this passage. The outputs of the *PM* and *SP* are combined using *(F) Passage Driver Target (PDT)*, which shall transmit the passage's coordinates to the *Passage Driver (PD)*. The latter shall further process the coordinates and finally send them to the output of the *(G) Mediator* (see Fig. 10b), which groups[7] the classic path planner and the passage behaviours.

It is important that always only one navigation component may send commands to the lower control layer. Hence, an order of precedence is needed, leading to the following requirements.

---

[7] RAVON's control system contains over 500 behaviours. In order to improve the structure of the system, many behaviours are combined in groups.

R1) Only one of the components shall be able to provide target coordinates to the robot at the same time.

R2) *(G) LPP* has precedence over the high-level navigation component, thus it is allowed to deactivate *(F) Nav. DPA Interface* and *(F) Nav. PAO Interface.*

R3) The behaviour realising an oriented point access *(PAO)* is able to overrule the direct point access *(DPA Input).*

R4) *NP* together with *PM* shall have precedence over *SP.*

R5) *SP* shall have precedence over *(G) LPP.*

Using the following UPPAAL queries along with UPPAAL's verifier it is shown that the network fulfills all of the above-mentioned requirements:

R1: To verify the system with respect to this requirement, it is checked whether one of the behaviours used by the high-level navigation layer is active at the same time as the group *(G) Mediator*.

```
E<> ( ((F_Nav_DPA_Interface_a_value == 1) ||
(F_Nav_PAO_Interface_a_value == 1)) && (F_Mediator_a_value == 1) )
```

As expected, this query evaluates to false, indicating that either the high-level navigation or the *(G) Mediator* is active. It still has to be checked whether at most one of the components within the *(G) Mediator* can control RAVON at the same time. The following query evaluates to true, which yields that it is possible that the path planning as well as the passage components are active concurrently.

```
E<> ( ((SP_a_value == 1) || (NP_a_value == 1)) && (G_LPP_a_value == 1) )
```

However, the automaton modelling the activity of *(F) Mediator* never reaches the location indicating that both input behaviours are active (`Active_11`). So either *(G) LPP* or the passage subsystem is active. The reason for this is the inhibitory link connecting the activity output of *Passage Driver* with the inhibition input of *(G) LPP* (see Fig. 10b (1)). The corresponding query is:

```
E<> (F_Mediator_activity_calculation.Active_11) → false
```

The next result indicates that *SP* and *NP* can be active at the same time:

```
E<> ( (SP_a_value == 1) && (NP_a_value == 1) ) → true
```

But *SP* and *PM* cannot be active at the same time:

```
E<> ( (SP_a_value == 1) && (PM_a_value == 1) ) → false
```

Similar as above, the reason is the inhibitory link from *PM* to *SP* (see Fig. 10b (2)). As the former processes the outputs of *NP*, the result is that either *SP* or *NP* can provide a target to the lower layers.

R2: The prioritisation is realised using inhibitory links from *(G) Mediator* to *(F) Nav. DPA Interface* and *(F) Nav. PAO Interface* (see Fig. 10a (1) and (2)). This can be verified using the following three queries:

```
E<> ( (F_Nav_DPA_Interface_activation_calculation.Activated || F_Nav_PAO_
Interface_activation_calculation.Activated) && (G_LPP_a_value == 1) )
```

The above query will evaluate to false and thus prove that *(F) Nav. DPA Interface* or *(F) Nav. PAO Interface* are never activated when *(G) LPP* is active.

```
E<> ( (F_Nav_DPA_Interface_a_value == 1) && (G_LPP_activation_calculation.
Activated) )
```

```
E<> ( (F_Nav_PAO_Interface_a_value == 1) && (G_LPP_activation_calculation.
Activated) )
```

By contrast, these queries evaluate to true, which means that neither *(F) Nav. DPA Interface* nor *(F) Nav. PAO Interface* inhibits *(G) LPP*.

R3 This requirement is fulfilled with an inhibition between two behaviours.

```
E<> ( (PAO_activity_calculation.Active) &&
(!F_Point_Access_Mode_activity_calculation.Active_01) ) → false
```

`Active_01` is the location in which the only active behaviour connected to *(F) Point Access Mode* (*(F) PAM*) is *PAO* (cp. information about `FBActivity-Calculation` in Sec. 3.3). Hence, the result of the query shows that whenever *PAO* is active, no other input behaviour of *(F) PAM* can be active, too. This is realised by the link between the former and *(F) DPA Input* (see Fig. 10a (3)).

R4 The prioritisation is realised using the inhibitory link from *PM* to *SP* (see Fig. 10b (2)). Two queries can be used to verify this:

```
E<> ( (SP_a_value == 1) && (PM_activation_calculation.Activated) ) → true
```

```
E<> ( (SP_activation_calculation.Activated) && (PM_a_value == 1) ) → false
```

R5 This prioritisation is realised with the inhibitory link going from *PD* to *(G) LPP* (see Fig. 10b (1)). To verify this, similar queries as the ones above are used.

5   Conclusion and Future Work

In this paper, it has been demonstrated how model checking can help in verifying properties of behaviour networks. It has been explained how a behaviour-based system can be transformed automatically into a model consisting of finite-state automata and how these automata can be analysed with the help of UPPAAL. An example has been used to prove the applicability of the presented concepts to the control system of an autonomous off-road vehicle. It has shown that the approach helps in verifying a behaviour-based system.

Future work will deal with more sophisticated networks and additional specialised behaviours. A way of modelling a robot's collision avoidance system along with environmental features is currently developed in order to take the robot's reaction to changes in the environment into account when verifying its control system. Queries still have to be created manually, which is tedious and error-prone. In the future, an automatism for creating whole sets of queries and a graphical interface shall facilitate this task.

Acknowledgements. The authors gratefully acknowledge Prof. Roland Meyer from the Concurrency Theory Group[8] of the University of Kaiserslautern for his helpful comments and suggestions.

References

1. Alur, R., Dill, D.L.: A theory of timed automata. Theoretical Computer Science 126(2), 183–235 (1994)
2. Arkin, R.: Behaviour-Based Robotics. MIT Press (1998)
3. Armbrust, C., Braun, T., Föhst, T., Proetzsch, M., Renner, A., Schäfer, B.H., Berns, K.: RAVON – the robust autonomous vehicle for off-road navigation. In: Baudoin, Y., Habib, M.K. (eds.) Using robots in hazardous environments: Landmine detection, de-mining and other applications. Woodhead Publishing (2010)
4. Armbrust, C., Kiekbusch, L., Berns, K.: Using behaviour activity sequences for motion generation and situation recognition. In: Ferrier, J.L., Bernard, A., Gusikhin, O., Madani, K. (eds.) ICINCO 2011, July 28-31, vol. 2, pp. 120–127. INSTICC, SciTePress, Noordwijkerhout, The Netherlands (2011)
5. Armbrust, C., Schäfer, B.H., Berns, K.: Using passages to support off-road robot navigation. In: Filipe, J., Andrade-Cetto, J., Ferrier, J.L. (eds.) ICINCO 2009, pp. 189–194. INSTICC, Milan, Italy (July 2009)
6. Behrmann, G., David, A., Larsen, K.G.: A Tutorial on UPPAAL. In: Bernardo, M., Corradini, F. (eds.) SFM-RT 2004. LNCS, vol. 3185, pp. 200–236. Springer, Heidelberg (2004)
7. Clarke, E.M., Grumberg, O., Peled, D.A.: Model Checking. MIT Press (1999)
8. Eleftherakis, G., Kefalas, P., Sotiriadou, A., Kehris, E.: Modeling biology inspired reactive agents using x-machines. In: Okatan, A. (ed.) International Conference on Computational Intelligence 2004 (ICCI 2004), pp. 93–96. International Computational Intelligence Society, Istanbul, Turkey (December 2004)
9. Faber, J.: Fault tree analysis with Moby/FT. Tech. rep., Department for Computing Science, University of Oldenburg (2005), publication available at http://csd.informatik.uni-oldenburg.de/~jfaber/dl/ToolPresentationMobyFT.pdf
10. Juurik, S., Vain, J.: Model checking of emergent behaviour properties of robot swarms. Proceedings of the Estonian Academy of Sciences 60(1), 48–54 (2011)
11. Lowry, M., Havelund, K., Penix, J.: Verification and Validation of AI Systems that Control Deep-Space Spacecraft. In: Raś, Z.W., Skowron, A. (eds.) ISMIS 1997. LNCS, vol. 1325, pp. 35–47. Springer, Heidelberg (1997)
12. Proetzsch, M.: Development Process for Complex Behavior-Based Robot Control Systems. RRLab Dissertations, Verlag Dr. Hut (2010)
13. Proetzsch, M., Berns, K., Schuele, T., Schneider, K.: Formal verification of safety behaviours of the outdoor robot RAVON. In: Zaytoon, J., Ferrier, J.L., Andrade-Cetto, J., Filipe, J. (eds.) ICINCO 2007, Angers, France, pp. 157–164. INSTICC Press (May 2007)
14. Schäfer, A.: Combining Real-Time Model-Checking and Fault Tree Analysis. In: Araki, K., Gnesi, S., Mandrioli, D. (eds.) FME 2003. LNCS, vol. 2805, pp. 522–541. Springer, Heidelberg (2003)
15. Webster, M., Fisher, M., Cameron, N., Jump, M.: Model checking and the certification of autonomous unmanned aircraft systems. Tech. Rep. ULCS-11-001, University of Liverpool Department of Computer Science (2011)

---

[8] http://concurrency.cs.uni-kl.de/

Formal Semantics of Model Fields in Annotation-Based Specifications*

Bernhard Beckert and Daniel Bruns

Karlsruhe Institute of Technology (KIT), Department of Informatics

Abstract. It is widely recognized that abstraction and modularization are indispensable for specification of real-world programs. In source-code level program specification and verification, *model fields* are a common means for those goals. However, it remains a challenge to provide a well-founded formal semantics for the general case in which the abstraction relation defining a model field is non-functional.

In this paper, we discuss and compare several possibilities for defining model field semantics, and we give a complete formal semantics for the general case. Our analysis and the proposed semantics is based on a generalization of Hilbert's ε terms.

1 Introduction

Annotation-based specification. Recently, formal specification of programs at the source-code level has become increasingly popular with a wider community, where such specifications are used both in safety and security contexts. This is mainly due to the rise of a specification methodology where the boundaries between program proper and specification become blurred: specifications are written as annotations into program source files. The specifications languages extend the programming language's syntax, and their semantics is defined on top of the programming language's semantics. Particular examples include the Java Modeling Language (JML) [12] for Java, the ANSI/ISO C Specification Language (ACSL) [2] for C, and Spec# [1] for C#. This approach bears the clear advantage of being intuitively understandable to users who are not familiar with logic. At the same time, however, it has become far more laborious to come up with a sound semantical foundation.

Model fields. Even if programs are specified at the source-code level, abstraction and modularization are indispensable for handling real-word programs. For that purpose, the concept of model fields [9,14] is widely used. Model fields are abstractions of the program's memory state given in a syntactically convenient form (as fields in a class). The relation between the concrete state and the model fields, i.e., the abstraction relation, is specified by so-called *represents clauses*.

---

* This work was supported by the German National Science Foundation (DFG) under project "Program-level Specification and Deductive Verification of Security Properties" within priority programme 1496 "Reliably Secure Software Systems – RS³".

B. Glimm and A. Krüger (Eds.): KI 2012, LNCS 7526, pp. 13–24, 2012.
© Springer-Verlag Berlin Heidelberg 2012

In general, abstraction relations may be non-functional, and they may refer to entities which are not present in the concrete program (e.g., other model fields). Model fields are also commonly used to give implementation-independent specifications of abstract data types. In that case, the requirement specification only refers to model fields while the abstraction relation is part of the (hidden) implementation details.

Topic of this paper. There is yet no common understanding of what the semantics of model fields is in the general case. The semantics used by verification and runtime checking tools as well as the semantics defined in the literature is restricted to functional represents clauses, to model fields of a primitive type, or by restricting the syntax of represents clauses. The general case, however, raises several questions:

- On which memory locations does the value of a model field depend?
- What value is chosen if the represents clause is non-functional?
- Is there aliasing between model fields of a reference type?
- What does an unsatisfiable represents clause mean? Does it lead to an inconsistent axiom set?
- At what points in time does the value of a memory field change?
- In which cases are represents clauses well-defined? What about recursive represents clauses?

In this paper, we answer these questions by presenting a well-founded semantics for model fields in the general case, which is inspired by a generalization of ε terms. Although we primarily report on the situation in the Java Modeling Language (JML)—this is the specification language the authors know best— we expect the principles outlined here to apply to other specification languages which make use of model fields as well. In particular, the semantics is independent of any reasoning system. It is parameterized so that it can be instantiated in different ways in cases where different reasonable answers to the above questions exist.

Hilbert's ε terms. The concept of ε terms was first introduced by Hilbert in 1939 as an extension to classical first-order predicate logic [8]. An ε term $\varepsilon x.\varphi(x)$, where x is a variable and φ is a formula, stands for 'some domain element such that φ holds (if such exists)'. In general, this informal understanding is the only restriction on the value of an ε term; however, we will later see that further useful restrictions may be added. These terms can, for example, be used to represent instantiations of existentially quantified variables without assigning a concrete value (i.e., skolemization). The quantifier in $\exists x.\varphi(x)$ can be eliminated by replacing the formula $\exists x.\varphi(x)$ by $\varphi(\varepsilon x.\varphi(x))$.

In the course of this paper, we will review the discussion on restrictions to the valuation of ε terms, with a look for analogies in the discussion on model field semantics.

Structure of this paper. In Section 2, we give a short introduction to JML and, in particular, model fields in JML. We however expect the results presented here to apply to other specification languages as well. In Section 3, we give a formal semantics for JML expressions *without model fields*. Before extending this semantics to model fields, we review the discussion on semantics of ε terms and develop an n-ary generalization of ε terms (Section 4). Then, in Section 5, we present a first approach to model field semantics inspired by ε terms. In Section 5.1, we discuss some of the desired properties of this approach. We discuss one deficiency in Section 5.2 and propose a solution in a second, extended approach based on our generalized ε terms from Section 4.1.

2 The Java Modeling Language

The Java Modeling Language (JML) [12] was conceived to be both easily accessible to the 'common programmer'—who might *not* be skilled in formal modeling—and "capable of being given a rigorous, formal semantics" [11]. JML specifications, i.e., primarily method contracts (including frame conditions) and class invariants, are written in a Java-like expression language as comments in source files. Due to this advantage, JML has quickly become one of the most popular specification languages, which is employed in numerous program verification and runtime checking methods and tools. Despite good intuitive understanding of JML, there is yet no canonized formal semantics. Some have been presented before [4,5,6,10], including one of the authors' own. But, semantics of model fields, in particular, are subject to an ongoing debate.

In addition to plain Java expressions, JML expressions are enriched with quantification and special constructs, such as \result to access the return value of a method invocation, or \old to refer to pre-state values of expressions (in a method's post-state) as well as quantification over primitive and reference types.

Model fields in JML are declared similarly to regular Java fields, but within specifications. They may occur as either non-static (i.e., instance) or static fields. A model field is declared with the additional modifier model. This does not yet give any information on the value of the field but only type information. To impose a constraint on the possible values of a model field, a (separate) represents clause is provided. It comes in two variations: a functional form, in which a model field points to exactly one value depending on the memory state, and a relational form, in which it is constrained to values satisfying a boolean expression. Obviously, the functional form is a special case of the relational form. The functional form is indicated by the assignment operator =, while a relational definition is indicated by the keyword \such_that; see Fig. 1 for an example. Since they are not describing the relationship between two states, represents clauses are not allowed to contain \old or \result. Otherwise, their syntax is not restricted. They may, for example, contain references to other model fields. We will call such references the *dependencies* of the model field.

```
public class List {                                          1
    private int[] theList;                                   2
    /*@ model int bound;                                     3
    @ model int idxMax;                                      4
    @ represents bound \such_that                            5
    @       (\forall int i; 0 <= i &                         6
    @           i < theList.length;                          7
    @               bound >= theList[i]);                    8
    @ represents idxMax \such_that                           9
    @       theList[idxMax] == bound;                        10
    @*/ }                                                    11
```

Fig. 1. Two model fields with non-functional represents clauses. While there are always multiple possible values for **bound**, the relation for **idxMax** may be empty.

3   Semantics of JML Expressions

In this section, we summarize the framework given in [4] to evaluate JML expressions that do *not* contain references to model fields. This semantics is then extended to the case of model fields in Section 5.

We assume that a closed Java program is given that is annotated with JML specifications. This program provides a type hierarchy, i.e., a partially ordered set $(\mathcal{T}, \sqsubseteq)$ of types, and a *universe* $\mathcal{U}$. The universe $\mathcal{U}$ consists of all semantical objects which may be referenced in the program. In particular, it includes the mathematical integers and truth values tt (true) and ff (false). For each reference type $T \sqsubseteq \texttt{Object}$ there is a countably-infinite subset $V_T \subset \mathcal{U}$ which serves as a reservoir and contains the elements of that type and a special element *null*; $T' \sqsubset T$ implies $V_{T'} \subset V_T$. When needed, we denote the set of *direct instances* by V_T^0, with the property $V_T^0 \cap V_{T'}^0 = \emptyset$ if $T \neq T'$. For a primitive type T, V_T and V_T^0 are identical and map directly to the corresponding mathematical entities, e.g., $V_{\texttt{int}} = \{z \in \mathbb{Z} \mid -2^{31} \leq z < 2^{31}\}$. We also require that $\mathcal{T} \subset \mathcal{U}$ in order to allow types (i.e., classes and interfaces) to act as the receiver of a static field or method. The declared type of a field identified by x is denoted by *typeof*(x). Let *Id* denote the set of valid Java identifiers and *Expr* the set of syntactically well-formed JML expressions. See [12, Appendix A] for the complete syntax.

A *(system) state* s is the union of functions η and σ, which represent the heap and the stack memory, respectively. $\eta : \mathcal{U} \times Id \to \mathcal{U}$ maps pairs of *receiver objects* and field identifiers (these pairs are also called *locations*) to a value. $\sigma : Id \cup \{\texttt{this}\} \to \mathcal{U}$ evaluates local variables. For now, we assume both η and σ to be total functions.[1] For a total function f and a partial function p, we use the notation $f \oplus p$ to indicate that p overrides f, i.e., $(f \oplus p)(x) = p(x)$ if $x \in \mathrm{Id}(p)$ and $f(x)$ otherwise. We omit $\oplus$ where the notion is clear.

---

[1] This can be achieved through underspecification of otherwise undefined values.

We define the evaluation function $val : \mathcal{S}^2 \times Expr \to \mathcal{U}$ that, given a pair of system states, maps expressions to elements of the universe. The two state parameters represent the state referred to by the \old operator (pre-state) and the current state (post-state), respectively. Table 1 shows the valuation function for some exemplary parameters. For a comprehensive definition, the reader is referred to [4, Appendix A]. For the sake of simplicity, we disregard the fact here that JML even allows pure methods to have certain side-effects.

Table 1. Valuation function val for some representative expressions where a and b are expressions and x is an identifier

field access:	$val(s_0, s_1, a.x) = \eta(val(s_0, s_1, a), x)$	where $s_1 = (\eta, \_)$
variable:	$val(s_0, s_1, x) = \sigma(x)$	where $s_1 = (\_, \sigma)$
constant:	$val(s_0, s_1, \mathtt{true}) = tt$	

identity: $\quad val(s_0, s_1, a\ \mathtt{==}\ b) = \begin{cases} tt & val(s_0, s_1, a) = val(s_0, s_1, b) \\ \mathit{ff} & \text{otherwise} \end{cases}$

logical and: $\quad val(s_0, s_1, a\ \&\&\ b) = \begin{cases} tt & val(s_0, s_1, a) = val(s_0, s_1, b) = tt \\ \mathit{ff} & \text{otherwise} \end{cases}$

implication: $\quad val(s_0, s_1, a\ \mathtt{==>}\ b) = \begin{cases} tt & val(s_0, s_1, a) = \mathit{ff} \vee val(s_0, s_1, b) = tt \\ \mathit{ff} & \text{otherwise} \end{cases}$

quantification: $val(s_0, s_1, (\backslash\mathtt{forall}\ \mathtt{T}\ \mathtt{x};\ a;\ b))$
$\qquad = \begin{cases} tt & \forall y \in V_T \setminus null : val(s_0\{x \mapsto y\}, s_1\{x \mapsto y\}, a\ \mathtt{==>}\ b) = tt \\ \mathit{ff} & \text{otherwise} \end{cases}$

old state: $\quad val(s_0, s_1, \backslash\mathtt{old}(a)) = val(s_0, s_0, a)$

4 Semantics of ε Terms

When Hilbert first introduced ε terms, he provided only a vague informal understanding of their semantics. This has led to some interesting discussions on a formalization. In this section, we mainly reprise the account given in [7].

A *pre-structure* of first-order logic with ε terms is a triple $\mathfrak{S} = (\mathcal{U}, \mathcal{I}, \mathcal{A})$ consisting of a domain $\mathcal{U}$, an interpretation $\mathcal{I}$ of predicates and functions as in classical logic, and additionally an ε-*valuation function* $\mathcal{A}$. The function $\mathcal{A}$ maps a term $\varepsilon x.\varphi$ and a variable assignment β to a value $\mathcal{A}(\varepsilon x.\varphi, \beta) \in \mathcal{U}$. To gain a 'more semantical' ε-valuation, *intensional* and eventually *extensional* semantics have been introduced.

Definition 1. *An* intensional structure $\mathfrak{S} = (\mathcal{U}, \mathcal{I}, \mathcal{A})$ *is a pre-structure in which the valuation of an ε term $\varepsilon x.\varphi$ only depends on the valuation of free variables occurring in φ, and $\mathcal{A}$ points to a value that actually satisfies φ if such a value exists:*

- *If* $\beta_1|_{fv(\varphi)} = \beta_2|_{fv(\varphi)}$ *then* $\mathcal{A}(\varepsilon x.\varphi, \beta_1) = \mathcal{A}(\varepsilon x.\varphi, \beta_2)$
  (where $\beta_i|_{fv(\varphi)}$ is the restriction of β_i to the free variables in φ).
- *If* $\mathfrak{S}, \beta \models \exists x.\varphi$ *then* $\mathfrak{S}, \beta\{x \mapsto \mathcal{A}(\varepsilon x.\varphi, \beta)\} \models \varphi$.

Intensional semantics may still assign different values to syntactically different but logically equivalent terms. *Extensional* structures, on the contrary, are built on a deterministic (total) choice function on the set of applicable values, the *extension*.

Definition 2. *The* extension Ext *of an ε term w.r.t. a structure and an assignment is defined as*

$$Ext(\mathfrak{S}, \beta, \varepsilon x.\varphi) := \{u \in \mathcal{U} \mid (\mathfrak{S}, \beta\{x \mapsto u\}) \models \varphi\} \ .$$

An intensional structure $\mathfrak{S} = (\mathcal{U}, \mathcal{I}, \mathcal{A})$ *with the following property is called an* extensional structure:

- *If* $Ext(\mathfrak{S}, \beta, \varepsilon x.\varphi) = Ext(\mathfrak{S}, \beta, \varepsilon y.\psi)$ *then* $\mathcal{A}(\varepsilon x.\varphi, \beta) = \mathcal{A}(\varepsilon y.\psi, \beta)$.

Note that extensions may be empty; in that case, $\mathcal{A}$ yields an arbitrary element of the universe. Extensional semantics are strictly stronger than intensional semantics, in the sense that they have more valid formulas. Take, for instance, the formula $\varepsilon x.\varphi \doteq \varepsilon x.\neg\neg\varphi$. It is valid in any extensional structure, but not in all intensional structures.

4.1 A Generalization of ε Terms

As we will further discuss in Section 5.2, model field specifications—in contrast to formulae in logic—are highly non-modular as represents clauses may depend on each other. Therefore, it is not always possible to express the value of a model field in terms of an ε term. In the following, we introduce the notion of *generalized ε terms*, which denote values for non-empty finite sequences of variables instead of single variables.

Definition 3 (Generalized ε term, syntax). *Let $\bar{x}$ be a non-empty finite sequence of pairwise distinct variables, let $i \in \mathbb{N}$, and let φ be a formula.*
    Then $\varepsilon\bar{x}_i.\varphi$ is a generalized ε term.

Definition 4 (Generalized extension). *The* generalized extension Ext *of a generalized ε term $\varepsilon\bar{x}_i.\varphi$ w.r.t. a structure and an assignment is defined as*

$$Ext(\mathfrak{S}, \beta, \varepsilon\langle x_0, \ldots, x_{n-1}\rangle_i.\varphi) :=$$
$$\{\langle u_0, \ldots, u_{n-1}\rangle \in \mathcal{U}^n \mid \mathfrak{S}, \beta\{x_j \mapsto u_j \mid 0 \le j < n\} \models \varphi\}$$

Note that the generalized extension contains n-tuples and is independent of the index i. We now extend the definition of structures to the case of generalized ε terms. The conditions imposed on the ε-evaluation function $\mathcal{A}$ in the following definition implies both the requirements made in Definitions 1 and 2, i.e., every generalised ε structure is extensional:

Definition 5 (Generalized ε term, semantics). *A pre-structure $\mathfrak{S} = (\mathcal{U}, \mathcal{I}, \mathcal{A})$ with the following properties is called a generalized ε structure:*

- **(Intensionality)**   If $Ext(\mathfrak{S}, \beta, \varepsilon \bar{x}_0.\varphi) \neq \emptyset$ then

$$\langle \mathcal{A}(\varepsilon \bar{x}_0.\varphi, \beta), \dots, \mathcal{A}(\varepsilon \bar{x}_{|\bar{x}|-1}.\varphi, \beta) \rangle \in Ext(\mathfrak{S}, \beta, \varepsilon \bar{x}_0.\varphi)$$

- **(Extensionality)**   If $Ext(\mathfrak{S}, \beta, \varepsilon \bar{x}_0.\varphi) = Ext(\mathfrak{S}, \beta, \varepsilon \bar{y}_0.\psi)$ then $\mathcal{A}(\varepsilon \bar{x}_i.\varphi, \beta) = \mathcal{A}(\varepsilon \bar{y}_i.\psi, \beta)$ for any i.

5   A Novel Approach to Model Field Semantics

We return to the evaluation of expressions in JML and present a first approach to model field semantics that is inspired by extensional ε term semantics (without using ε terms explicitly). As commonly accepted, program references can be approximately identified with variables in logic, as system states can be identified with valuations. In a way similar to the ε-valuation function $\mathcal{A}$ introduced above, we define a model field valuation function $\varepsilon : \mathcal{S} \times \mathcal{U} \times Id \times Expr \to \mathcal{U}$, which takes a state, a receiver object, a model field's identifier, and a constraining expression (from the represents clause) as parameters. We then build the definition of an extended valuation function val_ε for JML expressions on top.

Let us first define the *extension*, i.e., the set of semantical objects for which a state s validates a boolean JML expression φ with a field identifier x and receiver object o which simulates a heap location (o, x), in a way reminiscent to the above definition:

Definition 6 (Extension).

$$Ext_\varepsilon(s, o, \text{x}, \varphi) := \{ u \in V_{typeof(\text{x})} \mid val_\varepsilon(s, s\{\text{this} \mapsto o, (o, \text{x}) \mapsto u\}, \varphi) = t\!t \}$$

The extension is defined w.r.t. only one state. The reason is that the \old operation may not occur in represents clauses.

An extensional ε-valuation function is independent of the syntactical shape of the constraining formula but only depends on its extension. It therefore can be seen as a deterministic choice function $\chi : 2^{\mathcal{U}} \to \mathcal{U}$ applied on the extension set.[2] This seems plausible—except that in program specification, this is against the intuitive view that different locations hold values which are independent of each other. In other words: all model fields with logically equivalent represents clauses would be ==-equal. Therefore, we introduce (possibly) different choice functions for different model fields through a weaker version of extensionality and instead use a *family* of choice functions that contains a choice function $\chi_{(T,i)}$ for each type $T \in \mathcal{T}$ and identifier $i \in Id$.

Let T' be the type where x is declared. Then, an ε-valuation w.r.t. a choice function $\chi_{(T',i)}$ is defined by:

$$\varepsilon(s, o, \text{x}, \varphi) := \chi_{(T', \text{x})}(Ext_\varepsilon(s, o, \text{x}, \varphi)) \ .$$

---

[2] Note that χ is a total function and, in particular, yields an underspecified value $\chi(\emptyset)$.

In addition to the above mentioned information, we need to extract representation clauses from the annotated program. Let $rep(T, \mathbf{x})$ denote the represents clause declared in type T constraining model field $\mathbf{x}$. We are finally able to extend our definition of val from Sect. 3 to val_ε to include model field validation:

Definition 7. *If* $\mathbf{x}$ *is a model field, then*

$$val_\varepsilon(s_0, s_1, a.\mathbf{x}) := \varepsilon(s_1, val_\varepsilon(s_0, s_1, a), \mathbf{x}, rep(val_\varepsilon(s_0, s_1, a), \mathbf{x}))$$

Although extension and valuation are defined mutually recursively, this definition is well-founded since there is only a finite number of model fields which are referenced in a single expression.

5.1   Discussion

Frame properties. Framing is an essential means to specify and verify programs in a modular way. With the following remark, our approach for defining the semantics of model fields allows framing, i.e., restricting the possible assignments for fields. This is a purely semantical criterion—without (syntactically) naming dependencies explicitly.

Assuming a fixed choice function χ and, thus, a fixed valuation ε, there is only one possible object value for each model field as long as the values of its concrete dependencies remain unchanged, even if other parts of the state change.

The value for a model field can be observed in *any* state without additional care. While some authors [13,15,16] define model field semantics only for states in which the receiver object's invariant holds, our definition is independent of the particular semantics of invariants.

Handling undefinedness. Our definition of semantical evaluation of model fields is independent of how undefinedness in expressions is handled (e.g., division by zero or null pointer references). In JML—as in Java—an expression φ is only well-defined if its subexpressions are themselves well-defined, namely those which are relevant in a short-circuit evaluation read from left to right. On the top level, a boolean expression is considered valid if it is well-defined and yields the value tt. This can be seen as a non-symmetric, conservative three-valued logic. One could easily extend this notion of well-definedness to model fields where a reference expression is well-defined only if there is a non-empty extension.

Applications. Up to now, there exist various tools which use annotation-based languages as specification input: runtime checkers, static analyzers, and formal deductive verification tools. As our semantics is independent from any verification methodology, we believe that it can be used to check whether those applications implement model fields in a consistent way. For runtime-checking, however, it may be necessary to fix a certain choice function which is easy to compute, e.g., to choose the least element w.r.t. some order.

5.2   An Improved Approach

The above approach works well in most cases—even when a represents clause contains references to other model fields. However, the evaluation is local to single model fields in the sense that it only establishes the relations between a model field and its dependencies. In the case where references are cyclic, the relation between model fields are ignored. Consider the following two represents clauses:

represents x \such_that x >= y; represents y \such_that y >= x;

Both are clearly satisfiable, but when evaluated separately, it is not implied that x and y are assigned the same value. For a sound evaluation in that case, instead of making a choice from a set of *values*, we need to make a choice from the set of *valuations* conforming with all represents clauses simultaneously. Let $\mathcal{L}_s$ be the (finite) set of model field locations (i.e., pairs of receiver objects/classes and field identifiers) whose receiver object is created in state s (or has been statically initialized). Then, the *heap extension HExt*, as motivated by generalized extensions (Def. 4), can be given as follows. It consists of functions from locations to values—the same domain as the heap—under which all represents clauses valuate to true. This means that those functions extend the actual heap. Since there is a valuation for each model field, only one choice function is required.

Definition 8 (Generalized model field valuation). *Let $\bar{\chi}$ be a fixed choice function on $\mathcal{U}^{\mathcal{U} \times Id}$. Then define heap extension $HExt(s)$ and valuation $val_{\bar{\varepsilon}}$:*

$$HExt(s) := \left\{ h \in \mathcal{U}^{\mathcal{U} \times Id} \mid \forall (o, \mathbf{x}) \in \mathcal{L}_s . \, val_{\bar{\varepsilon}}(s, s \oplus h \oplus \{\mathbf{this} \mapsto o\}, rep(o, \mathbf{x})) = t\! t \right\}$$
$$val_{\bar{\varepsilon}}(s_0, s_1, a.\mathbf{x}) := (\bar{\chi} HExt(s_1)) (val_{\bar{\varepsilon}}(s_0, s_1, a), \mathbf{x})$$

The heap extension set may lead to fewer values for a particular model field when compared with the simple extension defined above. Those belonged to a partial (local) solution in which not *all* represents clauses are satisfied simultaneously. However, all aspects which we discussed in Sect. 5.1 still apply to this definition.

```
public class LinkedList {                                       1
    private /*@ nullable @*/ LinkedList next;                   2
    private Object contents;                                    3
    /*@ model int index;                                        4
    @ represents index \such_that                               5
    @                 next == null || index < next.index; @*/   6
}                                                               7
```

Fig. 2. Non-functional represents clause: index of a linked list

Example 1. Figure 2 shows an implementation of a linked list. In JML, it is necessary to add the modifier `nullable` to the `next` list element because as the default all object references must not point to `null` unless declared explicitly.

The represents clause of the model field `index` guarantees that the list is actually acyclic as its value needs to be strictly less than `index` of the next element. Let us determine the value of `this.index` in a state $s = (\eta, \sigma)$ where

$$\sigma(\mathtt{this}) = ll_0, \quad \eta(ll_0, \mathtt{next}) = ll_1, \quad \eta(ll_1, \mathtt{next}) = ll_2, \quad \eta(ll_2, \mathtt{next}) = null$$

and $ll_0, ll_1, ll_2 \in V_{\mathtt{LinkedList}}$ are the only objects created in s. From this it follows that $\mathcal{L}(s) = \{(ll_0, \mathtt{index}), (ll_1, \mathtt{index}), (ll_2, \mathtt{index})\}$. Then

$$HExt(s) = \left\{ h \in (V_{\mathtt{int}})^{\mathcal{U} \times Id} \mid h(ll_0, \mathtt{index}) < h(ll_1, \mathtt{index}) < h(ll_2, \mathtt{index}) \right\} \ ,$$

which is clearly not empty and some function can be chosen.

6   Related Work

Even though JML is designed to be interchangeably used with various specification and program analysis techniques, the issue of handling model fields is still subject to an on-going debate. There are several approaches to integrate model fields into verification. There, semantics are mostly implicit in the respective methodology or calculus. A preliminary version of the semantics in this work has also appeared in [4, Sect. 3.1.5].

Substitution-based Approaches. Breunesse and Poll [3] present a semantics using substitutions in expressions. The clear advantage of this technique is that no additional evaluation rules are needed. Given a model field x of type T with a represents clause ψ and a JML expression φ which contains x, the following transformation is applied: $\varphi \quad \rightsquigarrow \quad (\texttt{\\forall } T \texttt{ x; } \psi; \varphi) \texttt{ \&\& } (\texttt{\\exists } T \texttt{ x; true; } \psi)$

In the result, φ appears as the body of a quantifier expression with the model field x as the quantified variable. This transformation is done for every model field declared in the program. The resulting expression asserts both that φ holds if the represents clause ψ is true as well as the existence of a value that satisfies ψ.

However, this approach is syntactically restricted since the order in which an expression is transformed does matter. Moreover, model fields may depend on each other, so if ψ contains a reference to another model field y, the scope of quantification of y has to include ψ. Thus, the semantics of model fields is only well-defined if there exists a linear ordering of dependencies and an upper bound on their length. .

Concrete Instantiations. There are two approaches by Leino and Müller [13] and Tafat et al. [15], respectively, based on ownership methodology, which is used in Spec# and ACSL among other languages. Model field values are stored on the heap, like concrete or ghost fields. In contrast to JML, they are defined not to change their value instantaneously when the locations change on which they depend, but at given program points, namely upon invoking the special `pack` operation on its owner.

In these works, represents clauses are not allowed to contain calls to pure methods, and references to other model fields only in a few restricted cases. It is not clear whether there are restrictions on the chosen values in case the represents clause is not functional. Thus it may be possible, according to this definition, that the value of a model field spontaneously changes upon packing even though all dependencies retain their values.

Axiomatic Semantics. Weiß [16] presents a dynamic logic with explicit heap objects. Model fields are translated to function symbols. Represents clauses are introduced through logical axioms. As a simple solution to avoid an inconsistent axiom set, they are guarded by an existentially quantified assumption, which guarantees that the single represents clause is satisfiable. Mutually recursive represents clauses may, however, give rise to inconsistent axiom sets.

Frame Conditions. Much of the above is dedicated to how model fields gain their values. Another important property is to specify when a model field's value does *not change*, known as a frame condition. To this end, Weiß introduces contracts for model fields [16], similar to frame conditions on methods, which have to be respected by implementing represents clauses. Here, the argument of a frame condition is an expression of type \locset ('set of locations') which is dynamically valuated. This approach, known as *dynamic frames* theory, is particularly useful when the concrete fields on which a model field depends are not known on the abstract level.

7   Conclusion and Outlook

In this paper, we have presented a semantics for model fields in annotation-based specification languages. The first version is strongly inspired by the notion of ε terms as introduced by Hilbert. We have demonstrated the connection between those two concepts—one from an established theory and one as a current challenge in formal methods in software engineering. While this semantics exposes a 'good behavior' in most cases, the general case requires a different methodology. This second version covers the complete expression sub-language of JML.

To the best of our knowledge this is the first contribution in which model fields are described in all their extent and in an application-independent way. This means that the results can be applied to any verification paradigm. It also provides the basis to independently give a definition of well-definedness.

Model fields are a powerful instrument in code-level specification which hides behind the familiar syntactical guise. However, it is debatable whether there is a real demand for non-functional relations. Commonly, within the technique of abstraction, there are several concrete entities which are related to *one* abstract representation. In the vast majority of instances, there is always a sensible functional representation. In Fig. 2 for instance, we have seen an example where the represents clause exposes a kind of weakly functional behavior, while it would not do any harm to overspecify the relation and provide values to any case which is yet left undefined.

References

1. Barnett, M., Leino, K.R.M., Schulte, W.: The Spec# Programming System: An Overview. In: Barthe, G., Burdy, L., Huisman, M., Lanet, J.-L., Muntean, T. (eds.) CASSIS 2004. LNCS, vol. 3362, pp. 49–69. Springer, Heidelberg (2005)
2. Baudin, P., Cuoq, P., Filliâtre, J.C., Marché, C., Monate, B., Moy, Y., Prevosto, V.: ACSL: ANSI/ISO C Specification Language, Version 1.5 (2010)
3. Breunesse, C.B., Poll, E.: Verifying JML specifications with model fields. In: Formal Techniques for Java-like Programs (FTfJP), pp. 51–60. No. 408 in Technical Report, ETH Zurich (July 2003)
4. Bruns, D.: Formal Semantics for the Java Modeling Language. Diploma thesis, Universität Karlsruhe (2009)
5. Darvas, Á., Müller, P.: Formal encoding of JML level 0 specifications in JIVE. Tech. Rep. 559, ETH Zürich (2007)
6. Engel, C.: A translation from JML to JavaDL. Studienarbeit, Fakultät für Informatik, Universität Karlsruhe (February 2005)
7. Giese, M., Ahrendt, W.: Hilbert's ε-Terms in Automated Theorem Proving. In: Murray, N.V. (ed.) TABLEAUX 1999. LNCS (LNAI), vol. 1617, pp. 171–185. Springer, Heidelberg (1999)
8. Hilbert, D., Bernays, P.: Grundlagen der Mathematik, vol. II. Springer (1939)
9. Hoare, C.A.R.: Proof of correctness of data representations. Acta Informatica 1, 271–281 (1972)
10. Jacobs, B., Poll, E.: A logic for the Java Modeling Language (JML). Tech. Rep. CSI-R0018, University of Nijmegen, Computing Science Institute (November 2000)
11. Leavens, G.T., Baker, A.L., Ruby, C.: Preliminary design of JML: A behavioral interface specification language for Java. ACM SIGSOFT Software Engineering Notes 31(3), 1–38 (2006)
12. Leavens, G.T., Poll, E., Clifton, C., Cheon, Y., Ruby, C., Cok, D., Müller, P., Kiniry, J., Chalin, P., Zimmerman, D.M.: JML Reference Manual (July 13, 2011)
13. Leino, K.R.M., Müller, P.: A Verification Methodology for Model Fields. In: Sestoft, P. (ed.) ESOP 2006. LNCS, vol. 3924, pp. 115–130. Springer, Heidelberg (2006)
14. Leino, K.R.M., Nelson, G.: Data abstraction and information hiding. ACM Transactions on Programming Languages and Systems 24(5), 491–553 (2002)
15. Tafat, A., Boulmé, S., Marché, C.: A Refinement Methodology for Object-Oriented Programs. In: Beckert, B., Marché, C. (eds.) FoVeOOS 2010. LNCS, vol. 6528, pp. 153–167. Springer, Heidelberg (2011)
16. Weiß, B.: Deductive Verification of Object-Oriented Software — Dynamic Frames, Dynamic Logic and Predicate Abstraction. Ph.D. thesis, Karlsruhe Institute of Technology (January 2011)

Searching with Partial Belief States
in General Games with Incomplete Information

Stefan Edelkamp[1], Tim Federholzner[1], and Peter Kissmann[2]

[1] TZI Universität Bremen, Germany
{edelkamp,tif}@tzi.de
[2] Universität des Saarlandes, Saarbrücken, Germany
kissmann@cs.uni-saarland.de

Abstract. In this paper we present a full-fledged player for general games with incomplete information specified in the game description language GDL-II. To deal with uncertainty we introduce a method that operates on partial belief states, which correspond to a subset of the set of states building a full belief state. To search for a partial belief state we present depth-first and Monte-Carlo methods. All can be combined with any traditional general game player, e.g., using mini-max or UCT search.

Our general game player is shown to be effective in a number of benchmarks and the UCT variant compares positively with the one-and-only winner of an incomplete information track at an international general game playing competition.

1 Introduction

General game playing (GGP) urges the computer to process the rules of the game and start to play, thus operating without including expert knowledge of the game that is played. In the context of international GGP competitions [6] the rules are specified in a logical formalism, called the game description language (GDL) [12]. The games are played on a server, which connects with GGP agents via TCP/IP. After some startup time the game starts and according to a play clock moves have to be issued. Moves are executed on the server and reported to the players in order to continue.

As randomness and handling incomplete information is a necessity for playing many games (e.g., card games), with the extension GDL-II [19] (for GDL with incomplete information) both recently became part of the accepted standard for general game playing. It has been shown that GDL-II can be mapped to situation calculus [17], while [15] highlights connections of GDL/GDL-II and epistemic logic.

Only few players have been developed so far, and documentation is rare. At the only international GGP competition that supported incomplete information games in GDL-II, Schiffel's FLUXII was clearly the best. The name indicates that the player is based on the internationally very successful FLUXPLAYER [18].

Currently, the number of GDL-II benchmark problems incorporating incomplete information is rather small. Even though all specified games can be played, current players often have difficulties handling some of their complexities, especially due to the additional efforts required to handle incomplete information. Players act in the so-called belief state space and some assumptions of the current state might become invalid due to incoming information provided by the server.

B. Glimm and A. Krüger (Eds.): KI 2012, LNCS 7526, pp. 25–36, 2012.
© Springer-Verlag Berlin Heidelberg 2012

In this paper we provide insights to the design and implementation of our GDL-II player NEXUSBAUM. We start with a brief introduction to general game playing (Section 2), where we address existing players and their techniques to play classical GDL games, and turn to the problems encountered when addressing incomplete information. For these problems we provide search solutions (Section 3) that act on subsets of the actual sets building the belief states. In the experiments (Section 4) we see that using these strategies for simple single-player GDL-II games (such as MEMORY and the MONTY HALL problem) NEXUSBAUM plays almost perfectly. Moreover, we show that in a two-player scenario our approach can meet the effectiveness of FLUXII. Finally we will draw some conclusions and point to possible extensions in the future (Section 5).

2   General Game Playing

2.1   GDL

As the description of syntax and semantics in GDL [12] is involved we prefer a set-based definition of a general game.

Definition 1 (General Game). *A general game can be described by a tuple of the form* $(P, S, s_0, T, S, M, L, succ, reward)$, *where*

- *P is the set of roles (the players),*
- *S is the set of all states,*
- *$s_0 \in S$ is the (unique) initial state,*
- *$T \subseteq S$ is the set of terminal states,*
- *M is the set of moves,*
- *$L \subseteq M \times P \times S$ is the set of legal moves for the specified player in the specified state,*
- *$succ$ is a mapping $L^{|P|} \times S \to S$ for the calculation of the successor states, and*
- *$reward$ is a mapping $P \times T \to \{0, \ldots, 100\}$ that defines the rewards of the players upon reaching a terminal state.*

In the first two GGP competitions, players making use of *Minimax* search [14] were prevalent, such as CLUNEPLAYER [3] and FLUXPLAYER [18], the winners of the first two international GGP competitions. The difficulty of the minimax based approaches is to find a good evaluation function that will work well for any game, as most games cannot be fully analyzed in the available time.

Since 2007, the most successful GGP agents such as CADIAPLAYER [5] or ARY [13] use *UCT* [10] to calculate the next move to play. UCT is a simulation based method that stores only small parts of the actual game tree in memory. Each simulation run starts at the root node and selects as the next move to take the one maximizing the UCT formula

$$UCT(s, m) = Q(s, m) + C\sqrt{\frac{\log N(s, m)}{N(s)}},$$

with $UCT(s, m)$ being the UCT value of move m in state s, $Q(s, m)$ the average reward achieved when choosing move m in state s, C a constant for controlling the

```
(role random)
(<= (legal random (flip ?coin1 ?coin2))
    (coin ?coin1) (coin ?coin2)
)
(coin heads) (coin tails)
```

Fig. 1. Legal moves of random in the coin flipping example

exploration versus exploitation ratio, $N(s)$ the number of times state s was expanded, and $N(s, m)$ the number of times move m was chosen in state s.

As an example of the portfolio of UCT search control heuristics, we refer to the *killer heuristic* [1], a method originally introduced to minimax based algorithms to improve pruning. The list of moves is sorted according to the success of pruning. This can be ported to UCT by sorting the moves according to the statistics of rewards similar to [4]. However, the effect is not always as big as in Minimax.

2.2   GDL-II

Syntactically, GDL-II [19] is a small extension, as it mainly adds two keywords. The first one is an additional role in P, called *random*, which chooses its moves uniformly at random. The other one is the predicate *sees* that defines the visibility of information to the players. While in GDL the players were informed of the moves that all participating players have chosen, in case of GDL-II the players are informed only of what they can see. Nevertheless, the players should always be able to determine the set of legal moves they currently may choose and should also be able to determine a terminal state.

Let us consider some fragments of a simple coin flipping example. At any time, the random player can only flip two coins (cf. Figure 1). The two possibilities for each coin are *heads* and *tails* and for each coin they are independent of the other. As it is the random player, we know that it will choose each of the four possible moves with the same probability.

The first coin determines what the first player may do, the second one decides what the second player may do. If a coin shows *heads* and the corresponding player has chosen *go*, it is moving forward (cf. Figure 2). However, if the coin shows *tails*, the player is blocked and thus does not change the position. If it chose to *stay* it will stay at the previous position as well independent of the outcome of the coin throw.

To determine if the players were able to move the observations are sent according to the *sees* rule (cf. Figure 3). Here it informs the players only about the results of the coin flip performed by the random player, so that the actual position of the own player has to be evaluated based on the performed moves, while that of the opponent is unknown, as a player does not know if the opponent chose to go or stay.

Concerning GDL-II search control heuristics there is a much wider spectrum of possibilities. One can maximize the own flexibility, i.e., prefer nodes with large branching factor, in order not to get stuck too quickly, or minimize the branching factor of the opponent. Such heuristics are to be implemented with care. While flexibility is often good for games like CHESS, in CHECKERS pieces are sacrificed too quickly because

```
(<= (next (position white ?n2))
    (does white go)  (does random (flip heads ?other))
    (true (position white ?n1))  (next_pos ?n1 ?n2)
)
(<= (next (position white ?n))
    (does white go)  (does random (flip tails ?other))
    (true (position white ?n))
)
(<= (next (position white ?n))
    (does white stay)
    (true (position white ?n))
)
```

Fig. 2. Update of the positions of white player in the coin flipping example. The update for the black player is analogue.

```
(<= (sees ?r (did random (flip ?coin1 ?coin2)))
    (role ?r)
    (does random (flip ?coin1 ?coin2))
)
```

Fig. 3. The information the players see in the coin flipping example

the players are required to capture opponent's pieces whenever they can. A better rule of thumb for GDL-II games is to maximize the own knowledge, and minimize the one offered to the opponents. However, the former can also lead to too many sacrifices, e.g., in KRIEGSPIEL, and the latter to avoid conflict that has to be resolved. As with the no-free lunch theorems in optimization there is hardly a heuristic that is effective for all games.

3 Handling Incomplete Information

When playing incomplete information games a player is confronted with the problem that it does not know the precise state. A first idea to get as much information as possible concerning the current state might be to evaluate all the observations based on the *sees* rules it has received during play. However, evaluating the corresponding rules often does not yield enough information.

Another approach is to handle *belief states*. A belief state is a set of states that the player believes might be true. The actual situation is one of the states building the belief state, but we do not know which element of the entire set it is. In this paper we propose two approaches: First, to always store the full belief states, and secondly to store only a subset of the set building the belief state, which we call a *partial belief state* and update it after a move or whenever we find that some state cannot hold anymore.

Algorithm 1. Finding the full belief state

Input: General Game, belief state of last step BS_{i-1}, set of observations of last step
Obs_{i-1}.
Output: Belief state of this step BS_i.

1 $BS_i \leftarrow \emptyset$;
2 **for all** $bs \in BS_{i-1}$ **do**
3 $\quad$ determine all possible joint moves JM;
4 $\quad$ **for all** $jm \in JM$ **do**
5 $\quad\quad$ $Obs' \leftarrow observe(bs, jm)$;
6 $\quad\quad$ **if** $Obs' = Obs_{i-1}$ **then**
7 $\quad\quad\quad$ $bs' \leftarrow succ(bs, jm)$;
8 $\quad\quad\quad$ $BS_i \leftarrow BS_i \cup \{bs'\}$;

9 **return** BS_i;

3.1 Full Belief States

At the beginning of each playing phase we must generate the new belief state BS_i based on the one of the previous step BS_{i-1} (cf. Algorithm 1). While several datastructures such as POMDPs [9,20] or BDDs [2] for the handling belief states have been used in the past, for this first implementation we decided to stick to an explicit representation. For each state $bs \in BS_{i-1}$ we determine all the moves of all other players – we of course know our own move – and calculate all possible joint moves JM. For each of these joint moves we check if the observations we would have achieved if these were the actual moves played equal those we did receive (Obs). If they do, we know that this joint move might really have been performed, so that we compute the corresponding successor state bs' and add it to BS_i.

While at first glance it seems great to have the full belief states in order to en-hance the performance of the player, it comes at a high cost. Take the game of POKER with three players. Each player knows only the five cards it owns, so that there are $\binom{47}{5,5,37} = 1,304,872,821,252$ possible states building the full belief state after dealing the cards. Storing all of these and efficiently operating on them is very expensive and the calculation of the next move might take more than the available play clock. Thus, for more complex games it seems better to store only a subset of all possible states.

3.2 Partial Belief States

If we do not want to store the full belief states we instead store a tree that allows us to find new possible states when we have to discard impossible ones. We call this tree the *belief state tree*. Each node of the belief state tree corresponds to a state the player believes to be possible (or mark it as being impossible), each edge to a joint move. The root of the tree is the initial state of the game, which we know to be the only state possible at the start of the game. For each node representing a possible state we store the full set of possible successor states. Each node can have one of three different values.

possible. We have evaluated that state and found that the observations we get when performing the ingoing joint move are equal to those we actually observed.

impossible. We have evaluated that state and either the observations when taking the joint move leading to it do not match the observed ones or all its successors are marked as impossible.

unknown. We have not yet evaluated that state and thus do not know if it is possible or not.

In order to find a subset of the possible states after a move was performed we distinguish two approaches, one based on depth-first search, which we call *depth-first belief state search* (DFBSS), and the other based on random choice, which we call *Monte-Carlo belief state search* (MCBSS). Such a subset then builds the partial belief state we use in order to determine the next move to take.

Depth-First Belief State Search (DFBSS). Starting at the root of the belief state tree, i.e., layer 0, we continue in a depth-bounded DFS manner until either the current layer i contains the desired number of possible states ($size$) or the full tree has been evaluated (cf. Algorithm 2).

When we reach a node with unknown value we evaluate it. If it is possible we continue further along that node. Otherwise we mark it as impossible and continue with its siblings.

When we reach a node representing a possible state we continue either to the first possible successor we have not visited in this search, or – if there is none – to the first successor with unknown value.

Upon reaching the current layer and evaluating the reached state as possible we store it in BS_i, the partial belief state in the current layer i, and continue with its siblings.

Monte-Carlo Belief State Search (MCBSS). A disadvantage of DFBSS is that it often has to evaluate large parts of the belief state tree. Especially when a layer is reached where the size of the full belief state is smaller than the subset size we wish to store, DFBSS has to search the entire tree. Thus, the main bottleneck of DFBSS we found in preliminary experiments is that it still is too slow. To overcome this problem we came up with a Monte-Carlo based search in the belief state tree (cf. Algorithm 3).

Instead of performing depth-first search we use several Monte-Carlo runs, each starting at the root node, the initial state of the game. When a state is reached that is marked as possible we randomly choose one of its successors and continue from that. If a state with unknown value is reached we must evaluate it. If it is impossible we mark it as such, recursively remove it and its predecessors if those now only have impossible successors, and afterward restart at the root node. If the node is evaluated as being possible we continue from that node. Whenever we reach a possible node in the current layer i we add the corresponding state bs to the partial belief state for the current step BS_i.

The algorithm stops when the specified number of states ($size$) is found. Note that these states do not have to be different – otherwise we might run into the same problem

---

Algorithm 2. Depth-First Belief State Search (DFBSS)

Input: General game, belief state tree BST, set of observations of all steps Obs, current
       step i, size of partial belief state $size$.

Output: Updated belief state tree BST, current partial belief state BS_i.

1 $layer \leftarrow 0$; $bs \leftarrow root(BST)$; $BS_i \leftarrow \emptyset$;
2 **while** $|BS_i| < size$ **and** $(hasMorePossibleSuccs(bs)$ **or** $hasUnknownSucc(bs))$ **do**
3     $jm \leftarrow jointMoveTo(bs)$;
4   **if** $isUnknown(bs)$ **then**
5       $Obs' \leftarrow observe(bs, jm)$;
6   **if** $Obs' = Obs_{layer}$ **then**
7         $\lfloor$ $markPossible(bs)$;
8   **else**
9         $markImpossible(bs)$;
10        $bs \leftarrow parent(bs)$;
11        $layer \leftarrow layer - 1$;

12   **if** $isPossible(bs)$ **then**
13   **if** $layer = i$ **then**
14         $\lfloor$ $BS_i \leftarrow BS_i \cup \{bs\}$;
15   **else if** $hasMorePossibleSuccs(bs)$ **then**
16         $bs \leftarrow nextPossibleSucc(bs)$;
17         $layer \leftarrow layer + 1$;
18   **else if** $hasUnknownSucc(bs)$ **then**
19         $bs \leftarrow firstUnknownSucc(bs)$;
20         $layer \leftarrow layer + 1$;
21   **else**
22   **if** $allSuccsImpossible(bs)$ **then**
23          $\lfloor$ $markImpossible(bs)$;
24         $bs \leftarrow parent(bs)$;
25         $layer \leftarrow layer - 1$;

26 **return** BST, BS_i;

---

as with DFBSS, because we would have to evaluate the entire belief state tree if the full belief state is smaller than $size$.

While in most cases MCBSS is a lot faster than DFBSS, memory consumption tends to be greater. In DFBSS only those nodes leading to possible states in the current layer remain, while in MCBSS we often store paths that are not fully evaluated to the current layer but rather ended in one state being impossible.

3.3 Choosing a Move for a (Full or Partial) Belief State

No matter if we manage the full belief state or only a partial one, each state of the set can be seen as the initial state of a classical GDL game and thus be handled by classical GGP approaches such as Minimax or UCT, similar to the sampling approaches used in BRIDGE [7] or SKAT [11].

Algorithm 3. Monte-Carlo Belief State Search (MCBSS)

Input: General game, belief state tree BST, set of observations of all steps Obs, current
        step i, size of partial belief state $size$.

Output: Updated belief state tree BST, current partial belief state BS_i.

1 $layer \leftarrow 0;\ bs \leftarrow root(BST);\ BS_i \leftarrow \emptyset;$
2 **while** $|BS_i| < size$ **do**
3 $\quad$ $jm \leftarrow jointMoveTo(bs);$
4 $\quad$ **if** $isUnknown(bs)$ **then**
5 $\quad\quad$ $Obs' \leftarrow observe(bs, jm);$
6 $\quad\quad$ **if** $Obs' = Obs_{layer}$ **then**
7 $\quad\quad\quad$ $markPossible(bs);$
8 $\quad\quad$ **else**
9 $\quad\quad\quad$ $markImpossible(bs);$
10 $\quad\quad\quad$ **while** $isImpossible(bs)$ **do**
11 $\quad\quad\quad\quad$ $bs \leftarrow parent(bs);$
12 $\quad\quad\quad\quad$ **if** $allChildrenImpossible(bs)$ **then**
13 $\quad\quad\quad\quad\quad$ $deleteAllChildren(bs);$
14 $\quad\quad\quad\quad\quad$ $markImpossible(bs);$
15 $\quad\quad$ $bs \leftarrow root(BST);$
16 $\quad\quad$ $layer \leftarrow 0;$

17 $\quad$ **if** $layer = i$ **then**
18 $\quad\quad$ $BS_i \leftarrow BS_i \cup \{bs\};$
19 $\quad\quad$ $bs \leftarrow root(BST);$
20 $\quad\quad$ $layer \leftarrow 0;$
21 $\quad$ **else**
22 $\quad\quad$ $bs \leftarrow randomSucc(bs);$
23 $\quad\quad$ $layer \leftarrow layer + 1;$

24 **return** $BST, BS_i;$

To determine which move to choose the results of the games must be combined. For
a minimax based approach the move maximizing

$$eval(m) = \frac{\sum_{bs \in BS_i} reward(bs, m)}{|BS_i|},$$

with m being a legal move and $reward(bs, m)$ being the estimated reward for move m
in state bs, is chosen.

For a simulation based approach the same function might be used. However, it is
possible to improve by integrating the number of simulation runs into the evaluation:

$$eval(m) = \frac{\sum_{bs \in BS_i} reward(bs, m) \times N(bs, m)}{\sum_{bs \in BS_i} N(bs, m)},$$

with $N(bs, m)$ being the number of times move m was evaluated in state bs. In other
words, the evaluations are weighted by their reliability. The results that were evaluated
more often are weighted higher than those evaluated only rarely.

Weighted MCBSS. A problem of MCBSS (as well as DFBSS) is that the partial belief state for the current step BS_i does not necessarily contain the true current state. Furthermore, it might even be that all the states in BS_i share only very few fluents with the current state.

To overcome this problem we can use the rules for determining the opponents' rewards. The estimated rewards determined for the various states in the evaluation process are stored together with the corresponding states within the belief state tree.

Instead of choosing a successor node uniformly at random, *weighted MCBSS* uses a probability distribution corresponding to those estimated rewards. Thus, a possible state with greater stored reward values for the opponents will be chosen with higher probability than one with smaller reward values. The idea here is that the opponents would typically perform a move that will ensure a higher reward in the end. The probability to choose a move is given by

$$P\left(\{m_{1i_1}, m_{2i_2}, \ldots, m_{pi_p}\}\right) = \prod_{k=1}^{p} \frac{estReward\,(m_{ki_k})}{\sum_{j=1}^{n_k} estReward\,(m_{kj})},$$

with p being the number of players, m_{ki_k} the move chosen by player k, $estReward(m_{ki_k})$ the estimated reward for player k when choosing move m_{ki_k}, and n_k the number of legal moves of player k. Note that our player's chosen move is known, so that, assuming we are player x and have chosen the yth move, the estimated rewards for our moves can be set to 100 for move m_{xy} and to 0 for all moves m_{xz} with $z \neq y$.

4 Experiments

So far, not many GDL-II games incorporating incomplete information have been published, and often they are either too simple or too hard. We selected the known benchmark MONTY HALL [16] and added the two games MEMORY and STRATEGO for evaluation.

According to a private communication with Stephan Schiffel, the competitor FLUXII uses full belief states. It has been implemented in *ECLiPSe-Prolog 6.0* and was added to the FLUXPLAYER infrastructure. During the startup time, static analyses are conducted to improve the performance during the search. Once the belief state is computed, UCT is applied. Afterward, results are merged.

Our player NEXUSBAUM stores only a subset of the belief states and applies MCBSS or weighted MCBSS to update it. The setup of the player including the calculation of the partial belief states and the accumulation of the results is implemented in *Java* using *SWI-Prolog*, while for performance reasons the Monte-Carlo simulations are implemented in *C++* using *ECLiPSe-Prolog 6.0*.

For the experiments we used a personal computer with an Intel Core $i7$ 920 CPU with 2.67 GHz and 12 GB RAM. Overall, the experiments took more than a full month.

4.1 Games Played

The MONTY HALL problem [16] has received much interest when it was first proposed. In that game we have a host (here modeled as the random player) and a player who has to decide which door to take. The host places a car behind one door, which the player is supposed to find, and goats behind the other two. After the player has chosen a door, the host opens one of the unchosen doors containing a goat, and allows the player to switch to the other unopened door. Actually, this switching is the best move the player can take, resulting in a probability of 2/3 to find the car.

In MEMORY (*engl.* CONCENTRATION) the random player deals four pairs of cards, which the player cannot see. The player is supposed to find the corresponding pairs in as few moves as possible. In each move it may choose two cards. If they match they are removed, otherwise they remain on the board. In case a player gets lucky four moves suffice. However, the general best case is eight moves, which results in the full 100 points.

Our version of STRATEGO (*orig.* L'ATTAQUE) is played with six pieces for each player on a 3×6 board. Pieces are captured according to fixed precedence rules, similar to the original game. The goal is to take the opponent's flag before running out of steps. Otherwise, both players receive 50 points.

4.2   Results in the Games

For MONTY HALL we played a total of 100 games using a partial belief state size of 10 states, a startup time of 10 seconds and a play clock of 20 seconds. Overall, NEXUS-BAUM scored an average of 67 points, which relates well to the theoretical knowledge that the player will find the car with a probability of 2/3 if it switches the chosen door. Indeed, in all the 100 runs it chose to switch the door.

For MEMORY we also played a total of 100 games and used a partial belief state containing 10 states. Concerning the times, we used 10 seconds for the startup time and 120 seconds for the play clock. Overall, NEXUSBAUM played optimally in most cases. However, in a few runs it took nine or ten moves to find the correct pairs, which correspond to 75 and 50 points, respectively, resulting in a total average of 95 points.

In STRATEGO we first of all played 50 matches against a random player, half of them as first and the other half as second player. We used a partial belief state of size 10, a startup time of 30 seconds and a play clock of 60 seconds. Overall, NEXUSBAUM was able to win most of the time; only one match ended in a draw.

After these preliminary results in STRATEGO we decided to play against a real opponent, i.e., FLUXII. We used three different versions of NEXUSBAUM, one using only Monte-Carlo Belief State Search (MCBSS), one using weighted MCBSS (WMCBSS), both of which use a simple Monte-Carlo approach as the underlying player. However, in a final set of experiments we switched to using a UCT based player (WMCBSS+UCT). All versions played 50 matches against FLUXII, 25 as the first and 25 as the second player. The results are depicted in Table 1.

Concerning only MCBSS we can see that the results differ a lot with different play clocks. With smaller play clock the version using a partial belief state size (pbs size) of only 10 is clearly inferior to using a size of 15. However, with a play clock of 120 seconds using a size of 10 is a bit better than 15. This is quite surprising as the player sometimes actually has problems finding the 15 possible states in the available time. Given more time it should be able to find them more often and thus have more time to evaluate them.

Table 1. Results of the matches against FLUXII in STRATEGO

NEXUSBAUM version	start clock	play clock	pbs size	average reward for NEXUSBAUM
MCBSS	10	60	10	35.0
MCBSS	10	90	10	25.0
MCBSS	10	120	10	44.0
MCBSS	10	60	15	43.0
MCBSS	10	90	15	50.0
MCBSS	10	120	15	39.0
WMCBSS	10	60	10	38.0
WMCBSS	10	90	10	43.0
WMCBSS	10	60	15	44.0
WMCBSS	10	90	15	43.0
WMCBSS+UCT	10	60	10	56.0
WMCBSS+UCT	10	90	10	63.0

For WMCBSS we can see that using a play clock of 60 seconds and a pbs size of 10 or 15 or using a play clock of 90 seconds and a pbs size of 10 the average results achieved against FLUXII are better for the weighted version. However, when using a play clock of 90 seconds and a pbs size of 15 the unweighted MCBSS is superior. In fact, when using only a Monte-Carlo based player we can see that using unweighted MCBSS with a play clock of 90 seconds and a pbs size of 15 resulted in the highest average outcome. This is the only setting where NEXUSBAUM played with a strength comparable to FLUXII, resulting in an average of 50 points.

Finally, we turned on UCT search as well, and here we can see that we clearly can win against FLUXII. When using a pbs size of 10 and a play clock of 90 seconds we achieve an average reward of 63 points. Thus, it seems that in this setting our approach of managing only partial belief states is better than using the full belief states.

5   Conclusions and Future Work

The challenge of playing general games is to program autonomous agents that can play on a high level. For the new standard GDL-II that includes incomplete information games this paper proposes a competitive full-fledged GDL-II player, which – besides parsing, game controlling and some efficiency tricks – comes with a new game engine for handling (partial) belief states.

Handling randomness and incomplete information is computationally hard. Even for single-player general games, which can be cast to contingent action planning problems [8], it is known that complexities rise drastically.

Our player NEXUSBAUM maintains partial belief states and works best with weighted Monte-Carlo belief state search using an underlying UCT based player. It plays single-player games like MONTY HALL and MEMORY almost perfectly, and – for our case study of the complex game STRATEGO – it is shown to outperform Schiffel's FLUXII.

We found that calculating the desired number of possible states sometimes takes more time than the available play clock. This suggests future work in order to cut off evaluation of moves even if the partial belief state does not yet contain the desired number of states in order to further tune the implementation, and to parallelize the search.

References

1. Akl, S.G., Newborn, M.M.: The principal continuation and the killer heuristic. In: Annual ACM Conference, pp. 466–473 (1977)
2. Bertoli, P., Cimatti, A., Roveri, M., Traverso, P.: Strong planning under partial observability. Artificial Intelligence 170(4-5), 337–384 (2006)
3. Clune, J.: Heuristic evaluation functions for general game playing. In: AAAI, pp. 1134–1139 (2007)
4. Finnsson, H., Björnsson, Y.: Learning Simulation Control in General-Game-Playing Agents. In: AAAI, pp. 954–959 (2010)
5. Finnsson, H., Björnsson, Y.: Simulation-based approach to general game playing. In: AAAI, pp. 259–264 (2008)
6. Genesereth, M.R., Love, N., Pell, B.: General game playing: Overview of the AAAI competition. AI Magazine 26(2), 62–72 (2005)
7. Ginsberg, M.L.: GIB: Imperfect information in a computationally challenging game. JAIR 14, 303–358 (2001)
8. Hoffmann, J., Brafman, R.: Contingent planning via heuristic forward search with implicit belief states. In: ICAPS, pp. 71–80 (2005)
9. Kaebling, L.P., Littman, M.L., Cassandra, A.R.: Planning and acting in partially observable stochastic domains. Artificial Intelligence 101(1-2), 99–134 (1998)
10. Kocsis, L., Szepesvári, C.: Bandit Based Monte-Carlo Planning. In: Fürnkranz, J., Scheffer, T., Spiliopoulou, M. (eds.) ECML 2006. LNCS (LNAI), vol. 4212, pp. 282–293. Springer, Heidelberg (2006)
11. Kupferschmid, S., Helmert, M.: A Skat Player Based on Monte-Carlo Simulation. In: van den Herik, H.J., Ciancarini, P., Donkers, H.H.L.M(J.) (eds.) CG 2006. LNCS, vol. 4630, pp. 135–147. Springer, Heidelberg (2007)
12. Love, N.C., Hinrichs, T.L., Genesereth, M.R.: General game playing: Game description language specification. Tech. Rep. LG-2006-01, Stanford Logic Group (April 2006)
13. Méhat, J., Cazenave, T.: A parallel general game player. KI – Künstliche Intelligenz (Special Issue on General Game Playing) 25(1), 43–48 (2011)
14. von Neumann, J., Morgenstern, O.: Theory of Games and Economic Behavior. Princeton University Press (1944)
15. Ruan, J., Thielscher, M.: The Epistemic Logic Behind the Game Description Language. In: AAAI, pp. 840–845 (2011)
16. vos Savant, M.: Ask Marilyn. Parade Magazine (1990)
17. Schiffel, S., Thielscher, M.: Reasoning About General Games Described in GDL-II. In: AAAI, pp. 846–851 (2011)
18. Schiffel, S., Thielscher, M.: Fluxplayer: A successful general game player. In: AAAI, pp. 1191–1196 (2007)
19. Thielscher, M.: A general game description language for incomplete information games. In: Fox, M., Poole, D. (eds.) 24th AAAI Conference on Artificial Intelligence (AAAI), pp. 994–999. AAAI Press (2010)
20. Wolfe, J., Russell, S.: Exploiting belief state structure in graph search. In: ICAPS-Workshop on Planning in Games (2007)

A Machine-Learning Framework
for Hybrid Machine Translation

Christian Federmann

Language Technology Lab,
German Research Center for Artificial Intelligence,
Stuhlsatzenhausweg 3, D-66123 Saarbrücken, Germany
cfedermann@dfki.de

Abstract. We present a Machine-Learning-based framework for hybrid
Machine Translation. Our approach combines translation output from
several black-box source systems. We define an extensible, total order on
translation output and use this to decompose the n-best translations into
pairwise system comparisons. Using joint, binarised feature vectors we
train an SVM-based classifier and show how its classification output can
be used to generate hybrid translations on the sentence level. Evaluations
using automated metrics shows promising results. An interesting finding
in our experiments is the fact that our approach allows to leverage good
translations from otherwise bad systems as the combination decision is
taken on the sentence instead of the corpus level. We conclude by summarising our findings and by giving an outlook to future work, e.g., on
probabilistic classification or the integration of manual judgements.

Keywords: Hybrid Machine Translation, System Combination, Machine
Learning, Support Vector Machines, Feature-Based Classification.

1 Introduction

Research on the automatic translation of written texts or *machine translation*
(MT) has resulted in many different MT paradigms, each having individual
strengths and weaknesses. Amongst others, there are:

a) *statistical machine translation* (SMT) which aims at learning translation
   probabilities from large amounts of parallel data, working on non-linguistic
   phrases;
b) *rule-based machine translation* (RBMT) which relies on hand-crafted parsers
   and grammars that transform a given input sentence into a foreign language
   translation output; and
c) *hybrid machine translation* approaches which focus on creating translations
   from several source systems, based on the assumption that the different MT
   paradigms' individual strengths and shortcomings are often complementary
   which implies that a clever combination of their translations would yield an
   overall better translation output.

B. Glimm and A. Krüger (Eds.): KI 2012, LNCS 7526, pp. 37–48, 2012.
© Springer-Verlag Berlin Heidelberg 2012

Regardless of the actual methodology of a given MT system, the production of the translations usually involves a lot of heterogeneous features. These range from simple language model scores, parser or phrase table probabilities, and confidence estimates to hierarchical parse trees or even full parse forests. This makes it very difficult to *intuitively* understand the inner workings of the MT engine in question; it is hence clear that research on the optimal combination of different machine translation systems into better, hybrid MT systems is of utmost importance to the field. To overcome the problem of incomprehensible feature values, we propose a method that applies Machine Learning (ML) tools, leaving the exact interpretation and weighting of features to the ML algorithms.

The remainder of this paper is structured as follows. After having introduced the matter of investigation in this section, we present related work in Section 2 before defining and explaining in detail our Machine-Learning-based framework for hybrid MT in Section 3. We first give an overview on the basic approach in Section 3.1 and then discuss its most important components: the extensible, total order on translations is defined in Section 3.2 while the notion of joint, binarised feature vectors for Machine Learning is introduced in Section 3.3. In Section 4 we present the experiments we have conducted in order to measure the proposed method's performance; results from this assessment are presented in Section 5. We conclude by summarising our findings and by discussing future research questions in Section 6.

2   Related Work

Hybrid translation approaches and system combination methods have received a lot of research attention over the last decade. There is general consensus that it is possible to combine translation output from different systems reaching an improvement over the individual baseline systems, e.g., [8,15,20].

Confusion Networks can be used for system combination [4,7,16]. One of the MT systems is chosen to become the *backbone* or *skeleton* of the hybrid translation, while other translations are connected via word alignment techniques such as GIZA++ [17]. Together, the systems then form a network with different paths through the network resulting in different translations. An open-source system combination toolkit like this is described in [2].

As the combination of translation output using phrase-based methods may not preserve the syntactic structure of the translation backbone, there also are methods which perform *Sentence-based Combination*, trying to select the best of several black-box translations for a given source text. This is similar to *Re-ranking Approaches* in SMT. See [1,9,20].

Finally, there are *Machine-Learning-based Combination* methods which train classifiers using, e.g., Support Vector Machines [22] to determine if a translation output is good or bad. Recent work such as [11,12] applies Machine Learning tools to estimate translation quality and re-rank a given set of candidate translations on the sentence level. Of course, there also exist various combinations of the aformentioned methods, e.g., [1,18].

3   Methodology

3.1   Classification-Based Hybrid Machine Translation

In this section, we describe a Machine-Learning-based framework for hybrid machine translation. Given a set of n translations from several, black-box systems and a tuning set including reference text, we perform the following steps to produce a hybrid translation for some given test set:

1. Compute a system ranking on the tuning set using some order relation based on quality assessment of the translations with automatic metrics. This can be extended to also include results from manual evaluation;
2. Decompose the aforementioned system ranking into a set of pairwise comparisons for any two pairs of systems A, B. As we do not allow for ties in our system comparisons, the two possible values $A > B$, $A < B$ also represent our *Machine-Learning classes* $+1/-1$, respectively;
3. Annotate the translations with feature values derived from natural language processing tools such as *language models*, *part-of-speech taggers*, or *parsers*;
4. Create a data set for training an SVM-based classifier that can estimate which of two systems A, B is *better* according to the available features[1];
5. Train an SVM-based classifier model using, e.g., libSVM, see [3];

Steps 1–5 represent the *training phase* in our framework. They require the availability of a tuning set including references to allow the definition of the order relation which subsequently defines the training instances for the SVM-based classifier. After training, we can use the classifier as follows:

6. Apply the resulting classification onto the candidate translations from the given test set. This will produce pairwise estimates $+1/-1$ for each possible combination of systems A, B;
7. Perform *round-robin playoff* elimination to determine the single-best system from the set of candidate translations on a per sentence level[2];
8. Synthesise the final, hybrid translation output.

Steps $6-8$ represent the *decoding phase* in which the trained classifier is applied to a set of *unseen* translations without any reference text available. By computing pairwise *winners* for each possible pair of systems and each individual sentence of the test set, we determine the single-best system on the sentence level. This is similar to SVMRank[3] and it will be an interesting extension of the work described in this paper comparing the performance of the two approaches.

---

[1] We had used decision trees learnt on annotated data in previous work with moderate success. For the experiments reported in this paper, we hence focused on SVM-based classification instead in order to learn about its performance in our problem setting.

[2] This may introduce problems such as loss of contextual information. For the work described in this paper, we ignore any such problems leaving them to future work.

[3] See http://cs.cornell.edu/people/tj/svm_light/svm_rank.html

3.2　An Extensible, Total Order on Translations

In order to rank the given source translations, we first need to define an *ordering relation* over the set of translation outputs. For this, we apply three renowned MT evaluation metrics which are the *de-facto standards* for automated assessment of machine translation quality. We consider:

1. The Meteor score, both on the sentence and on the corpus level, see [5];
2. The NIST n-gram co-occurence score on the corpus level, see [6]; and
3. The BLEU score which is the most widely used evaluation metric, see [19].

While both the BLEU and the NIST scores are designed to have a high correlation with judgements from manual evaluation on the corpus level (denoted by suffix C), the Meteor metric can also be used to meaningfully compare translation output on the level of individual sentences (denoted by suffix S). We make use of this property when defining our order $ord(A, B)$ on translations, as shown in Equations 1–5:

$$ord_{BLEU_C}(A, B) \stackrel{\text{def}}{=} \begin{cases} 1 & \text{if } A_{BLEU_C} > B_{BLEU_C} \\ -1 & \text{if } A_{BLEU_C} < B_{BLEU_C} \\ 0 & \text{else} \end{cases} \tag{1}$$

$$ord_{NIST_C}(A, B) \stackrel{\text{def}}{=} \begin{cases} 1 & \text{if } A_{NIST_C} > B_{NIST_C} \\ -1 & \text{if } A_{NIST_C} < B_{NIST_C} \\ ord_{BLEU_C}(A, B) & \text{else} \end{cases} \tag{2}$$

$$ord_{Meteor_C}(A, B) \stackrel{\text{def}}{=} \begin{cases} 1 & \text{if } A_{Meteor_C} > B_{Meteor_C} \\ -1 & \text{if } A_{Meteor_C} < B_{Meteor_C} \\ ord_{NIST_C}(A, B) & \text{else} \end{cases} \tag{3}$$

$$ord_{Meteor_S}(A, B) \stackrel{\text{def}}{=} \begin{cases} 1 & \text{if } A_{Meteor_S} > B_{Meteor_S} \\ -1 & \text{if } A_{Meteor_S} < B_{Meteor_S} \\ ord_{Meteor_C}(A, B) & \text{else} \end{cases} \tag{4}$$

$$ord(A, B) \stackrel{\text{def}}{=} ord_{Meteor_S}(A, B) \tag{5}$$

Note that the we called our order $ord(A, B)$ an *extensible, total order*. It can easily be extended to include, e.g., results from manual evaluation of translation output. In fact, this would be a very welcome addition as it would allow to bring in knowledge from domain experts. However, as a manual annotation campaign for n systems is both very time-consuming and expensive, we leave the integration of manual judgements into our ordering relation to future work.

3.3   Machine Learning Using Joint, Binarised Feature Vectors

As previously mentioned in Section 2, many Machine-Learning-based approaches for system combination use classifiers to estimate the quality or *confidence* in an individual translation output and compare it to other translations afterwards. This means that the feature vector for a given translation A is computed solely on information available in A, not considering any other translation B. Formally, this can be expressed by defining $vector_{single}(A) \in \mathbb{R}^n$ as follows:

$$vec_{single}(A) \overset{\text{def}}{=} \begin{pmatrix} feat_1(A) \\ feat_2(A) \\ \vdots \\ feat_n(A) \end{pmatrix} \tag{6}$$

We take a different approach here and compute feature vectors for all possible, *pairwise comparisons* of translations A, B, storing *binary feature values* to model if a given feature value $feat_x(A)$ for system A is better or worse than the corresponding feature value $feat_x(B)$ for the competing system B. Effectively, this means that we compare translations *directly* when constructing the set of feature vectors required for training our ML classifier. Equation 7 shows our definition of a *joint, binarised* feature $vector_{joint}(A, B) \in \mathbb{B}^n$:

$$vec_{joint}(A, B) \overset{\text{def}}{=} \begin{pmatrix} feat_1(A) > feat_1(B) \\ feat_2(A) > feat_2(B) \\ \vdots \\ feat_n(A) > feat_n(B) \end{pmatrix} \tag{7}$$

The reason to store binary features values $feat_x \in \mathbb{B}$ lies in the fact that these can be processed more efficiently during SVM training. Also, previous experiments have shown that using the actual feature values $feat_x \in \mathbb{R}$ does not give any additional benefit so that we decided to switch to binary notation instead. We have also run experiments using only joint feature vectors by concatenating feature values for systems A, B and using the corresponding feature vectors of length $2 * n$ for classifier training. As the comparison $A > B$ between systems could not be taken using the resulting classifier we started investigating the binarised model.

Note that the order in which features for translations A, B are compared does not strictly matter. For the sake of consistency, we have decided to compare feature values using simple $A > B$ operations, leaving the actual interpretation of these values or their polarity to the Machine Learning toolkit. This assumes that feature values are ordered in some way; which holds for the selected set of features. In future work, we plan to extend this introducing *feature-specific comparison* operators.

3.4   Feature Set for Training a Binary Classifier

We create the data set for classifier training using a selection of *features*. While there are many features which could be added to this feature set, we restricted ourselves to the following choice, leaving changes to future work:

1. Float values $\in [0.0, 1.0]$
   - ratio of target/source tokens;
   - ratio of target/source parse tree nodes;
   - ratio of target/source parse tree depth;
2. Integer values $\in \{0, 1, \ldots, \}$
   - number of target tokens;
   - number of target parse tree nodes;
   - number of target parse tree depth;
3. *log* probabilities
   - n-gram score for order $n \in \{1, \ldots, 5\}$;
   - inverse phrase translation probability $\rho(f|e)$
4. perplexity for order $n \in \{1, \ldots, 5\}$.

The selected features represent a combination of (shallow) parsing and language model scoring and are derived from the set of features that are most often used in the Machine-Learning-based system combination literature [1,9,11,12,18].

3.5   Creating Hybrid Translations Using an SVM Classifier

Given an SVM classifier trained on joint, binary feature vectors as previously described, we can now create hybrid translation output. The basic algorithm is depicted in Figure 1. It estimates the single-best translation for each sentence in the test set, based on the $+1/-1$ output of the classifier.

For each sentence, we create a dictionary that stores for some system X the set of systems which were outperformed by X according to our classifier. To do so, we consider each pairwise comparison of systems A, B and compute the corresponding feature vector which is then classified by the SVM. Only systems winning at least once in these pairwise comparisons end up as keys in our dictionary. The cardinality of the set of outperformed systems implicitly represents the number of wins for a system X.

Finally, we compute the single-best translation for a sentence by sorting the system_wins dictionary so that systems with a larger number of wins come first. There are three cases to consider:

1. If there is only one top-ranked system, this becomes the winning translation for the current sentence;
2. If two systems are top-ranked, the winner depends on the comparison of these. As we do not allow for ties in our comparisons, this is guaranteed to determine a single winner;
3. If more than two systems are top-ranked, we check if one of the systems outperforms the others. This may not yield a unique winner, in which case we fall back to scoring the systems with $ord_{Meteor_C}(A, B)$, effectively using the corpus level system rankings obtained on the tuning set to reach a final decision on the best translation for the current sentence.

```
 1: for s_id in 1..len(sentences):
 2:   system_wins = {}
 3:   for (A, B) in system_pairs:
 4:     joint_feature_vector = compute_feature_vector(A, B, s_id)
 5:     classification_result = classify(joint_feature_vector)
 6:     if classification_result == "+1":
 7:       system_wins[A].append(B)
 8:     else:
 9:       system_wins[B].append(A)
10:   compute_best_system(system_wins)
```

Fig. 1. Pseudo-code illustrating how an SVM classifier can be used to determine the single-best translation using round robin playoff elimination. This operates on the sentence level, `compute_best_system()` finally computes the system with most "wins" over the competing systems. If two systems A, B have scored the same number of wins, the algorithm falls back to the comparison of these two systems. As we do not allow for ties in our system comparisons, the algorithm is guaranteed to terminate and will always return the—*according to the classifier used*—single-best system for a sentence.

4   Experiments

In order to assess the performance of the proposed approach, we conduct several experiments and measure the translation quality of the resulting hybrid output. Note that in the data sets used for experimentation individual system names are anonymised as the translation output is part of a shared translation task.

We train SVM classifier models for two language pairs: Arabic→English and Chinese→English. For the first pair we work on translation output generated by $n = 10$ different systems, for the latter pair there are $n = 15$ systems to consider. The source text originates from the news domain.

As training data, we receive a tuning set including reference text as well as a test set without reference. We apply our order relation on the given translations to determine a system ranking on the sentence level. Using this information, we then compute pairwise system comparisons as SVM class labels and annotate individual translations with parser output and language model scores. We use the Stanford Parser [10,13,14] to process the source text and the corresponding translations. For language model scoring, we use the SRILM toolkit [21] training a 5-gram target language model for English. We do not consider source language language models in this work.

Figure 2 shows the optimisation grids we obtained during SVM tuning, using 5-fold cross validation an interval width $step = 1$, as implemented in *grid.py* from libSVM. They show which settings for C and γ result in the best prediction rate. Note how the graphs are similar regarding the *optimal area*. We train our final SVM classifiers with parameters from this area, giving preference to smaller values for both C and γ to reduce computational cost and thus training time.

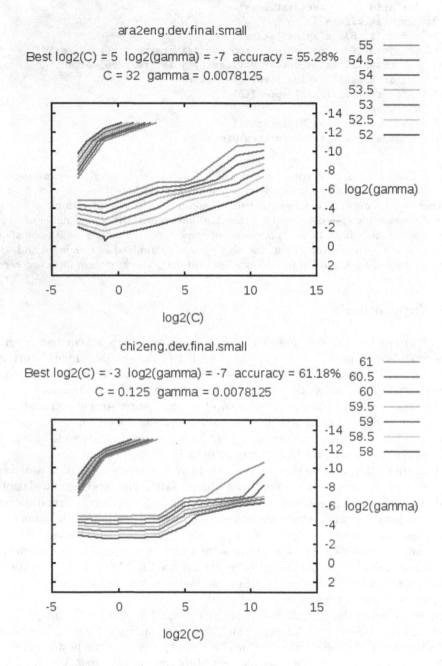

Fig. 2. Optimisation grids of SVM parameters C and γ for language pairs Arabic→English and Chinese→English. Note the similarity of the grids, indicating that our feature vectors are not depending on language-specific characteristics.

5   Evaluation

5.1   Automatic Metrics' Scores

We evaluated the translation quality of our hybrid MT system (referred to as *SVM-combo* in tables and figures) using BLEU and NIST, both of which are predominantly used in MT evaluation. Given the relatively small feature set and the sub-optimal prediction rate of the SVM classifier we achieve promising results for both language pairs.

For Arabic→English we achieved a NIST score of 10.3584 and a BLEU score of 0.4523. The single-best NIST score for the same language pair was 11.5046, for BLEU it was 0.4951 For Chinese→English we achieved a NIST and BLEU scores of 7.7636 and 0.2663, respectively, with single-best scores reported as 9.2705 and 0.3372. To correctly interpret these scores, it is important to note that our main focus lies on performance wrt. Meteor, as described in Section 3.2; here, the method performed better, with a result of 0.327 (best score 0.330) for Arabic→English and 0.307 (best score: 0.318) for Chinese→English.

5.2   System Contribution

Another interesting aspect related to the quality of the proposed method is the *system contribution* of the individual source systems. In order to better understand how much each of the systems added to the hybrid translation output, we compare the expected and the actual contribution in the translation result.

Expected contribution is computed as the average of the ranks assigned to each system by the metrics used in our order relation $ord(A, B)$, namely BLEU, NIST, and Meteor. Actual contribution is computed from the relative frequency of translations a system added to the hybrid translation output. We measure the difference between expected and actual contribution as Δ; positive values $+x$ mean that a system contributed more to the hybrid translation than we had expected, negative values $-y$ denote the opposite. Table 1 shows the comparison of system contribution for Arabic→English, table 2 for Chinese→English.

Table 1. System contribution for language pair Arabic→English

Rank	System									
	s01	s03	s05	s06	s07	s08	s11	s12	s16	s18
BLEU	3	10	7	2	1	6	8	9	4	5
NIST	2	10	6	1	3	5	7	9	4	8
Meteor	4	10	7	1	2	5	9	8	3	6
Expected	3	10	7	1	2	5	8	9	4	6
Combo	3	6	4	2	1	7	10	9	8	5
Δ		+4	+3	−1	+1	−2	+2		−4	+1

Table 2. System contribution for language pair Chinese→English

Rank	System														
	s01	s02	s04	s06	s07	s08	s09	s10	s12	s13	s14	s15	s16	s17	s18
BLEU	2	14	15	1	3	8	13	11	5	12	7	10	9	6	4
NIST	3	15	14	1	2	9	13	10	5	11	7	12	8	6	4
Meteor	4	15	14	1	2	9	13	11	6	12	7	10	8	5	3
Expected	3	15	14	1	2	9	13	10	5	12	7	10	8	6	4
Combo	1	14	7	9	11	8	13	6	2	3	4	14	12	10	5
Δ	+2	+1	+7	−8	−9	+1		+4	+3	+9	+3	−4	−4	−4	−1

6 Conclusion

6.1 Summary of Findings

We have described a Machine-Learning-based framework for hybrid MT. We defined a total order on translation output that can be applied during feature vector generation. Our method differs from previous work as we consider joint, binarised feature vectors instead of separate feature vectors for each of the source systems. We proposed an algorithm to make use of an SVM-based classifier trained on these feature vectors for the creation of hybrid translations.

In our experiments for language pairs Arabic→English and Chinese→English, we could observe promising results according to Meteor scores. We also analysed the expected contribution of the source systems to the hybrid translation output and found that our classifier was able to make use of good sentence translations from systems which performed bad on the corpus level. We observed interesting differences between expected and actual contribution ranks.

6.2 Outlook on Future Work

The total order on translation defined in Section 3 can be extended to make use of results from manual judgements regarding the quality of candidate translations. It is not yet clear how the SVM model's prediction rate and the quality of the final translation are interrelated or how changes of the former would alter the latter, leaving room for future research work. We also intend to invest effort into a large, manual evaluation campaign to examine in more detail what translations are selected by our combination method and if these are actually the best (or at least a good) translation considering the given source sentence.

Acknowledgments. This work has been funded under the Seventh Framework Programme for Research and Technological Development of the European Commission through the T4ME contract (grant agreement no.: 249119). The author would like to thank Sabine Hunsicker and Yu Chen for their support with the experiments, and Hans-Ulrich Krieger as well as Geert-Jan Kruijff for their helpful comments. We are grateful to the anonymous reviewers for their valuable feedback.

References

1. Avramidis, E.: DFKI System Combination with Sentence Ranking at ML4HMT-2011. In: Proceedings of the International Workshop on Using Linguistic Information for Hybrid Machine Translation (LIHMT 2011) and of the Shared Task on Applying Machine Learning Techniques to Optimise the Division of Labour in Hybrid Machine Translation (ML4HMT). META-NET, Barcelona (2011)
2. Barrault, L.: Many: Open source machine translation system combination. Prague Bulletin of Mathematical Linguistics, Special Issue on Open Source Tools for Machine Translation 1(93), 145–155 (2010), http://www-lium.univ-lemans.fr/sites/default/files/Barrault-MANY2010.pdf
3. Chang, C.C., Lin, C.J.: LIBSVM: A Library for Support Vector Machines. ACM Transactions on Intelligent Systems and Technology 2, 27:1–27:27 (2011), Software available at http://www.csie.ntu.edu.tw/~cjlin/libsvm
4. Chen, Y., Eisele, A., Federmann, C., Hasler, E., Jellinghaus, M., Theison, S.: Multi-engine machine translation with an open-source SMT decoder. In: Proceedings of the Second Workshop on Statistical Machine Translation, pp. 193–196. Association for Computational Linguistics, Prague (2007), http://www.aclweb.org/anthology/W/W07/W07-0726
5. Denkowski, M., Lavie, A.: Meteor 1.3: Automatic Metric for Reliable Optimization and Evaluation of Machine Translation Systems. In: Proceedings of the Sixth Workshop on Statistical Machine Translation, pp. 85–91. Association for Computational Linguistics, Edinburgh (2011), http://www.aclweb.org/anthology-new/W/W11/W11-2107
6. Doddington, G.: Automatic Evaluation of Machine Translation Quality Using n-gram Co-occurrence Statistics. In: Proceedings of the Second International Conference on Human Language Technology Research, HLT 2002, pp. 138–145. Morgan Kaufmann Publishers Inc., San Francisco (2002), http://www.itl.nist.gov/iad/mig/tests/mt/doc/ngram-study.pdf
7. Eisele, A., Federmann, C., Saint-Amand, H., Jellinghaus, M., Herrmann, T., Chen, Y.: Using Moses to integrate multiple rule-based machine translation engines into a hybrid system. In: Proceedings of the Third Workshop on Statistical Machine Translation, pp. 179–182. Association for Computational Linguistics, Columbus (2008), http://www.aclweb.org/anthology/W/W08/W08-0328
8. Frederking, R., Nirenburg, S.: Three Heads are Better Than One. In: Proceedings of the Fourth Conference on Applied Natural Language Processing, ANLC 1994, pp. 95–100. Association for Computational Linguistics, Stroudsburg (1994), http://ww2.cs.mu.oz.au/acl/A/A94/A94-1016.pdf
9. Gamon, M., Aue, A., Smets, M.: Sentence-level MT Evaluation Without Reference Translations: Beyond Language Modeling. In: Proceedings of the 10th EAMT Conference "Practical Applications of Machine Translation", pp. 103–111. European Association for Machine Translation (May 2005), http://research.microsoft.com/research/pubs/view.aspx?pubid=1426
10. Green, S., Manning, C.D.: Better Arabic Parsing: Baselines, Evaluations, and Analysis. In: Proceedings of the 23rd International Conference on Computational Linguistics, COLING 2010, pp. 394–402. Association for Computational Linguistics, Stroudsburg (2010), http://dl.acm.org/citation.cfm?id=1873826
11. He, Y., Ma, Y., van Genabith, J., Way, A.: Bridging SMT and TM with Translation Recommendation. In: Proceedings of the 48th Annual Meeting of the Association for Computational Linguistics, ACL 2010, pp. 622–630. Association for Computational Linguistics, Stroudsburg (2010), http://aclweb.org/anthology-new/P/P10/P10-1064.pdf

12. He, Y., Ma, Y., Way, A., van Genabith, J.: Integrating N-best SMT Outputs into a TM System. In: Proceedings of the 23rd International Conference on Computational Linguistics, COLING 2010, pp. 374–382. Association for Computational Linguistics, Stroudsburg (2010), http://doras.dcu.ie/15799/1/ Integrating_N-best_SMT_Outputs_into_a_TM_System.pdf

13. Klein, D., Manning, C.: Accurate Unlexicalized Parsing. In: Proceedings of the 41st Meeting of the Association for Computational Linguistics, ACL 2003, vol. 1, pp. 423–430. Association for Computational Linguistics, Stroudsburg (2003), http://acl.ldc.upenn.edu/P/P03/P03-1054.pdf

14. Levy, R., Manning, C.: Is it harder to parse Chinese, or the Chinese Treebank? In: Proceedings of the 41st Annual Meeting of the Association for Computational Linguistics, ACL 2003, pp. 439–446. Association for Computational Linguistics, Stroudsburg (2003), http://www.aclweb.org/anthology/P03-1056

15. Macherey, W., Och, F.J.: An Empirical Study on Computing Consensus Translations from Multiple Machine Translation Systems. In: Proceedings of the 2007 Joint Conference on Empirical Methods in Natural Language Processing and Computational Natural Language Learning (EMNLP-CoNLL), pp. 986–995. Association for Computational Linguistics, Prague (2007), http://www.aclweb.org/anthology/D/D07/D07-1105

16. Matusov, E., Ueffing, N., Ney, H.: Computing Consensus Translation from Multiple Machine Translation Systems Using Enhanced Hypotheses Alignment. In: Conference of the European Chapter of the Association for Computational Linguistics, pp. 33–40. Association for Computational Linguistics, Stroudsburg (2006), http://acl.ldc.upenn.edu/E/E06/E06-1005.pdf

17. Och, F.J., Ney, H.: A Systematic Comparison of Various Statistical Alignment Models. Computational Linguistics 29(1), 19–51 (2003), http://acl.ldc.upenn.edu/J/J03/J03-1002.pdf

18. Okita, T., van Genabith, J.: DCU Confusion Network-based System Combination for ML4HMT. In: Proceedings of the International Workshop on Using Linguistic Information for Hybrid Machine Translation (LIHMT 2011) and of the Shared Task on Applying Machine Learning Techniques to Optimise the Division of Labour in Hybrid Machine Translation (ML4HMT). META-NET, Barcelona (2011)

19. Papineni, K., Roukos, S., Ward, T., Zhu, W.J.: BLEU: A Method for Automatic Evaluation of Machine Translation. In: Proceedings of the 40th Annual Meeting of the Association for Computational Linguistics, ACL 2002, pp. 311–318. Association for Computational Linguistics, Stroudsburg (2002), http://acl.ldc.upenn.edu/P/P02/P02-1040.pdf

20. Rosti, A.V., Ayan, N.F., Xiang, B., Matsoukas, S., Schwartz, R., Dorr, B.: Combining Outputs from Multiple Machine Translation Systems. In: Human Language Technologies 2007: The Conference of the North American Chapter of the Association for Computational Linguistics; Proceedings of the Main Conference, pp. 228–235. Association for Computational Linguistics, Rochester (2007), http://www.aclweb.org/anthology/N/N07/N07-1029

21. Stolcke, A.: SRILM - An Extensible Language Modeling Toolkit. In: Proceedings of the International Conference on Spoken Language Processing, pp. 257–286 (November 2002)

22. Vapnik, V.N.: The Nature of Statistical Learning Theory. Springer-Verlag New York, Inc., New York (1995)

Using Equivalences of Worlds for Aggregation Semantics of Relational Conditionals*

Marc Finthammer and Christoph Beierle

Department of Computer Science, FernUniversität in Hagen, 58084 Hagen, Germany

Abstract. For relational probabilistic conditionals, the so-called aggregation semantics has been proposed recently. Applying the maximum entropy principle for reasoning under aggregation semantics requires solving a complex optimization problem. Here, we improve an approach to solving this optimization problem by Generalized Iterative Scaling (GIS). After showing how the method of Lagrange multipliers can also be used for aggregation semantics, we exploit that possible worlds are structurally equivalent with respect to a knowledge base $\mathcal{R}$ if they have the same verification and falsification properties. We present a GIS algorithm operating on the induced equivalence classes of worlds; its implementation yields significant performance improvements.

1 Introduction

In probabilistic reasoning, conditionals of the form $(B|A)[x]$, expressing *if A then B with probability x*, may be used. There are various approaches where A, B are not just propositional, but first-order formulas (see e.g. [3,8]) While probabilistic reasoning under maximum entropy exibits many desirable commonsense properties [13,9,10], it requires to solve a complex optimization problem, and the size of this optimization problem increases significantly when moving from a propositional to a relational setting.

Example 1. Consider a population of monkeys. The predicate *feeds*(X, Y) expresses that a monkey X feeds another monkey Y and *hungry*(X) says that a monkey X is hungry. The knowledge base $\mathcal{R}_{mky}$ contains conditionals expressing generic knowledge as well as specific knowledge about the monkey *charly*. E.g., r_1 states that if X is not hungry but Y is, X feeds Y with probability 0.8.

$$r_1 : (feeds(X, Y) \mid \neg hungry(X) \land hungry(Y)) \; [0.80]$$
$$r_2 : (\neg feeds(X, Y) \mid hungry(X)) \; [0.999]$$
$$r_3 : (\neg feeds(X, Y) \mid \neg hungry(X) \land \neg hungry(Y)) \; [0.90]$$
$$r_4 : (feeds(X, charly) \mid \neg hungry(X)) \; [0.95]$$
$$r_5 : (feeds(X, X) \mid \top) \; [0.001]$$

In virtually all approaches assigning a formal semantics to a relational knowledge base like $\mathcal{R}_{mky}$, the ground instances of the atoms or of the conditionals have

---

* The research reported here was partially supported by the DFG (grant BE 1700/7-2).

B. Glimm and A. Krüger (Eds.): KI 2012, LNCS 7526, pp. 49–60, 2012.
© Springer-Verlag Berlin Heidelberg 2012

to be taken into account, causing a severe complexity problem. For instance, for the knowledge base $\mathcal{R}_{mky}$ with *charly* and two additional constants, there are 4,096 possible worlds, while with 4 constants there are already 1,048,576 worlds.

In this paper, we will consider *aggregation semantics* [12], which aggregates the probabilities of worlds verifying a conditional and divides them by the aggregated probabilities of worlds satisfying the conditional's premise.

Up to now, only a single practical implementation has been developed for computing the maximum entropy inference operator under aggregation semantics [4]. Here, we extend and improve the approach of [4] that employs the Generalized Iterative Scaling (GIS) technique [2] in two directions. In a first step, we show how the method of Lagrange multipliers [1] can also be used for aggregation semantics and present an algorithm $\mathrm{GIS}_{\odot}^{\alpha}$ returning a compact representation of the maximum entropy solution specified by the optimization problem. As the main contribution of this paper, by exploiting Kern-Isberner's concept of conditional structures of worlds with respect to a knowledge base [9], we use the structural equivalence of worlds to refine $\mathrm{GIS}_{\odot}^{\alpha}$ to an algorithm $\mathrm{GIS}_{\odot}^{\equiv \mathcal{R}}$ that operates on equivalence classes of worlds rather than on single worlds, yielding significant performance improvements.

After recalling the basics of aggregation semantics (Sec. 2) and its normalized optimization problem [4] (Sec. 3), we present the $\mathrm{GIS}_{\odot}^{\alpha}$ algorithm (Sec. 4) and use conditional structures to define equivalence classes of worlds (Sec. 5). These are used by the algorithm $\mathrm{GIS}_{\odot}^{\equiv \mathcal{R}}$ in Sec. 6, where also an implementation and a first evaluation of $\mathrm{GIS}_{\odot}^{\alpha}$ and $\mathrm{GIS}_{\odot}^{\equiv \mathcal{R}}$ is presented. In Sec. 7 we conclude.

2   Background: Aggregation Semantics

We consider a first-order signature $\Sigma := (Pred, Const)$ consisting of a set of first order predicates *Pred* and a finite set of constants *Const*. So Σ is a restricted signature since it only contains functions with an arity of zero. Let p/k denote the predicate $p \in Pred$ with arity k. The set of atoms $\mathcal{A}$ over *Pred* with respect to a set of variables *Var* and *Const* is defined in the usual way. $\mathcal{L}$ denotes the quantifier-free first-order language defined over Σ and the junctors $\neg, \wedge, \vee$. We will also use the notation AB to abbreviate a conjunction $A \wedge B$. For a formula A, $\mathrm{gnd}(A)$ denotes the set of ground instances of A.

Definition 1 (Conditional). *Let* $A(\boldsymbol{X}), B(\boldsymbol{X}) \in \mathcal{L}$ *be first-order formulas with* $\boldsymbol{X}$ *containing the variables of* A *and* B*, and let* $d \in [0, 1]$ *be a real number.* $(B(\boldsymbol{X})|A(\boldsymbol{X}))$ *is a* conditional, *and* $(B(\boldsymbol{X})|A(\boldsymbol{X}))[d]$ *is a probabilistic conditional with probability* d*. If* $d \in \{0, 1\}$ *then the probabilistic conditional is called* hard, *otherwise it is a called* soft*. The set of all conditionals (resp. probabilistic conditionals) over* $\mathcal{L}$ *is denoted by* $(\mathcal{L}|\mathcal{L})$ *(resp. by* $(\mathcal{L}|\mathcal{L})^{prob}$*).*

A set of probabilistic conditionals is also called a *knowledge base*. If it is clear from context, we will omit the "probabilistic" and just use the term "conditional".

Given $\mathcal{L}$, $\mathcal{H}$ denotes the *Herbrand base*, i.e. the set containing all ground atoms constructible from *Pred* and *Const*. A *Herbrand interpretation* ω is a subset of the ground atoms, that is $\omega \subseteq \mathcal{H}$. Using a closed world assumption, each ground atom $p_{\text{gnd}} \in \omega$ is interpreted as true and each $p_{\text{gnd}} \notin \omega$ is interpreted as false; in this way a Herbrand interpretation is similar to a complete conjunction in propositional logic. $\Omega = \mathfrak{P}(\mathcal{H})$ denotes the set of all possible worlds (i.e. Herbrand interpretations), where $\mathfrak{P}$ is the power set operator.

Definition 2 (Set of Grounding Vectors). *For a conditional* $(B(\boldsymbol{X})|A(\boldsymbol{X})) \in (\mathcal{L}|\mathcal{L})$, *the set of grounding vectors of* $(B(\boldsymbol{X})|A(\boldsymbol{X}))$ *is given by:*
$$\mathcal{H}^{\boldsymbol{x}(A,B)} := \{(a_1,\ldots,a_s) \,|\, a_1,\ldots,a_s \in Const, \, (B(\boldsymbol{a})|A(\boldsymbol{a})) \in \text{gnd}\,((B(\boldsymbol{X})|A(\boldsymbol{X})))\}$$

Let $P : \Omega \rightarrow [0,1]$ be a probability distribution over possible worlds and let $\mathcal{P}_\Omega$ be the set of all such distributions. P is extended to ground formulas $A(\boldsymbol{a})$, with $\boldsymbol{a} \in \mathcal{H}^{\boldsymbol{x}(A)}$, by defining $P(A(\boldsymbol{a})) := \sum_{\omega \models A(\boldsymbol{a})} P(\omega)$.

Definition 3 (Aggregation Semantics Entailment Relation [12]). *The entailment relation* $\models_\odot$ *between a probability distribution* $P \in \mathcal{P}_\Omega$ *and a conditional* $(B(\boldsymbol{X})|A(\boldsymbol{X}))[d] \in (\mathcal{L}|\mathcal{L})^{prob}$ *with* $\sum_{\boldsymbol{a} \in \mathcal{H}^{\boldsymbol{x}(A,B)}} P(A(\boldsymbol{a})) > 0$ *is defined as:*

$$P \models_\odot (B(\boldsymbol{X})|A(\boldsymbol{X}))\,[d] \qquad \text{iff} \qquad \frac{\displaystyle\sum_{\boldsymbol{a} \in \mathcal{H}^{\boldsymbol{x}(A,B)}} P(A(\boldsymbol{a})B(\boldsymbol{a}))}{\displaystyle\sum_{\boldsymbol{a} \in \mathcal{H}^{\boldsymbol{x}(A,B)}} P(A(\boldsymbol{a}))} = d \qquad (1)$$

Thus, the aggregation semantics resembles the definition of a conditional probability by summing up the probabilities of all respective ground formulas. Note that both sums of the fraction run over the same set of grounding vectors and therefore the same number of ground instances, i.e. a particular probability $P(A(\boldsymbol{a}))$ can be contained multiple times in the denominator sum.

If $P \models_\odot r$ holds for a conditional r, we say that P *satisfies* r or P *is a model of* r. P satisfies a set of conditionals $\mathcal{R}$ if it satisfies every element of $\mathcal{R}$, and $\mathcal{S}(\mathcal{R}) := \{P \in \mathcal{P}_\Omega \,|\, P \models_\odot \mathcal{R}\}$ denotes the set of all probability distributions satisfying $\mathcal{R}$. $\mathcal{R}$ is *consistent* iff $\mathcal{S}(\mathcal{R}) \neq \emptyset$. The *entropy* $H(P) := -\sum_{\omega \in \Omega} P(\omega) \log P(\omega)$ of a probability distribution P measures the indifference within P. The principle of *maximum entropy* (*ME*) chooses the distribution P where $H(P)$ is maximal among all distributions satisfying $\mathcal{R}$ [13,9].

Definition 4 (ME$_\odot$ Inference Operator [12]). *The ME-inference operator* ME$_\odot$ *based on aggregation semantics for a consistent set* $\mathcal{R}$ *of conditionals is:*

$$\text{ME}_\odot(\mathcal{R}) := \arg \max_{P \in \mathcal{P}_\Omega : P \models_\odot \mathcal{R}} H(P) \qquad (2)$$

Since (2) has a unique solution [16], ME$_\odot(\mathcal{R})$ is well defined. To avoid cumbersome distinctions of cases, for the rest of this paper we will consider only soft probabilistic conditionals since they guarantee that ME$_\odot(\mathcal{R})$ is strictly positive using Paris' *open-mindedness principle* [13]:

Proposition 1. *1. For any consistent set of soft probabilistic conditionals* $\mathcal{R}$, *there exists a positive probability distribution which satisfies* $\mathcal{R}$.
2. If a set of probabilistic conditionals $\mathcal{R}$ *can be satisfied by a positive probability distribution, then* ME$_\odot(\mathcal{R})$ *is a positive probability distribution.*

3 Normalized Optimization Problem for ME$_\odot$ Operator

For propositional conditionals, the satisfaction relation can be expressed by using feature functions (e. g. [6]). The following definition defines feature functions for the relational case where the groundings have to be taken into account.

Definition 5 (Counting Functions, Feature Function). *For a conditional* $r_i = (B_i(\boldsymbol{X})|A_i(\boldsymbol{X}))\,[d_i]$ *the counting functions* $ver_i, fal_i : \Omega \to \mathbb{N}_0$ *are given by:*

$$ver_i(\omega) := \left|\left\{ \boldsymbol{a}_i \in \mathcal{H}^{\boldsymbol{x}(A_i,B_i)} \mid \omega \models A_i(\boldsymbol{a})B_i(\boldsymbol{a}) \right\}\right|$$

$$fal_i(\omega) := \left|\left\{ \boldsymbol{a}_i \in \mathcal{H}^{\boldsymbol{x}(A_i,B_i)} \mid \omega \models A_i(\boldsymbol{a})\overline{B_i(\boldsymbol{a})} \right\}\right| \tag{3}$$

$ver_i(\omega)$ *indicates the number of groundings of* $\omega \in \Omega$ *which* verify r_i, *whereas* $fal_i(\omega)$ *specifies the number of groundings which* falsify r_i. *The* feature function *of* r_i *is the linear function function* $f_i : \Omega \to \mathbb{R}$ *with:*

$$f_i(\omega) := ver_i(\omega)(1 - d_i) - fal_i(\omega)d_i \tag{4}$$

Proposition 2 ([4]). *For* $(B_i(\boldsymbol{X})|A_i(\boldsymbol{X}))\,[d_i]$ *with* $\sum_{\boldsymbol{a}\in\mathcal{H}^{\boldsymbol{x}(A,B)}} P(A(\boldsymbol{a})) > 0$ *we have:*

$$P \models_\odot (B_i(\boldsymbol{X})|A_i(\boldsymbol{X}))\,[d_i] \quad \text{iff} \quad \sum_{\omega \in \Omega} P(\omega)f_i(\omega) = 0 \tag{5}$$

Proposition 2 shows that under aggregation semantics a conditional induces a linear constraint which has to be met by a satisfying probability distribution. The *expected value* $\mathbb{E}(f_i, P)$ of a function f_i under a distribution P is defined as $\mathbb{E}(f_i, P) := \sum_{\omega \in \Omega} f_i(\omega)P(\omega)$. Thus, (5) states that the expected value of the feature function f_i must be 0 under every satisfying distribution. Since feature functions play a central role in the sequel, we assume the following:

Notation: For the rest of the paper, $\mathcal{R} = \{r_1, \ldots, r_m\}$ will always denote a consistent set of m soft probabilistic conditionals

$$r_i = (B_i(\boldsymbol{X})|A_i(\boldsymbol{X}))\,[d_i], \text{ with } d_i \in (0,1), 1 \le i \le m \tag{6}$$

and f_i will always denote the feature function of r_i according to Def. 5. Furthermore, P_U with $P_U(\omega) = \frac{1}{|\Omega|}$ for $\omega \in \Omega$ denotes the uniform distribution over Ω, and $P_{\mathcal{R}}^*$ denotes the maximum entropy distribution, i.e. $P_{\mathcal{R}}^* = \mathrm{ME}_\odot(\mathcal{R})$.

Instead of maximizing the entropy as in (2), one can also minimize the relative entropy with respect to P_U. The *relative entropy* $K(P,Q)$ (also called *Kullback-Leibler divergence* or *information divergence*) between two distributions P and Q is defined as $K(P,Q) := \sum_{\omega \in \Omega} P(\omega) \log \frac{P(\omega)}{Q(\omega)}$. Since $K(P, P_U) = \log|\Omega| - H(P)$ holds, entropy is just a special case of relative entropy, and we have:

$$\arg \min_{P \in \mathcal{S}(\mathcal{R})} K(P, P_U) = \arg \max_{P \in \mathcal{S}(\mathcal{R})} H(P)$$

The *Generalized Iterative Scaling (GIS)* algorithm technique [2] allows to solve the corresponding optimization problem defined by a set of linear constraints, each enforcing the expected value of a feature function, i. e., for given feature

functions and given expected values the distribution minimizing the relative
entropy is determined. The GIS algorithm requires the feature functions and
expected values to meet a normalized form, which can be achieved by an appropriate transformation and by adding an additional correctional feature function.
[4] shows that the following normalized optimization problem can be used.

Normalized Optimization Problem OptAggNorm($\mathcal{R}$):

$$\text{minimize} \quad K(P, P_U)$$

$$\text{subject to} \sum_{\omega \in \Omega} P(\omega)\hat{f}_i(\omega) = \hat{\varepsilon}_i, \, 1 \leq i \leq \hat{m}$$

$$\sum_{\omega \in \Omega} P(\omega) \quad = 1 \tag{7}$$

$$P(\omega) \quad > 0, \, \forall \omega \in \Omega$$

with the *normalized feature functions* $\hat{f}_i$ and their *expected values* $\hat{\varepsilon}_i$ given by

$$\hat{f}_i(\omega) = \frac{f_i(\omega) + d_i G_i^{\#}}{\mathcal{G}^{\#}}, \, \forall \omega \in \Omega \qquad\qquad \hat{\varepsilon}_i = \frac{d_i G_i^{\#}}{\mathcal{G}^{\#}},$$

for $1 \leq i \leq m$, where the *number of groundings of the conditional* r_i and the
total number of groundings of all conditionals in $\mathcal{R}$, respectively, is denoted by:

$$G_i^{\#} := |\mathcal{H}^{\boldsymbol{x}(A_i, B_i)}| \qquad\qquad \mathcal{G}^{\#} := \sum_{i=1}^{m} G_i^{\#} \tag{8}$$

For $\hat{m} := m + 1$, the *correctional feature function* $\hat{f}_{\hat{m}}$ and its *expected value* $\hat{\varepsilon}_{\hat{m}}$
are given by:

$$\hat{f}_{\hat{m}}(\omega) = 1 - \sum_{i=1}^{m} \hat{f}_i(\omega), \, \forall \omega \in \Omega \qquad\qquad \hat{\varepsilon}_{\hat{m}} = 1 - \sum_{i=1}^{m} \hat{\varepsilon}_i$$

In [4], it is shown that applying GIS to OPTAGGNORM($\mathcal{R}$) yields $P_{\mathcal{R}}^*$.

4   A GIS Algorithm for ME$_\odot$ Using Lagrange Multipliers

By applying the well-known *method of Lagrange multipliers* [1], a compact representation of the probability distribution $P_{\mathcal{R}}^*$ in terms of a Gibbs distribution
[7] can be derived using $\alpha_i = \exp(\lambda_i)$ with λ_i being a Lagrange multiplier:

Proposition 3. *There exist values* $\alpha_0, \alpha_1, \ldots, \alpha_m \in \mathbb{R}$ *such that for all* $\omega \in \Omega$:

$$P_{\mathcal{R}}^*(\omega) = \alpha_0 \prod_{i=1}^{m} \left(\alpha_i^{1-d_i}\right)^{ver_i(\omega)} \prod_{i=1}^{m} \left(\alpha_i^{-d_i}\right)^{fal_i(\omega)} = \alpha_0 \prod_{i=1}^{m} \alpha_i^{f_i(\omega)} \tag{9}$$

with $\alpha_0 = \frac{1}{\sum_{\omega \in \Omega} \prod_{i=1}^{m} \alpha_i^{f_i(\omega)}}$ *being a normalization value.*

Thus, $P_{\mathcal{R}}^*$ can be represented by m alpha-values $\alpha_1, \ldots, \alpha_m$. Note that since there
is just one alpha-value α_i for each conditional, the number of alpha-values is independent of the number of groundings of the conditionals. If these alpha-values
are at hand, the probability $P_{\mathcal{R}}^*(\omega)$ of a world ω can be determined according to
(9), since d_i and $ver_i(\omega)$ and $fal_i(\omega)$ are given by $\mathcal{R}$.

Input: a consistent set $\mathcal{R}$ of m soft probabilistic conditionals
Output: alpha-values $\alpha_0, \alpha_1, \ldots, \alpha_m$ determining the ME-distribution $P_{\mathcal{R}}^*$

1. for each $1 \leq i \leq \hat{m}$: initialize $\hat{\alpha}_{(0),i} := 1$

2. for each $\omega \in \Omega$: initialize $P_{(0)}(\omega) := \frac{1}{|\Omega|}$

3. initialize $k := 0$

4. repeat until an abortion condition holds (e.g. $|1 - \beta_{(k),i}| <$ a given threshold):

   (a) $k := k + 1$ // increase iteration counter

   (b) for each $1 \leq i \leq \hat{m}$:   // calculate scaling factors
   $$\beta_{(k),i} := \frac{\hat{\varepsilon}_i}{\displaystyle\sum_{\omega \in \Omega} P_{(k-1)}(\omega) \hat{f}_i(\omega)}$$

   (c) for each $\omega \in \Omega$:   // scale all probabilities
   $$P'_{(k)}(\omega) := P_{(k-1)}(\omega) \prod_{i=1}^{\hat{m}} \left(\beta_{(k),i}\right)^{\hat{f}_i(\omega)}$$

   (d) for each $\hat{\alpha}_{(k),i}, 1 \leq i \leq \hat{m}$:   // scale all $\hat{\alpha}$-values
   $\hat{\alpha}_{(k),i} := \hat{\alpha}_{(k-1),i} \cdot \beta_{(k),i}$

   (e) for each $\omega \in \Omega$:   // normalize probability values
   $$P_{(k)}(\omega) := \frac{P'_{(k)}(\omega)}{\displaystyle\sum_{\omega \in \Omega} P'_{(k)}(\omega)}$$

5. for each $1 \leq i \leq \hat{m}$: define $\hat{\alpha}_i := \hat{\alpha}_{(k),i}$ // denote final $\hat{\alpha}$-values

   define $\hat{\alpha}_0 := \left(\displaystyle\sum_{\omega \in \Omega} \prod_{i=1}^{\hat{m}} \hat{\alpha}_i^{\hat{f}_i(\omega)}\right)^{-1}$

6. for each $1 \leq i \leq m$: define $\alpha_i := \left(\frac{\hat{\alpha}_i}{\hat{\alpha}_{\hat{m}}}\right)^{\frac{1}{G^\#}}$ // determine α-values

   define $\alpha_0 := \hat{\alpha}_0 \hat{\alpha}_{\hat{m}} \prod_{i=1}^{m} \alpha_i^{d_i G_i^\#}$

Fig. 1. Algorithm $\mathrm{GIS}_{\odot}^{\alpha}$ for Aggregation Semantics computing alpha-values

By employing the basic GIS template of [2], we developed the algorithm $\mathrm{GIS}_{\odot}^{\alpha}$ (Fig. 1) computing the alpha values for the solution $P_{\mathcal{R}}^*$ of OPTAGGNORM$(\mathcal{R})$. $\mathrm{GIS}_{\odot}^{\alpha}$ starts with the uniform distribution as initial distribution (line 2). In the k-th iteration step, for each feature function $\hat{f}_i$ the current ratio $\beta_{(k),i}$ between its given expected value $\hat{\varepsilon}_i$ and its current expected value $\sum_{\omega \in \Omega} P_{(k-1)}(\omega) \hat{f}_i(\omega)$ under the current distribution $P_{(k-1)}$ is determined (line 4b). So $\beta_{(k),i}$ is the factor required to scale $P_{(k-1)}$ appropriately so that the expected value $\hat{\varepsilon}_i$ of $\hat{f}_i$ would be met exactly. Since the actual scaling of $P_{(k-1)}$ (line 4c) has to be performed with respect to all scaling factors $\beta_{(k),1}, \ldots, \beta_{(k),\hat{m}}$, the scaled distribution $P_{(k)}$ cannot fit all expected values immediately, but it is guaranteed by the GIS approach that a distribution iteratively computed that way converges to the correct solution. Note that the constraint $\sum_{\omega \in \Omega} P(\omega) = 1$ given in (7) is not explicitly encoded as a constraint in $\text{GIS}_\odot^\alpha$. Instead, the scaled probability values $P'_{(k)}(\omega)$ are normalized in each iteration step (line 4e), so that $P_{(k)}$ is a proper probability distribution (which is important to determine the correct $\beta_{(k+1),i}$ with respect to $P_{(k)}$). In line 4d, each $\hat{a}_{(k),i}$ value is scaled accordingly by its actual scaling factor $\beta_{(k),i}$. For the final $\hat{a}$-values (line 5) we have:

Proposition 4. *The $\hat{a}$-values $\hat{a}_0, \ldots, \hat{a}_{\hat{m}}$ computed by $\text{GIS}_\odot^\alpha$ determine $P_{\mathcal{R}}^*$ with respect to the normalized feature functions $\hat{f}_1, \ldots, \hat{f}_{\hat{m}}$ by $P_{\mathcal{R}}^*(\omega) = \hat{a}_0 \prod_{i=1}^{\hat{m}} \hat{a}_i^{\hat{f}_i(\omega)}$.*

Given the $\hat{m} = m+1$ final $\hat{a}$-values for the $\hat{m}$ normalized and correctional feature functions $\hat{f}_i$, the m α-values corresponding to the m original feature functions f_i are determined (line 6), i.e., each α_i value corresponds to a conditional $r_i \in \mathcal{R}$.

Proposition 5. *The α-values $\alpha_0, \ldots, \alpha_m$ computed by $\text{GIS}_\odot^\alpha$ determine $P_{\mathcal{R}}^*$ with respect to the feature functions $f_1, \ldots, f_m$ by $P_{\mathcal{R}}^*(\omega) = \alpha_0 \prod_{i=1}^{m} \alpha_i^{f_i(\omega)}$.*

A practical abortion condition as needed in line 4 of $\text{GIS}_\odot^\alpha$ is to stop after iteration step k if $|1 - \beta_{(k),i}| < \delta_\beta$ holds for $1 \leq i \leq \hat{m}$, with δ_β being an appropriate accuracy threshold.

5   Equivalences of Worlds

The core loop of the algorithm $\text{GIS}_\odot^\alpha$ in Figure 1 iterates over the set Ω of all worlds. This causes a redundancy for two different worlds ω, ω' if ω and ω' necessarily have the same ME probability with respect to $\mathcal{R}$. In [9], Kern-Isberner investigates the behaviour of worlds with respect to conditionals and introduces the concept of *conditional structure* of a world with respect to a set of propositional conditionals $\mathcal{R}^{\text{prop}}$. Formally, the conditional structure of ω with respect to $\mathcal{R}^{\text{prop}}$ is given by a product in a free abelian group with generators a_i^+, a_i^- where a_i^+ (resp. a_i^-) indicates that ω verifies (resp. falsifies) the i-th conditional in $\mathcal{R}^{\text{prop}}$. Kern-Isberner's idea of a conditional structure carries over to the relational case by employing the functions ver_i, fal_i counting the number of verifying and falsifying groundings. Here, we will extend the conditional structure of a world to the relational setting by using ordered tuples instead of a free abelian group notation (cf. [11]).

Definition 6 (vf-Pair, Conditional Structure). *For a world ω, the pair $(ver_i(\omega), fal_i(\omega)) \in \mathbb{N}_0 \times \mathbb{N}_0$ is called the vf-pair of ω with respect to conditional r_i. The conditional structure $\gamma_{\mathcal{R}}(\omega)$ of ω with respect to $\mathcal{R}$ is the m-tuple:*

$$\gamma_{\mathcal{R}}(\omega) := ((ver_1(\omega), fal_1(\omega)), \ldots, (ver_m(\omega), fal_m(\omega))) \in (\mathbb{N}_0 \times \mathbb{N}_0)^m \quad (10)$$

Example 2. Consider $\mathcal{R}_{\text{mky}}$ from Ex. 1 with $Const = \{andy, bobby, charly\}$. We abbreviate predicates and constants by their first character and consider the worlds $\omega' = \{f(a, c), f(a, a), f(a, b), f(c, c), h(a)\}$, $\omega'' = \{f(b, c), f(b, a), f(b, b), f(c, c), h(b)\}$, $\omega''' = \{f(c, a), f(c, b), f(c, c), h(c)\}$. We get $\gamma_{\mathcal{R}}(\omega') = \gamma_{\mathcal{R}}(\omega'') = ((0, 2), (0, 3), (3, 1), (1, 1), (2, 1))$ and $\gamma_{\mathcal{R}}(\omega''') = ((0, 2), (0, 3), (4, 0), (0, 2), (1, 2))$.

Note that the conditional structure $\gamma_{\mathcal{R}}(\omega)$ does not take any probabilities into account, i. e. it just considers the logical part of the conditionals in $\mathcal{R}$. Since in (9), $\alpha_0, \alpha_1, \ldots, \alpha_m$ and $d_1, \ldots, d_m$ are fixed values, the probability $P_{\mathcal{R}}^*(\omega)$ of ω merely depends on the values of the m vf-pairs $(ver_i(\omega), fal_i(\omega))$. Thus, worlds having the same conditional structure have the same probability under $P_{\mathcal{R}}^*$, motivating the following definition:

Definition 7 (Structural Equivalence). *Two worlds $\omega_1, \omega_2 \in \Omega$ are structurally equivalent with respect to $\mathcal{R}$, denoted by $\omega_1 \equiv_{\mathcal{R}} \omega_2$, iff $\gamma_{\mathcal{R}}(\omega_1) = \gamma_{\mathcal{R}}(\omega_2)$. With $[\omega_l]_{\equiv_{\mathcal{R}}} := \{\omega \in \Omega \mid \omega \equiv_{\mathcal{R}} \omega_l\}$ we denote the equivalence class of $\omega_l \in \Omega$, with $\Omega/\equiv_{\mathcal{R}} := \{[\omega]_{\equiv_{\mathcal{R}}} \mid \omega \in \Omega\}$ the set of all equivalence classes, and with $|[\omega_l]_{\equiv_{\mathcal{R}}}|$ the cardinality of the equivalence class $[\omega_l]_{\equiv_{\mathcal{R}}}$.*

Corollary 1. *For $\omega_1, \omega_2 \in \Omega$, $\omega_1 \equiv_{\mathcal{R}} \omega_2$ implies $P_{\mathcal{R}}^*(\omega_1) = P_{\mathcal{R}}^*(\omega_2)$.*

Similar to the conditional structure of ω given by an m-tuple of vf-pairs, we can consider the tuple of values of ω for the m different feature functions.

Definition 8 (Feature Function Structure). *The feature function structure $f_{\mathcal{R}}(\omega)$ of a world ω with respect to $\mathcal{R}$ is given by:*

$$f_{\mathcal{R}}(\omega) := (f_1(\omega), \ldots, f_m(\omega)) \in \mathbb{R}^m \tag{11}$$

Note that $f_{\mathcal{R}}(\omega)$, in contrast to $\gamma_{\mathcal{R}}(\omega)$, also depends on the probabilities of the probabilistic conditionals in $\mathcal{R}$.

Definition 9 (Feature Function Equivalence). *Worlds $\omega_1, \omega_2 \in \Omega$ are feature function equivalent with respect to $\mathcal{R}$, denoted $\omega_1 \equiv_{f_{\mathcal{R}}} \omega_2$, iff $f_{\mathcal{R}}(\omega_1) = f_{\mathcal{R}}(\omega_2)$.*

Corollary 2. *For $\omega_1, \omega_2 \in \Omega$, $\omega_1 \equiv_{f_{\mathcal{R}}} \omega_2$ implies $P_{\mathcal{R}}^*(\omega_1) = P_{\mathcal{R}}^*(\omega_2)$.*

Thus, both structural equivalence and feature function equivalence imply that worlds have the same ME probability. However, the equivalences do not coincide: The next proposition shows that $\equiv_{\mathcal{R}}$ is a finer equivalence relation than $\equiv_{f_{\mathcal{R}}}$.

Proposition 6 ($\equiv_{\mathcal{R}} \subsetneq \equiv_{f_{\mathcal{R}}}$).

For all worlds $\omega_1, \omega_2 \in \Omega$: $\omega_1 \equiv_{\mathcal{R}} \omega_2 \;\Rightarrow\; \omega_1 \equiv_{f_{\mathcal{R}}} \omega_2$ $\qquad$ (12)

There are worlds $\omega_1, \omega_2 \in \Omega$ with: $\omega_1 \equiv_{f_{\mathcal{R}}} \omega_2 \;\not\Rightarrow\; \omega_1 \equiv_{\mathcal{R}} \omega_2$ $\qquad$ (13)

Proof. (12) is easy to show. For (13), consider $Pred = \{q/1\}$, $Const = \{a, b\}$, and the knowledge base $\{r_1\}$ consisting of the single conditional $r_1 = (q(Y)|q(X))[0.5]$. There are four groundings of r_1: $(q(a)|q(a))[0.5]$, $(q(b)|q(a))[0.5]$, $(q(a)|q(b))[0.5]$, $(q(b)|q(b))[0.5]$. For the worlds $\omega_1 = \{\}$ and $\omega_2 = \{q(a)\}$, the counting functions ver_1 and fal_1 of r_1 yield $ver_1(\omega_1) = 0$, $fal_1(\omega_1) = 0$, $ver_1(\omega_2) = 1$, $fal_1(\omega_2) = 1$. Thus, for the feature function $f_1(\omega) = ver_1(\omega)(1 - 0.5) - fal_1(\omega)0.5$ of r_1 we get

$$f_1(\omega_1) = 0 \cdot (1 - 0.5) - 0 \cdot 0.5 \;=\; 0 = \; f_1(\omega_2) = 1 \cdot (1 - 0.5) - 1 \cdot (0.5)$$

and thus $\omega_1 \equiv_{f_{\mathcal{R}}} \omega_2$ holds. However, we have $\gamma_{\mathcal{R}}(\omega_1) = ((0, 0)) \neq ((1, 1)) = \gamma_{\mathcal{R}}(\omega_2)$ and therefore $\omega_1 \not\equiv_{\mathcal{R}} \omega_2$. $\qquad\square$

6   A GIS Algorithm Using Equivalence Classes of Worlds

According to Corollary 1, all worlds in an equivalence class have the same probability under the distribution $P_{\mathcal{R}}^*$. We describe how the $\mathrm{GIS}_\odot^\alpha$ algorithm can be modified to operate on equivalence classes instead of all worlds, thereby exploiting the fact that $\Omega/\equiv_{\mathcal{R}}$ is typically much smaller than Ω.

Definition 10 (Feature Function on Equivalence Classes). *For $r_i \in \mathcal{R}$ the feature function $f_i^{\Omega/\equiv_{\mathcal{R}}} : \Omega/\equiv_{\mathcal{R}} \to \mathbb{R}$ is defined by $f_i^{\Omega/\equiv_{\mathcal{R}}}([\omega]_{\equiv_{\mathcal{R}}}) := f_i(\omega)$.*

Definition 11 ($\equiv_{\mathcal{R}}$-Representation of a Distribution). *Let P be a probability distribution on Ω such that for all $\omega_1, \omega_2 \in \Omega$, $\omega_1 \equiv_{\mathcal{R}} \omega_2$ implies $P(\omega_1) = P(\omega_2)$. Then the function $P^{\Omega/\equiv_{\mathcal{R}}} : \Omega/\equiv_{\mathcal{R}} \to [0,1]$ with $P^{\Omega/\equiv_{\mathcal{R}}}([\omega]_{\equiv_{\mathcal{R}}}) = P(\omega)$ is called the $\equiv_{\mathcal{R}}$-representation of P.*

It is easy to show that the functions $f_i^{\Omega/\equiv_{\mathcal{R}}}$ and $P^{\Omega/\equiv_{\mathcal{R}}}$ on $\Omega/\equiv_{\mathcal{R}}$ are well-defined. To simplify our notation, in the following, we omit the index $\Omega/\equiv_{\mathcal{R}}$ in both $f_i^{\Omega/\equiv_{\mathcal{R}}}$ and $P^{\Omega/\equiv_{\mathcal{R}}}$, writing just f_i and P, since the domain of the function will always be clear from its argument. Note that Def. 10 covers feature functions in general and therefore also applies to normalized feature functions.

Using the structural equivalence of worlds and the functions defined in Def. 10 and 11, we developed the algorithm $\mathrm{GIS}_\odot^{\equiv_{\mathcal{R}}}$ (Fig. 2) operating on equivalence classes of worlds. Its structure is based on $\mathrm{GIS}_\odot^\alpha$ (Fig. 1), and in order to ease a comparison we have highlighted all differences to $\mathrm{GIS}_\odot^\alpha$. Apart from the additional step determining the set of equivalence classes (line 0), the two algorithms perform the same operations. Generally speaking, each occurrence of $\omega \in \Omega$ in $\mathrm{GIS}_\odot^\alpha$ has been replaced by $[\omega]_{\equiv_{\mathcal{R}}} \in \Omega/\equiv_{\mathcal{R}}$ (lines 2, 4b, 4c, 4e, and 5), and the cardinality of an equivalence class $[\omega]_{\equiv_{\mathcal{R}}}$ occurs as a factor in each sum over $\Omega/\equiv_{\mathcal{R}}$ (lines 4b, 4e, and 5).

An in-depth comparison of both algorithms reveals that, despite the differences, the operations of the $\mathrm{GIS}_\odot^{\equiv_{\mathcal{R}}}$ algorithm produce the same result as the $\mathrm{GIS}_\odot^\alpha$ algorithm. For instance, in line 4b, the scaling factors are calculated. In $\mathrm{GIS}_\odot^\alpha$, the sum in the denominator runs over Ω, whereas the sum in $\mathrm{GIS}_\odot^{\equiv_{\mathcal{R}}}$ runs over $\Omega/\equiv_{\mathcal{R}}$. Since the correct calculation of the scaling factor requires that the probability of each $\omega \in \Omega$ is summed up, each value $P_{(k-1)}([\omega]_{\equiv_{\mathcal{R}}})$ must be multiplied by the cardinality of the equivalence class $[\omega]_{\equiv_{\mathcal{R}}}$. That way, $\mathrm{GIS}_\odot^{\equiv_{\mathcal{R}}}$ computes exactly the same scaling factor values as $\mathrm{GIS}_\odot^\alpha$. In line 4c, the actual calculation of probabilities is performed. Since all worlds in an equivalence class have the same feature functions values, they also have the same scaled probability value; thus it is sufficient in $\mathrm{GIS}_\odot^{\equiv_{\mathcal{R}}}$ to calculate just one scaled probability value for each equivalence class.

Extending the analysis of $\mathrm{GIS}_\odot^{\equiv_{\mathcal{R}}}$ to all other differences to $\mathrm{GIS}_\odot^\alpha$ shows that Propositions 4 and 5 carry over to $\mathrm{GIS}_\odot^{\equiv_{\mathcal{R}}}$. In particular, $\mathrm{GIS}_\odot^{\equiv_{\mathcal{R}}}$ computes the correct alpha-values for $P_{\mathcal{R}}^*$:

Proposition 7. *The α-values $\alpha_0, \ldots, \alpha_m$ computed by $\mathrm{GIS}_\odot^{\equiv_{\mathcal{R}}}$ determine $P_{\mathcal{R}}^*$ with respect to the feature functions $f_1, \ldots, f_m$ by $P_{\mathcal{R}}^*(\omega) = \alpha_0 \prod_{i=1}^m \alpha_i^{f_i(\omega)}$.*

Input: a consistent set $\mathcal{R}$ of m soft probabilistic conditionals

Output: alpha-values $\alpha_0, \alpha_1, \ldots, \alpha_m$ determining the ME-distribution $P_{\mathcal{R}}^*$

0. determine the set of equivalence classes $\Omega/\equiv_{\mathcal{R}}$

1. for each $1 \leq i \leq \hat{m}$: initialize $\hat{\alpha}_{(0),i} := 1$

2. for each $[\omega]_{\equiv_{\mathcal{R}}} \in \Omega/\equiv_{\mathcal{R}}$: initialize $P_{(0)}([\omega]_{\equiv_{\mathcal{R}}}) := \frac{1}{|\Omega|}$

3. initialize $k := 0$

4. repeat until an abortion condition holds (e. g. $|1 - \beta_{(k),i}| <$ a given threshold):

   (a) $k := k + 1$ $//$ *increase iteration counter*

   (b) for each $1 \leq i \leq \hat{m}$: $//$ *calculate scaling factors*

   $$\beta_{(k),i} := \frac{\hat{\varepsilon}_i}{\displaystyle\sum_{[\omega]_{\equiv_{\mathcal{R}}} \in \Omega/\equiv_{\mathcal{R}}} |[\omega]_{\equiv_{\mathcal{R}}}| P_{(k-1)}([\omega]_{\equiv_{\mathcal{R}}}) \hat{f}_i([\omega]_{\equiv_{\mathcal{R}}})}$$

   (c) for each $[\omega]_{\equiv_{\mathcal{R}}} \in \Omega/\equiv_{\mathcal{R}}$: $//$ *scale all probabilities*

   $$P_{(k)}'([\omega]_{\equiv_{\mathcal{R}}}) := P_{(k-1)}([\omega]_{\equiv_{\mathcal{R}}}) \prod_{i=1}^{\hat{m}} \left(\beta_{(k),i}\right)^{\hat{f}_i([\omega]_{\equiv_{\mathcal{R}}})}$$

   (d) for each $\hat{\alpha}_{(k),i}, 1 \leq i \leq \hat{m}$: $//$ *scale all $\hat{\alpha}$-values*
   $$\hat{\alpha}_{(k),i} := \hat{\alpha}_{(k-1),i} \cdot \beta_{(k),i}$$

   (e) for each $[\omega]_{\equiv_{\mathcal{R}}} \in \Omega/\equiv_{\mathcal{R}}$: $//$ *normalize probability values*

   $$P_{(k)}([\omega]_{\equiv_{\mathcal{R}}}) := \frac{P_{(k)}'([\omega]_{\equiv_{\mathcal{R}}})}{\displaystyle\sum_{[\omega]_{\equiv_{\mathcal{R}}} \in \Omega/\equiv_{\mathcal{R}}} |[\omega]_{\equiv_{\mathcal{R}}}| P_{(k)}'([\omega]_{\equiv_{\mathcal{R}}})}$$

5. for each $1 \leq i \leq \hat{m}$: define $\hat{\alpha}_i := \hat{\alpha}_{(k),i}$ $//$ *denote final $\hat{\alpha}$-values*

   $$\text{define } \hat{\alpha}_0 := \left(\sum_{[\omega]_{\equiv_{\mathcal{R}}} \in \Omega/\equiv_{\mathcal{R}}} |[\omega]_{\equiv_{\mathcal{R}}}| \prod_{i=1}^{\hat{m}} \hat{\alpha}_i^{\hat{f}_i([\omega]_{\equiv_{\mathcal{R}}})} \right)^{-1}$$

6. for each $1 \leq i \leq m$: define $\alpha_i := \left(\frac{\hat{\alpha}_i}{\hat{\alpha}_{\hat{m}}}\right)^{\frac{1}{G^{\#}}}$ $//$ *determine α-values*

   $\text{define } \alpha_0 := \hat{\alpha}_0 \hat{\alpha}_{\hat{m}} \prod_{i=1}^{m} \alpha_i^{d_i G_i^{\#}}$

Fig. 2. Algorithm $\mathrm{GIS}_{\odot}^{\equiv_{\mathcal{R}}}$ for Aggregation Semantics operating on equivalence classes

Is is important to notice that the $\mathrm{GIS}_{\odot}^{\equiv_{\mathcal{R}}}$ algorithm does not consider the exponentially large set Ω at any iteration step. Merely the cardinality of Ω appears in the initial value $\frac{1}{|\Omega|}$, and the set $\Omega/\equiv_{\mathcal{R}}$ has to be determined in the initialization phase (lines 0 and 1). Applying a straight-forward approach requires to run over Ω once to determine $\Omega/\equiv_{\mathcal{R}}$. In contrast, GIS^{α} has to run over Ω in *every iteration step*, and the iterative computation of $P_{\mathcal{R}}^*$ with acceptable precision can require several ten thousands of such steps. Therefore, if

Table 1. Computations times of $\text{GIS}_{\ominus}^{\alpha}$ and $\text{GIS}_{\ominus}^{\equiv_{\mathcal{R}}}$ for different knowledge bases

Knowl. Base	Const	Size of Ω	$\Omega/\equiv_{\mathcal{R}}$	Iteration Steps	Computation Time $\text{GIS}_{\ominus}^{\alpha}$	$\text{GIS}_{\ominus}^{\equiv_{\mathcal{R}}}$
$\mathcal{R}_{\text{mky}}$	3	4,096	546	20,303	26 sec	4 sec
$\mathcal{R}_{\text{mky}}$	4	1,048,576	4,661	33,914	2 h 25 min	147 sec
$\mathcal{R}_{\text{syn}}$	8	65,536	80	731	16 sec	1 sec
$\mathcal{R}_{\text{syn}}$	9	262,144	99	810	58 sec	6 sec
$\mathcal{R}_{\text{syn}}$	10	1,048,576	120	892	199 sec	29 sec
$\mathcal{R}_{\text{flu}}$	3	4,096	32	257	1 sec	< 1 sec
$\mathcal{R}_{\text{flu}}$	4	1,048,576	91	686	152 sec	39 sec

the set $\Omega/\equiv_{\mathcal{R}}$ is significantly smaller than Ω as it is typically the case, the $\text{GIS}_{\ominus}^{\equiv_{\mathcal{R}}}$ algorithm will provide a much better performance than the $\text{GIS}_{\ominus}^{\alpha}$ algorithm.

We implemented the algorithms $\text{GIS}_{\ominus}^{\alpha}$ and $\text{GIS}_{\ominus}^{\equiv_{\mathcal{R}}}$ in Java as plugins for the KREATOR system, an integrated development environment for representing, reasoning, and learning with relational probabilistic knowledge [5]. In the following, we apply both algorithms to different knowledge bases. All results which are summarized in Table 1 were computed with an accuracy threshold of $\delta_{\beta} = 0.001$ (cf. Sec. 4) using an Intel Core i5-2500K CPU (4 cores, 3.3 Ghz).

Reconsider the knowledge base $\mathcal{R}_{\text{mky}}$ (Example 1) with *charly* and two other constants. There are $2^{12} = 4,096$ worlds, but only 546 equivalence classes. $\text{GIS}_{\ominus}^{\equiv_{\mathcal{R}}}$ takes just 4 seconds to compute the solution, while $\text{GIS}_{\ominus}^{\equiv_{\mathcal{R}}}$ needs 26 seconds. With 4 constants, the size of Ω is $2^{20} = 1,048,576$, compared to 4,661 equivalence classes. The corresponding difference in run time is almost 2 and a half hours vs. 147 seconds.

For $\mathcal{R}_{\text{syn}} = \{(r(X)|q(X))[0.7], (q(X))[0.2], (q(a))[0.6]\}$, Table 1 shows the corresponding results for 8, 9, and 10 constants. Note that here the number of iterations steps compared to $\mathcal{R}_{\text{mky}}$ is much smaller, while the benefit of using $\text{GIS}_{\ominus}^{\equiv_{\mathcal{R}}}$ is still significant.

Also the results for $\mathcal{R}_{\text{flu}} = \{(\mathit{flu}(X))[0.2], (\mathit{flu}(X)|\mathit{contact}(X,Y)\wedge\mathit{flu}(Y))[0.4]\}$ illustrate the performance improvements obtained by $\text{GIS}_{\ominus}^{\equiv_{\mathcal{R}}}$. All computation times include the constant amount of time needed for preprocessing steps, e. g. 36 sec for $\mathcal{R}_{\text{flu}}$ and 4 constants., i. e. this preprocessing time is independent of the number of iteration steps.

Whereas Ω always grows exponentially in the number of constants, it becomes clear from the result in Table 1 that the size of $\Omega/\equiv_{\mathcal{R}}$ grows much slower, thereby significantly reducing the complexity of each iteration step.

7 Conclusions and Further Work

For probabilistic reasoning with relational conditionals under aggregation semantics according to the principle of maximum entropy, we refined a generalized iterative scaling approach to compute the ME inference operator in two steps:

$\mathrm{GIS}_{\odot}^{\alpha}$ computes a compact representation of the maximum entropy distribution using alpha values, and, more importantly, $\mathrm{GIS}_{\odot}^{\equiv_{\mathcal{R}}}$ operates on equivalence classes induced by structural equivalences of worlds. An implementation and first evaluation of both algorithms demonstrates significant performance gains; further experiments and theoretical investigations are still needed. In future work, we will study to what extend equivalence classes can be exploited to perform lifted inference [14,15]. We will also extend our approach to cover other variants of maximum entropy semantics and by allowing deterministic knowledge in a knowledge base $\mathcal{R}$.

References

1. Boyd, S., Vandenberghe, L.: Convex Optimization. Cambridge University Press, New York (2004)
2. Darroch, J.N., Ratcliff, D.: Generalized iterative scaling for log-linear models. In: Annals of Mathematical Statistics. Institute of Mathematical Statistics (1972)
3. De Raedt, L., Kersting, K.: Probabilistic Inductive Logic Programming. In: De Raedt, L., Frasconi, P., Kersting, K., Muggleton, S. (eds.) Probabilistic ILP 2007. LNCS (LNAI), vol. 4911, pp. 1–27. Springer, Heidelberg (2008)
4. Finthammer, M.: An Iterative Scaling Algorithm for Maximum Entropy Reasoning in Relational Probabilistic Conditional Logic. In: Hüllermeier, E., Link, S., Fober, T., Seeger, B. (eds.) SUM 2012. LNCS (LNAI), vol. 7520, pp. 351–364. Springer, Heidelberg (2012)
5. Finthammer, M., Thimm, M.: An integrated development environment for probabilistic relational reasoning. Logic Journal of the IGPL (to appear, 2012)
6. Fisseler, J.: Learning and Modeling with Probabilistic Conditional Logic. Dissertations in Artificial Intelligence, vol. 328. IOS Press, Amsterdam (2010)
7. Geman, S., Geman, D.: Stochastic relaxation, gibbs distributions, and the bayesian restoration of images. IEEE Transactions on Pattern Analysis and Machine Intelligence 6, 721–741 (1984)
8. Getoor, L., Taskar, B. (eds.): Introduction to Statistical Relational Learning. MIT Press (2007)
9. Kern-Isberner, G.: Conditionals in Nonmonotonic Reasoning and Belief Revision. LNCS (LNAI), vol. 2087. Springer, Heidelberg (2001)
10. Kern-Isberner, G., Lukasiewicz, T.: Combining probabilistic logic programming with the power of maximum entropy. Artificial Intelligence, Special Issue on Nonmonotonic Reasoning 157(1-2), 139–202 (2004)
11. Kern-Isberner, G., Thimm, M.: A ranking semantics for first-order conditionals. In: Proc. 20th European Conference on Artificial Intelligence (to appear, 2012)
12. Kern-Isberner, G., Thimm, M.: Novel semantical approaches to relational probabilistic conditionals. In: Proc. of KR 2010, pp. 382–392. AAAI Press (May 2010)
13. Paris, J.: The uncertain reasoner's companion – A mathematical perspective. Cambridge University Press (1994)
14. Poole, D.: First-order probabilistic inference. In: Gottlob, G., Walsh, T. (eds.) Proc. of IJCAI 2003, pp. 985–991. Morgan Kaufmann (2003)
15. de Salvo Braz, R., Amir, E., Roth, D.: Lifted first-order probabilistic inference. In: Proc. of IJCAI 2005 (2005)
16. Thimm, M.: Probabilistic Reasoning with Incomplete and Inconsistent Beliefs. Ph.D. thesis, Technische Universität Dortmund (2011)

Developing of a Multimodal Interactive Training System in Therapeutic Calisthenics for Elderly People

Ben Hennig and Norbert Reithinger

German Research Center for Artificial Intelligence
Alt-Moabit 91c
10559 Berlin, Germany
{Ben.Hennig,Norbert.Reithinger}@dfki.de

Abstract. As a result of demographic developments and medical progress, the number of elderly and very old patients with multiple illnesses will increase in all areas of care. After stays at a clinic, it is important that rehabilitation exercises are continued at home. We developed an interactive training system to be installed in the homes of elderly people that should motivate and enhance the training experience at home. In this paper, we describe the simple-to-use multimodal interface of the system which facilitates the interactions with a virtual therapist. During various exercises, an integrated sensor system recognizes the user's movements. The multimodal visual feedback system supports and controls the exercises of the user and rates his performance. The system allows social interaction between the therapist, patient and/or other users via video conference and enables them to discuss problems as they arise. Furthermore, the therapist can remotely make adjustments to the users training protocol based on the monitored performance feedback.

1 Introduction

As a result of demographic developments and medical progress, the number of elderly and very old patients with multiple illnesses increases in all areas of care [2]. Further, medical care is more and more expensive, waiting times for treatments are getting longer and the patient has the problem to obtain the required therapy, the required count of therapy sessions for the real therapeutic goal. A home-based interactive therapeutic environment can be an important building block to continue the rehabilitation at home.

One part of such an environment is a user interface that hides the complexity of the interaction. A natural and easy interaction experience is crucial to control the system and to transmit feedback, especially for older people. During a therapy a user has to concentrate and perform the therapeutic exercises and the attention must not be absorbed by the system.

In this paper we will introduce the reader which need for developing and researching such systems exist, briefly in section 2. In section 3, we give an overview

B. Glimm and A. Krüger (Eds.): KI 2012, LNCS 7526, pp. 61–72, 2012.
© Springer-Verlag Berlin Heidelberg 2012

of the interactive training system. In section 4 we describe the requirement, concept and design of the multimodal interaction system as well as we describe the modules of interaction in section 5. Then we will introduce the reader by an example in section 6. And last but not least a short review, how we will evaluate the system within the project *SmartSenior*[1], in section 7.

2   Related Work

For physical therapy, several projects exist to increase physical activity and to support motivational factors.

Within the project *GestureTek Health*[2] different gesture-control technologies exist for disability, hospital, mental health and educational sectors. For a virtual reality physical therapy, *GestureTek Health* developed a system called IREX™ (Interactive Rehabilitation and Exercise System). The system involves the user into a virtual game environment, where they are do clinician prescribed therapeutic exercises. However it does not support a multimodal user interface.

A physical therapy system which based on the Nintendo® Wii™ system from Kaasa Health[3] is called *Physiofun Balance Training*. The system used the Wii including Wii Balance Board and a TV. A similar approach to therapeutic balance test and to comparable sensors is described by Dong et al. [4].

Ongoing projects for physical activities in rehabilitation are PAMAP[4] and MyRehab[5]. These systems analyze exercises and provides data for remote monitoring to evaluate by a medical supervisor. They helps patients to perform their rehabilitation and monitored their level of activity. A lot of more projects exist, like Silvergame [6], age@home [7] or KinectoTherapy [8]. However all systems do not support a multimodal user interface.

3   Overview of the Interactive Trainer

Our interactive training system integrates different sensor systems and multimodal input and output devices, controlled by a standard PC (see figure 1). To track the body movement we use a Kinect camera and a custom-built inertial 3D-body near sensor system[9]. The sensor platform was developed by Fraunhofer FIRST[10]. The body movements for the therapeutical exercises are mapped by a combination of

---

[1] http://www.smart-senior.de
[2] http://www.gesturetekhealth.com/
[3] http://www.kaasahealth.com/
[4] Physical Activity Monitoring for Aging People http://www.pamap.org/
[5] http://www.first.fraunhofer.de/home/projekte/myrehab/
[6] http://www.silvergame.eu/
[7] http://www.joanneum.at/index.php?id=4243&L=0
[8] http://www.kinectotherapy.in
[9] http://www.humotion.net/
[10] http://www.first.fraunhofer.de/

Fig. 1. Interactive training system, final prototype

both sensor types, Kinect and body sensors. The recognized sensor data are analyzed in real-time and mapped to a body model displayed on the display in front of the user. Green, yellow or red lines mark the body's contours and provide immediate feedback for correct or incorrect movements. Additional comments are provided both written and acoustically. Figure 2 shows the basic building blocks of the system. Using a therapy editor, the therapist initially configures an individual

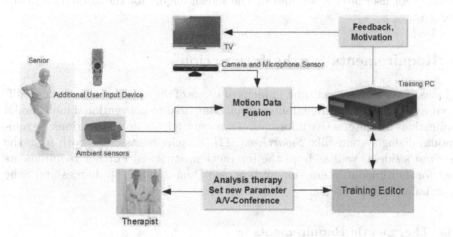

Fig. 2. Overview interactive training system

training plan for the senior [8]. Before starting a training session, the user gets his individual and actualized training plan from the online database at Charité's geriatric center, which is updated according to his personal training status. After the training session, the training results data are transmitted to the electronic health record in the safe and secure server back-end at the clinic. If needed, the system allows the patient also to get into contact with a therapist via A/V-communication as part of remote monitoring.

The design of the user interface including motivational elements is essential for user acceptance. To create familiarity with the training system in short time, we

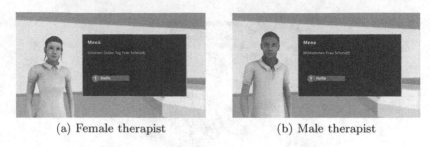

(a) Female therapist   (b) Male therapist

Fig. 3. Virtual therapist greets the user, avatar based design

used an avatar based approach (figure 3). The therapist avatar talks to the user and visualizes reference movements. He or she – depending on the preferences of the user – provides personal interaction. The user avatar is used to provide immediate feedback to his movements, functioning as a sort of mirror of the user. Immediate correctional feedback is provided through the color-coded body-parts (see above) and through comments from the therapist avatar. The GUI was designed and implemented by Nuromedia[11] and is controlled by the *Interaction Manager* for user interaction and by the sensor engine for the animation of the user avatar.

4   Requirements for the Interaction

In focus of our target group and in focus of usage of the application we have a different approach of multimodal interaction compared to conventional multimodal applications like interactive information systems, telephone applications, or multimodal dialog systems like *SmartKom* [11]. Requirements come both from the therapist's side as well as from the interaction situation. Further requirements exist for multimodal interaction system, see Dumas et al. [5], Jaimes and Sebe [7] or Lalanne et al. [1] e.g..

4.1   Therapeutic Requirements

In a first step, our clinical partner, the Geriatrics Research Group at Charité, held three focus group discussions about requirements of an interactive training device. As a result, an easy-to-use interactive device with individual adjustment possibilities and voice control, a therapeutic feedback system and game-based exercises were identified. Personal therapeutic feedback should take place approximately every four weeks [10].

Based on this study, we defined requirements from the point of view of therapists and end users, which also were relevant for the user interface. Most important is that the user interface do not disturb patients during therapeutic

---

[11] http://www.nuromedia.com/

activities: The users must not think about how to interact with the system. Therefore, a very easy to understand and operable user interface was necessary. We had to take into account that not every patient can react with all their senses, e.g. may have impaired hearing, or does not have fine control of his extremities. Therefore, we support modalities, well known to the user, like speech input and output. Additionally, simple input devices like a remote control should be supported, that are well known to the user from decade long operations.

4.2 Multimodal Interaction

On the multimodal input site, user interaction via speech or with an easy-to-use, but restricted input device like a remote control with number input is to be preferred. Gesture recognition to control the application by gesture is not supported, since gestures are neither natural in a therapeutic situation, nor possible, since arm movements of the patient are part of the therapeutical movement therapy. Additionally, control gestures must first be learned. For speech interaction we selected industry grade TTS (text-to-speech) and ASR (automatic speech recognition) components from SVOX and NUANCE, respectively. For ASR, we use a microphone placed close to the monitor: It cannot be expected that the user is able to attach a microphone correctly nor that the user can take care of the operations of a wireless microphone. A wired microphone will be in the way of the user's movements and is therefore not possible. Current commercial state-of-the-art ASR allows us to realize this requirement.

ASR and remote control are independent from each other, the user can choose between them freely. However, the dialog design has to take into account that the interaction has to be menu-like, and presented as text on the monitor in order to be able to be controlled by number input. Also, the prompts have to be visualized very clearly and in a big enough font-size so that visually impaired users can read them easily, if their hearing abilities are degraded.

In practice, the therapist will select the appropriate preferred multimodal input and output modes for the patient. If voice-control is not preferred, users can navigate through dialogs or menus with a senior-friendly remote control device, e.g. a device with fewer buttons and easy to operate layout.

To get therapeutically relevant improvements from the exercises, body movements in different regions of the body must be evaluated. Without delay, the interaction system has to provide feedback like *Keep your upper body upright.* or *Please keep your arms still.*. The patient has to get this instructions to correct the movements immediately. Therefore, the dialog control cannot rely on a turn based interaction sequence, it has to activate the feedback sequences immediately after the error signals are received from the senor system. Finally, the must not lose the fun in the exercises, which requires motivating intermediate feedback like *That was very good.* or *You have received all the stars.*.

5   Controlling the Interaction

In this section we will describe the modules of the interaction system, the *Interaction Manager* and the *Dialog Manager* including knowledge management.

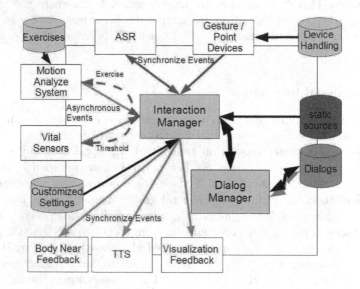

Fig. 4. Abstract Knowledge Management and Event System

5.1   The Interaction Manager

Figure 4 shows the general structure of the interaction system. In the center of the system is the *Interaction Manager*. It processes synchronous and asynchronous event from the user and the sensors. The core-setup, e.g., which multimodal I/O technology is to be used, comes from the *Customized Settings* knowledge source. If a specific device is connected, its messages will be posted and/or received. In case of input messages, the *Interaction Manager* delegates the processing to the *Dialog Manager*. The *Dialog Manager* interprets these message and generates the feedback for the user, which is handled back through the *Interaction Manager*. In a dialog state where speech input is possible, the ASR recognition process is started and the microphone is activated by the *Interaction Manager*. Therefore, no push-to-talk button is required, which is an absolute requirement in the training situation. The pointing gesture device is always activated. Once a message is received by either input modality, the *Interaction Manager* stops ASR and closes the microphone.

The interaction system uses two different event systems, the synchronous and asynchronous events. The synchronous events are used in direct user interaction. The user controls the interaction flow with menu dialogs and control dialogs, e.g. when talking about his health state. This corresponds to a standard turn-based interaction.

The asynchronous event system processes input from the Motion Analysis System or the Vital Sensors that can be posted anytime during the exercise. They notify about errors and special events and should initiate feedback to motivate, to correct, to inform, or to warn the user. The *Interaction Manager* forwards these events to the *Dialog Manager* immediately as they occur. The *Dialog Manager* process these events, irrespective of its current state and generates new user feedback events in order to supply instructions for the various output channels.

The challenge of the *Interaction Manager* is to handle and to synchronize all events for the dialog components. In default situations a user input via a pointing device has a higher priority than a posture message from Motion Analysis. However in case of warnings, alarm events have a higher priority than all other messages.

5.2   The Dialog Manager

The *Dialog Manager* controls the dialog flow. At its core we use *SceneMaker 3* [6], a toolkit to create *finite state machines* (FSM) for the design and execution of dialog automata. *SceneMaker 3* merges the advantages of dialog management based on FSMs and *frame based* knowledge representation, see e.g. [9,3].

For the dialog design we choose a mixture of *Command and Control-*, *Menu-* and free *Natural Language* dialogs. In a therapeutic scenario various requirements influence the interaction flow. E.g., we provide some menus where the user can choose the next path, e.g. the choice of a specific exercise scenarios, or to report the state of his health.

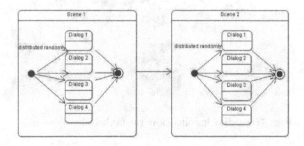

Fig. 5. Randomized dialog design for diversified dialogs

Additionally, to motivate the user and to make the interaction more interesting, we have implemented a randomized dialog design. A *scene* is a component where we define the *dialog flow*. A *dialog flow* has a start point and can have multiple end points for further *scenes*. Within the *dialog flow* we declare each sentence of the conversation as one *supernode* (figure 5). Inside a *supernode* we have the potential to define for one statement more than one sentence and/or question (figure 6), at which the activation of a *node* is randomized.

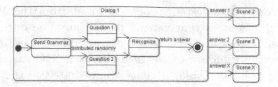

Fig. 6. Randomized question dialog diversified dialogs

The challenge is to match *supernodes* and its statement. For a small number of combination < 4 it is manageable for a native speaker. An example on the question of health is: *How are you?, How do you feel today?, Mr. Smith how you feel?* or *How are you today, Mr. Smith?*. On each of these questions, the user

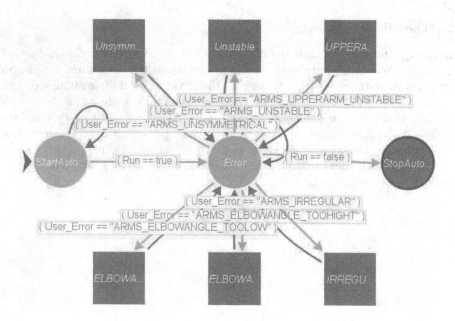

Fig. 7. Feedback collection by faulty arm posture

can respond with the same answer. *I'm fine* or *I feel bad.*, e.g.. Training exercises are tailored to a user or to user groups with the same rehabilitation needs. The development of an individual dialog is task of the specialists, the therapists in our case. The therapist in the normal training motivates or stimulates the user, corrects faulty postures and warn at fall risks. These dialogs have to be modeled in the dialog flow of our system.

Figure 7 shows the error and feedback handling for several incorrect arm movements. If an error message is received from the motion analysis system, we start the corresponding supernode. This corresponding message to the user can be realized in four different versions, as shown in figure 8.

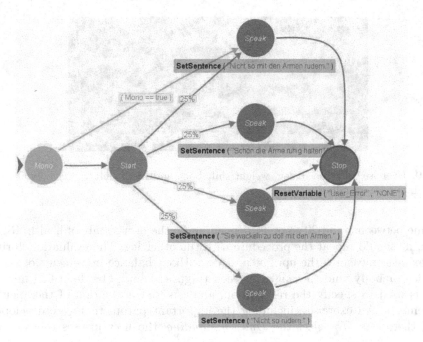

Fig. 8. Example of randomized feedback message of the same statement

6   Exemplary Multimodal Interactions

To provide an insight in the interaction with the system, we will describe a short walk-through of the *One leg standing* training exercise. The user starts the training system and is greeted by his virtual therapist (figure 3). Then he is asked if he feels good or bad. The microphone is activated by the system, and he can reply, e.g., with *I'm fine* or *I feel bad*[12]. As an alternative to speech, he can also use the remote control: Button 1 for *I'm fine* or button 2 for *I feel bad*. The alternatives are presented on the screen clearly to address every available modality. Should the user feel bad, he is asked in the next step if he wants to be connected with his therapist. If the user wishes a video call, is initiated by the system. Otherwise, the system ends the training session. In the case of the user feels well, the exercise selection starts (figure 9). The exercise selection only shows the exercises that were previously selected by the therapist for the patient.

As an example, we describe briefly the therapeutic exercise "one leg standing" to improve the balance (figure 10). In that exercise the goal is to get the user to stand stable with a correct body posture on one leg. Here, the upper part of the body, the arms and the free leg should be kept stable. It starts in the upright standing. To stay in balance, the arms should be kept lateral with a small distance to the body. The next step is to pull up one knee, so that the angle between thigh and hip is 90 degree. That position is to hold a certain period

---

[12] The dialog is in German and were translated for this purpose.

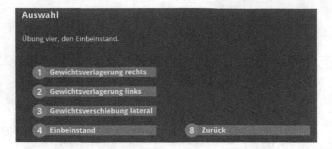

Fig. 9. Exercise selection dialog, weight shift back and forth (left/right), weight shift lateral, one leg standing

of time between 1 and 20 seconds, depending on the user's state of health. Right after, he should repeat the procedure with the other leg. The evaluation during the exercise measures the upright posture without balance movements of arms, free leg or body, and the angle between thigh and hip. The described motion flow is used to specify the recognition, analysis and evaluation of therapeutic movements. All exercises, including the important parameters were developed with therapists. To select the *One leg standing*, the user presses the number

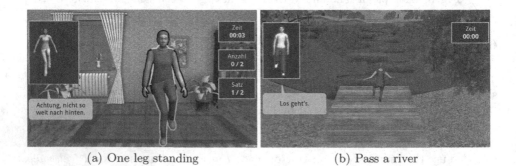

(a) One leg standing   (b) Pass a river

Fig. 10. Example of a therapeutic exercise and their corresponding game

4 on the remote control or voice commands *One leg standing*. If the user has selected an exercise it is explained to him, if desired. An exercise is started, first, a start counter counts down, so that the user can prepare himself for the exercise. Then he follows the prescribed motion, e.g. see figure 10(a), that is also visualized by the therapist's avatar. If the system detects a wrong move or a bad body posture, the user is immediately notified. We use different techniques simultaneously, voice announcement, acoustic signals and graphical feedback. When such an error occurs, the region with a bad posture is colored depending on the error level. The first error level is colored yellow. For example, in figure 10(a) the bearing of the upper part of the body is not correct. The user leans back slightly and at once he gets the friendly feedback not to lean back too far.

If a critical error is detected, for example, if the user just before falling down, the therapist gets a message immediately to inform him about the critical event.

After an exercise, the user gets a break and then repeats the exercise. The break time and repetitions are set by the therapist in the therapeutic editor. In the end, the user receives an evaluation which shows him whether he has improved or not. Afterwards he has the chance to make another exercise or game. If no further exercises are scheduled, the therapist's avatar will initiate a terminating dialog and the system shuts down.

Motivation and retention to the training is of utmost importance. In addition to the training exercises we developed a game for each therapeutic exercise that takes up the theme of the therapeutic goal but has a more playful content. The following exercises including games exist: *Weight shift back and forth* and *Drive a motorboat*, *Weight shift lateral standing* and *Slalom in standing*, *One leg standing* and *Pass a river*, *Weight shift lateral sitting* and *Slalom sitting*. For the corresponding game *Pass a river* of the exercise *One leg standing*, the same movement model is used. Also, the multimodal interaction is similar to the training exercise.

7   Conclusion and Future Work

We developed and implemented the concept of multimodal interaction, dialog management and design for an interactive trainer. The prototype was presented for one week on the CeBit 2012, where visitors could test the system. This also served as a pretest of the system before the final field test. Based on this experience, we now have a final prototype for the field test. This prototype comprises real therapeutic assessments developed by a therapist for physiotherapy. The assessments involve exercises for stroke patients and for people with an increased risk of fall.

Both, the interactive training system and the therapeutic assessments will be evaluated in our field test scenario at the end of the project. We deploy the system in 21 field-test apartments with users from the real target group ($\geq$ age of 50) in their home environment. The patient is alone and nobody can help him on site, once the system is installed. The evaluation period will be six weeks and will start in the second quarter of 2012.

The result of the field test will provide us with data about which feedback has the most influence, how much feedback is useful, and at which point the user is stressed by the system. Also we will get information about the use of modalities in real-life usage. It is a realistic test of usability and user acceptance of the system, and will give us important insight in the robustness of multimodal interaction in the target population of the system.

Acknowledgements. We thank our colleagues from SmartSenior, especially from Charité, FhG First and Nuromedia, for the collaboration in the development of the system. The development of the system was funded by the German Ministry for Education and Research within the SmartSenior project (contract number 16KT0902).

References

1. ACM: Fusion Engines for Multimodal Input: A Survey. In: Proceedings of the 2009 International Conference on Multimodal Interfaces (2009)
2. ADVISORY COUNCIL on the Assessment of Developments in the Health Care System. Coordination and integration – health care in an ageing society. Technical report, Bundesministerium für Gesundheit (2009)
3. Bui, T.H.: Multimodal dialogue management - state of the art. Technical Report TR-CTIT-06-01, Centre for Telematics and Information Technology University of Twente, Enschede (January 2006)
4. Dong, L., Tan, M.S., Ang, W.T., Ng, C.K.: Interactive rehabilitation. In: i-CREATe 2009 Proceedings of the 3rd International Convention on Rehabilitation Engineering & Assistive Technology (2009)
5. Dumas, B., Lalanne, D., Oviatt, S.: Multimodal Interfaces: A Survey of Principles, Models and Frameworks. In: Lalanne, D., Kohlas, J. (eds.) Human Machine Interaction. LNCS, vol. 5440, pp. 3–26. Springer, Heidelberg (2009)
6. Gebhard, P., Kipp, M., Klesen, M., Rist, T.: Authoring scenes for adaptive, interactive performance. In: Proceedings of the Second International Joint Conference on Autonomous Agents and Multiagent Systems (2003)
7. Jaimes, A., Sebe, N.: Multimodal human computer interaction: A survey. Computer Vision and Image Understanding 108(1-2), 116–134 (2007)
8. John, M., Klose, S., Kock, G., Jendreck, M., Feichtinger, R., Hennig, B., Reithinger, N., Kiselev, J., Gövercin, M., Kausch, S., Polak, M., Irmscher, B.: Smartsenior's interactive trainer - development of an interactive system for a home-based fall-prevention training for elderly people. Advanced Technologies and Societal Change 7, 305–316 (2012)
9. McTear, M.F.: Spoken dialogue technology: Enabling the conversational user interface. ACM Computing Surveys (CSUR) 34(1), 90–169 (2002)
10. VDE Verlag: Konzeption und Entwicklung eines interaktiven Trainingssystems zur häuslichen Sturzprophylaxe und Schlaganfallrehabilitation, Demographischer Wandel - Assistenzsysteme aus der Forschung in den Markt of Ambient Assisted Living - AAL - 4. Deutscher Kongress (January 2011)
11. Wahlster, W. (ed.): SmartKom: Foundations of Multimodal Dialogue Systems. Springer, Heidelberg (2006)

PAC-Learning with General Class Noise Models

Shahin Jabbari[1], Robert C. Holte[2], and Sandra Zilles[3]

[1] University of California, Los Angeles
shahin@cs.ucla.edu
[2] University of Alberta
holte@cs.ualberta.ca
[3] University of Regina
zilles@cs.uregina.ca

Abstract. We introduce a framework for class noise, in which most of the known class noise models for the PAC setting can be formulated. Within this framework, we study properties of noise models that enable learning of concept classes of finite VC-dimension with the Empirical Risk Minimization (ERM) strategy. We introduce simple noise models for which classical ERM is not successful. Aiming at a more general-purpose algorithm for learning under noise, we generalize ERM to a more powerful strategy. Finally, we study general characteristics of noise models that enable learning of concept classes of finite VC-dimension with this new strategy.

1 Introduction

Modeling noise in learning is a problem that has been widely addressed in the literature. Specific noise models have been formalized and studied with respect to their effect on learnability. Unfortunately, often noise models with strong positive learnability results are rather unrealistic models, whereas more realistic noise models leave little room for positive results. This trade-off has not been studied systematically—almost every previous study focuses on a specific noise model and produces results only for that model. To address this shortcoming, this paper provides a formal framework in which we can reason about a broad class of noise models, and presents quite general conditions on noise models in this class under which learnability in the PAC model [16] can be guaranteed.

The focus of this paper is on *class noise* (*e.g.*, [1]), which allows the labels of the examples given to the learner to be altered by noise, but not the instances themselves to be altered (in contrast to other types of noise, *e.g.*, [7]). In the class noise setting, for an instance x from input space $\mathcal{X}$, a distribution D over $\mathcal{X}$, and a target concept c, the *noise rate* of x given D and c is the probability that the wrong label for x is observed, given that x is sampled with respect to D.

Classical noise models, such as random classification noise [1], malicious classification noise [14], and constant partition classification noise (CPCN) [6], are rather restrictive. Random classification noise assumes that every instance x has the same noise rate, the latter being independent of D and c. Malicious classification noise allows different instances to have different noise rates but assumes

B. Glimm and A. Krüger (Eds.): KI 2012, LNCS 7526, pp. 73–84, 2012.
© Springer-Verlag Berlin Heidelberg 2012

a common upper bound on all the noise rates, which is independent of D and c. CPCN loosens these constraints by allowing the noise rate to depend on c as well as x, but not on D. This allows one to model the type of noise that arises in many natural settings when instances closer to the decision boundary have a larger noise rate than instances far away from the decision boundary. However, in CPCN the transition between these noise rates is not smooth, since noise rates are determined by a finite partitioning of the set of all possible labeled examples.

The literature studies these noise models separately. Though the statistical query model [9] gave a unified account of the learnability results of various noise models, it does not permit the definition of new noise models that overcome the limitations of the classical ones or to study general properties of noise that enable PAC-learning of certain concept classes under specific classes of distributions.

We introduce a formal definition of "class noise model" in which many classical models can be formulated. Our flexible framework allows noise rates to depend arbitrarily on x, D, and c. We then focus on the question of what makes learning under some noise models harder than learning under others, and try to gain insight into why all known noise models that produce general positive learnability results are rather unrealistic. We address this question by proposing formal properties *on noise models* under which PAC-learning is possible. Empirical Risk Minimization (ERM) strategies [17], which were previously used to prove that every PAC-learnable class is PAC-learnable under random classification noise, simply return a concept c' that minimizes the number of observed examples whose labels disagree with those of c'. In a noisy setting, this kind of strategy might not be generally successful, since the noise model might obfuscate the differences between concepts, *i.e.*, two dissimilar concepts might look very similar after applying noise, and vice versa. Therefore we generalize ERM to a strategy that picks a concept whose *expected behavior after applying noise* minimizes the number of disagreements with the sample. Under some additional assumptions on the noise model, we show that similar properties as in the classical ERM case are sufficient for PAC-learning with this generalized strategy.

To sum up: As opposed to the research on *agnostic learning*, we study the problem of finding a concept that approximates the underlying noise-free target concept c, instead of approximating the observed (noisy) data. Our results suggest that no *realistic* noise model will lead to a *general* solution to this problem in the distribution-free setting. Our goal is *not* to show that approximating c under severe noise is possible in general, but to study conditions on the noise models under which this is possible. The main contributions of this work are: *(i)* a formal basis for the design and study of new noise models as well as for classes of distributions that ease learning. *(ii)* formal conditions under which ERM still works; *(iii)* a generalization of ERM including conditions under which it solves the learning problem we propose.

2   Preliminaries

We denote by $\mathcal{X}$ a set called the *input space*. For most of this paper, $\mathcal{X} = \mathbb{R}^n$ for some $n \in \mathbb{N}$. A *concept* c is a subset of $\mathcal{X}$ or, equivalently, a binary-valued function on $\mathcal{X}$. A *concept class*, $\mathcal{C}$, is a set of concepts. A *probabilistic concept* (or a *noisy concept*) $c : \mathcal{X} \to [0,1]$ is a real-valued function that assigns to each element of $\mathcal{X}$ a value in the closed interval $[0,1]$. Hence, a concept can be considered as a special case of a probabilistic concept. Let D denote a probability *distribution* over $\mathcal{X}$ and $\mathcal{D}_{\mathcal{X}}$ denote the set of all distributions over $\mathcal{X}$. For a distribution D and probabilistic concept c, the *oracle*, $\mathrm{EX}(c, D)$, is a procedure that on each call returns a pair $(x, y) \in \mathcal{X} \times \{0, 1\}$, called an *example*, where *(i)* $x \in \mathcal{X}$ is drawn with respect to D and *(ii)* $y \in \{0, 1\}$ is drawn with respect to the Bernoulli distribution over $\{0, 1\}$ that assigns the probability $c(x)$ to 1 and the probability $1 - c(x)$ to 0. If c is a concept, then for every (x, y) returned by $\mathrm{EX}(c, D)$, $y = c(x)$. In any example (x, y), x is called the *instance* and y is called the *label*. Every multi-set $\mathcal{S}$ of examples is called a *sample*. We study learning in the framework of PAC-learning [16].

Definition 1. *[16] A concept class $\mathcal{C}$ is probably approximately correctly learnable (PAC-learnable), if there exists a learning algorithm $\mathcal{L}$ and a polynomial $m : \mathbb{R}^2 \to \mathbb{R}$ such that: for any target concept $c \in \mathcal{C}$, for any $\epsilon, \delta \in (0, 1/2)$ and for any distribution $D \in \mathcal{D}_{\mathcal{X}}$, if $\mathcal{L}$ is given access to $\mathrm{EX}(c, D)$ and inputs ϵ and δ, then with probability at least $1 - \delta$, after seeing a sample $\mathcal{S}$ of $\lceil m(1/\epsilon, 1/\delta) \rceil$ examples, $\mathcal{L}$ outputs a concept $c' \in \mathcal{C}$ satisfying $Pr_{x \sim D}[c'(x) \neq c(x)] \leq \epsilon$.[1]*

One criticism of the PAC model is the unrealistic assumption that the oracle always provides examples according to the true underlying distribution D and the true target concept c. Often in practice information sources are susceptible to noise. Several kinds of noise were proposed to remedy this problem. In our research we focus on class noise, *i.e.*, we assume in the examples returned by the noisy oracle, the instances x given to the learner are drawn with respect to D but with some probability η the labels may sometimes be flipped from $c(x)$ to $1 - c(x)$. η is called the *noise rate* and can vary with the instance, target concept and distribution. Previously studied class noise models were proven not to restrict PAC-learnability. Every PAC-learnable class is also PAC-learnable under a random classification noise oracle [1], a malicious classification noise oracle [14], or a CPCN oracle [13], as long as the noise rates are less than $1/2$.

3   A General Framework for Modeling Class Noise

Random classification noise and malicious classification noise involve noise rates that do not depend on the sampled instance x or on the target concept. In practice, this is unrealistic, since one might expect examples closer to the decision boundary to be more susceptible to noise than examples farther away [4]. For example, in optical character recognition, training examples for a certain character are more likely to be mislabeled the more similar they are to another character. The CPCN model addresses this issue, but does not allow for a smooth transition between noise rates when traversing the instance space. Moreover, the CPCN model does not allow the noise to depend on the distribution.

---

[1] Run-time efficiency issues are out of the scope of this paper. Further, note that Definition 1 is only sensible under mild measurability conditions.

One approach could be to introduce new noise models and compare them to existing ones. However, learnability results would then concern only the particular chosen noise models and might not provide much insight into what makes learning under noise difficult in general. Therefore, we abstract from specific noise models and introduce a framework that *(i)* captures most of the class noise models studied in the literature (Section 3.1), *(ii)* allows us to formalize new class noise models (Section 3.2), and *(iii)* allows us to study general properties of noise models that are sufficient or necessary for learnability (Section 4).

3.1   Class Noise Models

Class noise can be considered as a procedure that converts a concept to a probabilistic concept, because the correct label of an instance may be flipped.

Definition 2. *A* (class) noise model *is a mapping* $\Phi : 2^{\mathcal{X}} \times \mathcal{D}_{\mathcal{X}} \times \mathcal{X} \to [0,1]$.

Thus, noise can depend on the sampled instance x, the target concept c, and the distribution D. For every c and D, each instance x has a defined *noise rate* $\eta_{c,D}(x)$, *i.e.*, a probability with which its label is flipped, namely $\eta_{c,D}(x) = |c(x) - \Phi(c,D,x)|$. For example, random classification noise [1] can be defined by $\Phi(c,D,x) = 1 - \eta$, if $c(x) = 1$, and $\Phi(c,D,x) = \eta$, if $c(x) = 0$ where $\eta \in [0,1/2)$ is the noise rate. As another example, CPCN [6] can be defined as follows. If $\eta = (\eta_1, \ldots, \eta_k) \in [0,1/2)^k$, and $\pi = (\pi_1, \ldots, \pi_k) \subseteq (\mathcal{X} \times \{0,1\})^k$ is a k-tuple of pairwise disjoint sets such that $\pi_1 \cup \cdots \cup \pi_k = \mathcal{X} \times \{0,1\}$, then, for $(x, c(x)) \in \pi_i$, $\Phi(c,D,x) = 1 - \eta_i$, if $c(x) = 1$, and $\Phi(c,D,x) = \eta_i$, if $c(x) = 0$.[2]

Sampling according to c and D (via $\text{EX}(c,D)$), followed by applying the noise model Φ, is defined as sampling from the noisy concept $\Phi(c,D,\cdot)$. We then say that a class $\mathcal{C}$ is *learnable w.r.t.* Φ if $\mathcal{C}$ is PAC-learnable as in Definition 1, where the oracle $\text{EX}(c,D)$ is replaced by sampling from the noisy concept $\Phi(c,D,\cdot)$.

PAC-learning is distribution-free, *i.e.*, it requires the learner to be successful for any combination of target concept and underlying distribution. In the presence of noise, distribution-free learning may be difficult, and even impossible for many simple classes (see Proposition 1). Therefore, we sometimes restrict the class of distributions when dealing with noise. For any $\mathcal{D} \subseteq \mathcal{D}_{\mathcal{X}}$, we say $\mathcal{C}$ is learnable w.r.t. Φ and $\mathcal{D}$, if we require the learner to be successful only for distributions in $\mathcal{D}$, not for any distribution in $\mathcal{D}_{\mathcal{X}}$.

In our model, the learner is required to produce a concept that is similar to the target concept before it is corrupted by noise. This is a different task than agnostic learning [11], which requires the learner to find a concept that best

---

[2] Malicious classification noise [14] cannot be modeled by Definition 2. This can be easily fixed by using a mapping $\Phi : 2^{\mathcal{X}} \times \mathcal{D}_{\mathcal{X}} \times \mathcal{X} \to 2^{[0,1]}$ to a *set of values between 0 and 1*. This generalization allows defining malicious noise in which the adversary has the option of picking the value of Φ from a subset of $[0,1]$ that depends on the instance, the target concept and the distribution. Due to space constraints, we do not discuss such models any further. However, even this generalization cannot model noise that depends on the sequence of examples itself, *e.g.*, [5,9].

approximates the probabilistic (noisy) concept observed. An extra difficulty of our task arises from the fact that the noise process may generate two similar probabilistic concepts from two dissimilar concepts. In fact, unlike in the agnostic case, a necessary condition for PAC-learnability with any arbitrary error is that the noise model Φ does not "make two distinct concepts equal."

Lemma 1. *Let Φ be a noise model. Let C be a concept class, $c, c' \in C$ with $c \neq c'$ and $\mathcal{D} \subseteq \mathcal{D}_{\mathcal{X}}$. If there is some $D \in \mathcal{D}$ such that $\Phi(c, D, x) = \Phi(c', D, x)$ for all $x \in \mathrm{supp}(D)$, then the learner cannot distinguish between c and c' regardless of the number of examples it receives.*

An immediate consequence of Lemma 1 is that it implies a lower error bound of $Pr_{x \sim D}[c(x) \neq c'(x)]/2$ for learning C w.r.t. Φ and $\mathcal{D}$.

3.2 Defining New Noise Models

To illustrate the flexibility of our definition of noise, we introduce examples of noise models in which the noise rate depends on the target concept, the instance, and sometimes on the distribution. The first noise model was suggested by Shai Ben-David (personal communication) and is based on the idea that noise is often more likely when an instance lies close to the decision boundary.

In this model, the noise rate for an example $(x, c(x))$ is given by the probability of an instance in the vicinity of x being labeled by $1 - c(x)$, where c is the target concept. In other words, the probability of x being labeled 1 by the oracle equals the probability mass of the set of positively labeled instances in a ball around x, relative to the mass of the whole ball around x. There are different ways of defining the ball around an instance, e.g., the *distance ball* around x is defined as $\mathrm{DB}_\rho(x) = \{x' \in \mathcal{X} \mid \mathrm{dist}(x, x') < \rho\}$ for some metric dist.

Definition 3. *Let $\rho \geq 0$. The ρ-distance random classification noise model, $\Phi^{\mathrm{dr}(\rho)}$, is defined by*

$$\Phi^{\mathrm{dr}(\rho)}(c, D, x) = Pr_{x' \sim D}[c(x') = 1 \mid x' \in \mathrm{DB}_\rho(x)],$$

for $x \in \mathrm{supp}(D)$. $\Phi^{\mathrm{dr}(\rho)}(c, D, x) = 0$ for $x \notin \mathrm{supp}(D)$.

To gain some intuition about this new noise model, we show that the class of linear separators in $\mathbb{R}$ is learnable with respect to $\Phi^{\mathrm{dr}(\rho)}$, where the metric in the definition of the distance ball is the Euclidean distance.

Theorem 1. *Let $\mathcal{X} = \mathbb{R}$ and $\rho \geq 0$. Let C be the class of linear separators in $\mathbb{R}$. C is learnable w.r.t. $\Phi^{\mathrm{dr}(\rho)}$.*

Theorem 1 is proven by showing that the noisy concepts $\Phi^{\mathrm{dr}(\rho)}$ are all non-decreasing functions, *i.e.*, the probability of the label for x being 1 never decreases as x increases. Such probabilistic concepts can be approximated, with high probability, in a sample-efficient way [10], which helps to reconstruct the target concept approximately.

The second noise model follows a similar idea about the origin of noise but uses a different definition for the ball around an instance. The *weight ball*, $\text{WB}_\omega(x)$, around an instance x is the largest distance ball that has the mass of at most ω with respect to the distribution *i.e.*, $\text{WB}_\omega(x) = \text{DB}_\rho$ where $\rho = \sup \{\rho' \mid Pr_{x' \sim D}[x' \in \text{DB}_{\rho'}(x)] \leq \omega\}$.

Definition 4. *Let* $\omega \in [0,1]$. *The* ω-*weight random classification noise model,* $\Phi^{\text{wr}(\omega)}$, *is defined by*

$$\Phi^{\text{wr}(\omega)}(c, D, x) = \Pr_{x' \sim D}[c(x') = 1 \mid x' \in \text{WB}_\omega(x)],$$

for $x \in \text{supp}(D)$. $\Phi^{\text{wr}(\omega)}(c, D, x) = 0$ *for* $x \notin \text{supp}(D)$.

The idea behind the weight ball is that the expertise of the expert labeling the examples is built based on the same distribution with respect to which learning takes place. If x is close to the decision boundary, but in a dense area, the expert has more experience in the area around x and is thus less likely to make mistakes than in the case where the area around x is sparse.

In general, the new noise models introduced in this section are restrictive. The proof is based on Lemma 1 and is omitted due to space constraints.

Proposition 1. *For any of the noise models Φ introduced in Section 3.2, there exists a concept class C of finite VC-dimension that is not learnable w.r.t. Φ.*

The criteria for distribution-free learning seem too restrictive though for realistic settings; for example, often the distribution depends on the target concept. Thus, in cases where distribution-free learning is not possible, we have to ask ourselves whether the unrealistic requirements concerning unrestricted distributions are the actual reason for the negative learnability result.

One idea for limiting the distributions was recently proposed [2]. Recall that $f : \mathcal{X} \to \mathbb{R}$ is Lipschitz if $|f(x) - f(x')| \leq \gamma \cdot \text{dist}(x, x')$ for all $x, x' \in \mathcal{X}$, given a fixed $\gamma > 0$ and some metric dist. If f is a concept, the Lipschitz condition would make f constant. Relaxing the definition by requiring the Lipschitz condition to hold with some high probability, we can model situations in which no clear margin between instances with different labels around the boundary exists.

Definition 5. *[2] Let* $\psi : \mathbb{R} \to [0,1]$. *A function* $f : \mathcal{X} \to \mathbb{R}$ *is* ψ-*Lipschitz with respect to a distribution D if for all* $\gamma > 0$

$$Pr_{x \sim D}[\exists\ x' : |f(x) - f(x')| > \gamma \cdot \text{dist}(x, x')] \leq \psi(\gamma).$$

This gives us positive learnability results for classes that are not learnable if we do not limit the distributions, if we don't require that an arbitrarily low error can be achieved.

Theorem 2. *Let* $\mathcal{X} = \mathbb{R}^n$ *for some* $n \in \mathbb{N}$ *and* $\rho \geq 0$ *($\omega \in [0,1]$). Let C be the class of linear separators in $\mathbb{R}^n$. Let* $\mathcal{D} \subset \mathcal{D}_\mathcal{X}$ *such that for all $c \in C$ and $D \in \mathcal{D}$, c is ψ-Lipschitz with respect to D. Then for all $\gamma > 0$, C is learnable w.r.t. $\Phi^{\text{dr}(\rho)}$ ($\Phi^{\text{wr}(\omega)}$) and $\mathcal{D}$, with a lower bound of $\psi(\gamma)$ on the error bound.*

3.3 Noise Rates Different from 1/2

The positive results on learning in the classical noise models discussed above (random classification noise, CPCN, malicious classification noise) assume that the noise rate for any instance is always less than $1/2$ unless the noise rates for *all* the instances are always greater than $1/2$. (The latter case can be reduced to the former by flipping all the labels.)

The models introduced in Section 3.2 typically do not have this property. Noise rates can be greater than $1/2$ for some instance x and less than $1/2$ for another instance x', given the same distribution and target concept, or they can be greater than $1/2$ for some instance x given a particular distribution D, and less than $1/2$ for x under some other distribution $D' \neq D$. However, for finite instance spaces, learning under such noise models is still possible, namely if only the instance determines whether the noise rate is above or below $1/2$.

Theorem 3. *Let $\mathcal{X}$ be finite. Let $\mathcal{C}$ be a concept class over $\mathcal{X}$ and Φ a noise model such that $\eta_{c,D}(x) \neq 1/2$ for all $c \in \mathcal{C}$, $D \in \mathcal{D}_{\mathcal{X}}$, and $x \in \mathcal{X}$. If $[\eta_{c,D}(x) > 1/2 \iff \eta_{c',D'}(x) > 1/2]$ for all $c, c' \in \mathcal{C}$, $D, D' \in \mathcal{D}_{\mathcal{X}}$, and $x \in \mathcal{X}$, then $\mathcal{C}$ is learnable w.r.t. Φ.*

The idea behind the proof is that the probabilistic concepts generated by the noise model can be learned by repeatedly sampling a set of instances that contain an arbitrarily large portion of the distribution mass. The assumption that the noise rates are not equal to $1/2$ can be relaxed (at the cost of error values no longer approaching zero) if we assume the weight of the area with noise rate close to $1/2$ is bounded (*e.g.*, by applying Tsybakov's noise condition [15]).

4 Minimum Disagreement Strategies

ERM [17] refers to learning algorithms that pick a concept $c' \in \mathcal{C}$ that minimizes the number of examples in the given sample $\mathcal{S} = \{(x_1, y_1), \ldots, (x_m, y_m)\}$ that are labeled differently than c' would label them. In the absence of noise, $y_i = c(x_i)$ where c is the target concept. This means ERM picks a $c' \in \mathcal{C}$ that minimizes the empirical error, $1/m \sum_{i=1}^{m} |y_i - c'(x_i)|$. When the sample size grows, this corresponds to minimizing $\mathrm{err}_D(c', c) = Pr_{x \sim D}[c'(x) \neq c(x)]$, *i.e.*, the expected error of c', which is supposed to be kept small in PAC-learning. We call a learning algorithm that uses the ERM principle a *minimum disagreement strategy*. When c and D are clear from the context, we use $\mathrm{err}(c')$ instead of $\mathrm{err}_D(c', c)$ for brevity.

If $\mathcal{C}$ is infinite, it is in general impossible to compute a minimum disagreement strategy. Then an approximation strategy typically reduces $\mathcal{C}$ to a finite set $\mathcal{C}' \subset \mathcal{C}$ such that, for any target concept $c \in \mathcal{C}$, at least one concept $c' \in \mathcal{C}'$ differs from c by at most ϵ, and then applies the minimum disagreement strategy over $\mathcal{C}'$. If the target concept is the unique minimizer of the empirical error, every such approximation strategy is called a minimum disagreement strategy as well. This is used implicitly in the proofs of Theorems 4 and 6.

Given noise, a minimum disagreement strategy (with growing sample size) minimizes the difference between the concept c' and the noisy (probabilistic) concept $\Phi(c, D, x)$ resulting from the target c when applying the underlying noise model Φ, i.e., $\mathrm{err}_D(c', \Phi(c, D, .)) = E[|c'(x) - \Phi(c, D, x)|]$. When c and D are clear from the context, we use $\mathrm{err}(c', \Phi)$ instead of $\mathrm{err}_D(c', \Phi(c, D, .))$.

Minimum disagreement strategies, in the noise-free PAC case, are always successful for classes of finite VC-dimension [3]. This result carries over to learning from random classification noise [1]. The latter means that finding a concept with low error is accomplished by finding a concept that looks most similar to the noisy version of the target concept i.e., the minimizer of $\mathrm{err}(c, \Phi)$. Obviously, this is not possible in general (see Proposition 2). But if the noise model fulfills some advantageous properties, minimum disagreement strategies still work.

In the following subsection, we analyze properties of class noise models under which minimum disagreement strategies are successful. Since a minimum disagreement strategy in the presence of noise returns the same concept as an agnostic learner, these are properties under which the concept returned by an agnostic learner satisfies the learning criteria in our framework.

4.1   Disagreement between Concepts and Noisy Samples

One desirable property of a noise model is that it won't let two concepts $c, c' \in \mathcal{C}$ appear almost "equally similar" to the noisy version of the target concept, if c is "much more similar" to the target concept than c' is.

Definition 6. *Let $\mathcal{C}$ be a concept class, $\mathcal{D} \subseteq \mathcal{D}_{\mathcal{X}}$ a class of distributions and Φ a noise model. Φ is distinctive with respect to $\mathcal{C}$ and $\mathcal{D}$ if there exist polynomial functions $f : (0, 1/2) \to (0, 1/2)$ and $g : (0, 1/2) \to (0, 1)$ such that for any target concept $c \in \mathcal{C}$, for any $c', \bar{c} \in \mathcal{C}$, $D \in \mathcal{D}$ and $\epsilon \in (0, 1/2)$*

$$\mathrm{err}(c') < f(\epsilon) \wedge \mathrm{err}(\bar{c}) > \epsilon \Rightarrow \mathrm{err}(\bar{c}, \Phi) - \mathrm{err}(c', \Phi) \geq g(\epsilon).$$

An example of a distinctive noise model is random classification noise for any noise rate $\eta < 1/2$: Note that, in this model, $\mathrm{err}(c', \Phi) = \eta + (1 - 2\eta) \, \mathrm{err}(c')$ for all $c' \in \mathcal{C}$ [1]. Then $f(\epsilon) = \epsilon/2$ and $g(\epsilon) = \epsilon(1 - 2\eta)/2$ yield, as soon as $\mathrm{err}(c') < f(\epsilon)$ and $\mathrm{err}(\bar{c}) > \epsilon$, that $\mathrm{err}(\bar{c}, \Phi) - \mathrm{err}(c', \Phi) = (1 - 2\eta)(\mathrm{err}(\bar{c}) - \mathrm{err}(c')) \geq \epsilon(1 - 2\eta)/2 = g(\epsilon)$.

Distinctiveness guarantees learnability of classes of finite VC-dimension (of course, sample bounds are higher in the noisy setting).

Theorem 4. *Let $\mathcal{C}$ be a concept class of finite VC-dimension d and Φ a noise model. If Φ is distinctive with respect to $\mathcal{C}$ and $\mathcal{D}_{\mathcal{X}}$ then $\mathcal{C}$ is learnable w.r.t. Φ using a minimum disagreement strategy.*

Proof. A minimum disagreement strategy, $\mathcal{L}$, can learn any concept class of finite VC-dimension in the agnostic setting when the examples are drawn from any joint distribution over $\mathcal{X} \times \{0, 1\}$ [8]. Fix the target concept c, D, and $\delta, \epsilon \in (0, 1/2)$. Let $m(g(\epsilon)/2, \delta, d)$ and c' be the sample complexity and concept returned by $\mathcal{L}$ resp., when the examples are drawn from Φ. By the definition of agnostic learning, $\mathrm{err}(c', \Phi) \leq \min_{\bar{c} \in \mathcal{C}} \ \mathrm{err}(\bar{c}, \Phi) + g(\epsilon)/2$ with probability $\geq 1 - \delta$.

By distinctiveness, $\{c\} = \arg\min_{\bar{c}\in C} \operatorname{err}(\bar{c}, \Phi)$. Thus, $\operatorname{err}(c', \Phi) \leq \operatorname{err}(c, \Phi) + g(\epsilon)/2$. Hence, $\operatorname{err}(c') \leq \epsilon$ because otherwise $\operatorname{err}(c', \Phi) \geq \operatorname{err}(c, \Phi) + g(\epsilon)$, due to distinctiveness. Therefore, learning in the presence of noise is equivalent to agnostic learning under the assumptions of Theorem 4.   □

If both the concept class and the collection of distributions are finite, a weaker property can be proven to be sufficient for learning. It simply requires the target concept to always be the unique minimizer of $\operatorname{err}(c', \Phi)$, among all $c' \in C$. This property is necessary for learning with minimum disagreement strategies, since otherwise, for small enough ϵ, picking the minimizer of the disagreement could result in choosing a concept whose error is larger than ϵ, with high probability.

Definition 7. *Let C be a concept class, $D \subseteq D_{\mathcal{X}}$, and Φ a noise model. Φ is monotonic with respect to C and D if for any target concept $c \in C$, for any $D \in D$ and for any $c' \in C$: $\operatorname{err}(c') > 0 \Rightarrow \operatorname{err}(c', \Phi) > \operatorname{err}(c, \Phi)$.*

Monotonicity is implied by distinctiveness, since $g(\epsilon) > 0$ for all ϵ in the definition of distinctiveness. The sufficiency result mentioned above can be formulated as follows. The proof is omitted due to space constraints.

Theorem 5. *Let C be a finite concept class, $D \subseteq D_{\mathcal{X}}$ finite, and Φ a noise model. C is learnable w.r.t. Φ and D using a minimum disagreement strategy iff Φ is monotonic w.r.t. C and D.*

For random classification noise, minimum disagreement strategies are universal, *i.e.*, they are successful for every concept class that is PAC-learnable by *any* other learning algorithm [1]. This is not true for all noise models as stated in Proposition 2. (This result is due to [1], but we give our own proof).

Proposition 2. *There exists a concept class C, a distribution D, and a noise model Φ such that C is learnable w.r.t. Φ and $\{D\}$, but no minimum disagreement strategy can learn C w.r.t. Φ and $\{D\}$.*

Proof. Let $\mathcal{X} = \{x_1, x_2\}$, $C = \{c_1, c_2, c_3\}$ where $c_1 = \{x_1, x_2\}$, $c_2 = \{x_2\}$, and $c_3 = \{x_1\}$. Let $D \in D_{\mathcal{X}}$ be defined by $Pr_{x\sim D}[x = x_1] = 0.25$ and $Pr_{x\sim D}[x = x_2] = 0.75$. Let Φ be a noise model with $\Phi(c, D, x_1) = |c(x_1) - 0.75|$ and $\Phi(c, D, x_2) = |c(x_2) - 0.25|$ for any $c \in C$ and suppose c_2 is the target concept. Then $\Phi(c_2, D, x_1) = \Phi(c_2, D, x_2) = 0.75$, $\operatorname{err}(c_1) = 0.25$, $\operatorname{err}(c_3) = 1$, $\operatorname{err}(c_1, \Phi) = 0.25$, $\operatorname{err}(c_2, \Phi) = 0.375$, and $\operatorname{err}(c_3, \Phi) = 0.625$. Since $c_2 \notin \arg\min_{c\in C} \operatorname{err}(c, \Phi)$ ($\operatorname{err}(c_1, \Phi) = 0.25$ while $\operatorname{err}(c_2, \Phi) = 0.375$), Φ is not monotonic with respect to C and $\{D\}$ (Φ is not distinctive with respect to C and $\{D\}$ either.) By Theorem 5, no minimum disagreement strategy can PAC-learn C w.r.t. Φ and $\{D\}$.   □

This proof relies on the noise rates exceeding $1/2$, which might well happen in realistic noise models. The noise models defined in Section 3.2 can also yield noise rates greater than $1/2$ on parts of the instance space. So far, for noise rates exceeding $1/2$, we only dealt with strategies for special cases on finite $\mathcal{X}$ (Theorem 3). The following subsection deals with general strategies for learning under noise in cases where minimum disagreement strategies might fail.

4.2   Disagreement between Noisy Concepts and Noisy Samples

Minimum disagreement strategies return a concept c' that minimizes the disagreement with the sample. Thus they ideally minimize $\mathrm{err}(c', \Phi)$, i.e., the difference between c' and the noisy target concept. However, our goal is to return a concept that minimizes $E[\|\Phi(c', D, x) - \Phi(c, D, x)\|]$, i.e., whose *noisy version* is similar to the noisy target concept. When the target concept and the distribution are clear from the context, with a slight abuse of notation, we use $\mathrm{err}(\Phi(c'), \Phi)$ to denote $E[\|\Phi(c', D, x) - \Phi(c, D, x)\|]$.[3]

Note that the target concept, c, always minimizes $\mathrm{err}(\Phi(c'), \Phi)$ among all $c' \in \mathcal{C}$, since $\mathrm{err}(\Phi(c), \Phi) = E[\|\Phi(c, D, x) - \Phi(c, D, x)\|] = 0$. This is not the case for $\mathrm{err}(c', \Phi)$ (see the proof of Proposition 2).

A natural strategy for minimizing $\mathrm{err}(\Phi(c'), \Phi)$ is to pick a concept whose *noisy version* agrees best with the sample drawn from the noisy target concept.

Definition 8. *Let $\mathcal{C}$ be a concept class, $c \in \mathcal{C}$ the target concept, $D \in \mathcal{D}_{\mathcal{X}}$, and Φ a noise model. Let $\mathcal{S} = \{(x_1, y_1), \ldots, (x_m, y_m)\}$ be a sample of size m drawn from the noisy concept $\Phi(c, D, \cdot)$. For any $c' \in \mathcal{C}$, $\mathrm{err}(c', \Phi, \mathcal{S})$ is defined by*

$$\mathrm{err}(\Phi(c'), \Phi, \mathcal{S}) = \frac{1}{m} \sum_{i=1}^{m} \left| \Phi(c', D, x_i) - \frac{\#^+(x_i, \mathcal{S})}{\#(x_i, \mathcal{S})} \right|$$

where for all $x \in \mathcal{X}$, $\#^+(x, \mathcal{S}) = |\{j \in \{1, \ldots, m\} \mid x = x_j \wedge y_j = 1\}|$ and $\#(x, \mathcal{S}) = |\{j \in \{1, \ldots, m\} \mid x = x_j\}|$.

The term $\#^+(x_i, \mathcal{S})/\#(x_i, \mathcal{S})$ approximates $\Phi(c, D, x_i)$ for the target concept c. As sample size grows, $\#^+(x_i, \mathcal{S})/\#(x_i, \mathcal{S}) \to \Phi(c, D, x_i)$ and $\mathrm{err}(\Phi(c'), \Phi, \mathcal{S}) \to \mathrm{err}(\Phi(c'), \Phi)$. Unfortunately, to compute $\mathrm{err}(\Phi(c'), \Phi, \mathcal{S})$ for some c', the learning algorithm would have to know $\Phi(c', D, x)$—a probabilistic concept that depends on the unknown distribution D. The best we could hope for is that $\Phi(c', D, x)$ can be approximated using knowledge about D obtained from sampling.

Definition 9. *For any sample $\mathcal{S} = \{(x_1, y_1), \ldots, (x_m, y_m)\}$ of size m a distribution $D(\mathcal{S})$ is defined by $\mathrm{Pr}_{x' \sim D(\mathcal{S})}[x' = x] = \#(x, \mathcal{S}) \cdot \frac{1}{m}$ for all $x \in \mathcal{X}$, where $\#(x, \mathcal{S}) = |\{j \in \{1, \ldots, m\} \mid x = x_j\}|$.*

Replacing D by $D(\mathcal{S})$ in Definition 8 allows us to approximate $\mathrm{err}(\Phi(c'), \Phi, \mathcal{S})$.

Definition 10. *Let $\mathcal{C}$ be a concept class, $c \in \mathcal{C}$ the target concept, $D \in \mathcal{D}_{\mathcal{X}}$, and Φ a noise model. Let $\mathcal{S} = \{(x_1, y_1), \ldots, (x_m, y_m)\}$ be a sample of size m drawn from the noisy concept $\Phi(c, D, \cdot)$. For any $c' \in \mathcal{C}$, $\mathrm{err}(\Phi(c'), \Phi, \mathcal{S})$ can be estimated as follows (with $\#^+(x_i, \mathcal{S})$ and $\#(x_i, \mathcal{S})$ as in Definition 8).*

$$\widehat{\mathrm{err}}(\Phi(c'), \Phi, \mathcal{S}) = \frac{1}{m} \sum_{i=1}^{m} \left| \Phi(c', D(\mathcal{S}), x_i) - \frac{\#^+(x_i, \mathcal{S})}{\#(x_i, \mathcal{S})} \right|$$

---

[3] This quantity was first introduced as *variational distance* [10].

We call any algorithm that returns a concept minimizing $\widehat{\mathrm{err}}(\Phi(c'), \Phi, \mathcal{S})$ a *noisy minimum disagreement strategy*. In essence, it is a form of maximum likelihood process. Since $\widehat{\mathrm{err}}(\Phi(c'), \Phi, \mathcal{S})$ approximates $\mathrm{err}(\Phi(c'), \Phi, \mathcal{S})$ (which itself approximates $\mathrm{err}(\Phi(c'), \Phi)$), a noisy minimum disagreement strategy is expected to be successful only if the $\widehat{\mathrm{err}}(\Phi(c'), \Phi, \mathcal{S})$ provides a good estimate of $\mathrm{err}(\Phi(c'), \Phi)$.

Definition 11. Φ *is smooth with respect to concept class* $\mathcal{C}$ *and a class of distributions* $\mathcal{D}$ *iff there is a function* $M : (0, 1/2) \times (0, 1/2) \to \mathbb{N}$ *such that (1)* $M(\epsilon, \delta)$ *is polynomial in* $1/\epsilon$ *and* $1/\delta$, *for* $\epsilon, \delta \in (0, 1/2)$; *and (2) For all* $\epsilon, \delta \in (0, 1/2)$, *for all target concepts* $c \in \mathcal{C}$ *and for all* $D \in \mathcal{D}$: *if* $\mathcal{S}$ *is a sample of at least* $M(\epsilon, \delta)$ *examples drawn from the noisy oracle then, with probability of at least* $1 - \delta$, *for all* $c' \in \mathcal{C}$ *we obtain* $|\mathrm{err}(\Phi(c'), \Phi) - \widehat{\mathrm{err}}(\Phi(c'), \Phi, \mathcal{S})| < \epsilon$.

Distinctiveness and monotonicity can be generalized to the new setting by replacing $\mathrm{err}(c, \Phi)$ with $\mathrm{err}(\Phi(c), \Phi)$, resulting in *noise-distinctiveness* and *noise-monotonicity*, resp. It is not hard to show that random classification noise is both noise-distinctive (with $f(\epsilon) = \epsilon/2$ and $g(\epsilon) = \epsilon(1 - 2\eta)/2$) and noise-monotonic.

Sufficiency of noise-distinctiveness for learning of classes of finite VC-dimension is guaranteed if the smoothness property is fulfilled.

Theorem 6. *Let* $\mathcal{C}$ *be a concept class of finite VC-dimension* d *and* Φ *a noise model. If* Φ *is both noise-distinctive and smooth with respect to* $\mathcal{C}$ *and* $\mathcal{D}_{\mathcal{X}}$ *then* $\mathcal{C}$ *is learnable w.r.t.* Φ *using a noisy minimum disagreement strategy.*

Proof. Let f and g witness the noise-distinctiveness of Φ w.r.t. $\mathcal{C}$ and $\mathcal{D}$, and let $\epsilon, \delta \in (0, 1/2)$. We show that the noisy minimum disagreement strategy, with a sample $\mathcal{S}$ of at least $m = \max(m_1, m_2, m_3)$ examples, learns $\mathcal{C}$ w.r.t. Φ, where

$$m_1 = \left\lceil \max(\frac{4}{f(\epsilon)} \ln(\frac{8}{\delta}), \frac{8d}{f(\epsilon)} \ln(\frac{8d}{f(\epsilon)})) \right\rceil, \ m_2 = \left\lceil M(\frac{g(\epsilon)}{2}, \frac{\delta}{4}) \right\rceil, \ m_3 = \left\lceil \frac{8}{g(\epsilon)^2} \ln(\frac{3(m_1{}^d + 1)}{\delta}) \right\rceil.$$

m_1 examples suffice to find a set $\mathcal{C}_N$ of $N \leq m_1{}^d + 1$ concepts in $\mathcal{C}$ among which at least one has an error $\leq f(\epsilon)$ with probability $\geq 1 - \frac{\delta}{4}$ [12]. We show that the noisy minimum disagreement strategy will return one of these N concepts.

Since Φ is smooth for $\mathcal{C}$ and $\mathcal{D}_{\mathcal{X}}$, m_2 examples are sufficient to satisfy Definition 11 with ϵ and δ replaced by $g(\epsilon)/2$ and $1 - \delta/4$, resp. Finally, m_3 examples are sufficient for a noisy minimum disagreement strategy to select a concept in $\mathcal{C}_N$ that has an error $\leq \epsilon$ with probability $\geq 1 - \delta/2$ (cf. proof of Theorem 4). $\square$

In parallel to Theorem 5, it is not hard to show that noise-monotonicity is necessary for learning a finite concept class using a noisy minimum disagreement strategy when the class of distributions is finite.

Finally, we show that noisy minimum disagreement strategies are a proper generalization of minimum disagreement strategies.

Proposition 3. *There is a concept class* $\mathcal{C}$ *over a finite input space* $\mathcal{X}$ *and a noise model* Φ *such that* $\mathcal{C}$ *is learnable w.r.t.* Φ *using a noisy minimum disagreement strategy, but no minimum disagreement strategy learns* $\mathcal{C}$ *w.r.t.* Φ.

Proof. Let $\mathcal{C}$ and Φ be as in the proof of Proposition 2. Since $|\mathcal{X}| = 2$, each $D \in \mathcal{D}_{\mathcal{X}}$ is uniquely identified by the probability p with which x_1 is sampled.

It is then easy to prove that Φ is smooth and that $f(\epsilon) = \epsilon$ and $g(\epsilon) = \epsilon/2$ witness noise-distinctiveness of Φ w.r.t. $\mathcal{C}$ and $\mathcal{D}_\mathcal{X}$. Theorem 6 then proves the claim. $\square$

5 Conclusions

A high-level study of noise models, as our definition allows, gives insights into conditions under which learning under noise in general can be guaranteed. We hope that our formal framework and the insights gained from it will inspire the definition of new, potentially more realistic noise models and classes of distributions under which sample-efficient learning is possible.

Acknowledgements. This work was supported by the Alberta Innovates Centre for Machine Learning (AICML) and the Natural Sciences and Engineering Research Council of Canada (NSERC).

References

1. Angluin, D., Laird, P.: Learning from noisy examples. Machine Learning 2, 343–370 (1988)
2. Ben-David, S., Shalev-Shwartz, S., Urner, R.: Domain adaptation–can quantity compensate for quality? In: ISAIM (2012)
3. Blumer, A., Ehrenfeucht, A., Haussler, D., Warmuth, M.: Classifying learnable geometric concepts with the Vapnik-Chervonenkis dimension. In: STOC, pp. 273–282 (1986)
4. Bshouty, N., Eiron, N., Kushilevitz, E.: PAC learning with nasty noise. Theoretical Computer Science 288, 255–275 (2002)
5. Crammer, K., Kearns, M., Wortman, J.: Learning from data of variable quality. In: NIPS, pp. 219–226 (2005)
6. Decatur, S.: PAC learning with constant-partition classification noise and applications to decision tree induction. In: ICML, pp. 83–91 (1997)
7. Goldman, S., Sloan, R.: Can PAC learning algorithms tolerate random attribute noise? Algorithmica 14, 70–84 (1995)
8. Haussler, D.: Decision theoretic generalizations of the PAC model for neural net and other learning applications. Information and Computation 100, 78–150 (1992)
9. Kearns, M.: Efficient noise-tolerant learning from statistical queries. Journal of the ACM 45, 983–1006 (1998)
10. Kearns, M., Schapire, R.: Efficient distribution-free learning of probabilistic concepts. In: SFCS, pp. 382–391 (1990)
11. Kearns, M., Schapire, R., Sellie, L.: Toward efficient agnostic learning. Machine Learning 17, 115–141 (1994)
12. Laird, P.: Learning from Good and Bad Data. Kluwer Academic Publishers (1988)
13. Ralaivola, L., Denis, F., Magnan, C.: CN = CPCN. In: ICML, pp. 721–728 (2006)
14. Sloan, R.: Four types of noise in data for PAC learning. Information Processing Letters 54, 157–162 (1995)
15. Tsybakov, A.: Optimal aggregation of classifiers in statistical learning. Annals of Statistics 32, 135–166 (2004)
16. Valiant, L.: A theory of the learnable. In: STOC, pp. 436–445 (1984)
17. Vapnik, V.: The Nature of Statistical Learning Theory. Springer (1995)

Avoiding Moving Persons
by Using Simple Trajectory Prediction
and Spatio Temporal Planning

Jens Kessler, Jürgen Strobel, and Horst-Michael Gross

Neuroinformatics and Cognitive Robotics Lab, Ilmenau University of Technology,
98693 Ilmenau, Germany

Abstract. If a mobile robot operates within its environment, it should take other persons into account while moving around. This work presents an approach, which predicts the movements of persons in a very simple way, and uses the predicted trajectories to plan a motion path for the robot. The presented motion prediction and planning process is much faster than real time. A potential field is applied to predict the person's movement trajectory, and a modified Fast Marching planner is used for the planning process. The aim of this work is, to create an early avoiding behavior of the robot, when the robot passes a person, to signal a "busy"'-behavior towards the person.

1 Introduction

In the near future, the application space of mobile robots will be more and more enhanced towards home environments, public care centers, and shopping malls. In these environments, the behavior of a robot should equal human behavior, especially when interacting with non-expert users. In experiments [12] it could be shown, that humans tend to observe complex technical devices, like a robot, as social entities. This causes the user to expect human-like behavior from a mobile robot.

When investigating human-robot interaction, the scenario of "a robot interacting with a person" is the most common use-case. In our work, we want to emphasize the case of human-robot interaction, when the robot does *not* want to interact with a person. For example, in nursing homes or hospitals, when the robot is on a tour to collect food orders or drives to the charging platform, an interaction with a randomly passing persons is not wanted. Interestingly, if humans do not want to interact with each other, the spatial configuration between these non-interaction partners signals the intention of each partner. Those spatial behavior patterns are quite complex and are profoundly investigated by psychologists. One aspect of spatial configurations and their meaning is described in the theory of the personal space, created by Hall [4]. In our work, we use the spatial configuration (or distance) which corresponds to "non interaction". We use a simple mathematical model of the personal space, and combine this model with the predicted motion of an observed person. With this knowledge, a non-intrusive path towards a predefined goal, which does not touch the personal space of a person, is planned.

B. Glimm and A. Krüger (Eds.): KI 2012, LNCS 7526, pp. 85–96, 2012.
© Springer-Verlag Berlin Heidelberg 2012

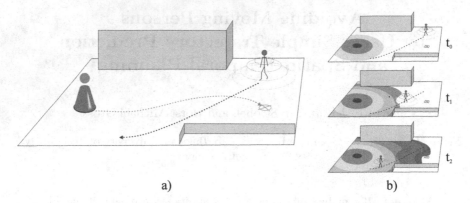

a)   b)

Fig. 1. The idea of the presented approach: the robot should be able to politely pass a moving person. To do so, the person path is predicted (see a)) and the personal space of the person is used in a spatio-temporal planning process to compute a feasible path. In b), a planning wave is propagated from the robot origin towards the goal (cross). This wavefront is deformed by the obstacles as well as the moving personal space from the predicted trajectory. When the goal is reached by the wavefront, the robot path could be extracted from calculated travel times.

Related work: A lot of work was done to investigate, if the model of the personal space, originally created from human-human interaction patterns, is also valid for human-robot interaction [2,17]. Indeed, spatial configurations carry information about the intention of interaction partners, and are similar to the findings of Hall. The personal space is used regularly in robotic applications to solve tasks like approaching a person [8,16] or path planning [15].

The benefit of the method of Svenstrup[16] is, to deal with changing person positions in a reactive way, but could get stuck in local minima due to the potential field motion control. The method of Sisbot[15] is only defined in an static environment, and does not consider time during the planning phase, so it could not incorporate moving persons. Anyhow, it uses the same simple personal space model than our approach. In [10], a rule based behavior was constructed to pass a person in a feasible distance in straight floors. Since this behavior was completely rule-based, it only works in floor-like environments and fails in unforeseen situations or environments, where the rules are not applicable. To our knowledge, there are no additional known publications on the topic of politely passing a moving person. However, there are many approaches which concern spatio-temporal path planning, which is a basic technique of our approach. The most advanced methods operate on planning trees. For example in [13,9], lattice graphs are used to create a tree with spatial and temporal information, as long as the motion prediction of the moving objects are certain. In case of uncertain predictions, the algorithm only uses static spatial knowledge to plan further. This algorithm is very time consuming and is not processable in real time on a robot system. Another approach is presented by [6] and [8], where expanding random trees are used to create an collision free path in space and time to steer a robot. These approaches are very powerful in terms of describing the spatio-temporal information in state space, but fail when the robot deviates from the planned path in space or time. In such cases, large parts of the tree have to be re-calculated. In this work, a modified version of the Fast Marching planner [14] is used to enable the robot to find an optimal path, even when minor deviations from the optimal path occur. When incorporating moving objects into the spatio-temporal planning process, one fundamental precondition is a sufficient prediction of the motion trajectory of that object. It depends on the given task, to what time interval this prediction has to be useful. In our task, the motion trajectory is predicted in a duration of 10 seconds. A large set of prediction algorithms exist, mostly using probability densities, which are build upon a large set of trajectory observations [7,1]. The disadvantage of these approaches is the need of an exhaustive data collection of trajectories over a long time. We prefer an out-of-the-box approach, where the trajectory of a person is predicted using the current motion direction and a potential field, presented in [6], to predict the person movement for the next few seconds.

Presented approach: A modified version of the Fast Marching Method (see [14]) is used to propagate a virtual traveling wave into the environment. The passing times of the wavefront through each point in space could be afterwards used to extract an optimal path. The passing time of the wavefront is determined by physical correct simulation of the wave. The travel speed in each point is directly related to the maximal driving speed of the robot, *and* the restrictions of traveling speed coming from the static and dynamic environment. The static restrictions are the obstacles. The dynamic restrictions of the environment are considered to come from the predicted motion trajectories of a person. A potential field method is used to predict the trajectory of the moving person. A brief overview of the key idea of the presented approach is shown in figure 1. The prediction method is described in detail in section 2, while the modified planning algorithm is presented in section 3. The paper is concluded by a set of experiments in section 4.

2   Prediction of the Person's Trajectory

In this section, the prediction of the person's trajectory is presented. A very simple, physically inspired model, also known as potential field, is proposed. This model is often used in robot navigation to avoid obstacles or approach a target, but here, it is used to predict near-future person movement for the next seconds. Note, that short time estimators, like the prediction step of a Kalman filter or the motion model of a particle filter, are not sufficient to predict a trajectory over several seconds. These approaches assume piecewise linear motion, like this approach also did, but the estimation is corrected by consecutive observations during each time step, which are not available on longer prediction periods. Our "correction" is done by the method of potential fields. The key idea is, to model the environment as a set of point like electric charges, which create an electrical field. This field could affect other charges by applying a force towards them. Two forces are modeled to predict the motion trajectory. First, the pushing force of obstacles is used to push a virtual person away to avoid collision. And second, the pulling force of an infinite virtual target line in front of the person is modeled to move the person forward. This line has a constant position, relative to the current person position. Next, a detailed description of the potential field model for an arbitrary configuration of charges is given.

2.1   The Potential Field

The presented approach uses two forces, which model the affected charges in different ways. The theoretical background, how charges could create a force, is identical in both cases. To calculate a force, coming from a generic set of charges at different positions x_i, the electric field at a position x is defined as:

$$E(x) = \sum_{i=0}^{n} Q_i^- \cdot \frac{x - x_i}{|x - x_i|^3}$$
(1)

The resulting force on a negative charge is proportional to the vector $E(x)$. To compute the pushing forces of the obstacles, a grid based world representation is used. If a cell contains an obstacle, a negative charge is defined there. A free cell does not contain any charge. The resulting vector of the electric field could be preprocessed in each free cell x_f by evaluating the obstacle cells in a circular neighborhood C of that cell.

$$E_{obs}(x_f) = \sum_{i=0}^{n} 1 \cdot \frac{x - x_i}{|x - x_i|^3} \ , \ (x_i \in C(x_f)) \cap (x_i = obstacle)$$
(2)

The person itself is attracted by an infinite virtual line of positive charges. The position of that line is constant relative to the person. An example setting is shown in figure 2. This pulling field is defined by the infinite virtual target line L in front of the person, consisting of an *infinite* number of charges. Theoretically, the equation of the resulting vector could be formulated as:

$$E_{target}(x_f) = \int_{i=-\infty}^{\infty} -1 \cdot \frac{x - x_i}{|x - x_i|^3} dx_i \ , \ x_i \in L(x_f)$$
(3)

If the line is always tangential towards the person's view direction, each point at line L could be paired with a corresponding (mirrored) point, where the sum of the corresponding field vectors directs towards the view direction. So, the final sum is an infinite number of vectors, pointing towards the view direction. Points, which are far away, apply nearly tangential forces, which are also very small, and so the sum of all these forces remains a finite number. Considering these facts, the resulting force from the tangential line could be *approximated* by a constant force in view direction of the person, where the strength is a parameter of the prediction algorithm. So, the overall resulting force is the vector sum of a force towards the current view direction, and a disturbing force, sourced by the obstacle configuration:

$$F(x) = Q^- (E_{obs}(x) + E_{target}(x))$$
(4)

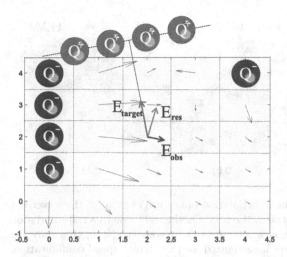

Fig. 2. This image shows the resulting vector field $E_{obs}(x)$, which is sourced by the negative charges of the obstacle cells. The resulting force on the moving person is defined by two components. The pushing field E_{obs} of the obstacles and the pulling force E_{target} of the virtual target line. This results in a field vector E_{res}, which is proportional to the applied force.

Since the vector field $E_{obs}(x)$ is only determined by the obstacle configuration, it could be processed off line. In such a way, the calculation of the resulting force $F(x)$ is a very efficient operation.

2.2   Motion Prediction

The idea of predicting the trajectory is simply, to simulate the movement of a zero-mass, charged particle by considering the force $F(x_j)$ in the currently predicted position x_j, applied to the particle. Here, only the preprocessed static electric field is needed and a valid person position and walking direction of the person. A sufficient prediction of the person's trajectory for the next ten seconds could be provided by calculating the motion of the charged "person particle". If the motion of a charged particle within the resulting force field should be processed, the well known momentum equation could be used for that:

$$m \cdot v_{t+1} = m \cdot v_t + F \cdot \Delta t$$
$$v_{t+1} = v_t + F/m \cdot \Delta t \tag{5}$$

Here, m denotes the mass of the charged particle, v_n denotes the speed at time n, and Δt is the time interval for one simulation step. It could be seen, that the mass influences the update of the speed. With a huge mass, the speed update is fairly slow and could lead to collisions. This changes, when the mass tends to small values, since than the speed tends to infinity and the speed vector tends to follow only the force vector F. Since a collision free path of the person should be constructed, the particle should mainly react on the resulting force F, and only an approximation of the momentum equation is used to update the current person speed:

$$v_{t+1} = 0 + |v_t| \cdot \frac{F}{|F|} \cdot \Delta t \tag{6}$$

It could be seen, that the mass of the particle is defined by $m = |F|/|v_t|$ and the speed direction of the previous motion step is not used. This assumption differs

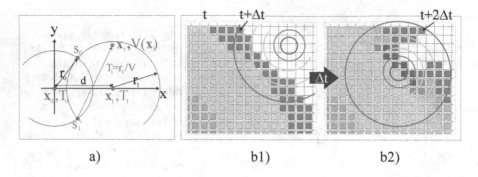

Fig. 3. In image a), the details of the interpolation of one cell element of the wavefront are shown. They are described in detail in the text. On the right side b) a full simulation step is shown, where the personal space intersects the wavefront. Note, that only the marked elements of the wavefront are investigated for the current speed configuration. The wavefront is only updated with the current configuration until the elements reach the simulation time $t + \Delta t$, shown in b1). Afterwards, the personal space configuration is updated to $t + \Delta t$ and the propagation of the wave is executed, until $t + 2\Delta t$ is reached (see b2)).

from a physical plausible approach. By re-defining the momentum equation, only the direction of the person prediction is influenced by the potential field and the absolute value of the person speed is left constant. The trajectory of the moving person is calculated by sequentially applying equation 6. The predicted person's path is used for the robot's motion planning.

3   The Adapted Fast Marching Planner

The most common planning approaches [3,5] use only binary values to encode cell traversability and have to create graphs from these binary information to compute optimal paths. In our approach, the Fast Marching Method from Setian [14] is used for robot path planning. It also operates on a regular grid. Each grid cell contains a cost value, that reflects the speed a wavefront is able to travel through this cell. Small values are assigned to cells, which should not be penetrated by the wavefront, like obstacles, whereas high values are assigned to free space and the wave can travel freely. Anyhow, all positive real values can be applied to the map cells, which is the major advantage of this planning method. Fast Marching computes to *which time* the wavefront crosses a cell. Our main idea is to calculate the cell crossing speed *at the time*, the cell is reached by the wavefront. This is the main difference to other approaches (e.g. E* [11]), where the travel speed of each cell is constant all the time. The benefit of the Fast Marching Method is the ability, to construct monotonical raising functions with *any* configuration of positive speed values, which is essential for a path planning algorithm to apply gradient descent for path following.

3.1 The Fast Marching Method

In the standard case, static velocity values are assigned for each cell, where free space is set to v_{max}, and near zero values are assigned to obstacle cells. The Fast Marching Method tries to find a numeric solution of the so called Eikonal equation $v(x) \cdot |\Delta T(x)| = 1$. The solution of this equation describes the evolution of a closed curve in time T, reacting on the different speeds $v(x)$ at the positions x. At most speed configurations, the solution could not be found in closed form. Fast Marching proposes a very simple numeric solution to solve this problem by sequntially interpolating small parts of the current wavefront to the next timestep. The "oldest" parts of the wavefront are propagated first. An expansion step is done by interpolating the wavefront for the current cell element x_i with the two neighboring elements with the smallest traveling times. For the interpolation of the cell element, the traveling times T_0, T_1 and positions x_0, x_1 of the two neighboring elements are considered. Also the current valid speed of that cell $v(x_i)$ has to be known and is static for the standard case. In the first step, the positions s_0, s_1 of possible sources of the wavefront are calculated. Details of the geometric interpretation of the used values are sketched in figure 3 a):

$$r_0 = v(x_i) * T_0$$
$$r_1 = v(x_i) * T_1$$
$$s_x = (d^2 + r_0^2 - r_1^2)/2d$$
$$s_y = \pm\sqrt{r_0^2 - s_x^2}$$
$$s_0 = \langle s_x \; ; \; +s_y \rangle$$
$$s_1 = \langle s_x \; ; \; -s_y \rangle$$

Here, d is the distance between x_0 and x_1 and defines the X-axis of the solution. As seen in figure 3a), there exist two possible sources s_0, s_1 of the wave origin to reach x_0 in T_0 and x_1 in T_1. The most distance source to our point x_i is chosen, since the point x_i would already have been interpolated if the nearest source is the correct one. With the correct source s_j, the interpolation of the wave crossing time at position x_i is easy:

$$T_i = \frac{|x_i - s_j|}{v(x_i)} \tag{7}$$

Note, that for very small values of the traveling speed, the passing time T_i will become very large and such elements are expanded very late in the propagation process. This is the case when the wave hits an obstacle cell, or the inner part of the personal space in our case.

3.2 Adaptation for Predicted Motions

To adapt the described interpolation method to time variant traveling speeds of $v(x_i, t)$, a number of changes are necessary. First, the planning direction is reversed. In our case, the traveling times of the wave have the physical meaning, that the robot could actually cross that cell at the calculated passing time. So, the current robot position is the source of the wavefront. Setting the wave source to the initial robot position also helps to fuse the motion prediction with the planning process, since it is also known, at which time the person is at which position, and therefor the planning has to be applied *forward* in time.

Second, the fusion process is the fundamental change in wavefront propagation. The system starts from a time t_0 and updates the prediction of the person movement *as well as* the propagation of the wavefront in time intervals Δt. This means for the n-th planning step, that only those elements from the open list are expanded, whose travel times are smaller than $t_0 + n \cdot \Delta t$ and *only* for the expanded elements, the dynamic speed function $v(\boldsymbol{x_i}, t_0 + n \cdot \Delta t)$ is evaluated.

The dynamic speed function consists of two parts: the static part $v_{st}(\boldsymbol{x_i})$ from the obstacle configuration, where the robot could drive in free space at a predefined speed (defined within each cell), and a dynamic part $v_{dyn}(\boldsymbol{x_i}, t_0 + n \cdot \Delta t)$, coming from the predicted motion trajectory of the person and their corresponding personal space:

$$v_{st}(\boldsymbol{x_i}) = \begin{cases} v_{max} \cdot \frac{d(\boldsymbol{x_i}) - d_{min}}{d_{max} - d_{min}} & , if \ d(\boldsymbol{x_i}) \leq d_{max} \\ v_{max} & , else \end{cases} \qquad (8)$$

$$v_{dyn}(\boldsymbol{x_i}, t_0 + n \cdot \Delta t) = 1 - exp\left(\frac{|\boldsymbol{x_i} - \boldsymbol{x_p}(t_0 + n \cdot \Delta t)|^2}{2\pi\sigma_p^2}\right) \qquad (9)$$

Here, $d(\boldsymbol{x_i})$ is the distance to the next obstacle cell, and $\boldsymbol{x_p}(t_0 + n \cdot \Delta t)$ is the predicted position of the person at the current simulation time. The personal space was defined by Hall [4] to be above 2.6 meters to symbolize non-interaction, and so, the value of σ_p is set to 2.6 meters. The fusion is done by a simple minimum operation:

$$v(\boldsymbol{x_i}, t_0 + n \cdot \Delta t) = min(v_{st}(\boldsymbol{x_i}), v_{dyn}(\boldsymbol{x_i}, t_0 + n \cdot \Delta t)) \qquad (10)$$

Note, that high values of the personal space have not the same influence on the wavefront like obstacles, since the wave could travel very slowly through these cells. In this way, the wavefront travels around a person without touching the personal space, when enough free space is available. If the environments gets more narrow, the wave starts to travel through the personal space and the robot is allowed to penetrate that space without changing the algorithm.

3.3   Following the Calculated Path

The planning is complete, if the wavefront has reached the predefined target cell. Now, each cell passed by the wavefront contains a passing time, where the resulting driving path is calculated by gradient descent from the target towards the robot's original position. The robot has to follow this path as good as possible with the defined speeds, also calculated during the planning process. If the person deviates to much from the predicted path in space or time, a replanning has to be performed. This is done, if the Euclidean distance $|(x_p^{pred} - x_p^{obs}), (y_p^{pred} - y_p^{obs}), (t^{pred} - t^{obs})|$ is above a certain threshold.

4   Experiments and Results

In our experiments two typical scenarios with different characteristics where evaluated. At the one hand, we evaluated the planning and prediction process regarding the quality of the path, and at the other hand, we evaluated the processing time, needed to create the path. The scenarios should only present a preliminary test of the feasibility of our method and do not present a full experimental coverage.

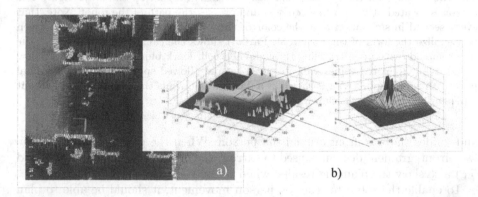

a)   b)

Fig. 4. In a), an example of the force field is shown, which is used for motion prediction. In b) the navigation function of the passing times of the wave from the wide space scenario is shown. The traveling time raises, when the wavefront hits the personal space of the person during planning. A detailed view of that part of the function is shown on the right.

The first scenario tests a passage with narrow space in our living lab. Here, a person moves on a straight line, and the robot has to cross this line by taking into account the currently measured walking speed of the person. In the second scenario, the person meets the robot in a wide corridor. The person moves also in a straight line and the robot should approach a goal behind the person by driving in the opposite direction. Here, the person should move directly towards the robots original position and the robot has to avoid the person. Both scenarios use the map of our lab for planning. The map has a resolution of 10cm per cell. The resulting planning function and the associated cell speeds, which correspond to the passing time of the wavefront, are shown in figure 5 for the narrow space scenario and figure 6 for the wider space passing scenario. It can be seen, that in both cases the personal space of the moving person slows down the wavefront

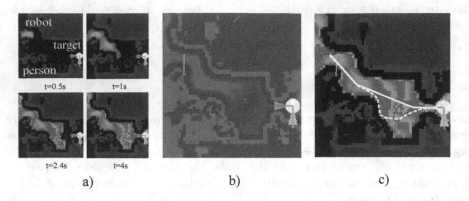

Fig. 5. In part a): snapshots of the propagation of the wavefront in a narrow passage. The robot starts on the left side and has to reach the goal on the lower right. The person is located at the bottom (circles) and crosses the path of the robot. Note, that every second in simulation time the color of the wavefront changes from red to green to visualize the form of the wavefront. Part b) shows the calculated travel speed, the robot should drive upon traveling through each cell. Dark blue values mean very slow speeds while light red values indicate the maximal allowed speed. In part c) the final path with avoiding behavior is shown as a dashed line, while the original path, without a person being present, is shown as a solid line.

and guides the wavefront around the person. When the goal is reached by the wavefront, gradient descent is used to extract the optimal path. Figures 6 c) and 5 c) also show the planning results, when no person is present.

To enable the robot to react on person movement, it should be able to plan the path much faster than real time. In fact, it must be possible to plan the path in a fraction of a second for multiple seconds beforehand. If not, the person has moved already when the path is calculated, and the estimation is not valid anymore at the time the robot starts moving.

We measure the average runtime of the algorithm with different prediction intervals Δt for a total prediction period of 10 seconds. Smaller time intervals Δt mean more accurate motion prediction and wave propagation. Table 1 shows the results of the runtime investigation. In average, the method is capable of predicting and planning 13 times faster than real time. We chose a simulation interval of 0.5 seconds for the motion prediction and the update of the planning function, since this time provides good accuracy by providing still good performance. The prediction and planning of ten seconds of motion can be done in 770 milliseconds.

The calculation of the force field E_{obs} is constant for the given map and is done once before the algorithm starts. Since this is a time consuming operation, it took 10.3 seconds for the given map of the lab to build the vector field. For the experiments a standard dual core mobile processor with 2.1 GHz was used. Only one core does the wavefront propagation since this is a highly sequential task and it is hard to parallelize this algorithm.

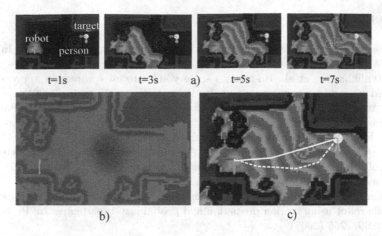

Fig. 6. Here, the wide space scenario is shown, where the person heads directly towards the robot original position and the robot has to avoid the person, since the robot's target lies behind the person. For a full description of a), b), and c), please refer to figure 5.

Table 1. Overview of the resulting computation times for different prediction intervals Δt for the person's trajectory prediction and wave propagation. Here, t_{avg} is the average computation time, while t_σ is the variance of the computation time per iteration step. On prediction steps up to 0.5 seconds, the system is able to predict and plan 13 times faster than real time. Only on small simulation steps, this factor begins to fall. In our scenario tests, a simulation time step of 0.5 seconds is chosen.

Simulation Step	Δt=3s	Δt=1.5s	Δt=0.5s	Δt=0.2s
t_{avg}	75ms	75ms	75ms	89.2ms
t_σ	72ms	35ms	18ms	13.4ms
Speed factor	13	13	13	11

5 Conclusion and Future Work

In this work, an approach for spatio-temporal path planning with regard of one moving person is shown. The main benefit is the possibility to create a path under all circumstances. If possible, the robot avoids the personal space of a person, when there is enough space. If not, the robot at least slows down. At the one hand, this behavior of the robot has to be investigated in further experiments. At the other hand, an investigation has to be done, what happens if the robot could not keep track of the planned path and planned time and deviates from the given task.

Acknowledgment. This work was financed by the project AAL-2009-2-049 "Adaptable Ambient Living Assistant" (ALIAS) co-funded by the European Commission and the Federal Ministry of Education and Research (BMBF) in the Ambient Assisted Living (AAL) program.

References

1. Bruce, A., Gordon, G.G.: Better motion prediction for people-tracking. In: Proc. ICRA (2004)
2. Dautenhahn, K., et al.: How may i serve you? a robot companion approaching a seated person in a helping context. In: Proc. HRI, pp. 172–179 (2006)
3. Dijkstra, E.W.: A note on two problems in connexion with graphs. Numerische Mathematik 1, 269–271 (1959)
4. Hall, E.T.: The hidden dimension. Doubleday, NY (1966)
5. Hart, E.P., Nilsson, N.J., Raphael, B.: A formal basis for the heuristic determination of minimum cost paths. IEEE Transactions on Systems, Science and Cybernetics 4, 100–107 (1968)
6. Hoeller, F., Schulz, D., Moors, M., Schneider, F.E.: Accompanying persons with a mobile robot using motion prediction and probabilistic roadmaps. In: Proc. IROS, pp. 1260–1265 (2007)
7. Kanda, T., Shiomi, M., Miyashita, Z., Ishiguro, H., Hagita, N.: A communication robot in a shopping mall. IEEE Transactions on Robotics 26(5), 897–913 (2010)
8. Kessler, J., Scheidig, A., Gross, H.-M.: Approaching a person in a socially acceptable manner using expanding random trees. In: Proc. ECMR, pp. 95–100 (2011)
9. Likhachev, M., Ferguson, D.: Planning long dynamically-feasible manuevers for autonomous vehicles. Int. Journal of Robotics Research 28(8), 933–945 (2009)
10. Pacchierotti, E., Christensen, H.I., Jensfelt, P.: Evaluation of passing distance for social robots. In: Proc. RO-MAN (2006)
11. Philippsen, R.: Motion Planning and Obstacle Avoidance for Mobile Robots in Highly Cluttered Dynamic Environments, PHD Thesis. Univ. of Toulouse, Ecole Polytechnique Federale de Lausanne (2004)
12. Reeves, B., Nass, C.: The Media Equation: How People Treat Computers, Television, and New Medial Like Real People and Places. CSLI Press, Stanford (1996)
13. Rufli, M., Siegwart, R.: On the application of the d* search algorithm to time-based planning on lattice graphs. In: Proc. ECMR, pp. 105–110 (2009)
14. Sethian, J.A.: A fast marching level set method for monotonically advancing fronts. Proc. Nat. Acad. Sci. 93(4), 1591–1595 (1996)
15. Sisbot, E.A.: Towards Human-Aware Robot Motions, PHD Thesis. Univ. of Toulouse, Toulouse (2006)
16. Svenstrup, M., Tranberg, S., Andersen, H.J., Bak, T.: Pose estimation and adaptive robot behaviour for human-robot interaction. In: Proc. ICRA, pp. 3571–3576 (2009)
17. Takayama, L., Pantofaru, C.: Influences on proxemic behaviours in human-robot interaction. In: Proc. IROS, pp. 5495–5502 (2009)

Unsupervised Nearest Neighbors with Kernels

Oliver Kramer

Computational Intelligence Group
Department of Computing Science
University of Oldenburg
oliver.kramer@uni-oldenburg.de

Abstract. In this paper we introduce an extension of unsupervised nearest neighbors for embedding patterns into continuous latent spaces of arbitrary dimensionality with stochastic sampling. Distances in data space are employed as standard deviation for Gaussian sampling in latent space. Neighborhoods are preserved with the nearest neighbor data space reconstruction error. Similar to the previous unsupervised nearest neighbors (UNN) variants this approach is an iterative method that constructs a latent embedding by selecting the position with the lowest error. Further, we introduce kernel functions for computing the data space reconstruction error in a feature space that allows to better handle non-linearities. Experimental studies show that kernel unsupervised nearest neighbors (KUNN) is an efficient method for embedding high-dimensional patterns.

1 Introduction

Efficient, and robust dimensionality reduction (DR) methods are required to process high-dimensional patterns, e.g., for visualization, as preprocessing for classification, and other methods like symbolic algorithms. With increasing data sets, and improved sensor systems, DR becomes an important problem class in machine learning. DR methods perform a mapping $\mathbf{F} : \mathbb{R}^d \to \mathbb{R}^q$ from a high-dimensional data space $\mathbb{R}^d$ to a latent space of lower dimensionality $\mathbb{R}^q$ with $q < d$. Non-parametric DR methods compute low-dimensional representations $\mathbf{X} = [\mathbf{x}_i]_{i=1}^N \in \mathbb{R}^{q \times N}$ for N high-dimensional observed patterns $\mathbf{Y} = [\mathbf{y}_i]_{i=1}^N \in \mathbb{R}^{d \times N}$. Famous DR methods are principal component analysis (PCA) [2] for linear manifolds, and isometric mapping (ISOMAP) [14], as well as locally linear embedding (LLE) [11] for non-linear dimensionality reduction. UNN is a fast approach that allows to iteratively construct low-dimensional embeddings in $\mathcal{O}(N^2)$, and has been introduced for embedding patterns in discrete latent topologies [3,5].

In this work we present extensions of UNN for embedding of patterns to manifolds of arbitrary dimensionality that preserve data space neighborhoods. The paper is structured as follows. Section 2 introduces a stochastic variant of UNN, and presents related work. Section 3 introduces kernel functions for computation of the data space reconstruction error in a feature space. An experimental

B. Glimm and A. Krüger (Eds.): KI 2012, LNCS 7526, pp. 97–106, 2012.
© Springer-Verlag Berlin Heidelberg 2012

comparison of all approaches, and a variety of kernel functions is presented in
Section 4. Conclusions are drawn in Section 5.

2 Unsupervised Nearest Neighbors

UNN is a fast approach for dimensionality reduction. It fits K-nearest neighbor
(KNN) regression into the framework of unsupervised regression. UNN iteratively constructs a solution by placing latent points at positions that minimize
the KNN data space reconstruction error (DSRE), which is defined by

$$E(\mathbf{X}) := \frac{1}{N}\|\mathbf{Y} - \mathbf{f}_{KNN}(\mathbf{X})\|_F^2, \tag{1}$$

where the output of KNN regression given the pattern matrix $\mathbf{X} = [\mathbf{x}_i]_{i=1}^N$ is a
matrix $\mathbf{f}_{KNN}(\mathbf{X}) = [\mathbf{f}_{KNN}(\mathbf{x}_i)]_{i=1}^N$, whose columns are the KNN mappings from
pattern $\mathbf{x}_i$ to data space $\mathbb{R}^d$. We define the contribution of latent position $\mathbf{x}_i$ to
the DSRE when embedding $\mathbf{y}'$ as

$$e(\mathbf{x}_i, \mathbf{y}', \mathbf{X}) := \|\mathbf{y} - \mathbf{f}_{KNN}(\mathbf{X})\|^2. \tag{2}$$

In the following, we introduce an UNN variant that can embed points into continuous latent spaces of arbitrary dimensionality, i.e., $q \geq 1$.

2.1 UNN with Stochastic Embeddings

The idea of UNN with stochastic embeddings is to randomly generate points
near the closest embedded points in latent space, and choose the position that
achieves the lowest DSRE with KNN. Algorithm 1.1 shows the pseudocode of
UNN with stochastic embeddings. Later, we extend the concept of neighborhood
relations in data space to a kernel-induced feature space.

Algorithm 1.1. UNN with stochastic embeddings

1: **input: Y**, K, κ
2: **repeat**
3:     choose $\mathbf{y}' \in \mathbf{Y}$
4:     look for closest pattern $\mathbf{y}^*$ with latent position $\mathbf{x}^*$
5:     **for** $i = 1$ **to** κ **do**
6:         $\mathbf{x}_i \sim \mathsf{N}(\mathbf{x}^*, \sigma)$ with $\sigma = \delta(\mathbf{y}', \mathbf{y}^*)$
7:     **end for**
8:     choose $\mathbf{x}' = \arg\min_{i=1,\dots,\kappa} e(\mathbf{x}_i, \mathbf{y}', \mathbf{X})$
9:     $\mathbf{Y} = \mathbf{Y}\backslash\mathbf{y}'$
10: **until Y** $= \emptyset$

Let $\mathbf{y}'$ be a pattern from the matrix $\mathbf{Y}$ of patterns that has to be embedded.[1]
The idea is to first look for the closest pattern $\mathbf{y}^*$ with latent position $\mathbf{x}^*$ among

---

[1] For the sake of a simple notation we use the notation for sets, e.g., $\mathbf{y}' \in \mathbf{Y}$ to express
that a column vector $\mathbf{y}'$ is randomly chosen from matrix $\mathbf{Y}$, and $\mathbf{Y}\backslash\mathbf{y}'$ to express
that column vector $\mathbf{y}'$ is removed from $\mathbf{Y}$.

the embedded patterns. Then, test κ random latent positions $\mathbf{x}_i$ with $i = 1, \ldots, \kappa$ sampled based on the Gaussian distribution

$$\mathbf{x}_i \sim \mathsf{N}(\mathbf{x}^*, \sigma). \tag{3}$$

The standard deviation σ is chosen according to the distance between pattern $\mathbf{y}'$, and the nearest embedded pattern $\mathbf{y}^*$ in data space

$$\sigma = \delta(\mathbf{y}', \mathbf{y}^*) \tag{4}$$

with distance measure $\delta(\cdot)$. This kind of sampling reflects valuable information about distance relations in data space. Patterns with large distances in data space are with a higher probability further away in latent space than points with low distances. The DSRE is computed for every latent position, and the latent position $\mathbf{x}'$ with minimal DSRE is chosen to embed $\mathbf{y}'$:

$$\mathbf{x}' = \arg \min_{i=1,\ldots,\kappa} e(\mathbf{x}_i, \mathbf{y}', \mathbf{X}) \tag{5}$$

This step is iteratively repeated until all patterns have been embedded. The result of the complete process depends on the order the patterns $\mathbf{y}' \in \mathbf{Y}$ are put into the iteratively growing manifold, on the number κ of positions that are tested, and also on the random values generated for sampling in latent space.

2.2 Related Work

UNN is based on unsupervised regression, which became famous for kernel density regression (e.g., cf [9]), but has also been applied to radial basis function networks [12], Gaussian processes [7], and neural networks [13]. Recently, we fitted nearest neighbor regression to the unsupervised regression framework [3] employing an iterative approach, and introduced extensions w.r.t. robust loss functions [5]. UNN is a fast approach that allows to iteratively construct one-dimensional embeddings in $\mathcal{O}(N^2)$ with KNN. It has been introduced for discrete latent space topologies, i.e., latent sorting [3]. The idea is to test all possible latent positions of embeddings on a line, and choose the position that leads to the lowest DSRE. Following this scheme a solution is iteratively constructed until all points are embedded. A faster variant only tests the dimensionality reduction errors of the neighbored positions of the latent point with the closest pattern in data space. Evolutionary continuous, and combinatorial variants have been analyzed in [4]. A related approach based on particle swarm embeddings has recently been introduced [6].

3   Kernel UNN

Kernel functions have become very popular in the last decade, and are important ingredients of many state-of-the-art methods in machine learning. The motivation for employing kernel functions is to cope with non-linearities in data space. In this section we extend the stochastic iterative embedding algorithm to the kernel variant KUNN.

3.1 Kernel Functions

Kernel methods take advantage of an interesting property of a reproducing kernel Hilbert space. The *kernel trick* is the effect that all operations in a feature space of higher dimensions can be expressed by scalar products. A kernel is a real-valued function of two input space elements that corresponds to a scalar product of its arguments mapped to some metric feature space. A kernel function $k : \mathbb{R}^d \times \mathbb{R}^d \to \mathbb{R}$ induces a feature mapping $\phi : \mathbb{R}^d \to \mathcal{F}$ into some potentially high-dimensional feature space $\mathcal{F}$ such that

$$k(\mathbf{y}, \mathbf{y}') := \langle \phi(\mathbf{y}), \phi(\mathbf{y}') \rangle. \tag{6}$$

Basis of many kernel methods is a kernel matrix $\mathbf{K}$ that contains the pairwise similarities of patterns. Often employed kernel functions are linear, polynomial, and Gaussian kernels. The linear kernel is based on the inner product

$$k(\mathbf{y}, \mathbf{y}') := \langle \mathbf{y}, \mathbf{y}' \rangle, \tag{7}$$

which is one in case of identity, and zero in case vectors are orthogonal. The polynomial kernel

$$k(\mathbf{y}, \mathbf{y}') := \langle \mathbf{y}, \mathbf{y}' \rangle^p \tag{8}$$

employs a polynomial function with $p \in \mathbb{N}$. An often employed kernel function, in particular for support vector classification and regression, is the radial basis function kernel (RBF-kernel)

$$k(\mathbf{y}, \mathbf{y}') := \exp\left(-\gamma \|\mathbf{y} - \mathbf{y}'\|^2\right) \tag{9}$$

with $\gamma > 0$, which is sometimes chosen as $\gamma = 1/\sigma^2$ with bandwidth σ. The hyperbolic tangent is another kernel function that is a bit less common. It is defined as

$$k(\mathbf{y}, \mathbf{y}') := \tanh(a \cdot \langle \mathbf{y}, \mathbf{y}' \rangle + b) \tag{10}$$

with $a > 0$, and $b < 0$. In the following, we employ kernel functions for the DSRE computation of UNN. The kernel functions will be experimentally analyzed in Section 4.

3.2 Kernelization of DSRE

In UNN the employment of kernel functions for computation of the DSRE allows to capture non-linear structures in data space corresponding to *non-linear Voronoi boundaries*. For each pattern $\mathbf{y}'$, and its mapping $\phi(\mathbf{y}')$ into feature space, we look for the closest embedded pattern $\phi(\mathbf{y}^*)$ in feature space. Similarity can directly be expressed with kernel function $k(\cdot)$:

$$\mathbf{y}^* = \arg\max_i k(\mathbf{y}', \mathbf{y}_i) \tag{11}$$

With a kernel the DSRE $e(\mathbf{x}, \mathbf{y}, \cdot)$ is computed in feature space as follows:

$$e(\mathbf{x}, \mathbf{y}, \cdot) = \|\phi(\mathbf{f}(\mathbf{x})) - \phi(\mathbf{y})\|^2 \qquad (12)$$

$$= \langle \phi(\mathbf{f}(\mathbf{x})), \phi(\mathbf{f}(\mathbf{x})) \rangle - 2 \langle \phi(\mathbf{f}(\mathbf{x})), \phi(\mathbf{y}) \rangle + \langle \phi(\mathbf{y}), \phi(\mathbf{y}) \rangle \qquad (13)$$

$$= k(\mathbf{f}(\mathbf{x}), \mathbf{f}(\mathbf{x})) - 2k(\mathbf{f}(\mathbf{x}), \mathbf{y}) + k(\mathbf{y}, \mathbf{y}) \qquad (14)$$

The kernel DSRE is the basis of the embeddings of the following experimental part.

4   Experimental Analysis

In the following experimental study we compare the behavior of the introduced methods on selected artificial data sets. Besides visualization, we compare the experimental results w.r.t. the DSRE, and the co-ranking-matrix measure E_{NX} introduced by Lee and Verleysen [8], measuring the fraction of preserved ranks in latent space within a neighborhood of size K. Neighborhood preserving embeddings achieve a high value. For a definition, and derivation of E_{NX} we refer to [8].

4.1   RBF-Kernel

One of the most frequently employed kernel functions is the RBF-kernel, on which we pay special attention in the following. We explore the influence of kernel bandwidth γ of the RBF-kernel in the following experimental analysis.

Table 1. Analysis of kernel bandwidth γ of KUNN with RBF-kernel on the *Digits* data set with $N = 300$ patterns, and settings $K = 10$, $\kappa = 30$. The best results are shown in bold, the second best in italic figures.

data	Digits		Boston	
γ	DSRE	E_{NX}	DSRE	E_{NX}
1.0	1.30 ± 0.01	0.30 ± 0.01	2.43 ± 0.10	0.29 ± 0.01
10^{-4}	*1.11 ± 0.02*	*0.45 ± 0.01*	*2.15 ± 0.12*	*0.42 ± 0.01*
10^{-8}	**0.91 ± 0.01**	**0.50 ± 0.01**	**1.14 ± 0.15**	**0.62 ± 0.04**

Table 1 shows the normalized DSRE[2], and E_{NX} of KUNN with RBF-kernel for three settings of γ, i.e., $\gamma = 1.0, 10^{-4}$, and 10^{-8}. The figures show the mean DSRE, and the corresponding standard deviation of 25 runs. The results show that the choice of γ has a significant influence on the learning result. The best embedding w.r.t. the DSRE has been achieved for $\gamma = 10^{-8}$ in case of data set *Digits*, and also $\gamma = 10^{-8}$ in case of *Boston*. As of $\gamma = 10^{-9}$ the achieved DSRE varies only after the tenth decimal place. Figures 1(a), and 1(b) show exemplary embeddings for the bandwidth settings $\gamma = 1.0$, and $\gamma = 10^{-6}$ on the *Digits* data set. The distribution of the majority of latent points is comparatively narrow for $\gamma = 1.0$ due to outliers, while for $\gamma = 10^{-6}$ the manifold becomes broader, and well distributed. The plots confirm the choice for γ determined in Table 1, i.e., the tendency towards smaller settings for γ (corresponding to a larger σ).

---

[2] The normalized 'kernel-free' DSRE is $E_N(\mathbf{X}) = \frac{1}{N} E(\mathbf{X})$.

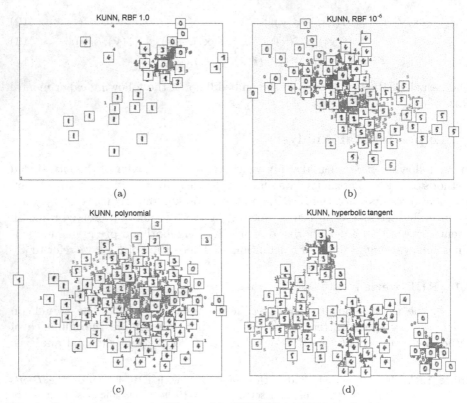

(a)   (b)

(c)   (d)

Fig. 1. Comparison of embeddings with KUNN for RBF-kernel with parameter settings (a) $\gamma = 1.0$, and (b) $\gamma = 10^{-6}$, as well as (c) a polynomial (p=4), and (d) a hyperbolic tangent kernel on the *Digits* data set ($a = 10^{-6}$, and $b = -10^{-2}$), and $K = 10$, $\kappa = 30$, $N = 1,000$

4.2   Kernel Function Comparison

The influence of the kernel function type on the embedding result is analyzed in the following. The comparison includes the linear kernel, the polynomial kernel, and the hyperbolic tangent kernel. Table 2 shows an experimental comparison of the three kernel functions on *Digits*, and *Boston* w.r.t. DSRE, and E_{NX}. The linear kernel is parameter-free. For the polynomial kernel we chose $p = 2$, and for the hyperbolic tangent we chose $a = 10^{-6}$, and $b = -10^{-2}$. We can observe that the polynomial kernel achieves better results than the linear kernel in minimizing the DSRE, and maximizing the co-ranking-matrix measure E_{NX} on the *Digits*, and vice versa on the *Boston* data set. But the co-ranking-matrix value is comparatively bad. Only the fraction of about 0.3 of the data space neighborhood is maintained in latent space. On the contrary, the hyperbolic tangent kernel shows surprisingly good results that even outperform the RBF-kernel on both data sets. Figures 1(c), and 1(d) show a visualization of exemplary embeddings of the polynomial kernel ($p = 4$), and the tangent kernel ($a = 10^{-6}$, and $b = -10^{-2}$). In particular, the hyperbolic tangent is able to separate the different classes.

Table 2. Comparison of linear, polynomial, and hyperbolic tangent kernel on *Digits*, and *Boston* with $N = 300$, $K = 5$, and $\kappa = 30$

kernel	linear		polynomial		tangent	
data	DSRE	E_{NX}	DSRE	E_{NX}	DSRE	E_{NX}
Digits	1.14 ± 0.03	0.31 ± 0.01	1.12 ± 0.01	0.32 ± 0.01	$\mathbf{0.85 \pm 0.02}$	$\mathbf{0.56 \pm 0.01}$
Boston	1.87 ± 0.04	0.31 ± 0.01	1.90 ± 0.08	0.31 ± 0.01	$\mathbf{1.00 \pm 0.07}$	$\mathbf{0.68 \pm 0.01}$

4.3 Comparison between KUNN, LLE, and ISOMAP

Last, we compare UNN with stochastic embeddings, and KUNN with kernel functions to ISOMAP, and LLE w.r.t. neighborhood size K. The embeddings of the *Digits* data set of UNN without kernel, and KUNN are shown in Figure 2 (a), and (b). Different classes are separated, and similar digits are neighbored. KUNN achieves a better separation of different classes than UNN without kernel. In comparison to the LLE result the embeddings are smoother. Also ISOMAP computes a smooth embedding with similar patterns lying close to each other in latent space.

Table 3. Comparison of DSRE, and E_{NX} with UNN, KUNN, LLE, and ISOMAP on the two test data sets *Digits*, and *Boston* with each $N = 300$ patterns. ISOMAP, and KUNN achieve the lowest DSRE, and show the best ability to preserve neighborhoods in latent space ($\kappa = 30$, and 25 repetitions)

Digits	UNN		KUNN		ISOMAP		LLE	
K	DSRE	E_{NX}	DSRE	E_{NX}	DSRE	E_{NX}	DSRE	E_{NX}
5	1.14 ± 0.02	0.31 ± 0.01	$\mathbf{0.86 \pm 0.01}$	$\mathbf{0.55 \pm 0.01}$	1.00	0.45	1.23	0.30
10	1.27 ± 0.03	0.31 ± 0.01	$\mathbf{1.03 \pm 0.01}$	0.53 ± 0.01	$\mathbf{1.03}$	$\mathbf{0.54}$	1.08	0.50
30	1.52 ± 0.01	0.40 ± 0.01	1.33 ± 0.02	0.57 ± 0.01	1.28	$\mathbf{0.64}$	1.42	0.51
Bost.	UNN		KUNN		ISOMAP		LLE	
K	DSRE	E_{NX}	DSRE	E_{NX}	DSRE	E_{NX}	DSRE	E_{NX}
5	1.94 ± 0.11	0.31 ± 0.01	$\mathbf{1.00 \pm 0.07}$	$\mathbf{0.68 \pm 0.01}$	1.05	0.67	2.56	0.35
10	2.32 ± 0.03	0.30 ± 0.02	1.57 ± 0.08	0.62 ± 0.01	$\mathbf{1.38}$	0.65	2.21	0.42
30	3.30 ± 0.04	0.37 ± 0.01	2.85 ± 0.18	0.56 ± 0.02	$\mathbf{2.05}$	$\mathbf{0.74}$	2.33	0.72

To evaluate the embeddings quantitatively, we again employ the DSRE, and E_{NX}. The experimental results can be found in Table 3. From the analysis of different kernels in Section 4.2, we choose the hyperbolic tangent kernel with parameters $a = 10^{-6}$, and $b = -10^{-2}$. Again, UNN, and KUNN have been run 25 times, and the corresponding mean values, and standard deviations are shown. Comparing UNN to KUNN we can observe that the employment of a kernel function can improve the embeddings achieving results that are statistically significant. KUNN achieves lower DSRE results, and larger neighborhood preserving values E_{NX}. In general, a low DSRE is strongly correlated to a high E_{NX} result. When we compare the UNN variants to ISOMAP, and LLE, we

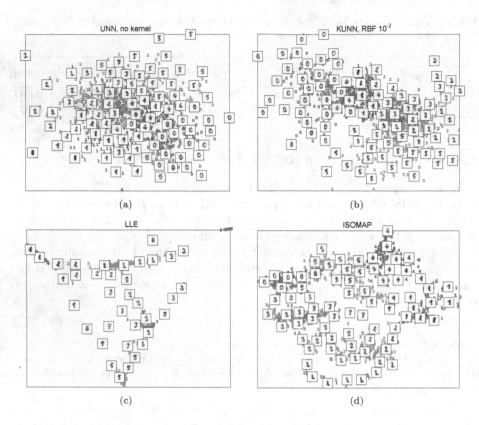

Fig. 2. Embeddings of (a) UNN, (b) KUNN employing an RBF-kernel with $\gamma = 10^{-2}$, (c) LLE, and (d) ISOMAP on the *Digits* data set ($K = 10$, $\kappa = 30$, $N = 1,000$)

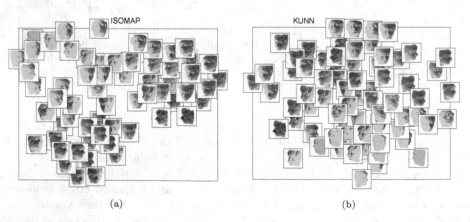

Fig. 3. Comparison of embeddings of the ISOMAP-*Faces* data set of (a) ISOMAP with $K = 50$, and (b) KUNN with RBF-kernel, and $\gamma = 10^{-4}$

can observe that KUNN is better on the *Digits* data set for small neighborhood sizes, i.e., $K = 5, 10$, while ISOMAP is superior in two cases on *Boston*. With one exception (*Boston*, and $K = 30$), KUNN is superior to LLE w.r.t. both measures.

In a last experiment we compare ISOMAP, and KUNN with RBF-kernel on the ISOMAP-*Faces* data set that is employed in the original ISOMAP article [14]. This data set contains images of a statue with different poses, and lights. Figure 3 shows the results of (a) ISOMAP with $K = 50$, and (b) KUNN using the RBF-kernel with setting $\gamma = 10^{-4}$, and neighborhood size $K = 5$. Both approaches compute topology preserving embeddings: similar poses, and lights of the statue are neighbored in latent space.

5   Conclusions

Dimensionality reduction has an important part to play in a world with a steadily growing information infrastructure. Many dimensionality reduction methods have been proposed in the past. But most are comparatively inefficient. In this paper we introduced a simple yet effective approach for embedding patterns to latent spaces of arbitrary dimensionality with an iterative KNN-based strategy. Neighborhoods are preserved employing the KNN-based DSRE, while distances are preserved by Gaussian sampling in latent space with variances based on distances in data space. The approach is extended by the concept of kernel-function induced features spaces to handle non-linearities in data space. Various kernel functions are employed: from linear to hyperbolic tangent kernels. The latter achieved surprisingly low DSRE, and high co-ranking-matrix values. The experiments have shown that KUNN is competitive with famous methods like ISOMAP, and LLE. Employing kernel functions for the DSRE turns out to improve the dimensionality reduction result significantly. While the runtime complexity of ISOMAP is $\mathcal{O}(N^2 \log N)$, and LLE takes $\mathcal{O}(N^2)$, KUNN is computing a manifold in $\mathcal{O}(N^2)$, and can be accelerated to $\mathcal{O}(N \log N)$ employing space partitioning data structures for the neighborhood queries in data, and latent space, e.g., k-d-trees [1], and balltrees [10].

References

1. Bentley, J.L.: Multidimensional binary search trees used for associative searching. Communications of the ACM 18(9), 509–517 (1975)
2. Jolliffe, I.: Principal component analysis. Springer series in statistics. Springer, New York (1986)
3. Kramer, O.: Dimensionalty reduction by unsupervised nearest neighbor regression. In: Proceedings of the 10th International Conference on Machine Learning and Applications (ICMLA), pp. 275–278. IEEE (2011)
4. Kramer, O.: On Evolutionary Approaches to Unsupervised Nearest Neighbor Regression. In: Di Chio, C., Agapitos, A., Cagnoni, S., Cotta, C., de Vega, F.F., Di Caro, G.A., Drechsler, R., Ekárt, A., Esparcia-Alcázar, A.I., Farooq, M., Langdon, W.B., Merelo-Guervós, J.J., Preuss, M., Richter, H., Silva, S., Simões, A.,

Squillero, G., Tarantino, E., Tettamanzi, A.G.B., Togelius, J., Urquhart, N., Uyar, A.Ş., Yannakakis, G.N. (eds.) EvoApplications 2012. LNCS, vol. 7248, pp. 346–355. Springer, Heidelberg (2012)

5. Kramer, O.: On unsupervised nearest-neighbor regression and robust loss functions. In: International Conference on Artificial Intelligence, pp. 164–170. SciTePress (2012)

6. Kramer, O.: A Particle Swarm Embedding Algorithm for Nonlinear Dimensionality Reduction. In: Dorigo, M., Birattari, M., Blum, C., Christensen, A.L., Engelbrecht, A.P., Groß, R., Stützle, T. (eds.) ANTS 2012. LNCS, vol. 7461, pp. 1–12. Springer, Heidelberg (2012)

7. Lawrence, N.D.: Probabilistic non-linear principal component analysis with gaussian process latent variable models. Journal of Machine Learning Research 6, 1783–1816 (2005)

8. Lee, J.A., Verleysen, M.: Quality assessment of dimensionality reduction: Rank-based criteria. Neurocomputing 72(7-9), 1431–1443 (2009)

9. Meinicke, P., Klanke, S., Memisevic, R., Ritter, H.: Principal surfaces from unsupervised kernel regression. IEEE Transactions on Pattern Analysis and Machine Intelligence 27(9), 1379–1391 (2005)

10. Omohundro, S.M.: Five balltree construction algorithms. Technical report, International Computer Science Institute (ICSI) (1989)

11. Roweis, S.T., Saul, L.K.: Nonlinear dimensionality reduction by locally linear embedding. Science 290, 2323–2326 (2000)

12. Smola, A.J., Mika, S., Schölkopf, B., Williamson, R.C.: Regularized principal manifolds. Journal of Machine Learning Research 1, 179–209 (2001)

13. Tan, S., Mavrovouniotis, M.: Reducing data dimensionality through optimizing neural network inputs. AIChE Journal 41(6), 1471–1479 (1995)

14. Tenenbaum, J.B., Silva, V.D., Langford, J.C.: A global geometric framework for nonlinear dimensionality reduction. Science 290, 2319–2323 (2000)

A Compact Encoding of Pseudo-Boolean Constraints into SAT

Steffen Hölldobler, Norbert Manthey, and Peter Steinke

Knowledge Representation and Reasoning Group
Technische Universität Dresden, 01062 Dresden, Germany
peter@janeway.inf.tu-dresden.de

Abstract. Many different encodings for pseudo-Boolean constraints into the Boolean satisfiability problem have been proposed in the past. In this work we present a novel small sized and simple to implement encoding. The encoding maintains generalized arc consistency by unit propagation and results in a formula in conjunctive normal form that is linear in size with respect to the number of input variables. Experimental data confirms the advantages of the encoding over existing ones for most of the relevant pseudo-Boolean instances.

1 Introduction

Due to various improvements in satisfiability testing (see e.g. [14,15,19,8]) SAT solvers are successfully applied to many domains like electronic design automation [12,6], periodic scheduling [11], or cryptography [10]. To encode a problem into SAT it is often necessary to translate cardinality constraints or general pseudo-Boolean (PB) constraints. In this work we focus on the latter.

PB constraints of the form $\sum_{i=1}^{n} w_i x_i \leq k$ are a special case of 0-1 integer linear programming [9], where k and w_i are integers, x_i are Boolean variables, and n is the number of variables. Besides translating PB constraints into SAT, there also exists solvers that handle these constraints natively. We show that native domain solvers can be outperformed by encoding PB and using SAT solvers, when appropriate encodings are applied.

There are different ways of translating a PB constraint into a SAT instance (see e.g. [2,5,9]), which differ in the size of the resulting formula and the properties, which help a SAT solver to find a solution in a smaller time span. Two properties are particularly important, both of which are related to unit propagation, the main inference rule within a modern SAT solver: (i) the ability to detect inconsistencies by unit propagation and (ii) maintaining general arc consistency by unit propagation. The former is achieved by running into a conflict as soon as an inconsistency is observed, whereas the latter is achieved if unit propagation assigns all variables that are not part of any solution of a constraint to false.

In particular, to encode PB constraints into SAT instances the following methods have been applied: *binary decision diagrams* (BDD) [2,9], *sorting* and *adder networks* [9] as well as the so-called *local watchdog* encoding [5]. BDDs and the

B. Glimm and A. Krüger (Eds.): KI 2012, LNCS 7526, pp. 107–118, 2012.
© Springer-Verlag Berlin Heidelberg 2012

local watchdog encoding maintain general arc consistency. The former requires $\mathcal{O}(n^3 log(k))$ clauses and variables, the latter uses $\mathcal{O}(n^3 log(n) log(k))$ clauses and $\mathcal{O}(n^2 log(n) log(k))$ variables w.r.t. a PB constraint of the form $\sum_{i=1}^{n} w_i x_i \leq k$. There also exist encodings that require much less clauses, namely sorting networks and adder networks, but these encodings do not maintain general arc consistency in general. Sorting networks encode a PB constraint with $\mathcal{O}(n \, log^2(n))$ clauses and maintain arc consistency only for cardinality constraints, which are a special case of PB constraints. Adder networks require $\mathcal{O}(n \, log(k))$ clauses.

The contributions of this paper are the following: We present a new translation from PB constraints into SAT instances, called the *sequential weight counter* (SWC) encoding. For a PB constraint of the form $\sum_i w_i x_i \leq k$, where $1 \leq i \leq n$, this encoding requires $\mathcal{O}(nk)$ clauses and auxiliary variables while preserving the ability to detect inconsistencies and to maintain general arc consistency by unit propagation. In contrast to the other encodings, the SWC encoding depends only linearly on n and k. Furthermore, its structure is simple and easy to understand compared to complex BDDs or sorting networks. Analyzing instances of recent PB competitions shows that for more than 99 % of the PB constraints the SWC encoding produces a smaller SAT formula than with BDDs of [2] or the watchdog encoding [5]. Finally, we provide an experimental analysis that empirically verifies the practicability of the new encoding.

The paper is structured as follows: the background of SAT and PB solving is given in Sect. 2. In Sect. 3 the sequential weight counter encoding is introduced, followed by an empirical evaluation in Sect. 4. Some final conclusions are presented in Sect. 5.

2   Preliminaries

Let V be a finite set of Boolean variables. The set of *literals* $V \cup \{\overline{x} \mid x \in V\}$ consists of positive and negative Boolean variables. A *clause* is a finite disjunction of literals and a *formula* (in *conjunctive normal form* (CNF)) is a finite conjunction of clauses. We sometimes consider clauses and formulas as sets of literals and sets of clauses, respectively. A *unit clause* is a clause that contains a single literal.

An *interpretation* J is a (partial or total) mapping from the set of variables to the set $\{1, 0\}$ of truth values; it is represented by a set J of literals, also denoted by J, with the understanding that a variable x is mapped to 1 if $x \in J$ and is mapped to 0 if $\overline{x} \in J$. If J can be determined from the context, then we simply write $x = 1$ or $x = 0$ in case of $J(x) = 1$ and $J(x) = 0$, respectively. If a variable x is neither mapped to 1 nor to 0 by J, we say the variable is *undefined* and write $J(x) = undef$ or, for short, $x = undef$. This notion can be easily lifted to literals. One should observe that $\{x, \overline{x}\} \not\subseteq J$ for any x and J.

A clause C is *satisfied* by an interpretation J if $J(l) = 1$ for some literal $l \in C$. An interpretation *satisfies* a formula F if it satisfies every clause in F. If there exists an interpretation that satisfies F, then F is said to be *satisfiable* or *consistent*, otherwise it is said to be *unsatisfiable* or *inconsistent*. The *reduct* $F|_J$

of a formula F with respect to an interpretation J is the formula obtained from F by evaluating F under J and simplifying the formula: all satisfied clauses are removed, and from all the remaining clauses all x with $J(x) = 0$ and all $\overline{x}$ with $J(x) = 1$ are removed.

In the sequel we will use gate representations for special propositional formulas, where the equivalence connective $\Leftrightarrow$ can be transformed according to the standard rules of propositional logic into conjunctive normal form. The conjunction $x \Leftrightarrow (x_i \wedge x_j)$ is represented by an *AND gate* with the *input bits* x_i and x_j and the *output bit* x. We will refer to AND gates with the symbol &. Similarly we represent the disjunction $x \Leftrightarrow (x_i \vee x_j)$ by an *OR gate*. Again, x_i and x_j are input bits and x is the output bit. The symbol used for OR gates is ≥ 1. Depending on the circuit, sometimes only a single direction of the equivalence needs to be encoded [20,16].

One of the most important inference rules in modern SAT solvers is *unit propagation* (UP) [7]. Let F be a formula and J be an interpretation, then unit propagation extends an interpretation if there is a unit clause in $F|_J$: $F, J \vdash_{up} F, J \cup \{l\}$ if $\{l\} \in F|_J$. Let $\vdash_{up}^*$ be the transitive and reflexive closure of $\vdash_{up}$. UP *detects a conflict* in a formula F and an interpretation J, if the resulting reduct contains the empty clause: $F, J \vdash_{up}^* F, J'$ and $\{\} \in F|_{J'}$.

A *pseudo-Boolean (PB)* constraint is defined over a finite set of Boolean variables x_i and has the form $\sum_i w_i x_i \triangleright k$, where w_i (called *weights*) and k are integers, $\triangleright$ is one of the following classical relational operators $=, >, <, \leq$ or $\geq$, and $1 \leq i \leq n$, where n is the number of variables in the PB constraint. W.l.o.g. in this work we consider only PB constraints that use the $\leq$ operator and where each weight is $1 \leq w_i \leq k$. As presented in [9,17], each PB constraint can be transformed into an equivalent PB constraint that matches this construction. This may introduce negative variables $\overline{x}$ that can be handled like positive literals in the constraint or that can be replaced by a fresh positive variable z. In the latter case $z \Leftrightarrow \overline{x}$ has to be encoded in the resulting formula. For more details we refer the reader to [17].

We define the multiplication of Boolean variables x and integers a, with respect to an interpretation J, as follows: for each integer $a \in \mathbb{Z}$ we define $a \cdot x = a$ if $J(x) = 1$ and $a \cdot x = 0$ if $J(x) = 0$. A PB constraint is *consistent* or *satisfiable* iff $\sum_{i=1} w_i x_i \leq k$ holds for some interpretation J, and is *inconsistent* otherwise. The *PB decision problem* asks if for a set of PB constraints there exists an interpretation such that all PB constraints are satisfied.

3   Sequential Weight Counter Encoding

In this section we present the *sequential weight counter* (SWC) encoding, which is a new encoding for PB constraints of the form $\sum_i w_i x_i \leq k$ into SAT. The SWC encoding is a modification of the sequential counter (SEQ) encoding [18], which translates cardinality constraints into SAT. The SWC encoding needs the same amount of clauses as the SEQ encoding, viz. at most $n(2k + 1)$ clauses and $(n - 1)k$ auxiliary variables, and – like SEQ – maintains generalized arc

Table 1. Distribution of k with respect to n in PB constraints

Number of Constraints	$k > n^2$	$n^2 \geq k > n$	$k \leq n$
22 014 154	0.56 %	0.23 %	99.2 %

consistency (GAC) by unit propagation. However, the SWC encoding needs more clauses and variables than an adder network for PB constraints, which requires $\mathcal{O}(n\,log(k))$ variables and clauses [9], but adder networks do not maintain GAC by unit propagation. On the contrary, if $k \leq n^2$ the SWC encoding needs less variables and clauses than the watchdog encoding [5] – which produces $\mathcal{O}(n^3\,log(n)\,log(k))$ clauses and $\mathcal{O}(n^2\,log(n)\,log(k))$ variables. The watchdog encoding is the currently best known encoding of PB constraints maintaining generalized arc consistency by unit propagation [5] with respect to asymptotic space complexity.

We have analyzed the set of PB instances from recent PB competitions, where we only considered PB constraints where at least one weight w_i is greater than 1. Table 1 shows the distribution of PB constraints in the instances of the PB benchmark 2011 and 2010.[1] The analysis reveals that $k \leq n$ holds for 99 % of the considered PB constraints. Comparing the two GAC encodings for the extreme case $k = n$, the SWC generates at most $2n^2 + n$ clauses and the watchdog encoding generates $\mathcal{O}(n^3\,log(n)\,log(n))$ clauses. In this case, our encoding has a quadratic complexity and the watchdog encoding a cubic complexity. Only in the rare case where $k \geq n^3$ the watchdog encoding results in less clauses. Hence the novel encoding improves the state of the art in practice.

In the following, we briefly discuss the SEQ encoding and define the SWC encoding in Sect. 3.1. In Sect. 3.2 we prove that the SWC encoding detects inconsistency and maintains GAC by unit propagation.

3.1 From Sequential Counters to Sequential Weight Counters

Sequential Counters.   Setting all weights w_i in a PB constraint to 1 results in a *cardinality constraint* $\sum_i x_i \leq k$, allowing at most k variables to be assigned to 1, where $1 \leq i \leq n$. These constraints and their encodings into SAT instances are well studied (see e.g. [18,4]).

The idea of the SEQ encoding is to sequentially count from left to right the number of variables which have been assigned to 1 by the current interpretation J. This process can be encoded by circuits [18]. Each intermediate sum is encoded by a unary representation with the help of auxiliary variables $s_{i,j}$, $1 \leq i \leq n$ and $1 \leq j \leq k$, such that $s_{i,k}$ is the most significant digit. The value of j is used to represent the value of the ith sum. Intuitively, if and only if among

---

[1] http://www.cril.univ-artois.fr/PB11/benchs/PB11-SMALLINT.tar
   http://www.cril.univ-artois.fr/PB11/benchs/PB11-BIGINT.tar
   http://www.cril.univ-artois.fr/PB10/benchs/PB10-selected-benchs.tar

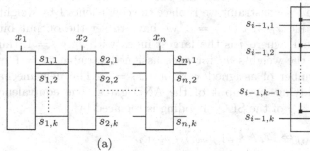 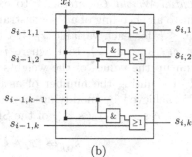

(a)   (b)

Fig. 1. SEQ encoding: (a) An overview over the whole circuit showing the connection of the input bits and output bits between the single circuits for each variable x_i. (b) The detailed circuit for a single input variable x_i.

the variables $x_1, x_2, \ldots, x_i$ of the PB constraint at least j variables are set to 1 by J, the variable $s_{i,j}$ should also be set to 1 by UP and the encoding. Therefore, we introduce a number $s_\geq^i$ for the ith sum that is defined as:

$$s_\geq^i := \begin{cases} j & \text{if } s_{i,j} = 1 \wedge s_{i,j+1} \neq 1 \wedge j < k \\ k & \text{if } s_{i,k} = 1 \\ 0 & \text{else} \end{cases}$$

Hence, $s_\geq^i$ represents the number of variables $x_1, x_2, \ldots, x_i$ which are assigned to 1 by $\bar{J}$ (see Fig. 1). As an example, consider the cardinality constraint $x_1 + x_2 + x_3 + x_4 \leq 3$, assume that the interpretation J maps $x_1 = x_3 = 1$ and $x_2 = x_4 = undef$, and suppose we are interested in the question how many of the first three variables are assigned to 1 by J. In this case, $s_{3,1} = s_{3,2} = 1$, $s_{3,3} = undef$, and $s_\geq^3 = 2$.

The counting mechanism is illustrated in Fig.1(a) and can be implemented by gates: An OR gate in Fig.1(b) ensures that if the input bit $s_{i-1,j}$ is set to 1, then the output bit $s_{i,j}$ is set to 1 as well. Thus, for the two sums $s_\geq^i$ and $s_\geq^{i+1}$ in unary representation we find that $s_\geq^i \leq s_\geq^{i+1}$ holds. An output bit $s_{i,j}$ is also set to 1 if the input variable x_i and the previous input bit $s_{i-1,j-1}$ are set to 1. This behavior is ensured by the AND gate.

For the encoding of the circuit the Tseitin transformation [20] is used. In addition a formula is added, which excludes the sum to become greater than k:

$$\begin{array}{ll} s_{i,1} \Leftrightarrow x_i \vee s_{i-1,1} & \text{for } 1 \leq i \leq n, \\ s_{i,j} \Leftrightarrow (x_i \wedge s_{i-1,j-1}) \vee s_{i-1,j} & \text{for } 1 \leq i \leq n,\ 1 < j \leq k, \\ \bot \Leftrightarrow x_i \wedge s_{i-1,k}, & \end{array}$$

where $\bot$ denotes a formula, that is always false. Because the OR and AND gates in the SEQ encoding occur only positively, only the $\Leftarrow$ directions are required for the transformation into conjunctive normal form [16]. For more information about the SEQ encoding we refer to [18].

Sequential Weight Counters. To extend the encoding of a cardinality constraint to an encoding of a PB constraint we replace the coefficients 1 by weights $1 \leq w_i \leq k$ for each variable x_i. If $J(x_i) = 1$ we have to set the output bits $s_{i,j+1}, s_{i,j+2}, \ldots, s_{i,j+w_i}$ to 1, where j is the largest index with $s_{i-1,j} = 1$, thus we sum up the values of the weights w_i for each assigned variable $x_i = 1$ instead of counting the number of assigned variables $x_i = 1$. The new mechanism is achieved by modifying one input of the AND gates. The equivalence $s_{i,j} \Leftrightarrow (x_i \wedge s_{i-1,j-1}) \vee s_{i-1,j}$ of the SEQ encoding is replaced by

$$s_{i,j} \Leftrightarrow (x_i \wedge s_{i-1,j-w_i}) \vee s_{i-1,j}.$$

If $j - w_i \leq 0$ we can skip the AND gate and just use the OR gate with $s_{i,j} \Leftrightarrow (x_i \vee s_{i-1,j})$. Fig.2(b) illustrates this substitution. The connections of the counters remains unchanged as shown in Fig.2(a). The final modification is to force the sum to be smaller or equal to k:

$$\bot \Leftrightarrow x_i \wedge s_{i-1,k+1-w_i}.$$

Since we have to ensure that the sum is smaller or equal than k, we can drop the circuit for x_n and the gates of the actual sum, because the formula

$$\bot \Leftrightarrow x_n \wedge s_{n-1,k+1-w_n}$$

already achieves this property. For a PB constraint $\sum_i w_i x_i \leq k$ with $1 \leq i \leq n$ and the Tseitin transformation the conjunction of the following formulas encodes the constraint into SAT:

$$\overline{s_{i-1,j}} \vee s_{i,j} \qquad \text{for } 2 \leq i < n,\ 1 \leq j \leq k, \qquad (1)$$

$$\overline{x_i} \vee s_{i,j} \qquad \text{for } 1 \leq i < n,\ 1 \leq j \leq w_i, \qquad (2)$$

$$\overline{s_{i-1,j}} \vee \overline{x_i} \vee s_{i,j+w_i} \qquad \text{for } 2 \leq i < n,\ 1 \leq j \leq k - w_i, \qquad (3)$$

$$\overline{s_{i-1,k+1-w_i}} \vee \overline{x_i} \qquad \text{for } 2 \leq i \leq n. \qquad (4)$$

Hence, the SWC encoding requires $2nk - 4k + w_1 + n - 1$ clauses and $k\,(n-1)$ auxiliary variables. As shown in Fig.2(b) the structure of the encoding is simple to understand and the formula can be easily encoded. We will show in Theorem 4 in the next section that the SWC encoding correctly encodes a PB constraint $\sum_{i=1}^{n} w_i x_i \leq k$, where $1 \leq w_i \leq k$ and $k \geq 1$.

3.2   Properties of the SWC Encoding

In this section, we prove properties of the SWC encoding, i.e., we show that it allows to detect inconsistencies as well as that it maintains GAC by unit propagation. For this, we first look at the generic definition of generalized arc consistency:

Following [3], in a constraint $C \subseteq D_1 \times \cdots \times D_k$ on the variables $x_1, \ldots, x_k$ with domains $D_1, \ldots, D_k$, a variable x_i is *generalized arc consistent (GAC)* – also known as *hyper-arc consistent* – if for every $a \in D_i$ there exists a $d \in C$

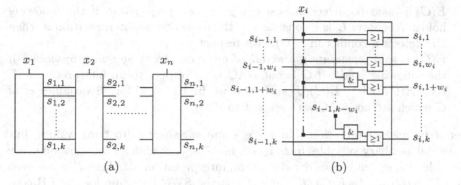

Fig. 2. SWC encoding: (a) Overview. (b) The detailed circuit for x_i.

such that $a = d[i]$, where $d[i]$ denotes the ith element of d. The constraint C is *generalized arc consistent (GAC)* if all variables x_j with $1 \le j \le k$ are GAC. One should observe that an inconsistent constraint C cannot be GAC because there does not exist any solution $d \in C$.

If a constraint C is not GAC, then there exist an element a in the domain of some variable x_i which can be removed from the domain of x_i without removing any solution of C. It is beneficial to remove such unnecessary elements as soon as possible in order to prune the search space.

Returning to PB constraints, we recall that the domain of each variable occurring in a PB constraint of the form $\sum_i w_i x_i \le k$ is initially the set $\{1, 0\}$. We define the minimum sum $min\_sum(C, J)$ of a PB constraint C with respect to an interpretation J as

$$min\_sum(C, J) = \sum \{w_i \mid J(x_i) = 1\},$$

where the sum of a finite set $\{e_1, e_2, \ldots, e_m\}$ of integers is $\sum_{i=1}^{m} e_i$.

We can now apply GAC to PB constraints: A variable x_i of a consistent PB constraint C of the form $\sum_i w_i x_i \le k$, where $1 \le w_i \le k$, is GAC with respect to an interpretation J if

(1) $J(x_i) = 0$
(2) $J(x_i) = 1$
(3) $min\_sum(C, J) \le k - w_i$.

In case (1) and (2), the variable x_i is already assigned and therefore this variable must be GAC because, otherwise, the PB constraint would not be consistent. Case (3) states that there exists a solution for the PB constraint where $x_i = 1$. Note that assigning a variable x_i to 0 in a consistent PB constraint in the given form always preserves consistency. We can assign to 0 every variable x_i which does not meet one of the conditions until the constraint is GAC without loosing a solution for the constraint.

Now we can define the properties that a PB encoding into SAT should meet. Let $E(C)$ be an encoding of a PB constraint C into a SAT instance, where C is of the form $\sum_{i=1}^{n} w_i x_i \le k$:

- $E(C)$ is said to *detect inconsistency by unit propagation* if the following holds: Whenever C is inconsistent with respect to an interpretation J, then UP detects a conflict in $E(C)$ with respect to J.
- $E(C)$ is said to *maintain generalized arc consistency by unit propagation* if the following holds: If C is not GAC with respect to an interpretation J, then $E(C), J \vdash_{up}^* E(C), J'$ such that we find $\overline{x_i} \in J'$ for all variables x_i of C which are not GAC with respect to J.

Let J be an interpretation that maps some variables x_i to truth values, but leaves all auxiliary variables unassigned, i.e. $J(s_{i,j}) = undef$. From now on every variable assignment is considered w.r.t. an interpretation J', where J' is achieved by UP: $E(C), J \vdash_{up}^* E(C), J'$ and $E(C)$ is the SWC encoding for the PB constraint C. This can be done w.l.o.g. because for each interpretation $J'' \supseteq J$ that satisfies $E(C)$, $J' \subseteq J''$ holds.

In the rest of this section we prove that the SWC encoding detects inconsistency and maintains GAC by UP.

Lemma 1. $\sum\{w_j \mid x_j = 1, 1 \leq j \leq i\} = s_{\geq}^i$.

If we arbitrarily assign 1 or 0 to the variables x_i, $s_{\geq}^i$ is the value of the sum $\sum\{w_j \mid x_j = 1, 1 \leq j \leq i\}$. This is obvious from the definitions of the encoding. The clauses (1),(2) and (3) imply the mapping for the auxiliary variables $s_{i,j}$ by UP for every variable x_i in exactly that way.

Now we can prove that SWC detects consistency by UP:

Corollary 2. *The Sequential Weight Counter encoding detects inconsistency by UP.*

Proof. With Lemma 1 and the clause $\overline{s_{i-1,k-w_i}} \vee \overline{x_i} \in E(C)$ this follows directly, since $\sum\{w_j \mid x_j = 1, 1 \leq j \leq n\} > k$ implies that there exists a variable $x_i = 1$ with $s_{\geq}^{i-1} + w_i \geq k$, hence $s_{i-1,k-w_i} = 1$.

In analogy to $s_{\geq}^i$ we define $s_{<}^i$, where $s_{\geq}^i$ is counting the sum from left to right, i.e.: $\sum_{a=1}^{i} w_a x_a$, and $s_{<}^i$ from right to left, i.e.: $\sum_{a=n}^{i+1} w_a x_a$.

$$s_{<}^i = \begin{cases} k - u + 1 & \text{where } u \text{ is the smallest number with } s_{i,u} = 0 \\ 0 & else \end{cases}$$

The auxiliary variable $s_{i,j}$ is set to 0 if and only if $\sum\{w_a \mid x_a = 1, i < j \leq n\} \geq k - j + 1$.

Lemma 3. $\sum\{w_j \mid x_j = 1, i < j \leq n\} = s_{<}^i$

Proof (sketch). We consider the sum $\sum\{w_j \mid x_j = 1, i < j \leq n\}$ as a fixed sequence of addends w_j in descending order according to j. Now we can prove the lemma by induction, starting with the first addend w_i in the sum (i.e. there exists no $x_l = 1$, with $l > i$). With $\overline{s_{i-1,k-w_i+1}} \vee \overline{x_i} \in E(C)$ we get $s_{<}^{j-1} = w_j = \sum\{w_j\}$. For the induction step we show that for each $x_a = 1$ with $a < i$ we find a clause

$\overline{s_{a-1,j}} \vee \overline{x_a} \vee s_{a,j+w_a} \in E(C)$ such that $s_{a,j+w_a} = 0$ is the previous addend of the sum:

$$s_<^{a-1} = w_a + s_<^a = w_a + \sum \{w_l \mid x_l = 1, a < l \leq n\}$$

For each $x_j \neq 1$ it follows from the definitions of SWC that $s_<^{i-1} = s_<^i$, since $\overline{s_{i-1,j}} \vee s_{i,j} \in E(C)$. $\square$

From Lemma 1 and 3 follows that:

$$x_i \neq 1 \Rightarrow s_\geq^{i-1} = s_\geq^i \tag{5}$$

$$s_\geq^i + s_<^i = min\_sum(C, J) \tag{6}$$

Now we can prove that SWC is an encoding for the PB constraint and that the SWC encoding maintains GAC by UP.

Theorem 4. *The SWC is an encoding for the PB constraint $\sum_{i=1}^n w_i x_i \leq k$ in CNF, requiring $\mathcal{O}(nk)$ clauses and $\mathcal{O}(nk)$ auxiliary variables.*

Proof. From the corollary 2 we know that setting the variables x_i such that the sum $\sum_{i=1}^n w_i x_i > k$ leads to an inconsistent formula by the encoding. Hence we only have to show that setting the variables x_i such that $\sum_{i=1}^n w_i x_i \leq k$ does not lead to a contradiction. Having only the clauses (1),(2) and (3), it follows that any assignment of the variables x_i does not lead to a contradiction, since $x_i = 1$ only implies the mapping for an auxiliary variable $s_{i,j}$ positively (i.e. $s_{i,j} = 1$) and in each of these clauses $s_{i,j}$ occurs positively. Setting $x_i = 0$ results in no implication, since x_i does not occur positively in any clause. Similar to the proof of lemma 3, we can prove that the implications of the clause (4) lead to a contradiction if and only if $\sum_{i=1}^n w_i x_i > k$. $\square$

Theorem 5. *The Sequential Weight Counter encoding maintains GAC by UP.*

Proof. Assume there is a variable x_i that is not GAC with respect to C, hence $x_i = $ undef. Since x_i is not GAC, $min\_sum(C, J) > k - w_i$ holds (i.e. we cannot assign $x_i = 1$). With (5) and (6) we have:

$$min\_sum(C, J) = s_\geq^i + s_<^i = s_\geq^{i-1} + s_<^i$$

Hence there exists a lower bound l for the ith sum that represents the value of the $i - 1^{th}$ sum ($l = s_\geq^{i-1}$ because $s_{i-1,l} = 1$) and an upper bound u for the ith sum $s_{i,u} = 0$ such that $u = k - s_<^i + 1$. If the difference between l and u is less equal than w_i, x_i needs to be set to $x_i = 0$:

$$s_\geq^{i-1} + s_<^i > k - w_i \Leftrightarrow$$
$$l + k - u + 1 > k - w_i \Leftrightarrow$$
$$l + w_i + 1 > u \tag{7}$$

case $u \leq w_i$
   with $\overline{x_i} \vee s_{i,u} \in E(C)$ this directly contradict our assumption.

case $u > w_i$

> with (7) we know that $l \geq 1$ and there exists a $j \leq l$ with $j + w_i = u$. With $\overline{s_{i-1,j}} \vee \overline{x_i} \vee s_{i,j+w_i} \in E(C)$ this contradicts our assumption. $\square$

4   Results

In this section we want to show the usefulness of the proposed sequential weight counter (SWC) encoding. The first advantage of the encoding is its simple structure. Compared to translating a PB constraint into SAT by a BDD [9,2], the presented algorithm is conceptionally easy.

As a basis for the experiments we use all decision PB instances of PB competitions 2010 and 2011.[1]Note, that from the *big int* PB instances none of the selected solving methods can solve a single instance within the timeout. Therefore, we decided to drop these instances from the benchmark. In total, there are 278 PB instances in the benchmark. The experiments have been performed on an AMD Opteron CPU with 2.66 GHz, a memory limit of 2 GB and a timeout of 1800 s.

Before all the single constraints are translated into SAT, we simplified them as follows: For a constraint $\sum_i w_i x_i \leq k$ we immediately assign x_i to 0, if $w_i > k$. Furthermore, all constraints with $\sum_i w_i \leq k$ are removed. Constraints of the form $\sum_i l_i \geq 1$ are encoded as a single clause. Finally, $\sum_i l_i \leq k$ is translated by an appropriate cardinality constraint encoding [4]. We have not used the watchdog encoding for several reasons: (i) this encoding almost always produces more clauses than the SWC encoding, (ii) the encoding is complex to implement and (iii) using the tool that has been used in [5] would also encode all special PBs with the watchdog encoding.

To compare the impact of the novel encoding, we translated all PB instances into SAT and solved them with the SAT solver GLUCOSE 2 because of its high performance in recent SAT competitions.[2] Table 2 compares the number of solved PB instances among the encodings and gives the average time that has been used to solve a single instance. Encoding PB constraints with BDD has been done according to [9]. We furthermore added the configuration BEST, that selects for each PB the encoding that produces the least number of clauses. By fixing the encoding, the solver with both BDD and SWC solve already a large number of instances. However, there is no clear benefit for either of the two encodings. By using SWC the solver can solve exactly the same instances as by using BDD and another three instances more. For 58 instances of the 126 commonly solved instances, with BDDs one can solve the instance faster whereas for the remaining 68 instances with SWC the answer is returned more quickly. As already seen in other fields, a portfolio approach usually increases the performance of solvers [21] and could be applied to PB solving as well. By choosing always the best encoding the configuration BEST solves another 12 instances and also decreases the run time per instance. Thus, for the translation to SAT the SWC encoding provides a clear benefit.

---

[2] We provide the tool at http://tools.computational-logic.org.

Table 2. Comparing the performance of PB solving approaches

Encoding	BDD	SWC	BEST	BSOLO	CLASP
Solved instances	126	129	**141**	98	120
Run time	180.49 s	193.74 s	142.77 s	136.43 s	138.08 s

Since PB can be solved also natively or by handling PB constraints inside a SAT solver, we furthermore compared our approach with successful systems of the last PB competition. BSOLO is a native PB solver [13] and CLASP [1] is a SAT solver that can handle PB constraints inside the solver without a translation to SAT. These solvers are also compared to the translation to SAT in Table 2. Again, the configuration BEST solves 21 more instances then the best of the native solvers, and solves all the instances that have been solved by the native solvers. Summarizing the evaluation it can be stated that adding the SWC encoding to the portfolio of available PB encodings results in a noticeable performance improvement for PB solvers.

5   Conclusion and Future Work

In this work we presented the SWC encoding, a new encoding for PB constraints of the form $\sum_{i=1}^{n} w_i x_i \leq k$ into SAT. The SWC encoding allows unit propagation to quickly prune the search space by maintaining GAC and needs at most $n(2k+1)$ clauses and $(n-1)k$ auxiliary variables. This is a significant improvement to the state of the art for PB constraints with $k \leq n^2$: To the best of our knowledge so far the local watchdog encoding generates the fewest clauses, namely $\mathcal{O}(n^3 \log(n) \log(k))$ clauses, while maintaining GAC. This contribution is highly relevant, because for 99 % of the PB constraints even $k \leq n$ holds.

The new encoding is not only a nice and simple encoding, but also provides a performance improvement for solving PB instances. By always choosing the encoding that requires the smallest number of clauses, our PB solver can solve 12 instances more than by forcing to use a single encoding only. With our approach 21 more instances of the PB benchmark can be solved compared to successful solvers from recent PB competitions.

For future work we leave a detailed comparison between the known encodings, the SWC, binary decision diagrams, local watchdog and the non-GAC encodings. With the help of a detailed empirical investigation we want to extend our current research to a competitive SAT-based PB solver that can also solve optimization instances fast.

References

1. Potsdam answer set solving collection, http://potassco.sourceforge.net/
2. Abío, I., Nieuwenhuis, R., Oliveras, A., Rodríguez-Carbonell, E.: BDDs for Pseudo-Boolean Constraints – Revisited. In: Sakallah, K.A., Simon, L. (eds.) SAT 2011. LNCS, vol. 6695, pp. 61–75. Springer, Heidelberg (2011)

3. Apt, K.: Principles of Constraint Programming. Cambridge University Press (2003)
4. Asín, R., Nieuwenhuis, R., Oliveras, A., Rodríguez-Carbonell, E.: Cardinality Networks and Their Applications. In: Kullmann, O. (ed.) SAT 2009. LNCS, vol. 5584, pp. 167–180. Springer, Heidelberg (2009)
5. Bailleux, O., Boufkhad, Y., Roussel, O.: New Encodings of Pseudo-Boolean Constraints into CNF. In: Kullmann, O. (ed.) SAT 2009. LNCS, vol. 5584, pp. 181–194. Springer, Heidelberg (2009)
6. Biere, A., Cimatti, A., Clarke, E.M., Fujita, M., Zhu, Y.: Symbolic model checking using SAT procedures instead of BDDs. In: Proc. DAC, pp. 317–320 (1999)
7. Davis, M., Logemann, G., Loveland, D.: A machine program for theorem-proving. Comm. ACM 5(7), 394–397 (1962)
8. Eén, N., Biere, A.: Effective Preprocessing in SAT Through Variable and Clause Elimination. In: Bacchus, F., Walsh, T. (eds.) SAT 2005. LNCS, vol. 3569, pp. 61–75. Springer, Heidelberg (2005)
9. Eén, N., Sörensson, N.: Translating pseudo-boolean constraints into SAT. JSAT 2(1-4), 1–26 (2006)
10. Eibach, T., Pilz, E., Völkel, G.: Attacking Bivium Using SAT Solvers. In: Kleine Büning, H., Zhao, X. (eds.) SAT 2008. LNCS, vol. 4996, pp. 63–76. Springer, Heidelberg (2008)
11. Großmann, P., Hölldobler, S., Manthey, N., Nachtigall, K., Opitz, J., Steinke, P.: Solving Periodic Event Scheduling Problems with SAT. In: Jiang, H., Ding, W., Ali, M., Wu, X. (eds.) IEA/AIE 2012. LNCS, vol. 7345, pp. 166–175. Springer, Heidelberg (2012)
12. Kaiss, D., Skaba, M., Hanna, Z., Khasidashvili, Z.: Industrial strength SAT-based alignability algorithm for hardware equivalence verification. In: Proc. FMCAD, pp. 20–26 (2007)
13. Manquinho, V.M., Marques-Silva, J.P.: On using cutting planes in pseudo-Boolean optimization. JSAT 2(1-4), 209–219 (2006)
14. Marques-Silva, J.P., Sakallah, K.A.: Grasp: A search algorithm for propositional satisfiability. IEEE Trans. Comput. 48(5), 506–521 (1999)
15. Moskewicz, M.W., Madigan, C.F., Zhao, Y., Zhang, L., Malik, S.: Chaff: engineering an efficient SAT solver. In: Proc. DAC, pp. 530–535 (2001)
16. Plaisted, D.A., Greenbaum, S.: A structure-preserving clause form translation. J. Symb. Comput. 2(3), 293–304 (1986)
17. Roussel, O., Manquinho, V.: Pseudo-Boolean and Cardinality Constraints, Frontiers in Artificial Intelligence and Applications, vol. 185, ch. 22, pp. 695–733. IOS Press (2009)
18. Sinz, C.: Towards an Optimal CNF Encoding of Boolean Cardinality Constraints. In: van Beek, P. (ed.) CP 2005. LNCS, vol. 3709, pp. 827–831. Springer, Heidelberg (2005)
19. Sörensson, N., Biere, A.: Minimizing Learned Clauses. In: Kullmann, O. (ed.) SAT 2009. LNCS, vol. 5584, pp. 237–243. Springer, Heidelberg (2009)
20. Tseitin, G.S.: On the complexity of derivation in propositional calculus. Studies in Constructive Mathematics and Mathematical Logic 2(115-125), 10–13 (1968)
21. Xu, L., Hutter, F., Hoos, H.H., Leyton-Brown, K.: Satzilla: portfolio-based algorithm selection for SAT. J. Artif. Int. Res. 32(1), 565–606 (2008)

Small Talk Is More than Chit-Chat
Exploiting Structures
of Casual Conversations for a Virtual Agent

Nikita Mattar and Ipke Wachsmuth

Artificial Intelligence Group, Bielefeld University
Universitätsstr. 25, 33615 Bielefeld, Germany
{nmattar,ipke}@techfak.uni-bielefeld.de

Abstract. An approach of improving the small talk capabilities of an existing virtual agent architecture is presented. Findings in virtual agent research revealed the need to pay attention to the sophisticated structures found in (human) casual conversations. In particular, existing dialogue act tag sets lack of tags adequately reflecting the subtle structures found in small talk. The approach presented here structures dialogues on two different levels. The micro level consists of meta information (speech functions) that dialogue acts can be tagged with. The macro level is concerned with ordering individual dialogue acts into sequences. The extended dialogue engine allows for a fine-grained selection of responses, enabling the agent to produce varied small talk sequences.

1 Introduction

Research in the field of Embodied Conversational Agents has shown that it is not sufficient to restrict conversations between agents and humans to task-oriented topics. Findings suggest that small talk supports the deepening of relationships between virtual agents and human interaction partners. Especially when dealing with interactions over the long run it is inevitable to enable the agent to develop a close relationship to the human interactant. This trend is reflected in the emergence of new research areas of "more sociable" agents like companion agents. For details cf. [3].

First attempts of integrating small talk into task-oriented dialogues were restricted to common topics like the weather. While this is sufficient to fill short gaps between tasks, recently the focus shifted towards more elaborate small talk capabilities in order to further enhance the bonding between agent and human.

In some cases, even small talk can be regarded as task-oriented. Since it serves the purpose of establishing relationships it might be a very important goal for people to successfully engage in small talk with others. While a lot of people might complain that they do not like to participate in small talk, others are not capable of doing it. Still these people might benefit from training small talk. To enable a virtual agent to coach a human interlocutor doing small talk, the agent has to have a clear representation of small talk. Furthermore, the agent should

B. Glimm and A. Krüger (Eds.): KI 2012, LNCS 7526, pp. 119–130, 2012.
© Springer-Verlag Berlin Heidelberg 2012

perform small talk on different levels of complexity and therefore must be able to select from different sequences and strategies for conducting small talk.

The paper is structured as follows. In the section to follow we discuss the nature of small talk and casual conversations in human dialogue and briefly review relevant research on this issue in the virtual agents domain. In Section 3, the main section, we introduce our approach on how to improve the small talk capabilities of a virtual agent architecture by tagging dialogue acts with meta information in order to achieve a variety of small talk sequences. In Section 4 we describe how we plan to evaluate our system, and present our ideas how this work is to be continued.

2   Related Work

2.1   Small Talk and Casual Conversations

Small talk has been defined as a "conversation about things which are not important, often between people who do not know each other well" [1]. According to Schneider [16] small talk can be classified as a special kind of casual conversation (which is influenced by social distance), in that small talk is more likely to happen if the social distance is greater, whereas casual conversation in general can be conducted between strangers or friends. Furthermore, small talk topics are much broader than commonly assumed. Schneider [16] suggests three situation categories from which topics can be chosen during small talk, but points out that use of topics differs among, and even within, cultures. He proposes a sequence for discussing a topic during small talk, consisting of an initial question/answer pair, followed by several further turns of question/acknowledgment or idling behavior, often referred to as "Schneiders sequence".

The main purpose of casual conversations is the maintenance of social identities and relations. Eggins and Slade [6] state that, while there are no restrictions of topic selection in casual conversations, the structure of casual conversations is an important part of the process of creating and maintaining social roles. They consider *speech functions* to be a fundamental part of discourse structure and present a network of speech functions intended to be used to annotate and analyze casual conversations. While the authors have in mind conversations between friends or workmates when talking about casual conversations, the common understanding of small talk is one of discourse mainly occurring between strangers, or at least people that are not close friends.

In conclusion, even when small talk is about things which are not important, the skill of conducting small talk is important in that it helps to establish social relations. Thus small talk is more than "chit-chat" in the sense of idle talk.

2.2   Virtual Agent Research

The idea to use human-like dialogues was early adopted in recommender systems. Those systems where intended to operate in a closed task domain and therefore only task specific dialogue capabilities were implemented.

With the emergence of virtual agents the need for more elaborate dialogue systems arose. Bickmore and Cassell [4] introduce the idea of implementing small talk in their agent REA, an embodied conversational agent for a real estate sales domain. In addition to pursuing its task-oriented goal, REA tries to accomplish non-task-oriented, interpersonal goals by engaging the interlocutor in small talk. The interpersonal goals mainly serve the purpose to prepare the interlocutor for the next task-oriented dialogue move, by making him feel more comfortable and relaxed. In [5] Bickmore and Cassell identified user trust to be most important for their scenario. With the aid of small talk, the agent is enabled to affect this dimension by e.g. establishing common ground and conducting "facework". An activation network-based approach is used for discourse planning, allowing for a fine grained control of REA's conversational strategies. However, since user responses are mainly ignored, there seems to be no need for structuring the dialogues on utterance level.

Meguro et al. [13] use an HMM-based approach to compare so called listening-oriented dialogues to casual conversations. They successfully trained HMMs to distinguish between the two dialogue types. Analysis of the HMMs gave further insight into the structural differences of listening-oriented dialogues and casual conversations, namely the frequency of tags and the transitions between them. Novielli and Strapparava [14] use HMMs for automatic dialogue act classification of utterances. They exploit differences in dialogue patterns for categorizing different types of users.

Klüwer [10] criticizes that, despite the fact that small talk has been acknowledged an important part of human-agent conversations, no computational model has been developed, and even the most prominent annotation schemes for dialogue acts lack a specialized tag set for social acts. The author presents a set of dialogue acts intended as an extension for existing tag sets. Her analysis of a dialogue corpus reveals the occurrence of several different sequences during small talk, supporting her claim that the use of a single sequence (e.g. Schneider's sequence) may not be sufficient.

Endrass et al. [7] investigate cultural differences in small talk and evaluate their findings using virtual agents. Summarizing literature they state that small talk dialogues in Asian and Western culture differ in structure, in that Western small talk dialogues tend to be more sequential than the Asian ones. Using Schneider's sequence as a basis for their computational model of small talk, they plan to adapt the sequences according to the cultural background of the interlocutor.

In conclusion, while there are many indications in the current literature that more elaborate small talk capabilities for virtual agents would seem advantageous, research on this issue has only begun. We consider the structuring of dialogue in varied small talk sequences an important starting point for further progress.

3   Structuring Dialogue

To motivate our aim to provide a fine grained structure for small talk dialogues, consider the short, fictitious example dialogue depicted in Fig. 1. In fact, several different dialogues can be constructed by omitting certain utterances. E.g. sequences consisting of the utterances *1,3*; *1,2,3*; *1,3,4,5*; *1,3,6,7*; *1,2,3,4,5,6,7*, etc. all resemble short conversations that make perfect sense. However, the complexity of the sequences differ. One could even argue that they not only differ in terms of structure, but in the level of commitment they convey. In fact, if the whole conversation only consists of Question-Answer (QA) pairs (like the *1,3* sequence) the dialogue could be considered rather superficial.

```
1. A:   Do you like soccer?
2. A:   I mean do you like watching it on tv?
3. B:   Sometimes.

4. A:   Uhh hu.
5. B:   I sometimes do watch world cup matches. I am
        not that much into watching every game that's on.

6. A:   So, you don't like soccer?
7. B:   Well not that much!
```

Fig. 1. Short example of a dialogue

3.1   Present System Architecture

The architecture of our agent consists of a BDI interpreter, based on JAM [9]. Beliefs about the world are stored as facts in the agent's world knowledge. Actions of the agent are guided by his internal goals, intentions, and external events. The agent is able to sense his environment through cameras and microphones. Percepts received through these sensors lead to reactive and deliberative behaviors of the agent.

While the agent is able to generate synthetic speech, interlocutors use a keyboard for input in the present setting. Utterances received as input through the keyboard are processed in the agent's deliberative component. The conversational behavior of the agent is realized within the deliberative component, either as response to the utterance of an interlocutor or as proactive behavior.

In order to generate a response to an utterance, the keyboard input is processed in several steps within the deliberative component. The first step is the interpretation of the textual input. Pattern matching rules classify the input among general semantic concepts [11]. In a second step a communicative function of the utterance is determined, by again employing rules matching certain features of the input. The communicative function consists of three parts – the *performative*, *reference*, and *content* part – covering semantic and pragmatic aspects of the utterance [11].

The original input and the assigned communicative function are passed on to the dialogue engine. Within the dialogue engine an appropriate response is determined from a set of rules. To be more precise, the plan with the highest utility for the current goal, among all BDI plans constituting the agent's dialogue knowledge, is selected and executed. As a last step, the behavior planner generates a multi-modal utterance that is then performed by the agent.

Our agent is employed as a museum guide, thus main effort was put into the design of the agent's presentation capabilities. Therefore, task-oriented dialogue knowledge is structured into small units [11], while small talk capabilities of the agent are mainly restricted to simple keyword matching and direct responses, resulting in short QA sequences. However, both types of dialogue rely on the communicative function in order to determine subsequent utterances.

In the following we present our approach of extending the dialogue engine to allow for a fine grained control of small talk and small talk sequences. In our approach, structuring of dialogues takes place on two different levels within our dialogue engine. The micro level consists of meta information that dialogue acts can be tagged with. Ordering of different dialogue acts into sequences, and therefore dialogues, is conducted on the macro level.

3.2   Micro Level

The concept of tagging dialogue acts with meta information is already present in the dialogue engine in terms of the communicative function. Extending this, we introduce another meta information – the *speech function*. Figure 2 depicts an utterance of the example dialogue as represented in the dialogue engine. The two types of meta information are discussed in the following.

```
<act communicative_function="askFor.content.dislikesSoccer"
     speech_function="rejoinder.track.probe" >
  So, you don't like soccer?
</act>
```

Fig. 2. XML notation of a dialogue act of our agent annotated with meta information.

Communicative Function. The *communicative function* meta information consists of three parts reflecting different information about the dialogue act of the agent and his interlocutors (see Fig. 3). Information about the speaker's intention is conveyed in the *performative* part. The *reference level* part determines the level of dialogue the act refers to: the *interaction*, *discourse*, and *content* level. The *content* part contains the semantic part of the dialogue act. E.g. it may contain the topic the utterance refers to (cf. [11]).

Only two different types, *provide* and *askFor*, are distinguished in the performative part of the function. These two types correspond to the *giving* and *demanding* speech roles used by Halliday [8]. While being applicable for simple small talk consisting of QA pairs, the distinction of only two performatives in the communicative function is not suitable to structure the conversation on a fine-grained level.

```
<performative>.<reference level>.<content>[arguments]
```

Fig. 3. Three independent parts constitute the communicative function of the dialogue engine [11]

Speech Function. The *speech function* meta information can be considered an extension of the communicative function further specifying the action of the dialogue act. Halliday [8] suggests four basic speech functions, two for each speech role, to capture the commodity and role of dialogue initiating moves (cf. [6]), and eight corresponding responding speech functions. Eggins and Slade [6] provide a finer subclassification of Halliday's basic speech functions, in order to account for the more subtle structure of casual conversations. Their speech functions are classified among four subcategories as illustrated in Fig. 4.

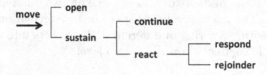

Fig. 4. Speech function network for casual conversations after [6]

As stated in Sect. 2.1 small talk is considered a subset of casual conversations. For this reason, we argue to exploit the speech functions for casual conversations in conversational agents that are to engage in more sophisticated small talk. In the initial implementation a subset of the speech functions suggested in [6] is used. An overview of the speech functions used in our dialogue engine is given in Table 1. In addition to the speech functions an example of an utterance, and its corresponding communicative function (if existent), is given. Note that some speech functions share the same communicative function.

3.3 Macro Level

The macro level is concerned with deciding how to select appropriate dialogue acts during conversation. One of the aims of using meta information is the reusability of generic utterances. E.g. utterances used as feedback channel, like "Uhh hu", can be used in a lot of situations, regardless of the content of prior utterances. On the other hand, related work (cf. Sect. 2.2) and the example given in Fig. 1 revealed that a variety of different sequences may occur within small talk conversations. Meguro et al. [13] demonstrated that even the type of conversation can be inferred from the transitions of dialogue acts.

As stated in Sect. 1, in some situations it may be crucial to reliably produce a certain sequence. E.g. in small talk training applications the agent should start with a very simple sequence, like Question-Answer. Over the course of training more complex sequences may have to be produced. Exploiting the introduced

Table 1. Subset of speech functions taken from Eggins and Slade [6]

Move Type	Speech Function	Communicative Function	Utterance
open	attending	provide.interaction.greeting	Hey!
	offer	provide.discourse .offer.guessingGame	Shall we play a funny guessing game?
	statement	provide.content.weather	The weather is really nice to-day.
	question	askFor.content.likesSoccer	Do you like soccer?
continue	monitor	askFor.content.confirmation	You know?
	elaborate	askFor.content.likesSoccer	I mean do you like watching it on tv?
respond	register		Mmm
	support.reply	provide.content.confirmation	Right!
	confront.reply	provide.content.disagree	No, sorry!
rejoinder	check	askFor.content.who	Who?
	confirm	askFor.content.confirmation	Did he?
	probe	askFor.content.dislikesSoccer	So, you dont like soccer?
	counter	askFor.content.confirmation	Does this even matter?

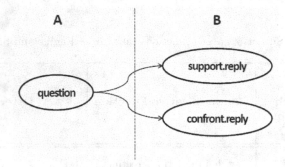

Fig. 5. Simple QA sequence. Dashed line represents the end of a turn.

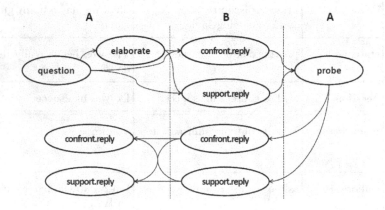

Fig. 6. Complex sequence. Dashed lines represent end of turns.

speech function meta information, a fine grained control of the course of conversations is possible. Figure 5 and Fig. 6 depict two possible sequences in our system, a simple QA, and a more complex sequence.

The following two problems have to be solved in order to enable the dialogue engine to select an appropriate response to an interlocutor's utterance:

1. **Utterance tagging:** Assign an appropriate speech function to interlocutor's utterance
2. **Utility adjustment:** Determine probability values for speech function candidates and adjust utility values of corresponding plans

Utterance Tagging. When annotating dialogues between two participants, the speech function of an utterance can be determined by only referring to the previous speech function (cf. [6]). But, as stated above, the dialogue engine should be able to produce structured sequences like the one presented in Fig. 6. It is obvious, that in this case, it is not sufficient to rely on the immediate predecessor of the current utterance. In the first case, the *reply* utterance of B is followed by a *probe* utterance. In the second case, it is followed by a *reply* utterance.

One option to assign speech functions to utterances would be to use a similar approach as used for deriving the communicative function, as described in [11]. However, this would require to provide dedicated rules for every possible sequence, resulting in a lot of redundant rules that only differ in the context of their sequence. Therefore, the process of assigning the speech function is done as a post processing step following the interpretation stage (cf. [11]) after every utterance of the agent's interlocutor. It is carried out by utilizing JAM's feature of employing Java methods. The Java part contains a representation of possible sequences, the sequence that is currently produced, the advancement in the current sequence, and a mapping of conversational to speech functions. The method for selecting the speech function is provided with the communicative function of the utterance that was determined during the interpretation stage. As output it returns the best matching speech function for the utterance. This way the communicative function is mapped to a corresponding speech function. By exploiting the sequence's history, utterances with similar communicative functions can be distinguished.

Algorithm 1 depicts the pseudo code for determining the speech function of an utterance. Given the communicative function CF and a set of speech functions `sequence_sfs` that are given due to the current position in the sequence, a set of possible speech functions is calculated. The speech function with the highest probability is selected and returned.

Algorithm 1. Pseudo code for selecting the speech function of an utterance

```
function SELECT_SF(CF : cfunction, sequence_sfs : {sfunction})
    possible_sfs = ∅

    for each sfunction SF with cfunction CF do
        possible_sfs = possible_sfs ∪ {SF}
    end for

    if possible_sfs ∩ sequence_sfs ≠ ∅ then
        return sfunction SF from (possible_sfs ∩ sequence_sfs)
                with probability(SF) == max
    else
        return sfunction SF from possible_sfs
                with probability(SF) == max
    end if
end function
```

Utility Adjustment. The BDI-based implementation of the dialogue engine allows for a flexible solution of providing alternatives for the agent's next dialogue contribution. Since utterances of our agent are represented within BDI plans, the utility values of these plans can be exploited to guide the agent's responses.

```
Plan:{
  NAME: "rule-0001 - continue.extend"
  GOAL: PERFORM match;
  PRECONDITION:
      (assign $util 10);
      (assign $util (* $util $continueextend));
      (FACT turn-holder "system");
  BODY:
    PERFORM collect-act
              (+ "<act sfunction=\"continue.extend\">
                  I mean do you like watching it on tv?
                </act>");
  UTILITY: $util;
}
```

Fig. 7. The utility value of a BDI plan is altered according to the probability of its speech function

The utility values define an order among plans. The plan with the highest utility value is selected as the most promising for fulfilling the current goal.

In contrast to the *utterance tagging* task described above, probabilities for possible following speech functions have to be determined after dialogue contributions of the agent and his interlocutor. Consider Fig. 6 with A being the agent. After A's first contribution A could try to hold the turn and continue with a further utterance. Accordingly, a probability value $\in [0, 1]$ is determined for every speech function known by the system (cf. Table 1) in the utility adjustment step after every utterance. To be accessible by the dialogue plans, the probabilities are stored as facts within the engine's dialogue knowledge.

Figure 7 depicts a simplified plan of our system. The utility value of the plan is multiplied by the corresponding speech function probability in the *precondition* part.

4   Conclusion and Future Work

In this paper an approach of improving small talk capabilities of an embodied conversational agent was presented. Speech functions of human casual conversations are used to tag utterances on the micro level. On the macro level, the tagged utterances can be ordered into arbitrary sequences found in human-human dialogues. Using these speech functions, our extended dialogue engine is able to produce various dialogue sequences as introduced in the example dialogue in Sect. 3.

In order to determine if the use of speech functions to structure dialogues on a fine-grained level actually leads to enhanced interactions, an evaluation with human interlocutors is planned. One possibility considered is to integrate the enhanced dialogue engine in the museum setting the agent daily operates in. Pfeiffer et al. [15] provide information about the mean length of dialogues (in terms of time and utterances) between the agent and his visitors in the museum setting. Following [2], an improvement in dialogue length could be judged to indicate an overall improvement of the system's acceptance due to its increased small talk capabilities. An accompanying questionnaire will be used to obtain additional hints about the qualitative changes. Since only a subset of the speech functions suggested for casual conversations in [6] was used to demonstrate the possibility of integrating speech functions into an existing dialogue engine, results of the evaluation could be used to assess if the full set of speech functions for casual conversations is actually needed.

In our initial approach speech functions are determined relying on the communicative function. An improvement could be the use of a machine learning approach to assign speech functions as described in [14]. Another option would be to focus on a more linguistically motivated approach. Following Halliday, Eggins and Slade [6] make use of mood and modality of the grammatical realizations of moves to identify speech functions.

The importance of being able to produce structured sequences in certain applications was stressed throughout this paper. However, the possibility to adapt the choice of sequences is important for an agent that engages in elaborate small talk to improve the relationship with his interlocutors. Bickmore and Cassell [5] found that the acceptance of an agent using small talk may also depend on the interlocutor's personality. Eggins and Slade state that conversations with close friends tend to be more confronting than the ones we have with work colleagues, because "conversations between close friends involve as much probing of differences between friends as confirming the similarities which brought them together as friends in the first place" [6]. Consequently, in future work we will focus on how information supplied by a Person Memory (cf. [12]) of an agent can be further used to improve the small talk conversation in terms of dialogue structure.

References

1. Small talk (2012),
   http://dictionary.cambridge.org/dictionary/british/
   small-talk?q=small+talk (accessed April 27, 2012)
2. Benyon, D., Hansen, P., Webb, N.: Evaluating human-computer conversation in companions. In: Proc. 4th International Workshop on Human-Computer Conversation (2008)
3. Benyon, D., Mival, O.: From human-computer interactions to human-companion relationships. In: Proceedings of the First International Conference on Intelligent Interactive Technologies and Multimedia, pp. 1–9. ACM (2010)
4. Bickmore, T., Cassell, J.: Small talk and conversational storytelling in embodied conversational interface agents. In: AAAI Fall Symposium on Narrative Intelligence, pp. 87–92 (1999)
5. Bickmore, T., Cassell, J.: Relational agents: a model and implementation of building user trust. In: Proceedings of the SIGCHI Conference on Human Factors in Computing Systems, pp. 396–403. ACM (2001)
6. Eggins, S., Slade, D.: Analysing Casual Conversation. Cassell (1997)

7. Endrass, B., Rehm, M., André, E.: Planning small talk behavior with cultural influences for multiagent systems. Computer Speech & Language 25(2), 158–174 (2011)
8. Halliday, M.: An Introduction To Functional Grammar, 2nd edn. Edward Arnold (1994)
9. Huber, M.: JAM: A BDI-theoretic mobile agent architecture. In: Proceedings of the Third Annual Conference on Autonomous Agents, pp. 236–243. ACM (1999)
10. Klüwer, T.: "I Like Your Shirt" - Dialogue Acts for Enabling Social Talk in Conversational Agents. In: Vilhjálmsson, H.H., Kopp, S., Marsella, S., Thórisson, K.R. (eds.) IVA 2011. LNCS, vol. 6895, pp. 14–27. Springer, Heidelberg (2011)
11. Kopp, S., Gesellensetter, L., Krämer, N.C., Wachsmuth, I.: A Conversational Agent as Museum Guide – Design and Evaluation of a Real-World Application. In: Panayiotopoulos, T., Gratch, J., Aylett, R.S., Ballin, D., Olivier, P., Rist, T. (eds.) IVA 2005. LNCS (LNAI), vol. 3661, pp. 329–343. Springer, Heidelberg (2005)
12. Mattar, N., Wachsmuth, I.: Who Are You? On the Acquisition of Information about People for an Agent that Remembers. In: ICAART 2012 - Proceedings of the 4th International Conference on Agents and Artificial Intelligence, pp. 98–105. SciTePress (2012)
13. Meguro, T., Higashinaka, R., Dohsaka, K., Minami, Y., Isozaki, H.: Analysis of listening-oriented dialogue for building listening agents. In: Proceedings of the SIGDIAL 2009 Conference: The 10th Annual Meeting of the Special Interest Group on Discourse and Dialogue, pp. 124–127. Association for Computational Linguistics (September 2009)
14. Novielli, N., Strapparava, C.: Dialogue Act Classification Exploiting Lexical Semantics. In: Conversational Agents and Natural Language Interaction: Techniques and Effective Practices, pp. 80–106. Information Science Reference (2011)
15. Pfeiffer, T., Liguda, C., Wachsmuth, I.: Living with a Virtual Agent: Seven Years with an Embodied Conversational Agent at the Heinz Nixdorf MuseumsForum. Group (2011)
16. Schneider, K.P.: Small talk: analysing phatic discourse. Hitzeroth (1988)

Clustering Based on Density Estimation
with Sparse Grids

Benjamin Peherstorfer[1], Dirk Pflüger[2], and Hans-Joachim Bungartz[1]

[1] Technische Universität München, Department of Informatics
Boltzmannstr. 3, 85748 Garching, Germany
[2] Universität Stuttgart, SimTech/Simulation of Large Systems, IPVS
Universitätsstr. 38, 70569 Stuttgart, Germany

Abstract. We present a density-based clustering method. The clusters
are determined by splitting a similarity graph of the data into connected
components. The splitting is accomplished by removing vertices of the
graph at which an estimated density function of the data evaluates to values below a threshold. The density function is approximated on a sparse
grid in order to make the method feasible in higher-dimensional settings
and scalable in the number of data points. With benchmark examples
we show that our method is competitive with other modern clustering
methods. Furthermore, we consider a real-world example where we cluster nodes of a finite element model of a Chevrolet pick-up truck with
respect to the displacements of the nodes during a frontal crash.

Keywords: clustering, density estimation, sparse grids.

1   Introduction

Clustering is one of the standard tasks in data mining. It is the process of dividing
data points of a set $S = \{x_1, \ldots, x_M\}$ into groups ("clusters") to reveal their
hidden structures. Here, we use a density-based notion of clusters and define a
cluster as a dense region ("where many data points are") surrounded by a region
of low-density ("where few data points are"), cf. [5]. However, there are almost
as many definitions of clustering and cluster as there are clustering methods, see,
e.g., the survey [18] and the references therein for further examples. Note that
in contrast to supervised learning tasks in data mining we do not have labels
associated to the data points in the set S. This means the grouping of the data
points into clusters has to be accomplished without additional knowledge about
the data.

One of the most prominent and also one of the oldest clustering methods is
k-means [8]. Nowadays there are many efficient implementations available, e.g.,
[12]. However, it is well-known that the initial guess of the cluster centers can
distinctly influence the outcome because the employed algorithms to solve the
underlying optimization problem typically find only a locally optimal solution.
Initialization strategies [1] can only remedy this problem for certain examples
and might not perform well in all situations. Furthermore, k-means can only find

B. Glimm and A. Krüger (Eds.): KI 2012, LNCS 7526, pp. 131–142, 2012.
© Springer-Verlag Berlin Heidelberg 2012

clusters with a convex shape. Thus, if a data set consists of clusters with non-convex boundaries, k-means fails to find a good partition. We will demonstrate this with our benchmark examples below.

Spectral clustering is a class of more recent clustering methods which can find clusters of non-convex shape. The data is represented by a similarity graph which is then partitioned such that the "flow" (the sum of weights of the edges) between clusters is minimized [13]. To solve the underlying graph partitioning problem an eigenproblem with dimension equaling the number of data points has to be solved. This is a major drawback if a large number of data points has to be clustered. By extending the method with sub-sampling techniques, this problem can be overcome to some extent [2,15].

Density-based clustering methods take the density of the data samples into account. They closely implement the idea that a cluster is a region of high-density surrounded by a region of low-density. Of the many clustering methods of this kind we consider the two arguably most prominent representatives DBSCAN [5] and DENCLUE [10]. Broadly speaking, DBSCAN finds clusters by determining so-called core objects which are points lying in a dense region. Core objects with overlapping neighborhood are then grouped into one cluster. Whereas DB-SCAN does not explicitly represent the density function corresponding to the data, DENCLUE employs kernel density estimation and hill-climbing to find local maxima, i.e. cluster centers. These methods again find clusters of arbitrary shape and are even well suited for large data sets. Furthermore, they do not need the number of clusters k as input parameter but can determine by themselves how many clusters are in the data. However, note that the number of clusters cannot be uniquely defined for a data set (see below) and thus the number determined by density-based clustering methods can only be considered as heuristical. Nevertheless, this is a huge advantage compared to k-means and spectral clustering methods.

Our method can be considered as a density-based clustering method as well, but whereas DBSCAN connects core objects and DENCLUE uses hill-climbing to find cluster centers, we pursue a more global approach. We first represent the data by a similarity graph. This is a standard task in machine learning. We then employ the nonparametric density estimation method [9] which uses a grid to approximate the density function. This means the method scales well with a large number of data points. Unfortunately, a straightforward grid-based discretization cannot be applied to problems with more than three or four dimensions ("curse of dimensionality"). Hence, we use sparse grids [3] to make it also scalable in the number of dimensions. Having the similarity graph and the estimated density function, we split the graph into various components by removing vertices at which the density function evaluates to values below a certain threshold. The components of the graph represent the cluster centers. In certain situations it might be useful to simple treat all data points corresponding to the deleted vertices as noise. But we will also see how we can easily assign those points to reasonable clusters if this is necessary. The method can again find clusters of arbitrary shape and, just as for DBSCAN and DENCLUE, the number of components gives a good indication of how many clusters we can expect to have in the data. Furthermore, as we will argue below, the method is again suited for large data sets.

We will report on several benchmark examples and show how our method performs compared to k-means, spectral clustering and DBSCAN. We will also present results of a real-world application where we cluster nodes of a finite element model of a car used for crash simulations.

2 Sparse Grids

Before we discuss in the next section the density estimation method on which our clustering method relies, we first need to summarize the most important facts about sparse grids. See [3] for a detailed description.

It is very common in machine learning algorithms to represent a function $f \in V$ as a linear combination of kernels associated to data points (kernel density estimation, kernel ridge regression, kriging, etc. [8]). In contrast, in a grid-based approach a function $f_N \in V_N$ can be represented as a linear combination $f_N(x) = \sum_{i=1}^{N} \alpha_i \phi_i(x)$ where the basis $\Phi = \{\phi_i\}_{i=1}^{N}$ comes from a grid and spans the function space V_N. Hence, the number of basis functions does *not* increase with the number of data points in contrast to classical approaches with kernels. However, a straightforward conventional discretization with 2^ℓ grid points in each dimension suffers the curse of dimensionality: The number of grid points is of the order $\mathcal{O}(2^{\ell d})$, depending exponentially on the dimension d. For sufficiently smooth functions, sparse grids enable us to reduce the number of grid points by orders of magnitude to only $\mathcal{O}(2^\ell \cdot \ell^{d-1})$ while keeping a similar accuracy as in the full grid case [3]. Note that we denote the sparse grid space of level $\ell \in \mathbb{N}$ with $V_\ell^{(1)}$ and that the level ℓ controls how many grid points are employed. Even though certain smoothness assumptions are required in theory, sparse grids have also been successfully applied for not so smooth functions in data mining, see, e.g., [7,17,16].

3 Density Estimation on Sparse Grids

The idea of our clustering method is to split the similarity graph representing the data into components by removing those vertices which lie in low-density regions. In order to find low-density regions we need to estimate the density function of our data. Whereas DBSCAN does not explicitly form an approximation of the density function and DENCLUE uses kernel density estimation, we employ the density estimation approach introduced in [9]. The idea is to start with a highly over-fitted initial guess f_ϵ and then use spline smoothing to obtain a smoother and more generalized approximation $\hat{f}$ of the density function of the underlying data $S = \{x_1, \ldots, x_M\}$. However, for us, the most crucial advantage of this approach is that the approximation $\hat{f}$ is discretized on grid points and *not* on kernels centered at the data points. This makes the method scalable in the number of data points. In this section, we give a brief description of the density estimation method [9] and show how to employ sparse grids in order to make the method not only scalable in the number of data points but also scalable in the number of dimensions.

Let f_ϵ be an initial guess of the density function of the data $S = \{x_1, \ldots, x_M\}$. We are then looking for $\hat{f}$ in a function space V such that

$$\hat{f} = \arg\min_{u \in V} \int_\Omega (u(x) - f_\epsilon(x))^2\, \mathrm{d}x + \lambda \|Lu\|_{L^2}^2,$$

where $\|Lu\|_{L^2}^2$ is a regularization or penalty term imposing a smoothness constraint. For example, L might be chosen to be ∇ but we will present another better suited regularization term below. The $\lambda \in \mathbb{R}$ is a regularization parameter and controls the trade-off between fidelity and smoothness. However, experience has shown that the method is not very sensitive to this parameter and $\lambda = 10^{-5}$ is a good choice, cf. Sec. 5 and Sec. 6. After some transformations we obtain the variational equation

$$\int_\Omega u(x)s(x)\mathrm{d}x + \lambda \int_\Omega Lu(x) \cdot Ls(x)\mathrm{d}x = \frac{1}{M}\sum_{i=1}^M s(x_i), \qquad \forall s \in V, \qquad (1)$$

with the test functions $s \in V$ and with $f_\epsilon = \frac{1}{M}\sum_{i=1}^M \delta_{x_i}$ where δ_{x_i} is the Dirac delta function centered on x_i. Note that other choices of f_ϵ are possible, see [9].

Instead of employing the finite element method with full grids, as proposed in [9], we employ sparse grids to find $\hat{f}$. Let $\Phi = \{\phi_1, \ldots, \phi_N\}$ be the (hierarchical) basis functions of a sparse grid space $V_\ell^{(1)}$ of level $\ell \in \mathbb{N}$, cf. Sec. 2. We are then looking for $\hat{f} \in V_\ell^{(1)}$. We set the test space to the sparse grid space $V_\ell^{(1)}$ and follow the usual Galerkin approach. We obtain the system of linear equations

$$(B + \lambda P)\alpha = f, \qquad (2)$$

where $B_{ij} = (\phi_i, \phi_j)_{L^2}$, $P_{ij} = (L\phi_i, L\phi_j)_{L^2}$ and $f_i = \frac{1}{M}\sum_{j=1}^M \phi_i(x_j)$. More details on the derivation of this system of linear equations can be found in [6].

Let us have a look at the system (2) from a computational perspective in the context of sparse grids. The matrices B and P of (2) are of size $N \times N$ where N is the number of grid points. Thus, the number of unknowns is *independent* from the number of data points. For example, if we have a grid consisting of only 5,000 grid points but we have 100,000 data points, we still need to solve a system of linear equations of the size 5,000 only. Furthermore, efficient algorithms exist to compute the matrix-vector product with the matrices B and P for the hierarchical basis Φ of a sparse grid space [16]. Additionally, it has been shown that in the case of the hierarchical basis and sparse grids the term $\sum_{i=1}^N \alpha_i^2$ is a very good choice for $\|Lu\|_{L^2}^2$, see [16]. The advantage of this choice is that the matrix P becomes the identity matrix I and thus the matrix-vector product becomes very cheap.

Note that we are not interested in any statistical properties (unit integrand, moments, etc.) of the estimated density. We only use it to indicate regions of low- and high-density.

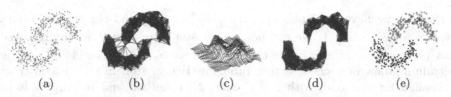

$$\text{(a)} \qquad\qquad \text{(b)} \qquad\qquad \text{(c)} \qquad\qquad \text{(d)} \qquad\qquad \text{(e)}$$

Fig. 1. Our density-based clustering method involves the following steps: representing the data (a) by a similarity graph (b), estimating the density function of the data (c), splitting the graph into components by removing vertices at which the density function evaluates to values below a threshold ϵ (d), assigning labels to the remaining vertices depending on their component, and classifying the data points which have been removed from the similarity graph (e).

4   Clustering with Estimated Densities

In this section, we describe in more detail our method based on density estimation with sparse grids. The idea is to represent the data by a similarity graph and to split this graph into several components by removing the vertices at which the estimated density function evaluates to values below a certain threshold. The steps of our method are visualized in Fig. 1.

In the first step, we represent the data $S = \{x_1, \dots, x_M\}$, see Fig. 1(a), by a similarity graph $G = (S, E)$ with vertices S and edges E, see Fig. 1(b). Note that the vertices are the data points. Here and in the following examples we always use nearest neighbor graphs with the Euclidean distance as similarity measure. This means we compute the Euclidean distances between the data points and connect the data points with their n nearest neighbors. Computing a nearest neighbor graph is a standard task in machine learning and can be performed with various implementations (e.g. BOOST[1], ANN[2]). Even though the construction of the graph is in $\mathcal{O}(M^2)$, it can be easily parallelized which makes processing of large amounts of data very easy. In step two, we compute the estimated density function $\hat{f}$ of our data with the approach described in the previous section, see Fig. 1(c). Again, this is scalable to many data points because we employ a grid-based discretization, cf. Sec. 3. Then (step three) we delete all vertices $\tilde{S}$ and the related edges $\tilde{E}$ of the graph G at which the estimated density function $\hat{f}$ evaluates to a value below a threshold ϵ. In other words, we remove those vertices $\tilde{S}$ (i.e. data points) of the graph which lie inside a region of low-density. Hence, the parameter ϵ controls what we consider to be a low-density region. The result is a graph $\hat{G} = (\hat{S}, \hat{E}) := (S \setminus \tilde{S}, E \setminus \tilde{E})$ which is split into several, say k, (connected) components each representing a cluster center, see Fig. 1(d). Thus, so far, we obtained a clustering of the data points $\hat{S} = S \setminus \tilde{S}$ remaining in the graph, i.e., we assign (step four) the labels $1, \dots, k$ to the components of the graph $\hat{G}$ (descending with the number of vertices in the component) and associate the label i to all data points in component i.

---

[1] http://www.boost.org/
[2] http://www.cs.umd.edu/~mount/ANN/

In the end, we have the labels $\hat{y}_1, \ldots, \hat{y}_{\hat{M}} \in \{1, \ldots, k\}$ and the clustered data point $\hat{S} = \{\hat{x}_1, \ldots, \hat{x}_{\hat{M}}\}$. We can now either stop here, and treat the removed data points $\tilde{S}$ as outliers, or we consider the set $\hat{S}$ and the labels $\hat{y}_1, \ldots, \hat{y}_{\hat{M}}$ as training data of a classification problem. Hence, step five is to construct a classifier for this data with any classification method and to employ it to classify the remaining data points $\tilde{S}$. Even though we have also tested more sophisticated classification approaches such as SVM [4] and sparse-grid-based classification [16], a simple and very fast nearest neighbor classifier based on approximated nearest neighbors (ANN[4]) has always worked well enough in the following examples[3]. As sketched in Fig. 1, the algorithm to cluster the data $S = \{x_1, \ldots, x_M\}$ can be summarized in the following five steps:

1. Construct a similarity graph $G = (S, E)$ to represent the data points in S.
2. Employ sparse-grid-based density estimation to compute $\hat{f}$, cf. Sec. 3.
3. Create graph $\hat{G} = (\hat{S}, \hat{E}) = (S \setminus \tilde{S}, E \setminus \tilde{E})$ with k (connected) components by deleting vertices $\tilde{S}$ and related edges $\tilde{E}$ at which the estimated density function $\hat{f}$ evaluates to values below threshold ϵ.
4. Depending on their component, assign labels $\hat{y}_1, \ldots, \hat{y}_{\hat{M}} \in \{1, \ldots, k\}$ to the remaining vertices (i.e. data points) in $\hat{S}$.
5. Optional: Train classifier on data $\hat{S}$ with labels $\hat{y}_1, \ldots, \hat{y}_{\hat{M}}$ and obtain labels for the data points in $\tilde{S}$.

Before we go on with the benchmark examples in the next section, we would like to make a few comments about the parameters of the method. For the density estimation, we have to choose the regularization parameter λ and the level (thus the number of grid points) of the sparse grid. For the similarity graph, we have to choose the number of neighbors n. And finally we need to determine the threshold ϵ to specify what is to be considered as a low-density region. Results have shown that the level of the sparse grid, the regularization parameter λ and the number of nearest neighbors n have only a minor effect on the clustering result and a reasonable guess is usually sufficient, see our examples in Sec. 5 and Sec. 6. Hence, we concentrate on the choice of the threshold ϵ. In Fig. 2(a) we plot the estimated density function of a data set with three clusters with different distinctiveness. In Fig. 2(d) we show the number of components against the threshold ϵ. On the one hand, we see that if we choose the threshold too low (< 0.2) then the two very distinctive clusters are not separated because the estimated density function is still above the threshold between them, see Fig. 2(b). On the other hand, if we choose the threshold too high (≥ 0.4) then we miss the small cluster because the estimated density function is not high enough at the not so strong cluster, see Fig. 2(f). However, we also see that we have a large region ($0.2 \leq \epsilon < 0.4$) where our method correctly predicts three clusters. Of course, there might be some outliers, see Fig. 2(e). We will see the same behavior in the benchmark and in real-world examples in the following sections.

---

[3] The number of neighbors has been automatically determined by cross validation.

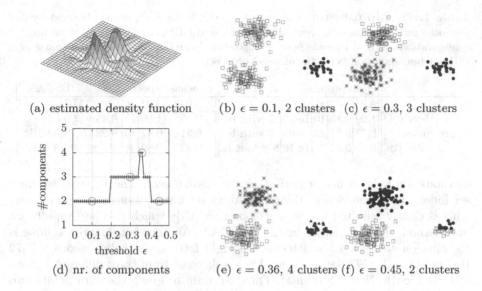

(a) estimated density function   (b) $\epsilon = 0.1$, 2 clusters   (c) $\epsilon = 0.3$, 3 clusters

(d) nr. of components   (e) $\epsilon = 0.36$, 4 clusters   (f) $\epsilon = 0.45$, 2 clusters

Fig. 2. This simple example demonstrates the effect of the threshold ϵ on the clustering. If the threshold is set too low (a) we may miss clusters with very many points, if it is set too high (f) we may not be able to capture clusters with just a few points. Note that we only plotted every tenth point of the data set in order to make the symbols better legible.

5   Benchmark Examples

In this section, we want to demonstrate the performance of our density-based clustering approach on some common benchmark examples. We compare our method to k-means, spectral clustering and DBSCAN for which we used the implementation in `scikit-learn` [14]. Tab. 1 shows the ARI (adjusted rand index) [11] corresponding to the cluster assignment obtained by our method and by k-means, spectral clustering and DBSCAN for three benchmark data sets. For spectral clustering we used the Gaussian kernel with bandwidth σ and an n-nearest neighbor graph. For DBSCAN we had to choose the threshold ϵ and the minimum number of points m required to form a cluster. The parameter configurations have been determined by running each method for a range of parameters. We kept the parameter configuration for which the method yielded the highest ARI. These parameter configurations are documented in Tab. 1. Note that this was only possible because we knew the cluster assignments. For our method, we give in Sec. 6 some motivation how to best choose the parameters in the more practical case where the clustering is not known beforehand.

The threeS data set [6] contains 675 data points of three spheres (three dimensions) of different size which are tangled with each other. It is clear that the three clusters (i.e. the three spheres) cannot be linearly separated. That is why k-means fails completely to detect the three clusters. However, all other

Table 1. The ARI (adjusted rand index) of the cluster assignment obtained by our proposed method, k-means, spectral clustering and DBSCAN and the used parameter configurations. ARI of 1 means perfect clustering. Note that we employed a sparse grid without boundary points for the olive oil data set.

	proposed method				k-means	spect. clust.			DBSCAN		
	ARI	ϵ	n	λ	ℓ	ARI	ARI	n	σ	ARI	ϵ	m
threeS [6]	1.00	0.15	10	1e-05	7 with b.	0.26	1.00	13	0.45	1.00	0.85	5
threeSnoise [6]	0.73	0.17	13	1e-05	7 with b.	0.31	0.87	13	9.23	0.73	0.93	18
olive [19]	0.97	0.02	5	1e-10	5 w/out b.	0.32	0.69	8	56.62	0.62	0.42	6

methods are able to find a perfect cluster assignment. The threeSnoise data set follows the same idea as the threeS data set but contains even more noise. This is clearly reflected in the corresponding ARIs which decrease rapidly for our method, spectral clustering and DBSCAN. Another benchmark example is the olive oil data set [19] which contains eight fatty acids (8 dimensions) of 572 Italian olive oils (572 data points). These oils come from three different regions in Italy (South, North, Sardinia). Thus, we want to group the data points into three clusters. The results are shown again in Tab. 1. Whereas spectral clustering and DBSCAN achieve an ARI of at most 0.70, our method handles the data set very well and we obtain a cluster assignment with ARI 0.97. In that case, the density estimation method might have played a decisive role because we set the regularization parameter λ to only 1e-10 and thus almost over-fitted our estimated density function to our data. We then had to use a very small threshold ϵ of only 0.02 in order to capture the third cluster. As we have demonstrated in the previous section and in Fig. 2, this means that the third cluster is very weak, i.e. the value of the estimated density function at the third cluster is very low compared to the two other clusters. This can also be verified by plotting the number of components versus the threshold ϵ, see Fig. 3(a). Clearly, only if we choose the threshold very small we have more than one component. The threshold $\epsilon = 0.02$ has been chosen because this is approximately the mean of the interval where we have exactly three components, i.e., where our method correctly predicts three clusters.

6   Clustering Car Crash Data

In this section, we consider a finite element model of a Chevrolet C2500 pick-up truck[4] which is used to simulate a frontal crash. We want to group the nodes of the finite element model with respect to the moving intensity and moving patterns of the nodes during the crash. Let $M \approx 66,000$ be the number of nodes $n_1, \ldots, n_M \in \mathbb{N}$ in the finite element model of the car. We compute the displacements $d_i = x_i^T - x_i^0 \in \mathbb{R}^3$ for all $i = 1, \ldots, M$ where x_i^0 and x_i^T denote the position of node n_i at the beginning of the crash (time 0) and at the end (time T), respectively. Our data set $S = \{d_1, \ldots, d_M\} \subset \mathbb{R}^3$ contains the displacements of the nodes during the crash.

---

[4] http://www.ncac.gwu.edu/

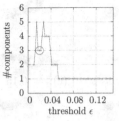
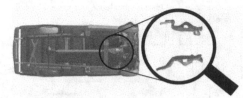

(a) Components for olive data set. (b) The position of the four beams in the car.

Fig. 3. In (a) the curve of the nr. of components versus the threshold ϵ shows that our method correctly predicts three clusters at $\epsilon \approx 0.02$ for the olive oil data set. In (b) we show the position of the four beams in the car model.

We first consider only four beams of the car model (with $\approx 7,000$ nodes), see Fig. 3(b), but their behavior during the crash distinctly influences the whole car. We apply our density-based clustering method on their displacements. Just as in the previous examples, we set the sparse grid level to 5 (with boundary points, 1,505 grid points), the regularization parameter λ to 1e-05 and the number of nearest neighbors for the similarity graph construction to 10. The threshold ϵ is in $[0.01, 0.25] \subseteq \mathbb{R}$, and to get an idea about how many clusters we should have a look for, we plot the number of components versus the threshold ϵ in Fig. 4(a). We can distinguish four intervals $[0.08, 0.11]$, $[0.14, 0.16]$, $[0.19, 0.21]$ and $[0.22, 0.25]$ at which our method distinctly predicts 6, 5, 3 and 2 clusters, respectively. They are marked by circles in Fig. 4(a). In Fig. 4(b)-(e) we also plot four cluster assignments, each of them corresponding to one of these intervals. For the smallest threshold $\epsilon = 0.1$ we have multiple clusters in the front of the beams but if we increase ϵ they disappear. This suggests that these clusters are not very strong, i.e. even though the estimated density function has local maxima in these regions they are rather small compared to local maxima corresponding to other clusters. Thus, if the threshold is set too high, we cannot capture them anymore. However, as described in Sec. 4 and Fig. 2, even if we loose clusters by increasing the threshold, we can also gain clusters: If local maxima corresponding to the clusters are very high, the peaks of the estimated density function might become only separated after a certain threshold. That is why new clusters appear in the rear of the beams if the threshold ϵ is increased from 0.1 (Fig. 4(b)) to 0.15 (Fig. 4(c)). Overall, the clusters in the rear of the beams seem to be more stable than the clusters in the front because they start to appear not until $\epsilon = 0.15$ and are still there at $\epsilon = 0.23$. From a car engineering point of view this is an interesting fact because this means that on the one hand the nodes in the front of the beams do not have a common moving pattern (e.g. they do not move in one direction), i.e., they are more or less scattered randomly. On the other hand, in the rear we find quite strong clusters which suggests a common moving pattern for all nodes in the rear. By visualizing the four beams during all time steps we can indeed verify that the front is crushed completely whereas the rear of the beams moves more smoothly, cf. again Fig. 3(b) for a visualization of the four beams at the last time step.

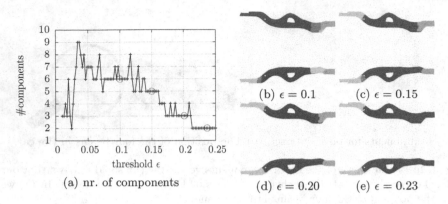

(a) nr. of components   (b) $\epsilon = 0.1$ (c) $\epsilon = 0.15$

(d) $\epsilon = 0.20$ (e) $\epsilon = 0.23$

Fig. 4. Cluster assignments of the four selected beams (b)-(e) with respect to different thresholds ϵ (a)

We now cluster all $\approx 66,000$ nodes of the whole car at once and we want to compare the result with the clustering of the four beams of the previous paragraph. A particular challenge in this setting is that the whole car exhibits many different effects leading to a large number of clusters, i.e. a large number of peaks in the estimated density function. In order to be able to represent each of these peaks, the estimated density function has to be approximated on a sparse grid with many grid points (i.e., we need a high level). Even though not considered in this work, adaptive sparse grids allow us to only refine certain parts of the sparse grid and thus a huge saving with respect to the number of grid points can be achieved, see, e.g., [16] for a discussion in the context of classification. Here, we simply increase the sparse grid level to 9 (18,943 grid points) and do not center points on the boundary. We do not need boundary points anymore because the data set contains so many noisy points scattered all over the domain that nothing important is happening near the boundary. The regularization parameter λ is set to 1e-08 to better fit the data. Again, this is useful because we have so many data points. All other parameters are kept as in the previous paragraph. In Fig. 5(a) we plot the number of components versus the threshold. We cannot find regions of ϵ where our method distinctly predicts a number of clusters anymore. However, if we plot the moving average of the previous ten data points, we can recognize a flat region of the moving average near $\epsilon = 0.2$. The corresponding cluster assignment of the four selected beams is shown in Fig. 5(b). We see that it consists of only three clusters. A few points are obviously not correctly clustered. Clearly, the clustering we find if we cluster the whole car with $\approx 66,000$ nodes at once (Fig. 5(b)) is similar to the one we find if we cluster only the four selected beams with only $\approx 7,000$ nodes (Fig. 4(b)-(e)). Again, we could find an appropriate threshold ϵ looking for flat regions in the curve which shows the number of components versus the threshold ϵ, see Fig. 5(a). On an Intel Core i7-870 with 8GB RAM clustering all nodes takes 37 seconds. If the threshold ϵ is changed, we do not have to recompute the graph or the density function and thus the new cluster assignment can be visualized within a few seconds.

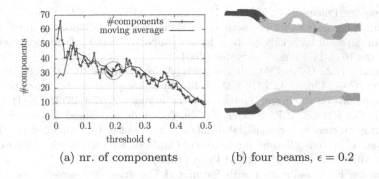

(a) nr. of components   (b) four beams, $\epsilon = 0.2$

Fig. 5. In (a) we show the number of components versus the threshold ϵ for the whole car, and in (b) the clustering of the four beams with threshold $\epsilon = 0.2$

7 Conclusions

We have presented a density-based clustering method which is distinctly different from other density-based clustering methods in two points: First, the density function is approximated on a grid. Thus, it is well suited for a vast number of data points. In order to make this grid-based approach feasible in higher dimensions, we employed sparse grids. Second, we determine clusters by splitting a similarity graph into connected components. This is a more global view instead of the local approaches of DBSCAN (connecting core objects) or DENCLUE (hill-climbing). Furthermore, creating the similarity graph and finding connected components are standard tasks and various efficient implementations exist. Thus, the implementational effort is kept at a minimum.

Just as other density-based methods, our method can find clusters with non-convex boundaries as well. Applying the method to benchmark examples has shown that this method performs well compared to k-means, spectral clustering and DBSCAN. We also applied the method to a real-world example where we clustered the nodes of a finite element model of a car. We demonstrated how we can use the number of components as a function of the threshold ϵ either to give an indication of the number of clusters in the data set (crash data) or as a means to find a good threshold ϵ if the number of clusters is known (olive oil). Furthermore, by comparing cluster assignments obtained with different threshold ϵ, we can determine how stable a cluster is. This is valuable information which goes beyond just providing a cluster assignment.

References

1. Arthur, D., Vassilvitskii, S.: k-means++: the advantages of careful seeding. In: Proceedings of the Eighteenth Annual ACM-SIAM Symposium on Discrete Algorithms, SODA 2007, pp. 1027–1035. SIAM, Philadelphia (2007)

2. Bengio, Y., Paiement, J., Vincent, P., Delalleau, O., Roux, N.L., Ouimet, M.: Out-of-sample extensions for lle, isomap, mds, eigenmaps, and spectral clustering. In: Thrun, S., Saul, L., Schölkopf, B. (eds.) Advances in Neural Information Processing Systems 16. MIT Press, Cambridge (2004)
3. Bungartz, H.J., Griebel, M.: Sparse grids. Acta Numerica 13, 147–269 (2004)
4. Chang, C.C., Lin, C.J.: LIBSVM: A library for support vector machines. ACM Transactions on Intelligent Systems and Technology 2, 27:1–27:27 (2011)
5. Ester, M., Kriegel, H.P., Sander, J., Xu, X.: A density-based algorithm for discovering clusters in large spatial databases with noise. In: Simoudis, E., Han, J., Fayyad, U.M. (eds.) Second International Conference on Knowledge Discovery and Data Mining, pp. 226–231. AAAI Press (1996)
6. Franzelin, F.: Classification with Estimated Densities on Sparse Grids. Master's thesis, Institut für Informatik, Technische Universität München (September 2011)
7. Garcke, J., Griebel, M., Thess, M.: Data mining with sparse grids. Computing 67(3), 225–253 (2001)
8. Hastie, T., Tibshirani, R., Friedman, J.: The Elements of Statistical Learning. Springer (2009)
9. Hegland, M., Hooker, G., Roberts, S.: Finite element thin plate splines in density estimation. ANZIAM Journal 42 (2009)
10. Hinneburg, A., Gabriel, H.-H.: DENCLUE 2.0: Fast Clustering Based on Kernel Density Estimation. In: Berthold, M., Shawe-Taylor, J., Lavrač, N. (eds.) IDA 2007. LNCS, vol. 4723, pp. 70–80. Springer, Heidelberg (2007)
11. Hubert, L., Arabie, P.: Comparing partitions. J. of Classification 2(1), 193–218 (1985)
12. Kanungo, T., Mount, D., Netanyahu, N., Piatko, C., Silverman, R., Wu, A.: An efficient k-means clustering algorithm: analysis and implementation. IEEE Transactions on Pattern Analysis and Machine Intelligence 24(7), 881–892 (2002)
13. von Luxburg, U.: A tutorial on spectral clustering. Statistics and Computing 17, 395–416 (2007)
14. Pedregosa, F., Varoquaux, G., Gramfort, A., Michel, V., Thirion, B., Grisel, O., Blondel, M., Prettenhofer, P., Weiss, R., Dubourg, V., Vanderplas, J., Passos, A., Cournapeau, D., Brucher, M., Perrot, M., Duchesnay, E.: Scikit-learn: Machine Learning in Python. Journal of Machine Learning Research 12, 2825–2830 (2011)
15. Peherstorfer, B., Pflüger, D., Bungartz, H.-J.: A Sparse-Grid-Based Out-of-Sample Extension for Dimensionality Reduction and Clustering with Laplacian Eigenmaps. In: Wang, D., Reynolds, M. (eds.) AI 2011. LNCS, vol. 7106, pp. 112–121. Springer, Heidelberg (2011)
16. Pflüger, D.: Spatially Adaptive Sparse Grids for High-Dimensional Problems. Verlag Dr. Hut, München (2010)
17. Pflüger, D., Peherstorfer, B., Bungartz, H.J.: Spatially adaptive sparse grids for high-dimensional data-driven problems. J. of Complexity 26(5), 508–522 (2010)
18. Xu, R., Wunsch II, D.: Survey of clustering algorithms. IEEE Transactions on Neural Networks 16(3), 645–678 (2005)
19. Zupan, J., Novic, M., Li, X., Gasteiger, J.: Classification of multicomponent analytical data of olive oils using different neural networks. Analytica Chimica Acta 292(3), 219–234 (1994)

A Comparison between Cognitive and AI Models of Blackjack Strategy Learning

Marvin R.G. Schiller and Fernand R. Gobet

Brunel University, London, UK
{marvin.schiller,fernand.gobet}@brunel.ac.uk

Abstract. Cognitive models of blackjack playing are presented and investigated. Blackjack playing is considered a useful test case for theories on human learning. Curiously, despite the existence of a relatively simple, well-known and optimal strategy for blackjack, empirical studies have found that casino players play quite differently from that strategy. The computational models presented here attempt to explain this result by modelling blackjack playing using the cognitive architecture CHREST. Two approaches to modeling are investigated and compared; (i) the combination of classical and operant conditioning, as studied in psychology, and (ii) SARSA, as studied in AI.

1 Introduction

Research in AI and cognitive science has made important contributions to understanding the difficulties underlying a myriad of learning tasks by devising and investigating learning algorithms. In this paper, we address the question of how human learning, which is governed by underlying psychological mechanisms, is modelled and investigated using a cognitive architecture (in our case, CHREST [1]). As the learning task, we use a game that relies both on chance and strategy, and for which empirical data shows that human players deviate from theoretically optimal strategies: blackjack. Models in CHREST simulate the information-processing of human players; they play the game, observe the outcomes, process and store the relationships between blackjack hands, actions and outcomes in long-term memory, and select actions accordingly. CHREST uses a mechanism that implements emotional memory, i.e. patterns of information in memory (chunks) may be associated with emotional tags, which are learned from experience with the environment. Using this basic framework, we investigate models based on theories in psychology and decision-making, and study how they compare to SARSA (cf. e.g. [2]), an AI algorithm modelling reinforcement learning, in explaining data from human casino players.

This paper is organised as follows. In Sect. 2 we discuss previous work investigating strategies in blackjack, both in psychology and AI. In Sect. 3 the cognitive architecture CHREST is introduced. Sect. 4 describes our modelling and Sect. 5 presents the results, which are discussed in Sect. 6.

B. Glimm and A. Krüger (Eds.): KI 2012, LNCS 7526, pp. 143–155, 2012.
© Springer-Verlag Berlin Heidelberg 2012

2 Blackjack Strategies: Modelling and the Role of Learning

Blackjack is played by one or several players (independently) against a dealer. At the start of a game, each player makes a bet and is dealt two cards face-up and their combined value is considered (figure cards count as 10 except the ace, which may count as 1 or 11, to the favour of the player). The dealer also obtains two cards, one of which is dealt face-up (the upcard). The goal of the player is to obtain a total that is as close to 21 as possible without exceeding 21, in which case the player immediately loses the game and thus the bet (going bust). If the initial two cards of the player add to 21 (blackjack), the player immediately wins the game and 2.5 times the amount of the original bet. Such hands that include an ace that may count as 11 without the total exceeding 21 are called soft (as opposed to hard) hands. Players may successively request to be dealt additional cards (hit) or to content themselves with the current total (stand). Further actions the player may take are splitting a pair hand, and doubling a bet (see e.g. [3, Sect. 3]), but these actions are not relevant for the remainder of this paper. After all players have made their choices, it is the dealer's turn to play according to a fixed rule (which may vary in different casinos); usually the dealer is required to hit at a total of 16 or less and to stand at 17. If the dealer busts, all players who have not bust receive 2 times the amount of the original bet (i.e. a net win of the size of the bet). If the dealer stands at a score of at most 21, the remaining players with a higher score win 2 times the original bet, otherwise they either draw (and receive back their bet) or lose their bet.

Wagenaar [4] notes that – even though strategies exist to maximise the returns of playing – the performance of blackjack players in the casino is not optimal. The question of what strategies people actually adopt when playing blackjack, and how they relate to learning, has not been answered conclusively. In this paper we propose a cognitive model (implemented using the cognitive architecture CHREST [1]) that relates blackjack strategy to theories in psychology and decision-making, and compare this to a traditional AI algorithm, SARSA.

2.1 Blackjack Strategies

Never bust is a strategy where the player hits at a total of 11 and below, and stands at a hard total of 12 or more. According to simulations [4], players using *never bust* are expected to lose 8% of their original investment on average. *Mimic the dealer* is a strategy where the player hits at 16 and stands at 17, like the dealer. The expected loss is 6% per game according to [4]. Both of these strategies are inferior to the *basic strategy* introduced by [5]. It can be represented in the form of decision tables taking into account the player's total and the dealer's upcard, and which prescribe one out of four actions (stand, hit, double, split). Different tables apply to hard hands, soft hands, and pair hands. Wagenaar [4] notes that this strategy can be learned very easily. It results in an expected loss of 0.4 % per game, which is relatively favourable for the player. In combination with a supplementary technique (card counting, as discussed by [4]), a positive expected return can be achieved. Sub-optimal play results in a larger house edge, i.e. expected losses of the player. Walker et al. [6] found that Australian players violated the basic strategy on 14.6% of the hands, resulting in a house edge of 2.4 % (instead of 0.8% with the basic strategy[1]).

To assess what type of strategy blackjack players in the casino are actually playing, Wagenaar studied the games[2] of 112 players and compared their play to the basic strategy. For each combination of the player's total and the dealer's upcard, it was established how often the players (on average) deviated from the basic strategy. Table 1 is adapted from [4] and shows the proportion of deviations from the basic strategy for hard non-pair hands (pair hands, which allow for splitting, were not further investigated in [4]). The table includes only players' totals from 12 to 17, since players always hit at 11 or less, and always stood at 18 or more. Wagenaar found that players are more likely to violate basic when they are required to hit (the underlined area) than when they are required to stand. Wagenaar discusses possible reasons for this kind of "conservatism" of standing where hitting offers a greater chance to win (e.g. regret minimisation, delaying bad news, blaming the dealer's luck). Wagenaar formulates this bias in the players' actions as a linear logistic model, but does not explore whether or how it might be related to learning.

2.2 Modelling Learning in Blackjack

A number of studies on blackjack strategies and learning have been contributed by researchers in mathematics and AI, who were either interested in optimal playing strategies or efficient machine-learning algorithms. Less is known about the blackjack skills of actual players, as investigated in [4], [6] and [7].

Work by mathematicians and statisticians (e.g. [5]) makes use of knowledge of the mechanics of blackjack (composition of decks, random drawing) in their search for optimality. In contrast, strategy acquisition in blackjack can be considered as a learning problem based solely on playing experience, which makes the analysis more challenging, and which is done in AI to investigate the capabilities of machine learning algorithms (e.g. bootstrapping [8] and evolutionary algorithms [3]). The work by Perez-Uribe and Sanchez [2] is interesting in that they use the SARSA algorithm, a reinforcement learning mechanism based on temporal difference learning and Q-learning. However, this work does not analyse the relationship between their models and the behaviour of human players. Furthermore, this work did not consider the value of the face-up dealer's card, and therefore it does not offer the possibility to compare the learned strategies to the basic strategy, one of the objectives of this paper.

Reinforcement learning in the context of decision-making tasks has been intensively studied with the Iowa Gambling Task, a kind of four-armed bandit problem (cf. [9]). Subjects have to select cards from four decks with different

---

[1] Differences wrt. the house edge reported in [4] are due to rule variations.
[2] Since observers had no control over the length of stay, the number of hands recorded for each player varies (median=74 hands, cf. [4]).

schedules of rewards and punishments. [10] and [9] propose an elaborate model for subjects' decision making behaviour on the task, the expectancy valence (EV) model. It models the learning of players' expectations and action selection via softmax selection/Boltzmann exploration. In this paper, we extend the use of some of these principles to the study of blackjack play.

3   CHREST

CHREST (Chunk Hierarchy and REtrieval STructures) is a cognitive architecture that enables the modelling of human processes of perception (in particular visual attention), learning and memory. CHREST is a symbolic architecture based on chunking theory [11] and template theory [12]. Chunking theory posits that information is processed, learned and retrieved in the form of patterns, which can be used as one coherent unit of knowledge, and which are referred to as chunks. CHREST is composed of an input analysis component, a short-term memory component (for different modalities: visual, auditory, action) and a long-term memory component which is organised in a network structure. Technically, patterns form nodes in the network structure of long-term memory. Retrieval is via an index structure referred to as discrimination network, which is learned incrementally. Furthermore, cross-links can be learned within long-term memory within and across chunks of different modalities. Patterns are formed when information is perceived via the input analysis component and passed on to short-term and long-term memory, where they are learned – i.e. integrated into the network structure – incrementally. Any chunk in long-term memory (LTM) can be associated with an emotional tag that is retrieved when the chunk is retrieved. In general, emotional tags in CHREST follow the paradigm of [13] and [14] by representing emotions as combinations on several dimensions of primary basic emotions (e.g. joy, acceptance, fear, surprise, sadness, disgust, anger, anticipation according to [14]). In this paper, however, we only use two dimensions of emotions (joy and sadness), in keeping with the parsimony of similar previous models for the Iowa Gambling Task (cf. Sect. 2.2). Emotional tags are learned via an association learning mechanism using a so-called Δ-rule (illustrated in the next section). This rule is part of psychological theories on classical conditioning [15] as well as the decision-theoretic model proposed by [10].

CHREST runs as a computer program in Java (with interfaces for scripts in other languages), to enable simulations and testing of cognitive models. CHREST has previously been used to model phenomena in various domains of human information-processing and expertise, including board games (Go, chess and awalé), language acquisition in children, and physics.

4   Modelling

CHREST models played blackjack, to investigate in how far the learning implemented by these models accounts for (i) the behaviour observed by Wagenaar [4] as described in Sect. 2, and (ii) the choices that the basic strategy prescribes instead. Since the actions of splitting and doubling are not relevant for modelling Wagenaar's data, our model is simplified by only considering hitting vs. standing (like [2]). As a further simplification, each game is dealt from a complete deck of cards. For simplicity we also assume that bets are held constant, and wins and losses are always represented as multiples of "1" bet. Our model is based on the hypothesis that players experience constant reinforcement and reward (of positive and negative valence) while playing, which follows a random ratio schedule. This experience is likely to enter the player's memory and to influence decision-making, in conflict or in addition to fixed strategies. For making an action, the model (i) visually recognises the total of the player's hand, (ii) visually recognises the value of the dealer's upcard, and (iii) retrieves the set of possible actions in action memory associated with that situation. Depending on previous experience, these situation-specific actions are associated with emotional tags of positive and/or negative valence. Depending on these values, the action to be performed is selected, the immediate outcomes are observed, and the model adjusts its expectations (using the Δ-rule).

4.1   CHREST Model (Model 1)

The model starts out with a representation of the possible losing and winning outcomes of blackjack. Monetary wins and losses carry emotional tags attached to these outcomes as follows; wins are directly represented in the "joy" dimension and losses in the "sadness" dimension. The possible outcomes are (i) losing (joy:0, sadness:1), (ii) blackjack win (joy:2.5, sadness:1), (iii) ordinary win (joy:2, sadness:1), (iv) push (joy:1, sadness:1). An alternative approach is to map the net wins onto a single dimension of "joy" (which can then also take negative values). The second approach assumes that players mentally offset bets and wins prior to experiencing their rewarding effect. We additionally included this variant of our model in the analysis, as discussed in the results.

Each game of blackjack requires the player to make one or several choices based on the current "state" of the game; i.e. the situation described by the player's cards and the dealer's upcard. Each game is terminated with a win, loss or draw after a finite number of iterations of the following steps.

1) **Recognition.** The model receives its own hand and the dealer's upcard as input. The model retrieves a chunk that represents the combination of its own total, together with an indicator whether the hand is soft or hard, and the dealer's upcard from long-term memory (e.g. "14-10-soft" if presented with Ace, 3 and dealer's upcard 10). If such a chunk does not exist or is incomplete, learning of such a chunk (according to chunking theory, cf. [1]) takes place instead. If the chunk has been linked to actions or carries an emotional tag (due to previous playing), these are retrieved. Any such "player's hand" or "state" chunk may have been linked with two different action chunks (hit/stand), each of which may have an emotional tag (resulting from previous experience with the action for that specific hand).

2) Action Selection. Based on the emotional tags for hit/stand actions linked to the chunk representing the player's hand in long-term memory, one is chosen over the other probabilistically via softmax selection as follows. For both options, the expected value of taking that action is taken to be the difference between the "joy" and "sadness" values of their emotional tags (and 0 otherwise). Let $Ev_{\text{STAND}}(x, y, z, t)$ denote the expected value of the STAND action for the hand characterised by a total of x, a dealer's upcard value of y, and the indicator for soft/hard hands z. Furthermore, assume that the model has previously encountered the current choice situation (e.g. "14-10-soft") t times. Then the probability that the model stands (rather than hits) is defined by the Boltzmann softmax:

$$Pr[\text{STAND}(x, y, z, t)] = \frac{exp(\theta(t) \cdot Ev_{\text{STAND}}(x, y, z, t))}{exp(\theta(t) \cdot Ev_{\text{STAND}}(x, y, z, t)) + exp(\theta(t) \cdot Ev_{\text{HIT}}(x, y, z, t))} \tag{1}$$

where $\theta(t) = (\frac{t}{10})^c$. The function $\theta(t)$ regulates the transition of the model from exploration in the beginning of learning (i.e. choosing actions at random with equal probability) towards exploitation of the learned values (where differences in the learned values Ev determine the choices to a large degree), cf. [9]. The parameter c represents the rigour with which the model transits from exploration to exploitation, if c is chosen to be positive (and vice versa otherwise). Thus, when nothing is known about both actions, chances of either being selected are fifty-fifty. With more experience, the model becomes more sensitive to the differences in the emotional tags and makes a more rigorous selection. The value $1/\theta(t)$ is called temperature [9]. This form of action selection is analogous to the use of softmax selection in modelling the Iowa Gambling Task with the EV model [9,10]. A difference, however, is that our model maintains individual temperatures for the different constellations of the player's and dealer's hand, whereas the temperature in the EV model is global. This way, we take into account the inherent imbalance in how often different constellations occur in blackjack.

3) Action and Reinforcement/Conditioning. The model carries out the selected action and obtains the results from the environment; either (i) the game ends with a win/loss/draw, or (ii) the model hits and remains in the game, and can thus make another choice. In both cases, association learning takes place, where the hand and the selected action are associated with positive and negative emotions based on the outcome. This uses the Δ-rule, which applies when a chunk x (a hand, or an action) is followed by a reward r. For each emotional dimension e, the emotional value of the chunk x is updated by the amount

$$\Delta x_e := \alpha(r_e - x_e). \tag{2}$$

The parameter α (with $0 \leq \alpha \leq 1$) is called the learning rate or update rate[3]. In case (i) the reward is a blackjack win/loss outcome as defined at the beginning of

---

[3] Low values of α represent slow learning and slow forgetting, whereas high values represent a bias towards recent events and a more limited memory [9,10].

this section, then both the (previous) hand and the action are credited this way (classical and operant conditioning). In case (ii), the reward is represented by the emotional tag associated with the new hand. For example, if the HIT action was chosen for the hand "14-10-soft", and the player is dealt a king, the new hand is "14-10-hard". The emotional tag associated with "14-10-soft" is updated with the Δ-rule and "14-10-hard" as a reward. Similarly, the emotional tag of the action chunk "14-10-soft→hit" is updated in the same way. Thus, the values of the emotional tags for hands propagate from those hands that are likely to receive immediate reward (or punishment) towards those that are more likely to represent an intermediate stage of the game. The model continues with the next choice as described by 1).

4.2   Attribution

In his analysis of casino players, Wagenaar [4] observed that the probability of hitting correlates with the probability of busting after drawing one card. As illustrated in Table 1, players are likely to hit at a hard hand of 12 and to be gradually more likely to stand as totals approach 16. This raises the question whether the behaviour of players can be conceived as "fitting" their decisions to the probability of busting, and ignoring other aspects of decision-making, and several hypotheses for this behaviour (attribution bias, delaying) are discussed by Wagenaar. We assume that affective conditioning requires stimuli to co-occur in short-term memory. This contiguity is playing an important role for crediting the player's actions with the emotional consequences (losing or winning). Perceptions that happen in between the player's action and the outcome (e.g. the dealer's actions), are likely to enter short-term memory and interfere with this contiguity. This results in a bias towards learning actions that are immediately punished or rewarded (busting or having blackjack) and against outcomes that involve the dealer's actions. In this paper, we use an explicit parameter that quantifies this bias, rather than model the perception of the dealer's actions in detail. We define an attribution bias $att \in [0, 1]$ that inhibits the learning of outcomes delayed by the dealer's actions. Technically, we use a reduced learning rate $\alpha' = \alpha(1 - att)$.

4.3   SARSA (Model 2)

The above described learning mechanism is similar, but not identical to a well-known reinforcement learning algorithm in AI, SARSA. Since SARSA has been described in detail elsewhere (e.g. [2]), we concentrate on the differences to the above algorithm. The simulations in this paper use a modification of Model 1 that implements a version of SARSA. Instead of using the above Δ-rule, actions are reinforced by the rule

$$\Delta x_e := \alpha(r_e + \gamma x'_e - x_e), \tag{3}$$

where x is the emotional tag associated with the action that has been taken, r is the emotional tag associated with the immediate reward (wins/loss/draw if the game has finished, nothing otherwise), and x' is the emotional tag associated with the next action that the model will take (according to action selection) if the model is allowed another choice (in case the game continues after hitting). This is done for all emotional dimensions indexed by e, sadness and joy. The parameter γ (in the range $[0,1]$) is used to tune down the contribution of the intermediate reward x' represented by staying in the game vis-a-vis actual reward r. Apart from the incremental learning of chunks, which we retain from the previous model, this implements a version of SARSA. In brief, the differences between the two variants of our model are the following:

- Model 1 maintains estimated values for both the player's hands and actions related to hands, Model 2 only for the latter.
- When Model 1 hits and is presented with a new choice, the hit action is credited by the general (action-unspecific) value of the new hand. Instead, Model 2 credits the action with the hypothetical value of the next action that will be chosen (i.e. it looks further ahead).
- The parameter γ regulates the contribution of expected vs. actual reward.

4.4 Model Fitting

Because the game of blackjack has an important stochastic element, for each of the models described above, and each set of parameters, we constructed ten instances with the same parameters, and calculated the fit relative to (i) the basic strategy, and (ii) the data from [4] in Table 1. Since this procedure is relatively time-consuming, and models have three parameters (α, c, and either att or γ) we performed a relatively coarse-grained grid search (550 combinations of parameters) to explore different models and to optimise their parameters (using the sum of squared errors of the models' percentages of standing in the different cases). We consider it more important to understand how the different models compare rather than pinpoint the exact location of the optimal parameters (which, due to the stochastic nature of the game, is very difficult anyway). We applied this procedure to models that played 10,000 blackjack games each (equivalent to roughly 194–333 hours of play, according to [4][4]). To ease the analysis, we assume that all models always hit at a total of less than 11, and stand at a hard total of at least 18. It is a plausible assumption that human players start off with a similar rule of thumb when learning blackjack, and Wagenaar's data shows that human players generally do not violate this simple rule.

5   Results

We measured in how far our models account for the learning of both (i) observed decision-making by casino players (as represented by Wagenaar's data in Table 1) and (ii) ideal decision making (as represented by the corresponding excerpt of the basic strategy, indicated by underlining in the table) by calculating r^2 (for

---

[4] Wagenaar [4] estimates that 30 hands in succession equal 35-60 minutes of playing.

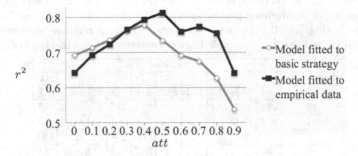

Fig. 1. Comparison illustrating the role of att for the fit of the CHREST model wrt. the basic strategy ($\alpha = 0.1$, $c = 3$) and Wagenaar's data ($\alpha = 0.2$, $c = 3$)

the percentage of standing, as opposed to hitting, in the different cases) and comparing the patterns in the decision tables. Table 2 shows the decision making pattern of Model 1 fitted to Wagenaar's empirical data, with $r^2 = 0.81$. The main phenomena in Wagenaar's data are present: when the dealer's total is low, players sometimes hit when they should stand. When the dealer's total is high, then the model is more likely to stand the higher the player's total.

Table 3 shows the decision making pattern of Model 1 fitted to the basic strategy. The fit is $r^2 = 0.79$. The model uses an attribution bias of 0.4. This bias is less than for the model fitted to the empirical data (as expected), but it is nevertheless surprising, since one would expect that a bias is likely to be detrimental to learning the optimal strategy. A possible explanation is that the attribution factor makes the model play more conservatively (i.e. stand rather than hit), and since the table contains more situations where the basic strategy mandates standing over hitting, our optimisation is slightly biased towards those situations (and thus, conservatism). Despite the relatively good fit, the model still falls noticeably short of attaining the basic strategy, illustrating how difficult it is to learn the strategy by playing. To assess the contribution of the attribution factor att, we compare the fit of the two models while varying att, as shown in Fig. 1. This shows that the attribution factor indeed contributes towards the fit of the model for Wagenaar's data. Interestingly, the model does not seem to depend on using separate dimensions of joy and sadness – a similar fit is obtained using only one emotional dimension where rewards reflect the net win only ($r^2 = 0.80$ for Wagenaar's data with $\alpha = 0.4$, $c = 3$, $att = 0.4$ and $r^2 = 0.76$ for the basic strategy, with $\alpha = 0.2$, $c = 5$, $att = 0.3$).

Table 4 shows the decision making pattern using Model 2 with parameters $\alpha = 0.2$, $c = 2$ and $\gamma = 0.1$, which results in an unexpectedly close fit to Wagenaar's data, $r^2 = 0.91$. In particular, this model exceeds the model in Table 2 by better representing the trend of players to hit at a low total and to stand at a high total when the dealer's upcard is high. The fact that γ is found to have a very low value means that the contribution of expected reward counts only with a factor of 0.1 relative to immediate reward, and thus represents a strong bias towards immediate reward. By contrast, our grid search produced only moderate results when fitting Model 2 to the basic strategy, not better than $r^2 = 0.6$.

Table 1. Percentage of decisions of casino players that violate the basic strategy for hard non-pair hands. Underlined percentages indicate those cases where the basic strategy requires hitting (in all other cases the basic strategy requires standing). Table adapted from [4] and shading was added (gray represents the percentage of hitting).

Player's total	Dealer's Upcard									
	2	3	4	5	6	7	8	9	10	11
12	14.5	33.7	47.7	44.1	29.9	9.4	9.0	9.3	7.7	3.7
13	49.5	23.3	17.4	8.2	8.2	28.2	22.5	17.6	17.8	8.3
14	24.5	10.4	4.0	1.3	4.8	35.7	38.1	39.1	47.4	27.8
15	6.3	3.6	2.5	4.1	3.5	77.6	78.4	63.9	71.5	48.1
16	3.0	0	0	0	0	89.7	86.2	82.8	89.6	71.6
17	0	0	0	0	0	0	1.2	0	0.5	1.2

Table 2. Percentage of deviations from the basic strategy of 100 instances of Model 1 with 10,000 games of training (each) during 1000 further games (each), fitted on Wagenaar's data in Figure 1, with parameters $\alpha = 0.2$, $c = 3$, $att = 0.5$

Player's total	Dealer's Upcard									
	2	3	4	5	6	7	8	9	10	11
12	57.7	54.4	31.8	27.9	32.9	33.7	26.0	36.9	16.5	15.1
13	32.0	26.9	19.4	14.5	24.5	35.4	37.1	41.7	21.0	19.7
14	20.6	14.8	13.9	13.0	13.8	52.0	39.8	55.7	26.7	22.2
15	18.6	15.6	7.6	9.8	11.8	48.5	55.9	64.2	55.5	35.6
16	11.8	12.4	7.0	5.0	10.8	57.2	67.1	62.5	67.3	49.4
17	3.8	1.7	1.6	3.4	2.1	2.2	10.9	9.2	5.1	21.1

Table 3. Percentage of deviations from the basic strategy of 100 instances of Model 1 with 10,000 games of training (each) during 1000 further games (each), fitted on the basic strategy ($\alpha = 0.1$, $c = 3$, $att = 0.4$)

Player's total	Dealer's Upcard									
	2	3	4	5	6	7	8	9	10	11
12	43.9	46.5	34.3	28.3	35.3	19.6	37.3	36.2	10.6	20.4
13	48.4	34.1	30.1	27.2	22.5	33.3	33.9	34.5	12.0	23.2
14	27.1	28.9	15.1	18.9	11.6	37.3	32.0	34.8	24.4	28.3
15	14.3	11.8	9.5	15.7	13.3	50.7	49.4	51.3	30.8	31.1
16	15.2	10.8	10.5	7.7	9.9	42.5	58.1	63.2	50.3	36.1
17	5.6	4.8	4.8	1.5	1.4	3.2	18.0	18.5	13.2	39.2

Table 4. Percentage of deviations from the basic strategy of 100 instances of Model 2 with 10,000 games of training (each) during 1000 further games (each), fitted on Wagenaar's data in Figure 1, with parameters $\alpha = 0.2$, $c = 2$, $\gamma = 0.1$

Player's total	Dealer's Upcard									
	2	3	4	5	6	7	8	9	10	11
12	36.8	36.5	50.0	47.2	46.7	17.8	13.9	6.8	3.0	4.4
13	40.7	42.0	32.8	31.8	27.4	25.5	21.6	20.2	9.7	8.6
14	23.7	23.0	18.5	13.2	20.9	50.4	49.1	36.2	18.7	22.3
15	13.8	14.7	13.8	12.6	8.7	70.0	53.3	63.8	55.0	32.4
16	12.5	8.2	9.7	8.2	8.1	84.8	77.4	74.3	83.3	61.9
17	4.9	5.0	1.6	1.0	1.8	2.1	5.8	3.1	0.7	6.5

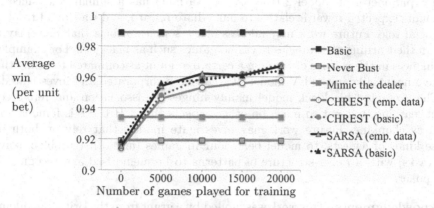

Fig. 2. Comparison between average wins of models and fixed strategies, relative to the amount of training

Fig. 2 presents the average wins achieved by the different models (evaluated in batches of 100, on 1000 different games each), relative to the number of games they are trained on, and relative to the unit bet. They perform quite similarly. In particular, their profitability falls in between the simple strategies and the basic strategy – similarly to the casino players in the empirical studies.

6   Conclusion

This paper has investigated in how far the behaviour of blackjack players in the casino can be modelled as being the result of learning. Our models were found to generate a behaviour similar to that observed by Wagenaar [4], which is half-way between the basic strategy and a bias to avoid busting. We compared the fit of two different approaches to modelling Wagenaar's data; which are mainly inspired by previous work on conditioning, decision making and SARSA. Whereas the fit of both investigated variants is very encouraging, the fit of the model combining SARSA and softmax turned out to be slightly superior in accounting for Wagenaar's data. However, one needs to be cautious with the interpretation, since our results also highlight the very stochastic nature of the game, which makes model fitting difficult. Furthermore, we used batches of models with the same parameters to model populations of players. In how far the models account for individual differences (e.g. use of explicit strategies) still needs to be tested. This work highlights how difficult it is for a player to learn blackjack by playing (rather than intentionally learning the basic strategy). Our models remain still far from optimal performance as compared to the basic strategy, even with parameters fitted for that goal and 10,000 hands of experience.

An important question raised in this paper is the role of biases on the learning of strategies. We found that a bias towards immediate outcomes (the attribution bias) contributed towards the fit of Model 1 to Wagenaar's empirical data.

The γ parameter of Model 2 (the SARSA-variant) has a similar role, since it discounts expected reward relative to immediate reward, and was found to play a crucial role. Future work may address other sources of bias that may play a role in the learning of strategies in casino games such as blackjack. For example, imbalances in the valence of winning a certain amount as compared to losing the same amount, like in the EV model [10], can be incorporated and investigated.

The presented blackjack model mainly hinges on association and reinforcement learning, but not so much on other aspects that CHREST is famous for, such as chunking. Future work may investigate models that rely on both of these kinds of aspects, to model behaviour in games (and other problem solving tasks) with a richer structure of patterns to be memorised and recognised, e.g. poker.

Acknowledgments. This work was funded by a grant from the British Academy, under contract number BR100096. We thank three anonymous reviewers for their useful comments.

References

1. Gobet, F., Lane, P.C.R., Croker, S., Cheng, P.C.H., Jones, G., Oliver, I., Pine, J.M.: Chunking mechanisms in human learning. Trends in Cognitive Sciences 5, 236–243 (2001)
2. Perez-Uribe, A., Sanchez, E.: Blackjack as a test bed for learning strategies in neural networks. In: IEEE International Joint Conference on Neural Networks, IJCNN 1998, vol. 3, pp. 2022–2027 (1998)
3. Kendall, G., Smith, C.: The evolution of blackjack strategies. In: The 2003 Congress on Evolutionary Computation, CEC 2003, vol. 4, pp. 2474–2481 (2003)
4. Wagenaar, W.: Paradoxes of gambling behaviour. Erlbaum, Hillsdale (1988)
5. Thorp, E.: Beat the dealer: A winning strategy for the game of twenty-one: A scientific analysis of the world-wide game known variously as blackjack, twenty-one, vingt-et-un, pontoon or Van John. Blaisdell Pub. Co. (1962)
6. Walker, M., Sturevska, S., Turpie, D.: The quality of play in Australian casinos. In: Finding the Edge: Mathematical Analysis of Casino Games. Institute for the Study of Gambling and Commercial Gaming (2000)
7. Chau, A.W.L., Phillips, J.G., Von Baggo, K.L.: Departures from sensible play in computer blackjack. Journal of General Psychology 127(4), 426–438 (2000)
8. Widrow, B., Gupta, N.K., Maitra, S.: Punish/reward: Learning with a critic in adaptive threshold systems. IEEE Transactions on Systems, Man and Cybernetics 3, 455–465 (1973)
9. Wetzels, R., Vandekerckhove, J., Tuerlinckx, F., Wagenmakers, E.J.: Bayesian parameter estimation in the expectancy valence model of the Iowa gambling task. Journal of Mathematical Psychology 54, 14–27 (2010)
10. Busemeyer, J.R., Stout, J.C.: A contribution of cognitive decision models to clinical assessment: Decomposing performance on the Bechara gambling task. Psychological Assessment 14, 253–262 (2002)

11. Simon, H.A., Chase, W.G.: Skill in chess: Experiments with chess-playing tasks and computer simulation of skilled performance throw light on some human perceptual and memory processes. American Scientist, 394–403 (1973)
12. Gobet, F., Simon, H.A.: Templates in chess memory: A mechanism for recalling several boards. Cognitive Psychology 31, 1–40 (1996)
13. Ekman, P.: Basic emotions. In: Handbook of Cognition and Emotion. Wiley (1999)
14. Plutchik, R.: Emotion: A psychoevolutionary synthesis. Harper & Row, New York (1980)
15. Rescorla, R.A., Wagner, A.R.: A theory of Pavlovian conditioning: Variations in the effectiveness of reinforcement and nonreinforcement. In: Black, A.H., Prokasy, W.F. (eds.) Classical Conditioning II: Current Research and Theory, pp. 64–99. Appleton-Century-Crofts, New York (1972)

Plan Recognition by Program Execution in Continuous Temporal Domains

Christoph Schwering, Daniel Beck, Stefan Schiffer, and Gerhard Lakemeyer

Knowledge-based Systems Group, RWTH Aachen University, Aachen, Germany
(schwering,beck,schiffer,gerhard)@kbsg.rwth-aachen.de

Abstract. Much of the existing work on plan recognition assumes that actions of other agents can be observed directly. In continuous temporal domains such as traffic scenarios this assumption is typically not warranted. Instead, one is only able to observe facts about the world such as vehicle positions at different points in time, from which the agents' plans need to be inferred. In this paper we show how this problem can be addressed in the situation calculus and a new variant of the action programming language Golog, which includes features such as continuous time and change, stochastic actions, nondeterminism, and concurrency. In our approach we match observations against a set of candidate plans in the form of Golog programs. We turn the observations into actions which are then executed concurrently with the given programs. Using decision-theoretic optimization techniques those programs are preferred which bring about the observations at the appropriate times. Besides defining this new variant of Golog we also discuss an implementation and experimental results using driving maneuvers as an example.

1 Introduction

Much of the work on plan recognition, e.g. [9,4,7,5,14], has made the assumption that actions of other agents are directly observable. In continuous temporal domains such as traffic scenarios this assumption is typically not warranted. Instead, one is only able to *observe facts* about the world such as vehicle positions at different points in time, from which the agents' actions and plans need to be inferred. Approaches which take this view generally fall into the Bayesian network framework and include [13,3,11]. One drawback of these approaches is that actions and plans can only be represented at a rather coarse level, as the representations are essentially propositional and time needs to be discretized.

On the other hand, action formalisms based on first-order logic are very expressive and are able to capture plans at any level of granularity, including parallelism, continuous change and time. As we will see, this makes it possible to model the behavior of agents directly in terms of actions such as changing the direction of a vehicle or setting a certain speed. In a sense, this expressiveness allows to combine actions into plans or programs, whose execution can be thought of as an abstract *simulation* of what the agents are doing. This and parameterized actions yield a huge flexibility in formulating possible agent plans. Plan

B. Glimm and A. Krüger (Eds.): KI 2012, LNCS 7526, pp. 156–167, 2012.
© Springer-Verlag Berlin Heidelberg 2012

recognition in this framework boils down to finding those plans whose execution are closest in explaining the observed data.

In this paper, we propose an approach to plan recognition based on the action programming language Golog [10], which itself is based on the situation calculus [12,16] and hence gives us the needed expressiveness. The idea is, roughly, to start with a plan library formulated as Golog programs and to try and match them online with incoming observations. The observations are translated into actions which can only be executed if the fact observed in the real world also is true in the model. These actions are executed concurrently with the given programs. Decision-theoretic optimization techniques are then used to select those among the modified programs whose execution bring about a maximum number of observations at just the right time.

Many of the pieces needed for a Golog dialect which supports this form of plan recognition already exist. These include concurrency [6], continuous change [8], stochastic actions [16], sequential time [15], and decision theory [2]. As we will see, these aspects need to be combined in novel ways and extended. The main contributions of the paper then are the definition of a new Golog dialect to support plan recognition from observations and to demonstrate the feasibility of the approach by applying it to traffic scenarios encountered in a driving simulator.[1] The rest of the paper is organized as follows. In the next section, we briefly outline our example traffic scenario. Section 3 introduces our new Golog variant prGolog, followed by a formal specification of an interpreter and a discussion of how plan recognition by program execution works in this framework. In Section 6, we present experimental results. Then we conclude.

2   Driving Maneuvers: An Example Domain

In this section we briefly introduce our example domain and some of the modeling issues it raises, which will motivate many of the features of our new Golog dialect.

In our simulator a human controls a vehicle on a two-lane road with other cars controlled by the system. The goal is to recognize car maneuvers involving both the human-controlled car and others on the basis of observed global vehicle positions which are registered twice a second. For simplicity we assume complete knowledge and noise-free observations. We would like to model typical car maneuvers such as one vehicle passing another in a fairly direct and intuitive way. For that it seems desirable to build continuous time and continuous change directly into the modeling language. Among other things, this will allow us to define constructs such as waitFor(behind($car1, car2$)), which lets time pass continuously until $car1$ is behind $car2$. To actually steer a car in the model, we will use actions to set the speed and to change the orientation (yaw). For simplicity and for complexity reasons, we assume that such changes are instantaneous and that movements are modeled by linear functions (of time) as in [8]. Concurrency comes into play for two reasons. For one, with multiple agents present they

---

[1] We remark that the only other existing work using Golog for plan recognition [7] is quite different as it assumes that actions are directly observable.

(a)   (b)

Fig. 1. Two cars driving straight with different tolerances

need to be able to act independently. For another, observations will be turned into special actions which are executed concurrently with the agents' programs. Technically we will make use of ConGolog's notion of interleaved concurrency [6].

To see where probabilities come into play, we need to consider a complication which results from a mismatch between a simple model of driving in a straight line and reality, especially when a human controls a car. Most likely the human will oscillate somewhat even when his or her plan is to drive straight, and the amount of oscillation may vary over time and among individuals (see Figure 1 for two examples). Since the observed data will also track such oscillations, a straight-line model is not able to explain the data. Instead we introduce tolerances of varying width and likelihood, where the width indicates that a driver will deviate at most this much from a straight line and the likelihood estimates the percentage of drivers which exhibit this deviation. Technically, this means that the action which changes the direction of a car is considered a stochastic action in the sense of [2,16]. We use a discretized log-normal distribution, where each outcome determines a particular tolerance. In a similar fashion, setting the speed introduces tolerances along the longitudinal axis to accommodate differences between the actual speed and the model.

3   The Action Language prGolog

prGolog is our new dialect of the action language Golog [10]. Golog is based on Reiter's version of the situation calculus [16] which is a sorted second-order language to reason about dynamic systems with actions and situations. A dynamic system is modeled in terms of a *basic action theory* (BAT) $\mathcal{D}$ which models the basic relationships of *primitive actions* and situation dependent predicates and functions, called *fluents*. A situation is either the initial situation S_0 or a term $do(a, s)$ where s is the preceding situation and a is an action executed in s. The main components of a BAT $\mathcal{D}$ are (1) precondition axioms $Poss(a, s) \equiv \rho$ that denote whether or not the primitive action a is executable in situation s, (2) successor state axioms which define how fluents evolve in new situations, and (3) a description of the initial situation S_0. A successor state axiom for a fluent $F(\boldsymbol{x}, s)$ has the form $F(\boldsymbol{x}, do(a, s)) \equiv \gamma_F^+(\boldsymbol{x}, a, s) \vee F(\boldsymbol{x}, s) \wedge \neg\gamma_F^-(\boldsymbol{x}, a, s)$ where γ_F^+ and γ_F^- describe the positive and negative effects on fluent F, respectively.

Our simple model of a car consists of primitive actions that instantaneously change the vehicle's velocity and yaw, respectively. Furthermore, there are fluents $x(v, s)$ and $y(v, s)$ for the x and y-coordinates of the car v. Here, the x-axis points in the forward/backward direction and the y-axis in the left/right direction.

prGolog offers the same programming constructs known from other Golog dialects: deterministic and stochastic actions, test actions $\phi?$, sequences $\delta_1; \delta_2$, nondeterministic branch $\delta_1 \mid \delta_2$ and choice of argument $\pi v . \delta$, interleaved concurrency $\delta_1 \parallel \delta_2$, and others like if-then-else and while-loops, which are not needed in this paper. Also, to simplify the presentation, we use procedures as macros.

The prGolog programs in the plan library describe the plans an agent could be following. A lane change of a car v can be characterized as follows:

> **proc** leftLaneChange(v, τ)
> $\quad \pi\theta . (0° < \theta \le 90°)?$; waitFor(onRightLane$(v), \tau$); setYaw$(v, \theta, \tau)$;
> $\quad\quad\quad \pi\tau'$. waitFor(onLeftLane$(v), \tau'$); setYaw$(v, 0°, \tau')$.

This program leaves certain aspects of its execution unspecified. The angle θ at which the car v steers to the left may be nondeterministically chosen between $0°$ and $90°$. While the starting time τ of the passing maneuver is a parameter of the procedure, the time τ' at which v gets back into the lane is chosen freely. The points in time are constrained only by means of the two waitFor actions in a way such that the car turns left when it is on the right lane and goes straight ahead when it is on the left lane. onRightLane and onLeftLane stand for formulas that specify what it means to be on the right and on the left lane, respectively. Using the procedure above an overtake maneuver can be specified as

> **proc** overtake(v, w)
> $\quad \pi\tau_1$. waitFor(behind$(v, w), \tau_1$); leftLaneChange(v, τ_1);
> $\quad \pi\tau_2 . \pi z$. setVeloc(v, z, τ_2);
> $\quad \pi\tau_3$. waitFor(behind$(w, v), \tau_3$); rightLaneChange(v, τ_3).

3.1 Stepwise Execution

To carry out plan recognition online, we will need to execute programs incrementally. ConGolog [6] introduced a transition semantics that does exactly this: a transition from a configuration (δ, s) to (δ', s') is possible if performing a single step of program δ in situation s leads to s' with remaining program δ'.

3.2 Time and Continuous Change

In the situation calculus, actions have no duration but are executed instantaneously. Hence, to get the position of a vehicle at a certain point in time, continuous fluents like $x(v, s)$ and $y(v, s)$ need to return *functions of time* which can be evaluated at a given time to get a concrete position. As in ccGolog [8], $y(v, s)$ returns a term $linear(a_0, a_1, \tau_0)$ which stands for the function of time $f(\tau) = a_0 + a_1 \cdot (\tau - \tau_0)$. The definition of successor state axioms for $x(v, s)$ and $y(v, s)$ to represent the effects of primitive actions is lengthy but straightforward.

We adopt sequential, temporal Golog's [15] convention that each primitive action has a timestamp parameter. Since these timestamped actions occur in situation terms, each situation has a starting time which is the timestamp of the last executed action. The precondition of a waitFor(ϕ, τ) action restricts the feasible timestamps$\tau$to points in time at which the condition $Poss(\text{waitFor}(\phi, \tau), s) \equiv \phi[s, \tau]$

holds. Here the syntax $\phi[s, \tau]$ restores the situation parameter s in the fluents in ϕ and evaluates continuous fluents at time τ. This precondition already captures the "effect" of waitFor, because just by occurring in the situation term, it shifts time to some point at which ϕ holds.

3.3   Stochastic Actions and Decision Theory

We include *stochastic actions* in prGolog which are implemented similarly to [16]. The meaning of performing a stochastic action is that nature chooses among a set of possible outcome actions. Stochastic actions, just like primitive actions, have a timestamp parameter. The setYaw action mentioned in the lane change program is a stochastic action. All outcomes for setYaw set the *yaw* fluent to the same value, they only differ in the width of the tolerance corridor described in Section 2 and Figure 1. In particular, the outcome actions are setYaw*$(v, \theta, \Delta, \tau)$ where Δ specifies the width of the tolerance corridor. Note that only the tolerance parameter Δ follows some probability distribution; the vehicle identifier v, the angle θ, and the timestamp τ are taken as they stand. We introduce a new fluent for the lateral tolerance, $\Delta y(v, s)$ whose value is the Δ of the last *setYaw** action. For setVeloc(v, z, τ) we proceed analogously.

Stochastic actions introduce a second kind of uncertainty in programs: while nondeterministic features like the pick operator $\pi v . \delta$ represent choice points for the *agent*, the outcome of stochastic actions is chosen by *nature*. To make nondeterminism and stochastic actions coexist, we resolve the former in the spirit of DTGolog [2]: we always choose the branch that maximizes a *reward function*.

4   The Semantics of prGolog

For each program from the plan library we want to determine whether or not it explains the observations. To this end we resolve nondeterminism (e.g., concurrency by interleaving) decision-theoretically: when a nondeterministic choice point is reached, the interpreter opts for the alternative that leads to a situation s with the greatest reward $r(s)$. To keep computation feasible only the next l actions of each nondeterminstic alternative are evaluated. In Section 5 a reward function is shown that favors situations that explain more observations. Thus program execution reflects (observed) reality as closely as possible.

The central part of the interpreter is the function $transPr(\delta, s, l, \delta', s') = p$ which assigns probabilities p to one-step transitions from (δ, s) to (δ', s'). A transition is assigned a probability greater zero iff it is an optimal transition wrt reward function r and look-ahead l; all other transitions are assigned a probability of 0. $transPr$ determines the optimal transition by inspecting all potential alternatives as follows: (1) compute all decompositions $\gamma; \delta'$ of δ where γ is a next *atomic action* of δ, (2) find a *best* decomposition $\gamma; \delta'$, and (3) execute γ. By *atomic action*, we mean primitive, test, and stochastic actions. A decomposition is considered *best* if no other decomposition leads to a higher-rewarded situation on average after l more transitions.

At first, we will define the predicate $Next(\delta, \gamma, \delta')$ that determines all decompositions $\gamma; \delta'$ of a program δ. We proceed with the function $transAtPr(\gamma, s, s') = p$ which holds if executing the atomic action γ in s leads to s' with probability p. Then, we define a function $value(\delta, s, l) = v$ which computes the estimated reward v that is achieved after l transitions of δ in s given that nondeterminism is resolved in an optimal way. $value$ is used to rate alternative decompositions. With these helpers, we can define $transPr(\delta, s, l, \delta', s') = p$.

In our definition we often use **if** $\exists x . \phi(x)$ **then** $\psi_1(x)$ **else** ψ_2 as a macro for $(\exists x . \phi(x) \wedge \psi_1(x)) \vee (\forall x . \neg\phi(x) \wedge \psi_2)$ where x is also visible in the then-branch.

4.1 Program Decomposition

$Next(\delta, \gamma, \delta')$ holds iff γ is a next atomic action of δ and δ' is the rest. It very much resembles ConGolog's *Trans* predicate except that it does not actually execute an action. Like ConGolog, we need to quantify over programs; for the details on this see [6]. Here are the definitions of *Next* needed for this paper:

$$Next(Nil, \gamma, \delta') \equiv False$$
$$Next(\alpha, \gamma, \delta') \equiv \gamma = \alpha \wedge \delta' = Nil \quad (\alpha \text{ atomic})$$
$$Next(\pi v . \delta, \gamma, \delta') \equiv \exists x . Next(\delta_x^v, \gamma, \delta')$$
$$Next(\delta_1; \delta_2, \gamma, \delta') \equiv \exists \delta_1' . Next(\delta_1, \gamma, \delta_1') \wedge \delta' = \delta_1'; \delta_2 \vee$$
$$Final(\delta_1) \wedge Next(\delta_2, \gamma, \delta')$$
$$Next(\delta_1 \parallel \delta_2, \gamma, \delta') \equiv \exists \delta_1' . Next(\delta_1, \gamma, \delta_1') \wedge \delta' = \delta_1' \parallel \delta_2 \vee$$
$$\exists \delta_2' . Next(\delta_2, \gamma, \delta_2') \wedge \delta' = \delta_1 \parallel \delta_2'.$$

δ_x^v stands for the substitution of x for v in δ. $Final(\delta)$ holds iff program execution may terminate, e.g., for $\delta = Nil$. We omit it for brevity.

4.2 Executing Atomic Actions

Now we turn to executing atomic actions with $transAtPr$. *Test actions* are the easiest case because the test formula is evaluated in the current situation:

$$transAtPr(\phi?, s, s') = p \equiv \text{if } \phi[s] \wedge s' = s \text{ then } p = 1 \text{ else } p = 0.$$

Primitive actions have timestamps encoded as parameters like in sequential, temporal Golog, which are of the newly added sort real [15]. The BAT needs to provide axioms $time(A(x, \tau)) = \tau$ to extract the timestamp τ of any primitive action $A(x, \tau)$ and the function $start(do(a, s)) = time(a)$ which returns a situation's start time. The initial time $start(S_0)$ may be defined in the BAT. Using these, $transAtPr$ can ensure monotonicity of time:

$$transAtPr(\alpha, s, s') = p \equiv$$
$$\text{if } time(\alpha[s]) \geq start(s) \wedge Poss(\alpha[s], s) \wedge s' = do(\alpha[s], s)$$
$$\text{then } p = 1 \text{ else } p = 0.$$

When a *stochastic action* β is executed, the idea is that nature randomly picks a primitive outcome action α. The axiomatizer is supposed to provide two macros $Choice(\beta, \alpha)$ and $prob_0(\beta, \alpha, s) = p$ as in [16]. The former denotes that α is a feasible outcome action of β, the latter returns the probability of nature actually choosing α in s. Probabilities are of sort real. The number of outcome actions must be finite. The axiomatizer must ensure that (1) any executable outcome action has a positive probability, (2) if any of the outcome actions is executable, then the probabilities of all executable outcome actions add up to 1, (3) no stochastic actions have any outcome action in common, and (4) primitive outcome actions do not occur in programs as primitive actions. The *transAtPr* rule returns the probability of the outcome action specified in s' if its precondition holds and 0 otherwise:

$$transAtPr(\beta, s, s') = p \equiv$$
$$\textbf{if } \exists \alpha, p' . \, Choice(\beta, \alpha) \wedge transAtPr(\alpha, s, s') \cdot prob_0(\beta, \alpha, s) = p' \wedge p' > 0$$
$$\textbf{then } p = p' \textbf{ else } p = 0.$$

4.3 Rating Programs by Reward

The function *value* uses *transAtPr* to determine the maximum (wrt nondeterminism) estimated (wrt stochastic actions) reward achieved by a program. For a program δ and a situation s, *value* inspects the tree of situations induced by stochastic actions in δ up to a depth of look-ahead l or until the remaining program is final and computes the weighted average reward of the reached situations:

$$value(\delta, s, l) = v \equiv$$
$$\textbf{if } \exists v' . \, v' = \max_{\{(\gamma, \delta') | Next(\delta, \gamma, \delta')\}} \sum_{\{(s', p) | transAtPr(\gamma, s, s') = p \wedge p > 0\}} p \cdot value(\delta', s', l - 1) \wedge$$
$$l > 0 \wedge (Final(\delta) \supset v' > r(s))$$
$$\textbf{then } v = v' \textbf{ else } v = r(s).$$

The expression $\max_{\{(\gamma, \delta') | Next(\delta, \gamma, \delta')\}} f(\gamma, \delta') = v$ stands for

$$\exists \gamma, \delta' . \, Next(\delta, \gamma, \delta') \wedge v = f(\gamma, \delta') \wedge (\forall \gamma', \delta'')(Next(\delta, \gamma', \delta'') \supset v \geq f(\gamma', \delta'')).$$

For an axiomatization of the sum we refer to [1].

4.4 Transition Semantics

Finally, *transPr* simply looks for an optimal decomposition $\gamma; \delta'$ and executes γ:

$$transPr(\delta, s, l, \delta', s') = p \equiv$$
$$\textbf{if } \exists \gamma . \, Next(\delta, \gamma, \delta') \wedge transAtPr(\gamma, s, s') > 0 \wedge$$
$$(\forall \gamma', \delta'' . \, Next(\delta, \gamma', \delta'') \supset value(\gamma; \delta', s, l) \geq value(\gamma'; \delta'', s, l))$$
$$\textbf{then } transAtPr(\gamma, s, s') = p \textbf{ else } p = 0.$$

The function is consistent, i.e., $transPr(\delta, s, l, \delta', s')$ returns a unique p, for the following reason: If a primitive or a test action is executed, the argument is trivial. If a stochastic action β is executed, this is reflected in $s' = do(\alpha, s)$ for some primitive outcome action α and the only cause of α is β due to requirements (3) and (4). We will see that $transPr$ is all we need for online plan recognition.

5   Plan Recognition by Program Execution

In our framework, plan recognition is the problem of executing a prGolog program in a way that matches the observations. An observation is a formula ϕ which holds in the world at time τ according to the sensors (e.g., ϕ might tell us the position of each car at time τ). For each of the, say, n vehicles, we choose a δ_i from the pre-defined programs as hypothetical explanation for the ith driver's behavior. These hypotheses are combined to a comprehensive hypothesis $\delta = (\delta_1 \| \ldots \| \delta_n)$ which captures that the vehicles act in parallel. We determine whether or not δ explains the observations. By computing a confidence for each explanation we can ultimately rank competing hypotheses.

To find a match between observations and program execution, we turn each observation into an action $\mathsf{match}(\phi, \tau)$ which is meant to synchronize the model with the observation. This is ensured by the precondition $Poss(\mathsf{match}(\phi, \tau), s) \equiv \phi[s, \tau]$ which asserts that the observed formula ϕ actually holds in the model at time τ. Hence, an executed match action represents an explained observation.

Plan recognition can be carried out online roughly by repeating two steps:
(1) If a new observation is present, merge the match action into the rest program.
(2) Execute the next step of the hypothesis program.
In practical plan recognition, it makes sense to be greedy for explaining as many observations as possible, with the ultimate goal of explaining all of them. This behavior can be easily implemented with our decision-theoretic semantics. Recall that the interpreter resolves nondeterministic choice points by opting for the alternative that yields the highest reward $r(s)$ after l further look-ahead steps. We achieve greedy behavior when we provide the reward function

$$r(s) = \text{number of } \mathsf{match} \text{ actions in } s.$$

While being greedy is not always optimal, this heuristic allows us to do plan recognition online. Since the interpreter can execute no more than l match actions during its look-ahead, nondeterminism is resolved optimally as long as the program contains at least l match actions. Thus, (2) is more precisely:
(2) If the program contains at least l match actions, execute the next step.

We now detail steps (1) and (2). Let δ be the hypothesis. The initial plan recognition state is $\{(\delta, S_0, 1)\}$ because, as nothing of δ has been executed yet, it may be a perfect hypothesis. As time goes by, δ is executed incrementally. However, the set grows because each outcome of a stochastic action must be represented by a tuple in the set.

Incoming observations are merged into the candidate programs by appending them with the concurrency operator. That is, when ϕ is observed at time τ we replace all configurations (δ, s, p) with new configurations $(\delta \| \mathsf{match}(\phi, \tau), s, p)$. When the number of match actions in δ is at least l, we are safe to update the configuration by triggering the next transition. Thus, upon matching the observation ϕ at time τ, a state $\mathcal{S}_i$ of the plan recognition evolves as follows:

$$\mathcal{S}_{i+1} = \{(\delta', s', p') \mid (\delta, s, p) \in \mathcal{S}_i, \delta \text{ contains } \geq l-1 \text{ match actions,}$$
$$\mathcal{D} \cup \mathcal{C} \models p \cdot transPr(\delta \| \mathsf{match}(\phi, \tau), s, l, \delta', s') = p' \wedge p' > 0\}$$
$$\cup \{(\delta \| \mathsf{match}(\phi, \tau), s, p) \mid (\delta, s, p) \in \mathcal{S}_i, \delta \text{ contains } < l-1 \text{ match actions}\}$$

where $\mathcal{D}$ is a BAT and $\mathcal{C}$ are the axioms of our language. To simplify the presentation we assume complete information about the initial situation S_0.

Finally, we roughly describe how hypotheses can be ranked. Generally the idea is to sum the probabilities of those executions that explain the observations. By this means the hypothesis go_straight is ranked very well in Figure 1a, whereas the wide oscillations in Figure 1b cut off many of the likely but small tolerances. A complication arises because $transPr$ does not commit to a single nondeterministic alternative if both are equally good wrt their reward. While our implementation simply commits to one of the branches which are on a par, $transPr$ returns positive probabilities for all of them. With requirements (3) and (4) from Subsection 4.2 it is possible to keep apart these alternative executions. For space reasons we only sketch the idea: let $U_i \subseteq \mathcal{S}_i$ be a set of configurations (δ, s, p) that stem from *one* of the optimal ways to resolve nondeterminism. Then the confidence of U_i being an explanation so far is $\sum_{(\delta,s,p)\in U_i} p \cdot \frac{r(s)}{r(s)+m(\delta)}$ where $m(\delta)$ is the number of match actions that occur in the program δ. This weighs the probability of reaching the configuration (δ, s, p) by the ratio of explained observations $r(s)$ in the total number of observations $r(s) + m(\delta)$. Since there are generally multiple U_i, the confidence of the whole hypothesis is $\max_{U_i} \sum_{(\delta,s,p)\in U_i} p \cdot \frac{r(s)}{r(s)+m(\delta)}$.

6   Classifying Driving Maneuvers

We have implemented a prGolog interpreter and the online plan recognition procedure in ECLiPSe-CLP,[2] a Prolog dialect. We evaluated the system with a driving simulation, TORCS,[3] to recognize driving maneuvers. Our car model is implemented in terms of stochastic actions like setVeloc and setYaw and fluents like x and y which are functions of the velocity, yaw, and time. The preconditions of primitive actions, particularly of waitFor and match, impose constraints on these functions. For performance reasons we restrict the physical values like yaw and velocity to finite domains and allow only timestamps to range over the full floating point numbers so that we end up with *linear equations*. To solve these linear systems we use the constraint solver COIN-OR CLP.[4] The look-ahead to resolve nondeterministic choice points varies between two and three.

---

[2] http://www.eclipseclp.org/
[3] http://torcs.sourceforge.net/
[4] http://www.coin-or.org/

We modified the open source racing game TORCS for our purposes as a driving simulation. Twice a second, it sends an observation of each vehicle's noise-free global position (X_i, Y_i) to the plan recognition system. According to our notion of robustness, it suffices if the observations are within the model's tolerance. The longitudinal and lateral tolerance of each driver V_i is specified by the fluents $\Delta x(V_i)$ and $\Delta y(V_i)$ (cf. Section 3). Therefore, TORCS generates formulas of the form

$$\phi = \wedge_i |x(V_i) - X_i| \le \Delta x(V_i) \wedge |y(V_i) - Y_i| \le \Delta y(V_i).$$

Thus, the plan recognition system needs to search for possible executions of the candidate programs that match the observed car positions. If a smaller tolerance is good enough to match the observations, the confidence in the candidate program being an explanation for the observation is higher.

In our experiments, the online plan recognition kept the model and reality in sync with a delay of about two to five seconds. A part of this latency is inherent to our design: a delay of (look-ahead)/(observations per second) seconds is inevitable because some observations need to be buffered to resolve nondeterminism reasonably. This minimal latency amounts to 1.5 s in our setting, the rest is due to computational limitations.

6.1   Passing Maneuver

In our first scenario, a human-controlled car passes a computer-controlled car. To keep the equations linear, both cars have nearly constant speed (about 50 km/h and 70 km/h, respectively). Six test drivers drove 120 maneuvers in total, 96 of which were legal passing maneuvers (i.e., overtake on the left lane) and 24 were random non-legal passing maneuvers. We tested only one hypothesis which consisted of a program overtake for the human driver and a program go_straight for the robot car. Note that even though the robot car's candidate program is very simple, it is a crucial component because the passing maneuver makes no sense without a car to be passed. Hence, this is an albeit simple example of multi-agent plan recognition.

We encountered neither false positives nor false negatives: For all non-passing maneuvers the candidate program was rejected (confidence 0.0). In case the driver indeed did pass the robot car, our system valued the candidate program by a clearly positive confidence: 0.54 on average with standard deviation ± 0.2.

6.2   Aggressive vs Cautious Passing

In the second experiment, the human may choose between two ways to pass another vehicle in the presence of a third one as depicted in Figure 2. Robot car A starts in the right lane and B follows at a slightly higher speed in the left lane. The human, C, approaches from behind in the right lane with the aim to pass A. C may either continuously accelerate and attempt to aggressively pierce through the gap between B and A. Alternatively, if C considers the gap to be too small,

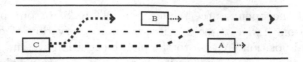

Fig. 2. While B passes A, C may choose between two maneuvers

he or she may decelerate, swing out behind B, and cautiously pass A. To keep the equations linear, we approximate acceleration by incrementing the velocity in the model iteratively instead of setting it just once. Our system compares two competing hypotheses, one for C driving cautiously and one for the aggressive maneuver. The candidates for A and B are simply go_straight again. Note that although the programs for A and B are very simple, they are crucial because otherwise A and B would not move in the model.

We conducted this experiment 24 times with two different test drivers for C, each driving aggressively and cautiously in equal shares. When C behaved cautiously, this hypothesis was rated 0.3 on average (±0.11) while the aggressive hypothesis was rated 0.0. When C drove aggressively, the aggressive program was rated 0.57 on average (±0.12) and the cautious hypothesis was rejected with 0.0. Hence, the system distinguished correctly between the alternative hypotheses.

7   Discussion and Conclusion

In this paper, we proposed a new action language for specifying the behavior of multiple agents in terms of high-level programs. Among other things, the language combines decision theory to resolve nondeterminism with concurrency, and it supports temporal flexibility as well as robustness using stochastic actions.

On top of this language, we built online *plan recognition by program execution*. Observations are translated into match actions which are executed concurrently with candidate programs. Based on the decision-theoretic component and the transition semantics, a greedy heuristic, which preferred a maximal number of matched observations, worked well in our experiments.

The handling of continuous time and robustness distinguishes our approach from others like [9,4,7,5,14]. Neither of the approaches supports continuous time and change. [7,5] also simulate candidate plans, but they require an action sensor, which is not given in continuous domains. Also, they do not provide any means to handle the mismatch between model and reality (cf. Section 2). While we use the plan library to reduce the space of explanations, [14] builds upon a pre-defined set of goals for which optimal plans (wrt a cost function) are computed and compared to the observed actions. This might lead to explanations that appear atypical to humans. We could achieve similar behavior with a program like $(\pi a\,.\,a)^*; \phi?$ which boils down to planning for goal ϕ. However, it is not clear whether or not [14] could handle fluent observations in continuous domains. Note that our approach also works if observations are sparser than in our experiments – the system just needs to match fewer observations.

However, much more needs to be done to deal with real-world traffic scenarios. We believe that recognition can be improved with more realistic models of acceleration and the like. Also, qualitative models like QTC [17] should be considered. The assumption of complete information also needs to be relaxed. Finally, we are interested not only in recognizing plans but to predict potentially dangerous future situations to assist the driver.

Acknowledgements. We thank the anonymous reviewers for their helpful suggestions. The first author is supported by the B-IT Graduate School.

References

1. Bacchus, F., Halpern, J.Y., Levesque, H.J.: Reasoning about noisy sensors and effectors in the situation calculus. Artificial Intelligence 111(1-2), 171–208 (1999)
2. Boutilier, C., Reiter, R., Soutchanski, M., Thrun, S.: Decision-theoretic, high-level agent programming in the situation calculus. In: Proc. of the 17th Nat'l Conf. on Artificial Intelligence (AAAI 2000), Menlo Park, CA, pp. 355–362 (July 2000)
3. Bui, H.H., Venkatesh, S., West, G.: Policy recognition in the abstract hidden markov model. Journal of Artificial Intelligence Research 17, 451–499 (2002)
4. Charniak, E., Goldman, R.: A probabilistic model of plan recognition. In: Proc. of the Ninth Nat'l Conf. on Artificial Intelligence (AAAI 1991), pp. 160–165 (1991)
5. Geib, C., Goldman, R.: A probabilistic plan recognition algorithm based on plan tree grammars. Artificial Intelligence 173, 1101–1132 (2009)
6. De Giacomo, G., Lespérance, Y., Levesque, H.J.: ConGolog, a concurrent programming language based on the situation calculus. Artif. Intell. 121, 109–169 (2000)
7. Goultiaeva, A., Lespérance, Y.: Incremental plan recognition in an agent programming framework. In: Geib, C., Pynadath, D. (eds.) Proc. of the AAAI Workshop on Plan, Activity, and Intent Recognition (PAIR 2007), pp. 52–59. AAAI Press (July 2007)
8. Grosskreutz, H., Lakemeyer, G.: cc-Golog – an action language with continuous change. Logic Journal of the IGPL 11(2), 179–221 (2003)
9. Kautz, H.A., Allen, J.F.: Generalized plan recognition. In: Proc. of the Fifth Nat'l Conf. on Artificial Intelligence (AAAI 1986), pp. 32–37 (1986)
10. Levesque, H., Reiter, R., Lespérance, Y., Lin, F., Scherl, R.: GOLOG: A logic programming language for dynamic domains. J. Log. Program. 31, 59–84 (1997)
11. Liao, L., Patterson, D.J., Fox, D., Kautz, H.: Learning and inferring transportation routines. Artificial Intelligence 171(5-6), 311–331 (2007)
12. McCarthy, J.: Situations, Actions, and Causal Laws. Technical Report AI Memo 2 AIM-2, AI Lab, Stanford University (July 1963)
13. Pynadath, D.V., Wellman, M.P.: Accounting for context in plan recognition, with application to traffic monitoring. In: Proc. of the Eleventh Annual Conf. on Uncertainty in Artificial Intelligence (UAI 1995), pp. 472–481. Morgan Kaufmann (1995)
14. Ramirez, M., Geffner, H.: Plan recognition as planning. In: Proc. of the 21st Int'l Joint Conf. on Artificial Intelligence (IJCAI 2009), pp. 1778–1783 (2009)
15. Reiter, R.: Sequential, temporal GOLOG. In: Proc. of the Int'l Conf. on Principles of Knowledge Representation and Reasoning (KR 1998), pp. 547–556 (1998)
16. Reiter, R.: Knowledge in Action: Logical Foundations for Specifying and Implementing Dynamical Systems. The MIT Press (2001)
17. Van de Weghe, N., Cohn, A.G., Maeyer, P.D., Witlox, F.: Representing moving objects in computer-based expert systems: the overtake event example. Expert Systems with Applications 29, 977–983 (2005)

Modeling Human Motion Trajectories by Sparse Activation of Motion Primitives Learned from Unpartitioned Data

Christian Vollmer[1], Julian P. Eggert[2], and Horst-Michael Gross[1]

[1] Ilmenau University of Technology,
Neuroinformatics and Cognitive Robotics Lab,
98684 Ilmenau, Germany
christian.vollmer@tu-ilmenau.de
[2] Honda Research Institute Europe GmbH
63073 Offenbach/Main, Germany
julian.eggert@honda-ri.de

Abstract. We interpret biological motion trajectories as being composed of sequences of sub-blocks or *motion primitives*. Such primitives, together with the information, *when* they occur during an observed trajectory, provide a compact representation of movement in terms of events that is invariant to temporal shifts. Based on this representation, we present a model for the generation of motion trajectories that consists of two layers. In the lower layer, a trajectory is generated by activating a number of motion primitives from a learned dictionary, according to a given set of activation times and amplitudes. In the upper layer, the process generating the activation times is modeled by a group of Integrate-and-Fire neurons that emits spikes, dependent on a given class of trajectories, that activate the motion primitives in the lower layer. We learn the motion primitives together with their activation times and amplitudes in an unsupervised manner from unpartitioned data, with a variant of shift-NMF that is extended to support the event-like encoding. We present our model on the generation of handwritten character trajectories and show that we can generate good reconstructions of characters with shared primitives for all characters modeled.

Keywords: sparse coding, non-negative matrix factorization, motion primitives, spiking neurons.

1 Introduction

Studies in animal motor control suggest that the motor system consists of a control hierarchy, where a number of low-level motor primitives control muscle activations to perform small movements and a higher level controls the sequential activation of those motor primitives to perform complex movements [1]. In addition, motor primitives are shared amongst high-level motions.

B. Glimm and A. Krüger (Eds.): KI 2012, LNCS 7526, pp. 168–179, 2012.
© Springer-Verlag Berlin Heidelberg 2012

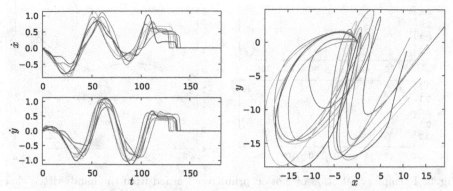

Fig. 1. Ten example handwritten character trajectories of the letter 'a' of our dataset, plotted as velocity space over time (left) and in pen space (right). Throughout this paper, training of the models and generation of trajectories is done in velocity space. The pen space representation is obtained by integrating the velocity over time. The pen space is shown for an intuitive visualization.

We present a model for the generation of motion trajectories that is inspired from those results. We demonstrate our model on the generation of handwritten character velocity trajectories (see Fig. 1).

We model a trajectory as being composed of short parts that are shared between different trajectories and form a dictionary. We call those parts *motion primitives*. In a generative interpretation, a motion primitive can be activated at a certain point in time to generate a characteristic temporal sequence of points in space for a short time period. This dictionary can be learned from data, as will be presented later. See Fig. 2 for an exemplary set of motion primitives that have been learned from handwritten character trajectories. Given a dictionary of motion primitives, a trajectory can then be represented by the activation times and amplitudes of those primitives for generating the trajectory (see Fig. 3). This representation provides an alternative encoding of the trajectory in terms of sparse events, also called a sparse code.

As will be shown later, for similar trajectories, the activation times and amplitudes are again similar. Thus, we can characterize different classes of trajectories, e.g. the character classes 'a', 'b', etc., by the typical activation times and amplitudes of the motion primitives for those classes. To generate a trajectory from a desired class, first the activations have to be sampled and then the motion primitives have to be activated according to those activations.

Thus, we have a two-layered model for character trajectory generation. In the lower layer, given a set of activation times, a trajectory is generated by activating a number of motion primitives, that have been learned beforehand. As learning algorithm, we use the Non-negative Matrix Factorization (NMF).

In the upper layer of our two-layered model, the exact order and timing of the primitives is controlled with a timing model that stores knowledge about the typical activation times and amplitudes of the primitives for a desired class of

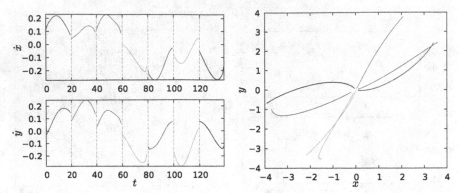

Fig. 2. Exemplary selection of motion primitives learned from the handwritten character data set in velocity space (left) and in pen space (right). In the left plot, the motion primitives (separated by dashed lines) have been appended to each other for visualization.

trajectories. The process generating the activation times is modeled by a group of Integrate-and-Fire (I&F) neurons (one for each motion primitive) that generate spikes, dependent on a given class of trajectories. The spikes are interpreted as activation times for the motion primitives in the lower layer. The input to the I&F neurons is the class-specific temporal activation density, which is also learned from the data.

We discuss related work in Sec. 2. Our approach is described in detail in Sec. 3. In Sec. 4, we show that we can generate visually appealing characters and illustrate some crucial parameter dependencies. Finally, we conclude our work in Sec. 5.

2   Related Work

There are a variety of approaches for sequencing of motion by means of motion primitives. The research in this area can be divided into two groups. In the first group, the existence of motion models is assumed that have been hand-crafted or learned in isolation in a supervised manner. In this group the most prominent approaches model motion primitives with Hidden Markov Models (see e.g. [6]) or Dynamic Movement Primitives (see e.g. [9]). Approaches in this group typically aim at a representation that can be used for reproduction on humanoid robots. In the second group, motion models are learned from the data in an unsupervised manner (see e.g. [12] and [5]). Those approaches typically aim at finding representations of data that are interpretable and uncover interesting features in the data. Our approach belongs to the second group.

In the domain of time series processing, sparse coding has been mainly used for auditory signal coding. In [8], the authors aim at computing a sparse representation of natural audio signals in form of spike trains, where the spikes mark activations of a fixed and hand-crafted set of basis functions. Given this set of basis functions, the amplitude and timing of their activations are learned.

The authors argue that such a representation provides a very efficient encoding and uncovers the underlying event-like structure of the signal. This work has been extended (e.g. in [11]) to also learn the basis functions to find an optimal dictionary or code of the signal. The authors show that the emerging basis functions can be compared to auditory receptors in animals and thus are naturally interpretable.

The main problem of such approaches is that the gradient-based techniques, used for optimization of the activations and the basis functions, lead to multiple adjacent activations with high values (activation traces; see Fig. 4 left), as opposed to sharply localized spikes desired for a sparse encoding. As a consequence, instead of optimizing the activations directly, heuristics like Matching Pursuit are used, where the subset of the activations is selected one after another by correlation with the basis functions and thresholding. We show in this paper, however, that temporally isolated activities can also be achieved without selection heuristics, but instead by directly formulating a penalty for adjacent activities and including this penalty as an additional energy-term for the basis vector decomposition model. During optimization, the penalty term naturally leads to a competition between rivaling activities, eliminating adjacent activations (see Fig. 4 right).

More recently, NMF has been applied to find patterns in data like neural spike trains [10] or walking cycles of human legs with constant frequency [5]. The length of the basis vectors must be specified manually and is typically chosen to be of the length of the expected patterns, e.g. a single spike pattern or a single walking cycle. However, for human movement data like handwriting, where a pattern in this sense is a whole character, NMF in this form can not be applied due to temporal variations of the underlying patters, like different speed profiles. Our approach is to interpret a pattern to be a combination of even smaller subparts (see Fig. 3), where the parts themselves have a lower temporal variability and the variability of the whole pattern is captured by shifting the parts in a small local region.

The above mentioned models address only the learning of basis functions and their activations. Our model additionally learns typical activation patterns for different classes of trajectories. In [12] an approach is presented, which is similar to our approach, but where the primitives in the lower layer are modeled by a factorial HMM (fHMM). To the contrary, we use a sparse coding framework, specifically the Non-negative Matrix Factorization (NMF), for learning the motion primitives, together with their activation times from unpartitioned training trajectories in an unsupervised manner. Further, in contrast to [12], where the layers are learned jointly, we separate the learning for the benefit of decreased computational complexity.

3   Method

In the following, the steps for learning the parameters of the layers in our model and for the generation of the trajectories will be described. The learning procedure consists of three stages. In the first stage motion primitives are learned from training trajectories in an unsupervised manner. In the second stage the activations of those motion primitives for all training trajectories in one class are temporally aligned. In the third stage, the aligned activities of all training trajectories in one class are used to learn class-specific intensity matrices (the activation density) of the I&F neurons that control the sequence of primitives.

3.1   Motion Primitive Learning

We formulate the motion primitive learning in the NMF framework. In general, with NMF one can decompose a set of N input samples into a small number $K \ll N$ of basis vectors and coefficients, called activations, to superimpose these to reconstruct the inputs. By imposing a non-negativity constraint and specific sparsity constraints on the activations, the resulting basis vectors are interpretable as parts that are shared amongst the inputs and constitute an alphabet (or dictionary) underlying the data [7].

We use a combination of two variants of NMF called semi-NMF and shift-NMF for learning the motion primitives from the handwritten character velocity profiles. Semi-NMF [3] relaxes the non-negativity constraint, such that only the activations are required to be non-negative. This allows the motion primitives to have positive and negative values, which we require for the velocity-based trajectory representation. Shift-NMF [4] introduces translation-invariant basis vectors. Thus, a basis vector can occur anywhere in the input, which is necessary for temporal signals with reoccurring patterns. See Fig. 3 for an example of the resulting representation.

For ease of notation, we separate the spatial dimensions ($\dot{x}$ and $\dot{y}$) of the trajectories into distinct matrices, denoted by the upper index d. Let $\mathbf{V}^d \in \mathbb{R}^{N \times T}$ denote the matrix of N training trajectories of length T (shorter trajectories are

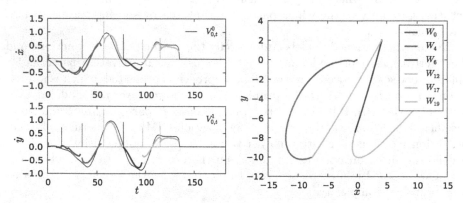

Fig. 3. Reconstruction of one character 'a' from the training data set after decomposition with NMF, according to eqs. 1 to 6. Left: reconstruction of the velocity profile of one input character (black line) by the learned parts (colored thick lines), scaled by their corresponding learned activations (vertical colored lines). The activations represent a sparse code of the trajectory. Right: velocity reconstruction (left) integrated over time, resulting in the position of the pen. The parts have also been colored. Note that shown here are the temporally integrated versions of the actual parts.

padded with zeros), with elements $V_{n,t}^d$. The single trajectories are denoted as vectors $\mathbf{V}_n^d$. Let $\mathbf{W}^d \in \mathbb{R}^{K \times L}$ be the matrix of K basis vectors of length L, with elements $W_{k,l}^d$. We denote the single basis vectors by $\mathbf{W}_k^d$. Let $\mathbf{H} \in \mathbb{R}^{N \times K \times T}$ be the tensor of activations $H_{n,k,t}$ of the k-th basis vector in the n-th reconstruction at time t. In semi-NMF the activations are constrained to be non-negative, and thus $\forall n, t, k : H_{n,k,t} \geq 0$.

We learn $\mathbf{W}^d$ and $\mathbf{H}$ with NMF by minimizing the following energy function

$$F = \frac{1}{2} \sum_d \left\| \mathbf{V}^d - \mathbf{R}^d \right\|_2^2 + \lambda_g \sum_{n,k,t} H_{n,k,t} + \lambda_h h(\mathbf{H}) \, . \tag{1}$$

The matrices $\mathbf{R}^d \in \mathbb{R}^{N \times T}$ are the reconstructions of the trajectories by activation of the basis vectors $\mathbf{W}^d$ through activations $\mathbf{H}$, which can be formulated as a temporal convolution

$$R_{n,t}^d = \sum_k \sum_{t'} H_{n,k,t'} \hat{W}_{k,t-t'}^d \, . \tag{2}$$

Here, we introduced *normalized basis vectors* $\hat{\mathbf{W}}_k^d$, where the normalization is done jointly over all dimensions d. This normalization is necessary during learning to avoid scaling problems as described in [4].

The first two terms of the energy function 1 formalize the standard approximation scheme commonly used for sparse non-negative matrix factorization (see e.g. [2]), where the first term is the distance measure and the second term is a penalization of the overall sum of activations. Additionally, we introduced the function h, which is crucial to get an encoding interpretable as spike-like activations and will be described later.

This optimization problem can be solved by alternatingly updating one of the factors $\mathbf{H}$ or $\mathbf{W}^d$, while holding the other fixed. For semi-NMF usually a combination of least-squares regression of the basis vectors and multiplicative update of the activations is used [3]. The former, however has very high computational demands in the case of shift-NMF and is not applicable for our problem. Thus, we have to resort to gradient descent techniques. The following steps are repeated iteratively until convergence after initializing $\mathbf{H}$ and $\mathbf{W}^d$ with Gaussian noise.

1. Build reconstruction according to Eq. 2
2. Update the activities by gradient descent and make them non-negative

$$H_{n,k,t} \leftarrow \max \left(H_{n,k,t} - \eta_H \nabla_{H_{n,k,t}} F, 0 \right) \tag{3}$$

$$\nabla_{H_{n,k,t}} F = - \sum_{d,t'} \left(V_{n,t'}^d - R_{n,t'}^d \right) \hat{W}_{k,t'-t}^d + \lambda_g + \lambda_h \nabla_{H_{n,k,t}} h \tag{4}$$

3. Build reconstruction according to Eq. 2
4. Update the basis vectors by gradient descent

$$W_{k,l}^d \leftarrow W_{k,l}^d - \eta_W \nabla_{W_{k,l}^d} F \tag{5}$$

$$\nabla_{W_{k,l}^d} F = - \sum_{n,d'} \sum_{t'} \left(V_{n,t'}^{d'} - R_{n,t'}^{d'} \right) H_{n,k,t'-l} \nabla_{W_{k,l}^d} \hat{W}_{k,l}^{d'} \tag{6}$$

The factors η_H and η_W are the learning rates. Note that the temporal correlations (all the sums over t') can be computed very efficiently in Fourier space. Note further, that expansion of the gradient in eq. 6 introduces dependencies between the dimensions. The derivation of the update equations by gradient descent from eq. 1 is straight forward and, thus, ommitted here.

Since two slightly shifted versions of the same basis vector are highly correlated with each other, typically, there are multiple non-zero activities at adjacent locations, which contradicts our idea of spike-like activations that are temporally isolated (see Fig. 4 (left)). Although non-isolated activities might give smoother trajectories, for the interpretation of the activities as temporal events that mark the beginning of motion parts, it is important to have clearly segregated activation peaks. In most approaches this is implemented by a heuristic like Matching Pursuit, which selects a subset of few activations beforehand. Instead, we enforce sharply localized activations directly by formulating a penalty for adjacent activations into the energy function by adding a term h that introduces a competition between adjacent activities. The competition is implemented by convolution of the activations with a triangular kernel function $z_H(k, k', t - t')$ that penalizes neighboring activities.

$$h(\mathbf{H}) = \sum_{n,k,t} H_{n,k,t} \sum_{k',t'} z_H(k, k', t - t') H_{n,k',t'} \qquad (7)$$

$$z_H(k, k', t - t') = \begin{cases} 0 & \text{if } k = k', t - t' = 0 \\ \left(1 - \left|\frac{t-t'}{w}\right|\right) \cdot I\left(\left|\frac{t-t'}{w}\right| < 1\right) & \text{otherwise} \end{cases}, \qquad (8)$$

where w is the kernel width, which we set to twice the length of the basis vectors. In the case of $k = k'$, activities of the same basis vector and adjacent to t are penalized, such that isolated spike-like activities emerge. In the case of $k \neq k'$, the activities of all other basis vectors that try to reconstruct the same part of the input are penalized. Thus, we enforce that approximately only one basis vector can be active during a time interval of L (the length of a basis vector) steps and that it can be active only once during that interval. See Fig. 4 for an illustration of the effect of the local activity competition.

After applying NMF to the data, we have a representation of the input in terms of learned basis vectors and activities. We interpret the basis vectors as motion primitives and their corresponding activities as temporal activations of the motion primitives. See Fig. 3 for an illustration of the resulting representation.

We observed that the activations are similar for trajectories of the same class. Thus, we can characterize a class by the average activations of a class. This will be used to build a model for the generation of activities for a given class.

3.2   Alignment of Activity Patterns

On top of the motion primitive layer we build a model for the generation of activations of motion primitives, given a character class. This model will be

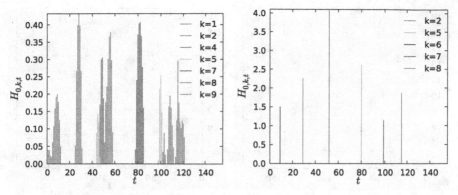

Fig. 4. Effect of the local activity competition. Without local activity competition (left), the activities (vertical colored lines) are distributed over adjacent locations. With the local sparsity extension (right), only one activity in a local cluster wins and all other activities are forced to zero.

parametrized by an intensity matrix $\mathbf{I} \in \mathbb{R}^{K \times T}$ which is the relative frequency of an activation greater than zero of primitive $\mathbf{W}_k$ at time t and a scaling matrix $\mathbf{S} \in \mathbb{R}^{K \times T}$, which is the average amplitude of an activation of the k-th primitive at time t

$$I_{k,t} = \frac{1}{N} \sum_n \bar{H}_{n,k,t} , \qquad S_{k,t} = \frac{\sum_n H_{n,k,t}}{N I_{k,t}}, \qquad (9)$$

where $\bar{H}_{n,k,t} = \Theta(H_{n,k,t})$ is the binarized activity and Θ is the Heavyside function.

The training trajectories in the data set, however, exhibit some variation in start time and average speed, which is also reflected in the activation patterns after the NMF step. This negatively affects the computation of $\mathbf{I}$ (see blue line in Fig. 5 (left)) and $\mathbf{S}$, because instead of having localized peaks, the intensities are spread over time. We align the activity patterns by associating with each training trajectory an offset a_n and stretching factor b_n and optimizing a_n and b_n iteratively by gradient ascent on the correlation between the individual activity pattern $\bar{H}_{n,k,t}$ and a linear interpolation of $I_{k,t}$. After this optimization, we apply eq. 9 again, but with the aligned activities, i.e. corrected by a_n and b_n to get the aligned intensity matrix $\hat{\mathbf{I}}$ and the aligned scaling matrix $\hat{\mathbf{S}}$.

3.3   Activity Generation

To model the generation of activities in the upper layer, we use a stochastic Integrate-and-Fire (I&F) model. For each motion primitive, there is one I&F neuron that activates the motion primitive by generating a spike. As input to the neurons, we use the average activations we computed earlier as the aligned intensity matrix $\hat{I}_{k,t}$ (see Sec. 3.2).

The k-th neuron generates spikes $v_{k,t} \in \{0,1\}$, which are interpreted as activation times of basis primitives, and thus are the generated counterpart of $\bar{H}_{n,k,t}$.

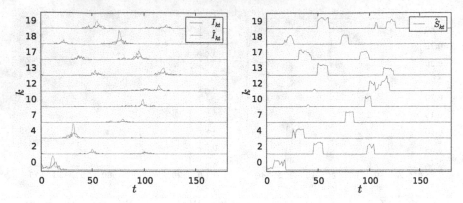

Fig. 5. Left: unaligned (**I**) and aligned (**Î**) intensity matrices for the character 'a' for the first ten basis vectors with highest maximum intensity. The intensities have been normalized to the maximum intensity of 0.235. Right: scaling matrix obtained from the aligned activity patterns for the same set of basis vectors. The scaling values have been normalized to the maximum value of 5.83.

The internal state $u_{k,t}$ of the k-th neuron is modeled by a leaky integrator

$$u_{k,t} = \begin{cases} u_{k,t-1} - \nu u_{k,t-1} + \hat{I}_{k,t} & : t - t' \geq \delta t_{ref} \\ \hat{I}_{k,t} - \nu u_{k,t-1} & : t - t' = 1 \\ 0 & : 1 < t - t' < \delta t_{ref} , \end{cases} \tag{10}$$

where t' is the time of the last spike before t, δt_{ref} is the absolute refractory time during which the load remains zero, and $\nu \in (0, 1)$ controls the amount of leakage. The neuron fires, i.e. $v_{k,t} = 1$, when $u_{k,t}$ exceeds a noisy threshold θ_t, which is sampled from a Gaussian during each simulation step.

After simulation of the I&F neurons, $v_{k,t}$ indicates the activation times for the motion primitives. For reconstruction of the actual trajectory, we also need the average amplitudes of the activations, which we computed earlier as the scaling matrix $\hat{\mathbf{S}}$ (see Sec. 3.2), since the generated spikes are only binary and they have to be scaled to actually use them as activations of the basis primitives. The generated trajectory, which we call $\tilde{\mathbf{R}}^d \in \mathbb{R}^T$, is then computed by the convolution of the basis vectors with the scaled spikes

$$\tilde{R}_t^d = \sum_k \sum_{t'} v_{k,t'} \hat{S}_{k,t'} \hat{W}_{k,t-t'}^d . \tag{11}$$

4   Results

We demonstrate our model on the Character Trajectories Data Set [12] available from the UJI Machine Learning Repository. We use the subset of all characters consisting of only one stroke, since there is no principled approach to deal with trajectories consisting of multiple strokes and, thus, having a large discontinuity, yet. This will be investigated in future research.

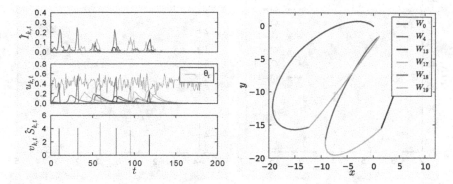

Fig. 6. Generation of trajectories through spiking neurons. Left: Process of spike generation, where the upper plot shows the aligned intensity matrix $\hat{I}$, the middle plot shows the resulting load $u_{k,t}$ from the integration by the I&F model according to eq. 10, and the lowest plot shows the spikes $v_{k,t}$ that are generated and scaled by $\hat{S}_{k,t}$. Right: the trajectory that results from the convolution of the basis vectors with the scaled spikes in pen space, according to eq. 11.

Figure 6 shows the results of the sampling of one character trajectory. It can be seen from the lowest plot on the left side, that exactly one spike is generated in regions of high intensity (as indicated by the upper plot on the left).

The most crucial parameter of our model is the number of motion primitives, which must be chosen manually, because it has great influence on the quality of the reconstructions in the NMF step (see Sec. 3.1). Figure 7 (left) shows the reconstruction error, which is a measure of the quality of the approximation of the input, dependent on the number of character classes $|C|$ (i.e. 'a', 'b', etc.) in the training data set and the number of basis components used. For a fixed number of classes, e.g. $|C| = 20$, the reconstruction error decreases with increasing number of motion primitives. From $K = 15$ to $K = 20$ there is only a minor decrease in reconstruction error. This indicates that $K = 20$ is sufficient for this data set. Note, however, that this is highly dependent on the data set. The necessity to manually choose the number of basis components is a restriction of our approach. However, one can automatize the selection process by running the optimization multiple times with increasing number of basis components and stop when the relative decrease in error through addition of a basis vector is small.

We tested the behavior of the reconstruction error, when the variability of the training data is reduced, by reducing the number of character classes $|C|$. As expected, for a smaller number of character classes, the reconstruction error saturates at smaller K. Thus, the less variability in the data set the fewer motion primitives are needed. Except for Fig. 7 (left), in all the simulations of this paper, we consistently used $K = 20$ motion primitives. Figure 7 (right) shows the 20 learned basis vectors in pen space. Note, that motion primitives that seem similar here differ in their speed of execution.

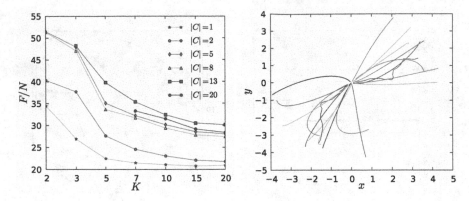

Fig. 7. Left: relation between cost F (normalized on the number of inputs N), number of basis vectors K and number of classes $|C|$. Choosing more than $K = 15$ basis vectors does not result in significant decrease of reconstruction error. Right: 20 learned basis primitives in pen space (i.e. temporally integrated). Overlapping basis vectors that appear very similar here, differ in the speed of execution.

Figure 8 shows a number of representatives of successfully generated characters for all classes. The quality of the generated characters is sensible on the mean of the Gaussian firing threshold (see Sec. 3.3). If it is is chosen too high, some parts are not activated and thus missing in the trajectory, which results in defects in some characters. Further the scaling of the basis vectors sometimes results in overlong strokes like in the characters 'l' and 'm'.

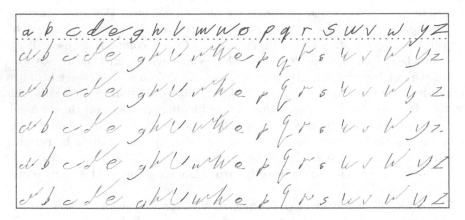

Fig. 8. The top row shows one example training character for each class from the training data set. The other rows show successfully generated samples for all 20 character classes. For some classes of the generated characters, like 'd' and 'z', small defects like missing parts can be observed.

5 Conclusion

We presented a model for learning the generation of handwritten characters based on a locally sparsified and translationally invariant NMF decomposition followed by an event-based activation through spiking neurons. The decomposition of the input patterns into smaller parts and their corresponding composition by learning their timing regime allows for an efficient handling of the temporal variations inherent in human movement data. We have shown that with the proposed model the handwritten characters can be successfully synthesized as a sequence of successive stroke parts.

The Integrate-and-Fire model for activation of primitives, however, sometimes results in defects in the resulting trajectories. Here we see room for improvement. The fact that our model delivers single, isolated spikes in regions with high intensity, invites for direct statistical models e.g. of Hidden Markov type. This will be investigated in future research.

References

1. Bizzi, E.: Modular organization of motor behavior in the frog's spinal cord. Trends in Neurosciences 18(10), 442–446 (1995)
2. Cichocki, A., Zdunek, R., Phan, A., Amari, S.: Nonnegative Matrix and Tensor Factorizations. Wiley (2009)
3. Ding, C., Li, T., Jordan, M.I.: Convex and semi-nonnegative matrix factorization for clustering and low-dimension representation (2006)
4. Eggert, J., Wersing, H., Körner, E.: Transformation-invariant representation and NMF. In: Proceedings of the 2004 IEEE International Joint Conference on Neural Networks, vol. 4, pp. 2535–2539. IEEE (2004)
5. Kim, T., Shakhnarovich, G., Urtasun, R.: Sparse Coding for Learning Interpretable Spatio-Temporal Primitives. In: Advances in Neural Information Processing Systems 22 (December 2010)
6. Kulic, D., Ott, C., Lee, D., Ishikawa, J., Nakamura, Y.: Incremental learning of full body motion primitives and their sequencing through human motion observation. International Journal of Robotics Research 31(2), 330–345 (2011)
7. Lee, D., Seung, H.: Learning the parts of objects by non-negative matrix factorization. Nature 401(6755), 788–791 (1999)
8. Lewicki, M.S., Sejnowski, T.J.: Coding time-varying signals using sparse, shift-invariant representations. In: Advances in Neural Information Processing Systems 11 (1999)
9. Meier, F., Theodorou, E., Stulp, F., Schaal, S.: Movement segmentation using a primitive library. In: 2011 IEEE/RSJ International Conference on Intelligent Robots and Systems (IROS), pp. 3407–3412. IEEE (2011)
10. Roux, J.L., de Cheveign, A., Parra, L.C.: Adaptive Template Matching with Shift-Invariant Semi-NMF. In: Advances in Neural Information Processing Systems 21 (2009)
11. Smith, E., Lewicki, M.S.: Efficient coding of time-relative structure using spikes. Neural Computation 17(1), 19–45 (2005)
12. Williams, B., Toussaint, M., Storkey, A.: A primitive based generative model to infer timing information in unpartitioned handwriting data. In: Proceedings of the 20th International Joint Conference on Artifical Intelligence, IJCAI 2007 (2007)

Nogoods in Qualitative Constraint-Based Reasoning

Matthias Westphal and Julien Hué

Department of Computer Science, University of Freiburg,
Georges-Köhler-Allee 52, 79110 Freiburg, Germany
{westpham,hue}@informatik.uni-freiburg.de

Abstract. The prevalent method of increasing reasoning efficiency in the domain of qualitative constraint-based spatial and temporal reasoning is to use domain splitting based on so-called tractable subclasses. In this paper we analyze the application of nogood learning with restarts in combination with domain splitting. Previous results on nogood recording in the constraint satisfaction field feature learnt nogoods as a global constraint that allows for enforcing generalized arc consistency. We present an extension of such a technique capable of handling domain splitting, evaluate its benefits for qualitative constraint-based reasoning, and compare it with alternative approaches.

1 Introduction

Qualitative Spatial and Temporal Reasoning (QSTR) is a knowledge representation discipline that deals with information about relations between objects defined on infinite domains, such as time and space. For example, two entities in space might "overlap" or one is a "part of" the other. A common reasoning task considered in QSTR is to solve constraint satisfaction problems over infinite domains with constraints from a fixed finite set of relations. With only a finite number of qualitative relations posing as constraints between entities, the idea is to employ inference techniques to tighten these constraints.

Constraint-based QSTR problems can be considered as entirely symbolic tasks where the qualitative relations are treated as symbols. Naturally, this leads to a constraint satisfaction problem on a finite domain where qualitative relations are possible values and constraint propagation enforces matching relation tuples. This type of QSTR has mostly benefited from the development of large tractable subclasses used by domain splitting branching rules [1,2].

Recently encodings of these problems into Boolean SAT-formulas have attracted considerable interest. The obtained benchmarking results [3,4] indicate that the constraint-based QSTR methods very often result in good runtime due to the use of fast, optimized constraint propagation algorithms and domain splitting. However, the results also show that the exploration of the search space is worse on very hard problems compared to SAT solvers on optimized encodings. This suggest that a blend of SAT/CSP and QSTR techniques should produce better results. More specifically, associated with runtime distributions is the

B. Glimm and A. Krüger (Eds.): KI 2012, LNCS 7526, pp. 180–192, 2012.
© Springer-Verlag Berlin Heidelberg 2012

technique of restarting search with learning so-called nogoods – parts of the search space that do not contain a solution.

We pursue the questions of the impact of nogood learning and restarts on QSTR problems and how nogood learning can beneficially be used with specialized constraint propagation and domain splitting. There is a number of different approaches that can be taken – here, we focus on solutions that put nogoods on top of arbitrary propagation techniques. In particular, we mainly discuss a lightweight solution that does not perform a conflict analysis at each conflict which has the benefit of being easier to integrate and causes almost no time overhead on easy problem instances. We only briefly discuss our experience with conflict analysis at each conflict.

The outline of this paper is as follows. In the next section we give standard definitions for concepts from constraint satisfaction. In Section 3 we give some background on QSTR and in Section 4 we introduce techniques to combine nogoods with domain splitting. Section 5 outlines our implementation and evaluates the proposed techniques. Finally, Section 6 gives our conclusions.

2   Notation

We define several standard concepts of CSPs.

Definition 1. *A* **finite constraint satisfaction problem** *(finite CSP) is an ordered tuple* $\langle \mathcal{V}, \mathcal{D}, \mathcal{C} \rangle$, *where (i)* $\mathcal{V}$ *is a finite set of variables, (ii)* $\mathcal{D}$ *is a finite set of values (the domain), (iii)* $\mathcal{C}$ *is a finite set of constraints, where each constraint* $((v_1, \ldots, v_n), R)$ *consists of a relation* R *on* $\mathcal{D}^n$ *and a scope* $v_1, \ldots, v_n \in \mathcal{V}$.

Definition 2. *A* **solution** φ *of a finite CSP* $\langle \mathcal{V}, \mathcal{D}, \mathcal{C} \rangle$ *is a function* $\varphi \colon \mathcal{V} \to \mathcal{D}$ *such that for each constraint* $((v_1, \ldots, v_n), R) \in \mathcal{C}$ *it holds* $(\varphi(v_1), \ldots, \varphi(v_n)) \in R$.

We consider depth-first search (DFS) with an inference algorithm ϕ. To this end, let $dom(v) \subseteq \mathcal{D}$ denote the set of remaining domain values of a variable $v \in \mathcal{V}$ at a search node. For backtracking search, we restrict ourselves to a 2-way branching scheme that employs a *domain splitting* branching rule [5] which restricts possible values of a domain rather than assigning a specific value.

Definition 3. *A* **decision** *on a variable* $v \in \mathcal{V}$ *during DFS on a finite CSP* $\langle \mathcal{V}, \mathcal{D}, \mathcal{C} \rangle$ *is a unary constraint on* v, *written* $v \leftarrow D = \{a_1, \ldots, a_n\} \subsetneq dom(v)$, *that restricts the remaining values of* v *at succeeding search nodes.*

In the 2-way branching scheme, we first perform a *positive decision* $v \leftarrow D$ at a search node, and once we backtrack to this node, a *negative decision* $v \not\leftarrow D$ which is a shorthand for $v \leftarrow dom(v) \setminus D$. Each branch of the search tree can be seen as a *sequence of decisions* $\langle v_1 \leftarrow D_1, \ldots, v_n \leftarrow D_n \rangle$, where at each search node i we apply ϕ after enforcing $v_i \leftarrow D_i$. The remaining values of each variable $v \in \mathcal{V}$ are restricted by ϕ and we backtrack whenever $dom(v) = \emptyset$.

In order to combine nogoods with domain splitting, we require generalized nogoods which cover not only assignments of single values to variables, but also arbitrary sets of values.

Definition 4 ([6]). *A* **generalized nogood** *of a finite CSP* $\langle V, D, C \rangle$ *is a sequence of decisions* $\langle v_1 \leftarrow D_1, \ldots, v_n \leftarrow D_n \rangle$ *such that there is no solution for* $\langle V, D, C \cup \{ (v_i, D_i) \mid 1 \leq i \leq n \} \rangle$.

3   Qualitative Constraint-Based Reasoning

Usually constraint satisfaction problems are assumed to be defined on a *finite* domain. Solutions (or a proof that none exists) are usually generated by explicitly assigning values to variables. In contrast, within constraint-based QSTR one considers constraints on infinite domains like time (e.g. the domain $\mathbb{Q}$) or space (e.g. the domain $\mathbb{Q}^2$). Hence, there is no basic default method like enumerating possible solutions to handle such problems. A key idea in QSTR is to consider as input constraint languages build on *finitely* many constraint relations. In this work, we consider input languages built on a *partition scheme* defined as follows.

Definition 5 ([7]). *A* **partition scheme** *on an infinite domain* D_∞ *is a finite set* B *of binary relations on* D_∞ *that forms a partition of* $D_\infty \times D_\infty$, *contains the identity relation* $\{ (x, x) \mid x \in D_\infty \}$, *and is closed under converses* $(B^{-1} := \{ (y, x) \mid (x, y) \in B \} \in B$ *for* $B \in B)$.

Relation	Example	Relation	Example
I before J	$\text{---}^I\text{\_\_}_J$	x disconnected y	
I meets J	$\text{---}^I\text{\_}_J$	x externally connected y	
I overlaps J	$\text{---}^I\text{\_}_J$		
I during J	$\text{---}^I{}_J$	x partially overlaps y	
I starts J	$\text{---}^I{}_J$	x non-tangential proper part y	
I finishes J	$\text{---}^I{}_J$		
I equals J	$\text{---}^I{}_J$	x tangential proper part y	
		x equals y	

Fig. 1. Base relations (without converses); *left*: Allen's Interval Calculus, *right*: RCC-8

Elements of B are called *base relations* of the partition scheme and exhaustively describe possible, distinct relations between entities. As an example consider the base relations of Allen's Interval Calculus [8] (AIC) for temporal reasoning and the Region Connection Calculus [9] with 8 base relations (RCC-8) for spatial reasoning in geographic information systems, depicted in Fig. 1.

To deal with indefinite knowledge we allow disjunctions of base relations to form relations between entities, e.g. if x_1 happened before or after x_2 we can write $(x_1 \text{ before } x_2 \vee x_1 \text{ after } x_2)$. We write B^* to denote the set of all possible disjunctions of base relations. This allows us to form logic statements about the relationship between multiple entities $x_1, \ldots, x_n \in D_\infty$ by a formula: $\bigwedge_{1 \leq i < j \leq n} (\bigvee_{1 \leq l \leq k} x_i B_{ij}^l x_j), B_{ij}^l \in B$. Such formulas are referred to as *qualitative constraint networks*.

The fundamental reasoning task for qualitative constraint networks is the *consistency problem*, i.e., deciding whether the input is consistent wrt. given inference rules. We here use the relation-algebraic approach that utilizes composition (denoted by $\circ$) on relations to establish local consistency on $\mathcal{D}_\infty$. The composition approach (often referred to as path consistency) is equivalent to a complete set of valid inference rules of the form

$$\forall x, y, z \in \mathcal{D}_\infty : (x\ R'\ y \wedge y\ R''\ z) \rightarrow \neg(x\ R\ z), \tag{1}$$

for $R, R', R'' \in \mathcal{B}^*$ and $R = \overline{(R' \circ R'')}$. In other words these rules remove those base relations from every triple that are not locally consistent. For example, we can conclude that $(x \prec y) \wedge (y \prec z) \wedge (x \succ z)$ is contradictory, since $(x \prec y \wedge y \prec z) \rightarrow \neg(x \succ z \vee x = z)$ is a valid rule. Thus, dealing with qualitative constraint networks can be cast as a *finite* constraint satisfaction problem. Here, $\mathcal{V} = \{\, x_{ij} \mid i < j \,\}, \mathcal{D} = \mathcal{B}^*, \mathcal{C} = \{\, \text{inference rules (1)} \,\}$, where x_{ij} refers to the relation between x_i and x_j. The latter can be used as an intensional constraint to avoid grounding the rules to tables for all triples. Enforcing these rules is equivalent to generalized arc consistency (GAC) (see, e.g. [3] for a discussion and related work). In general, the set of constraints $\mathcal{C}$ can be seen as a global constraint where the inference used is not necessarily built on rules in the form of (1), e.g. [10]. However, we stick to these rules in this work as it is a general approach to several qualitative formalisms. The nogood technique introduced herein is also applicable to specialized inference algorithms.

It is clear that valid rules in the form of (1) can be used to refute statements as every rule itself is a logically correct inference. The converse, however, is not necessarily true, as it depends on a "local-to-global" consistency property[1] of the used qualitative calculus (and $\mathcal{D}_\infty$). Whether there is such a set of rules that is *refutation complete*, depends on the used relations and $\mathcal{D}_\infty$. Problems of this type are in general undecidable, but both AIC and RCC-8 have good properties in this regard as we will briefly discuss next.

For both AIC and RCC-8, rules (1) are not refutation complete on the sets $\mathcal{B}^*$ (reasoning here is in fact NP-complete). However, the rules are refutation complete for $\mathcal{B}$. Moreover, these rules are refutation complete for the sets ORD-horn for AIC, and $\widehat{\mathcal{H}}_8$ for RCC-8. Both ORD-horn and $\widehat{\mathcal{H}}_8$ are strictly larger than the set of base relations and are maximal *tractable subclasses* (see [1,2] for detailed discussion and proofs). The set ORD-horn covers 868 of all the 8192 relations in AIC, $\widehat{\mathcal{H}}_8$ covers 148 of all the 256 relations in RCC-8. Such tractable subsets motivate the following approach for solving instances that has been used in qualitative reasoners: (a) use domain splitting to refine relations such that they are included in a fixed tractable set, (b) maintain local consistency by using the inference rules on qualitative relations. Wrt. (a), it has been shown [11] that decisions should need only to take place once per variable on a search branch.

---

[1] Not to be confused with "global consistency" which is a stronger property.

4   Nogoods in Constraint-Based QSTR

There exist different approaches to learning nogoods. We mainly consider the lightweight approach of Lecoutre et al. [12] where nogoods are only extracted from search once a solver restarts. Another approach is the work by Katsirelos and Bacchus [6] where nogoods are learnt from each conflict. We here analyze how the lightweight approach, originally only considering decisions as assignments of single values, can be extended to generalized nogoods and where this generalization worsens complexity bounds. For this we only briefly repeat discussion and arguments found in the work by Lecoutre et al. as our focus is on domain splitting. More details (without domain splitting) can be found in their paper. In the following, we assume a finite CSP $\langle \mathcal{V}, \mathcal{D}, \mathcal{C} \rangle$ and use the following notation for complexity bounds: n as the number of variables in $\mathcal{V}$, d as the size of the domain $\mathcal{D}$, $\mathcal{N}$ as the set of learnt nogoods.

4.1   Extracting Nogoods from Search

The easiest way to learn nogoods during search is to use the current sequence of decisions whenever backtracking occurs. Hence, we limit ourselves to nogoods that are (sub-)sequences of decisions starting from the root node of the search tree. This makes extracting and using nogoods easier, but also means that nogoods derived in this way are useless for the current DFS, because the 2-way branching scheme already incorporates information from such failures. For this reason, we use nogoods in combination with restarts of the DFS.

It is sufficient to only consider the last branch of the search to derive nogoods, since due to the 2-way branching scheme all previous decision failures are accounted for. To extract the set of nogoods, we consider all prefixes of the corresponding sequence of decisions that end in a negative decision. For each such sequence $\langle v_1 \leftarrow D_1, \ldots, v_i \nleftarrow D_i \rangle$, $\langle v_1 \leftarrow D_1, \ldots, v_i \leftarrow D_i \rangle$ was shown to be a nogood. All negative decisions can be stripped from each nogood since negative decisions were implied by the search. Additionally, we can try to minimize these nogoods by looking for a subset of its decisions where inference already finds a contradiction as in [12]. The number of nogoods derived from a search branch is unaffected by the generalization to domain splitting, unlike space complexity.

Proposition 1. *The space complexity of storing all nogoods that can be extracted from a search branch is $O(n^2 d)$ for singleton assignments [12] and $O(n^2 d^2)$ for domain splitting.*

Proof. We argue as in [12]: there are $O(nd)$ nogoods derived from the branch, each of them covering $O(n)$ positive decisions. Each decision (with domain splitting) requires $O(d)$ space and hence $O(n^2 d^2)$ space is required to store nogoods. □

4.2   Using Nogoods for Inference

Following the approach by Lecoutre et al., we treat nogoods as additional constraints and take them into account when establishing GAC. Each nogood

$\langle v_1 \leftarrow D_1, \ldots, v_n \leftarrow D_n \rangle$ constitutes the constraint $dom(v_1) \not\subseteq D_1 \vee \cdots \vee dom(v_n) \not\subseteq D_n$. For propagation, we consider a lazy data structure built on watched literals.

Unfortunately, our extension to generalized nogoods causes the original approach of [12] to be not directly applicable. For singleton assignments it is sufficient to check if a variable equals a previous decision. For decisions based on domain splitting, we need to check subset relations. We stick to the idea of watched literals and extend the original idea by Lecoutre et al. as follows. We associate two watched literals with each nogood, but a decision $v \leftarrow D$ is associated with a watched literal (v, a) where $a \notin D$. As long as a (v, a) is part of the network, the restriction associated with the decision $v \leftarrow D$ has not happened in the network and the watched literal is valid. Further, we need to make sure that both watched literals of a nogood are on different variables, since two valid watched literals guarantee GAC and otherwise restrictions on domain values apply.

Algorithm 1. Propagation with watched literals for nogood constraints.

1: **function** PROPAGATE(*queue*)
2:     **while** *queue* $\neq \emptyset$ **do**
3:         $v \leftarrow$ pick and remove variable from *queue*
4:         **for** each a removed by REVISE or REMOVED on v **do**
5:             **if** not REMOVED($v, a, queue$) **then**
6:                 **return false**
7:         **for** every constraint C involving v **do**
8:             **for** $w \in scope(C) \setminus \{v\}$ **do**
9:                 **if** REVISE(w, C) **then**
10:                     **if** $dom(w) = \emptyset$ **then**
11:                         **return false**
12:                     $queue \leftarrow queue \cup \{w\}$
13:     **return true**

Algorithm 1 gives the constraint propagation with GAC for generalized nogoods. It is a regular propagation function with a REVISE function that handles the constraints C and additional lines 4-6 that take care of learnt nogoods. The function REMOVED will handle the learnt nogoods and we invoke it $O(nd)$ times in our scheme, as opposed to the original algorithm by Lecoutre et al. which only invokes it if a domain becomes singleton (which only happens $O(n)$ times).

Algorithm 2 details REMOVED and shows how watched literals are managed and GAC performed on nogoods. In order to achieve a low time complexity, we note that the order of decisions in a nogood is originally unimportant, such that we can arrange them in a way where decisions that cannot be watched anymore are ordered before the currently watched ones. The consequence is that during constraint propagation every decision in a nogood is analyzed only until it cannot be watched anymore. This requires a preprocessing step before each constraint propagation that moves the currently watched decisions to the front of the nogood, and requires modifying the for-loop over decisions in REMOVED, such that only decisions behind the currently watched ones are considered (see [12]).

Algorithm 2. Enforce generalized arc consistency on $\mathcal{N}$.

1: **function** REMOVED($v, a, queue$)   ▷ a was just removed from $dom(v)$
2:     **for** each nogood N that watches (v, a) **do**
3:         Let (v', a') be the other watched literal in N
4:         Let D' be the assigned set in $v' \leftarrow D' \in N$
5:         **if** $dom(v') \cap D_{v'} \neq \emptyset$ **then**   ▷ applicable
6:             $changed \leftarrow$ **false**
7:             **for** each decision $v'' \leftarrow D'' \in N, v'' \neq v'$ **do**
8:                 **if** $dom(v'') \not\subseteq D''$ **then**
9:                     Let (v'', a''), such that $a'' \in dom(v'') \setminus D''$
10:                    Replace (v, a) with (v'', a'')
11:                    $changed \leftarrow$ **true**
12:                    **break**
13:            **if** not $changed$ **then**   ▷ enforce GAC
14:                $dom(v') \leftarrow dom(v') \setminus D'$
15:                **if** $dom(v') = \emptyset$ **then return false**
16:                $queue \leftarrow queue \cup \{v'\}$
17:     **return true**

Proposition 2. *Enforcing GAC with the watched literal approach for generalized nogoods adds an additional cost of $O(nd^2|\mathcal{N}|)$ to the time complexity of existing constraint propagation.*

Proof. Working on a decision of a nogood incurs a cost of $O(d)$ (set theoretic operations). Every decision of a nogood can only be considered $O(d)$ times. We obtain $O(nd^2)$ for each nogood, i.e., the overall complexity $O(nd^2|\mathcal{N}|)$.

5 Implementation and Evaluation of the Techniques

We have implemented the proposed lightweight nogood technique for domain splitting, the original technique by Lecoutre et al. [12], and further the extraction of nogoods via backchaining from conflicts by Katsirelos and Bacchus [6]. The proposed technique has been implemented in the qualitative constraint solver GQR [2] [13,3] and thus we have optimized constraint propagators for the inference rules. GQR represents domains as bitsets and assigns a predefined weight to each base relation estimating its restrictiveness wrt. composition [14,2]. These weights allow us to estimate the restrictiveness of remaining domain values by the sum of the elements' weights.

Further, we use 2-way branching and maintain GAC (cf. Section 3). The selection of variables is based on dom/wdeg [15], where domain size is replaced with the weight of the domain. Depending on the used branching strategy, value selection considers sets contained in a fixed predefined tractable subclass (cf. Section 3, domain splitting) or any included singleton value. We here choose a subset of the domain with maximum weight with cardinality used for tie-breaking.

---

[2] http://sfbtr8.informatik.uni-freiburg.de/R4LogoSpace/Resources/GQR

Propagation is handled by a coarse-grained scheme [16], as depicted in Algorithm 1. The queue used is a priority-queue that returns a variable where the weight of the domain is minimal [14].

For all nogood schemes, we perform unbounded learning, i.e., no extracted nogood is deleted or ignored. Restarts are based on a geometric restart policy based on the number of decision failures. The first DFS run is terminated after 10 failures and the limit for the next run is increased by a factor of 1.5.

We evaluate the discussed nogood approaches with the qualitative calculi AIC and RCC-8. Although we have implemented the generic approach for extracting nogoods from conflicts presented by Katsirelos and Bacchus [6], we do not detail here due to a lack of space and the observed running times significantly showing their generic method is unsuited to this framework.

We compare the following branching strategies with nogoods: (a) singleton assignments without restarts or nogoods (b) singleton assignments with the original nogood approach from [12], (c) domain splitting without restarts or nogoods, and (d) domain splitting with our presented nogood approach. For (c), (d) we use as tractable subclasses ORD-horn [1] for AIC and $\widehat{\mathcal{H}}_8$ [2] for RCC-8. We write $\mathcal{B}$ for (a), $\mathcal{B}+\mathcal{N}$ for (b), ORD-horn (or $\widehat{\mathcal{H}}_8$) for (c) and ORD-horn$+\mathcal{N}$ (or $\widehat{\mathcal{H}}_8 + \mathcal{N}$) for (d). To at least briefly illustrate the behaviour of SAT solvers, we include results for the specialized encoding of the AIC from [4] called IA2SAT which is based on network decomposition. We here use the simplification version of MiniSAT 2.2.0 [17] as backend.

Unfortunately, there is no large set of benchmark instances from applications, such that we have to rely on randomly generated qualitative constraint networks as in [1,2,3]. For AIC, we derive random instances by fixing the number of considered entities, e, the average number of non-trivial qualitative relations an entity is involved in, c, and the average size of variables' initial domain, l. This is the so-called A-model [1], and we write $A(e, c, l)$ to denote the corresponding set of problems. We set l to be half the number of base relations to obtain a uniform distribution of relation labels. The set of pairs of entities with non-trivially relations and the used qualitative relations are chosen randomly, such that they average around c and l, respectively. In particular, c controls the tightness of the constraint problem and we use it to obtain problems from the phase transition. For RCC-8, we use the H-model with the set of $\mathcal{NP}_8$ [1,2], which only differs from the A-model in requiring selected qualitative relations to be not included in $\widehat{\mathcal{H}}_8$. For each considered set we generated 1 000 problem instances. All experiments were conducted on an Intel Xeon CPU with 2.66 GHz, 4 GB memory, and a CPU time limit of 2 hours.

Tables 1-4 contain our obtained results where the best results are highlighted. As far as the runtime of the solver is concerned, we can conclude that both lightweight approaches have a positive impact. The addition of restarts and nogoods significantly lowers the average number of decisions and the runtime in every considered setup. We note here that changing the restarting strategy from the geometric scheme to the Luby sequence, changing the initial restart constant, or even applying minimization to the learnt nogoods as in [12] causes little change in the results. The presented results for domain splitting with restarts based on the geometric scheme without minimization are the best we have observed.

From the results, we further conclude that $\mathcal{B} + \mathcal{N}$ does not achieve the efficiency of ORD-horn or $\widehat{\mathcal{H}}_8$ approaches. The gap between singleton assignments and domain splitting remains significant and domain splitting with restarts and lightweight nogoods outperforms all other variants. For 100 entity networks, we can see the nogood approaches to achieve a speedup of about 25-50% for medium to hard instances with very little overhead on easy instances (Tables 1,3). The nogood approaches have an even more significant impact on larger networks, where we can observe reductions of more than 50% (see Tables 2,4). Here the given constraints in networks are less dense and thus (without learnt nogoods) perhaps less restrictive.

Finally, Fig. 2 gives a per instance instance comparison for the hardest set of problems in AIC, $A(150, 10.5, 6.5)$. We can see for both nogood techniques the runtime on satisfiable instances becomes scattered (most likely due to restarts), while runtimes on unsatisfiable instances deviate less but show a positive trend

Table 1. Times and decisions for AIC in each set $A(100, c, 6.5)$

c	approach	solved	average	percentiles (25-, 50-, 75-, 90-)			
10.0	$\mathcal{B}$	997	34 044.83d	395d	1 140d	7 976d	46 478d
			78.67s	0.28s	1.96s	17.96s	100.43s
	$\mathcal{B} + \mathcal{N}$	999	19 601.61d	403d	754d	2 736d	14 754d
			39.09s	0.24s	0.82s	4.68s	24.94s
	ORD-horn	1 000	3 646.24d	**102d**	368d	1 395d	5 771d
			6.87s	**0.11s**	0.60s	2.66s	10.62s
	ORD-horn $+ \mathcal{N}$	1 000	**2 111.70d**	129d	**336d**	**1 051d**	**3 014d**
			3.57s	0.12s	**0.38s**	**1.56s**	**4.96s**
10.5	$\mathcal{B}$	993	57 959.71d	113d	1 168d	13 451d	91 228d
			126.71s	0.15s	1.93s	27.12s	215.01s
	$\mathcal{B} + \mathcal{N}$	996	37 156.55d	86d	767d	5 249d	41 549d
			70.43 s	0.11s	0.98s	9.08s	82.20s
	ORD-horn	1 000	6 716.61d	**57d**	388d	2 230d	10 076d
			12.56s	**0.06s**	0.59s	4.18s	19.57s
	ORD-horn $+ \mathcal{N}$	1 000	**4 169.03d**	60d	**335d**	**1 344d**	**5 688d**
			7.03s	0.07s	**0.42s**	**2.08s**	**9.34s**
	IA2SAT	1 000	15 401.87d	2 016d	9 694d	22 680d	36 388d
			56.59s	34.15s	46.96s	65.91s	99.47s
11.0	$\mathcal{B}$	995	35 040.04d	23d	507d	4 477d	38 619d
			76.42s	0.03s	0.71s	7.76s	78.06s
	$\mathcal{B} + \mathcal{N}$	996	19 680.94d	25d	401d	2 781d	20 910d
			36.28s	0.03s	0.45s	4.48s	34.75s
	ORD-horn	1 000	3 839.38d	**13d**	209d	1 144d	5 694d
			7.23s	**0.02s**	0.29s	1.94s	10.57s
	ORD-horn $+ \mathcal{N}$	1 000	**2 882.40d**	18d	**198d**	**911d**	**4 354d**
			5.03s	0.03s	**0.25s**	**1.39s**	**7.31s**

Table 2. Times and decisions for AIC in the set $A(150, 10.5, 6.5)$

c	approach	solved	average	percentiles (25-, 50-, 75-, 90-)			
10.5	ORD-horn	889	161 697.01d	3 702d	39 021d	358 550d	–
			746.97s	16.38s	182.29s	1 632.30s	–
	ORD-horn + $\mathcal{N}$	929	135 370.43d	**2 424d**	**17 822d**	173 075d	1 089 146d
			578.11s	**9.25s**	**74.74s**	**727.24s**	4 695.58s
	IA2SAT	967	**98 011.87d**	32 152d	81 126d	**146 257d**	**252 273d**
			1 105.24s	377.95s	728.56s	1 446.35s	**3 155.23s**

Table 3. Times and decisions for RCC-8 in each set $H(100, c, 4.0)$

c	approach	solved	average	percentiles (25-, 50-, 75-, 90-)			
14.5	$\mathcal{B}$	1 000	5 941.69d	1 561d	1 922d	3 846d	9 903d
			7.92s	0.27s	0.98s	4.25s	14.34s
	$\mathcal{B} + \mathcal{N}$	1 000	3 442.47d	1 557d	1 824d	2 616d	5 740d
			3.26s	0.25s	0.54s	1.79s	6.73s
	$\widehat{\mathcal{H}}_8$	1 000	1 105.05d	**115d**	**303d**	951d	2 595d
			1.01s	**0.07s**	0.24s	0.83s	2.34s
	$\widehat{\mathcal{H}}_8 + \mathcal{N}$	1 000	**843.40d**	188d	364d	**727d**	**1 694d**
			0.63s	0.08s	**0.17s**	**0.48s**	**1.36s**
15.0	$\mathcal{B}$	1 000	8 790.21d	816d	1 989d	4 947d	16 149d
			12.87s	0.29s	1.47s	5.96s	24.56s
	$\mathcal{B} + \mathcal{N}$	1 000	7 182.89d	747d	1 854d	3 495d	8 805d
			9.19s	0.28s	0.93s	3.14s	10.48s
	$\widehat{\mathcal{H}}_8$	1 000	1 705.25d	**164d**	**478d**	1 500d	3 926d
			1.58s	0.11s	0.39s	1.33s	3.71s
	$\widehat{\mathcal{H}}_8 + \mathcal{N}$	1 000	**1 315.95d**	200d	511d	**1 200d**	**2 577d**
			1.08s	**0.10s**	**0.30s**	**0.88s**	**2.12s**
15.5	$\mathcal{B}$	1 000	6 537.62d	177d	1 412d	3 301d	10 673d
			9.58s	0.15s	0.68s	3.61s	14.90s
	$\mathcal{B} + \mathcal{N}$	1 000	4 339.76d	174d	1 225d	2 600d	6 541d
			5.60s	0.15s	0.57s	2.46s	7.93s
	$\widehat{\mathcal{H}}_8$	1 000	1 437.97d	**99d**	**315d**	1 031d	2 710d
			1.32s	**0.06s**	0.23s	0.92s	2.52s
	$\widehat{\mathcal{H}}_8 + \mathcal{N}$	1 000	**1 197.78d**	128d	352d	**954d**	**2 198d**
			1.01s	0.07s	**0.21s**	**0.72s**	**1.84s**

(cf. Fig. 2). We also have to acknowledge that the proposed technique does not strongly reduce the heavy-tailed behavior (cf. Fig. 2).

In summary, nogoods with restarts clearly improve the robustness and efficiency with little overhead on easy instances. The proposed technique is an improvement and clearly outperforms IA2SAT on instances with 100 entities, and for 150 entities with the exception of the hardest 10% of instances.

Table 4. Times and decisions for RCC-8 in the set $H(150, 16.0, 4.0)$

c	approach	solved	average	percentiles (25-, 50-, 75-, 90-)			
16.0	$\widehat{\mathcal{H}}_8$	989	105 926.94d	2 395d	11 043d	65 433d	273 493d
			226.87s	4.76s	23.12s	137.88s	604.58s
	$\widehat{\mathcal{H}}_8 + \mathcal{N}$	**992**	**57 999.05d**	**1 241d**	**3 802d**	**20 172d**	**116 095d**
			120.45s	**1.81s**	**7.10s**	**41.68s**	**232.59s**

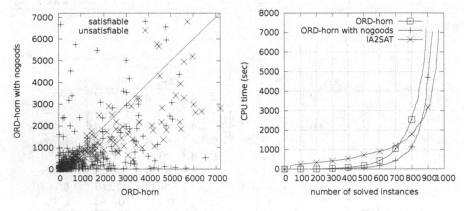

Fig. 2. Plotted data for AIC $A(150, 10.5, 6.5)$

6   Conclusion

In this paper, we have discussed and analyzed an extension of the nogood record-ing and inference technique presented by Lecoutre et al. [12] to a branching scheme with domain splitting. The overhead caused by the extension to domain splitting is low polynomial and the method is still efficient.

We have further shown how nogood techniques are applicable in the field of qualitative constraint-based reasoning and help to improve the efficiency of constraint solving. The profound impact of nogood learning and restarts that we demonstrate also helps to understand empirical results of recently studied SAT encodings. Our results show that the approach is well suited to improve qualitative reasoning procedures, in particular because it can be used with any inference algorithm on qualitative relations.

With regard to learning nogoods from conflicts, we note that while the generic method of Katsirelos and Bacchus [6] has not performed well in our case, we have not tried alternative, specialized methods tailored towards the considered constraints. It was shown by Katsirelos and Bacchus that it is often desirable to construct such specialized methods for extracting nogoods. Moreover, it would be interesting to consider the impact of structural restrictions as considered by Boolean SAT encodings [4] in the context of extracting nogoods.

Another interesting point for qualitative reasoning is the question whether a general approach building on inference rules as used here is desirable or if a focus on specialized inference methods for particular formalisms is more beneficial.

Acknowledgements. This work is an improved version of earlier work that appeared as a poster [18]. We are grateful for helpful comments from our previous coauthors Stefan Wölfl and Jason Li on work done for the poster. Further, we thank reviewers for suggestions and comments. This work was supported by DFG (Transregional Collaborative Research Center *SFB/TR 8 Spatial Cognition*, project R4-[LogoSpace]).

References

1. Nebel, B.: Solving hard qualitative temporal reasoning problems: Evaluating the efficiency of using the ORD-horn class. Constraints 1(3), 175–190 (1997)
2. Renz, J., Nebel, B.: Efficient methods for qualitative spatial reasoning. Journal of Artificial Intelligence Research (JAIR) 15, 289–318 (2001)
3. Westphal, M., Wölfl, S.: Qualitative CSP, finite CSP, and SAT: Comparing methods for qualitative constraint-based reasoning. In: Boutilier, C. (ed.) IJCAI 2009, pp. 628–633 (2009)
4. Li, J.J., Huang, J., Renz, J.: A divide-and-conquer approach for solving interval algebra networks. In: Boutilier, C. (ed.) IJCAI 2009, pp. 572–577 (2009)
5. van Beek, P.: Backtracking search algorithms. In: Rossi, F., van Beek, P., Walsh, T. (eds.) Handbook of Constraint Programming. Elsevier (2006)
6. Katsirelos, G., Bacchus, F.: Generalized nogoods in CSPs. In: Veloso, M.M., Kambhampati, S. (eds.) AAAI 2005, pp. 390–396. AAAI Press/The MIT Press (2005)
7. Ligozat, G., Renz, J.: What Is a Qualitative Calculus? A General Framework. In: Zhang, C., Guesgen, H.W., Yeap, W.-K. (eds.) PRICAI 2004. LNCS (LNAI), vol. 3157, pp. 53–64. Springer, Heidelberg (2004)
8. Allen, J.F.: Maintaining knowledge about temporal intervals. Communications of the ACM 26(11), 832–843 (1983)
9. Randell, D.A., Cui, Z., Cohn, A.G.: A spatial logic based on regions and connection. In: Nebel, B., Rich, C., Swartout, W.R. (eds.) KR 1992, pp. 165–176 (1992)
10. Bodirsky, M., Kára, J.: A fast algorithm and datalog inexpressibility for temporal reasoning. ACM Trans. Comput. Log. 11(3) (2010)
11. Condotta, J.-F., Ligozat, G., Saade, M.: Eligible and Frozen Constraints for Solving Temporal Qualitative Constraint Networks. In: Bessière, C. (ed.) CP 2007. LNCS, vol. 4741, pp. 806–814. Springer, Heidelberg (2007)
12. Lecoutre, C., Saïs, L., Tabary, S., Vidal, V.: Recording and minimizing nogoods from restarts. Journal on Satisfiability, Boolean Modeling and Computation 1(3-4), 147–167 (2007)
13. Westphal, M., Wölfl, S., Gantner, Z.: GQR: A fast solver for binary qualitative constraint networks. In: Proceedings of the AAAI 2009 Spring Symposium on Benchmarking of Qualitative Spatial and Temporal Reasoning Systems (2009)
14. van Beek, P., Manchak, D.W.: The design and experimental analysis of algorithms for temporal reasoning. Journal of Artificial Intelligence Research 4, 1–18 (1996)

15. Boussemart, F., Hemery, F., Lecoutre, C., Saïs, L.: Boosting systematic search by weighting constraints. In: de Mántaras, R.L., Saitta, L. (eds.) ECAI 2004, pp. 146–150. IOS Press (2004)
16. Bessière, C.: Constraint propagation. In: Rossi, F., van Beek, P., Walsh, T. (eds.) Handbook of Constraint Programming. Elsevier (2006)
17. Eén, N., Sörensson, N.: An Extensible SAT-solver. In: Giunchiglia, E., Tacchella, A. (eds.) SAT 2003. LNCS, vol. 2919, pp. 502–518. Springer, Heidelberg (2004)
18. Westphal, M., Wölfl, S., Li, J.J.: Restarts and nogood recording in qualitative constraint-based reasoning. In: Coelho, H., Studer, R., Wooldridge, M. (eds.) ECAI 2010, pp. 1093–1094. IOS Press (2010)

Stochastic Gradient Descent with GPGPU

David Zastrau and Stefan Edelkamp

Faculty 3—Mathematics and Computer Science, University of Bremen,
P.O. Box 330 440, 28334 Bremen, Germany

Abstract. We show how to optimize a Support Vector Machine and
a predictor for Collaborative Filtering with Stochastic Gradient Descent
on the GPU, achieving 1.66 to 6-times accelerations compared to a CPU-
based implementation. The reference implementations are the Support
Vector Machine by Bottou and the BRISMF predictor from the Netflix
Prices winning team. Our main idea is to create a hash function of the input data and use it to execute threads in parallel that write on different
elements of the parameter vector. We also compare the iterative optimization with a batch gradient descent and an alternating least squares
optimization. The predictor is tested against over a hundred million data
sets which demonstrates the increasing memory management capabilities
of modern GPUs. We make use of matrix as well as float compression to
alleviate the memory bottleneck.

1 Introduction

General Purpose GPU (GPGPU) computing is an ongoing field of research
that has been dynamically evolving over the last few years. The continuation
of Moore's Law seems to depend on the efficient application of parallel platforms. We support evidence that parallel programs on the GPU offer a growing
field of research for many machine learning [14] methods. The techniques have
been chosen by the criteria of accelerated *Stochastical Gradient Decent* (SGD)
search. Our main goal is to show that parallel SGD obtains adequate precision
while achieving proper speedups at the same time. We conduct two case studies.

Support Vector Machines (SVMs) belong to the most frequently applied machine learning techniques that can exploit SGD for training. SVMs are, however,
not typical applications for parallelization, due to data dependencies and high
memory requirements. In addition, there exist very efficient CPU implementations like Leon Bottou's SVM that significantly outperforms well-known libraries
for the given training data, so that we take it as an appropriate benchmark for
a fast sequential implementation. Bottou's implementation is already a factor of
about 50 faster than LIBSVM [1] (but can deal only with linear kernels). Catanzaro et al. [3] used CUDA to achieve a 9 to 35-times speedup compared to training
with LIBSVM. Classification was even 81 to 138-times faster. Both implementations used Sequential Minimal Optimization [8]. However, they didn't implement regression and no 32-bit-floating-point-arithmetic. The software package

---

[1] `http://www.csie.ntu.edu.tw/~cjlin/libsvm`

B. Glimm and A. Krüger (Eds.): KI 2012, LNCS 7526, pp. 193–204, 2012.
© Springer-Verlag Berlin Heidelberg 2012

by Carpenter [2] also uses Sequential Minimal Optimization to optimize SVMs and supports regression as well as 64-bit floating point arithmetic. Their code runs 13 to 73 times faster for training and 22 to 172 faster for classification than the CPU reference implementation.

Collaborative Filtering (CF) has become a relevant research subject since the public offer of the Netflix Price [12]. The original training data set poses a challenge to the GPU memory management capabilities. Furthermore, matrix factorization is well suited for parallel applications. We investigated if even those applications might benefit from GPGPU. Kato & Hosino [5] claim that they were able to speed up the training for Singular Value Composition by a factor of 20. In this work they use the same gradient as Webb and an own algorithm for matrix compression. However, they just use randomly generated data and they do not give information regarding the precision of the results.

Next, we present GPGPU essentials leading to the infrastructure we used. Then we consider SGD and its parallelization on the GPU and turn to the two scenarios with individual performance studies.

2   GPGPU Essentials

GPGPU programming refers to using the Graphical Processing Units (GPUs) for scientific calulations other than mere graphics. In contrast to Central Processing Units (CPUs), GPUs are programmed through kernels that are run on each core and executed by a set of threads. Each thread of the kernel executes the same code. Threads of a kernel are grouped in blocks. Each block is uniquely identified by its index and each thread is uniquely identified by the index within its block. The dimensions of the thread and the thread block are specified at the time of launching the kernel. Programming GPUs is facilitated by APIs and supports special declarations to explicitly place variables in some of the memories (e.g., shared, global, local), predefined keywords (variables) containing the block and thread IDs, synchronization statements for cooperation between threads, a runtime API for memory management (allocation, deallocation), and statements to launch functions on the GPU. This minimizes the dependency of the software from the given hardware.

The memory model loosely maps to the program thread-block-kernel hierarchy. Each thread has its own on-chip registers, which are fast, and off-chip local memory, which is quite slow. Per block there is also an on-chip shared memory. Threads within a block cooperate via this memory. If more than one block is executed in parallel then the shared memory is equally split between them. All blocks and threads within them have access to the off-chip global memory at the speed of RAM. Global memory is mainly used for communication between the host and the kernel. Threads within a block can communicate also via light-weight synchronization.

GPUs have many cores, but the computational model is different from the one on the CPU. A core is a streaming processor with some floating point and arithmetic logical units. Together with some special function units, streaming

Table 1. Comparison between several techniques for parallel programming

Properties		API				
		OpenMP	Pthreads	MPI	GPGPU	OpenGL
Architecture		MIMD	MIMD	MIMD	SIMD	SIMD
Synchronisation	• *lock-step*	+	+	+	+	+
	• *bulk*	+	+	+	+/-	-
	• *fine-Grain*	+	+	+	+/-	-
Model	Process-Interaction	*shared memory*	*shared memory*	*message passing*	*shared memory*	-
	• *Task Parallelism*	(+)	+	+	+	-
	• *Data Parallelism*	+	(+)	(+)	+	+
Scalability		+	-	-	+	-
Transparency		-	+	+	+	+
Overhead (implementation)		+	o	o	-	-
Overhead (resources)		+	+	o	-	-

processors are grouped together to form streaming multiprocessors. Programming a GPU requires a special compiler, which translates the code to native GPU instructions. The GPU architecture mimics a single instruction multiple data computer with the same instructions running on all processors. It supports different layers for accessing memory. GPUs forbid simultaneous writes to a memory cell but support concurrent reads.

On the GPU, memory is structured hierarchically, starting with the GPU's global memory called video RAM, or VRAM. Access to this memory is slow, but can be accelerated through coalescing, where adjacent accesses with less than word-width number bits are combined to full word-width access. Each streaming multiprocessor includes a small amount of memory called SRAM, which is shared between all streaming multiprocessors and can be accessed at the same speed as registers. Additional registers are also located in each streaming multiprocessor but not shared between streaming processors. Data has to be copied to the VRAM to be accessible by the threads.

Since frameworks like CUDA have enabled programmers to utilize the increased memory and thread management capabilities of modern GPUs, there is a wider selection of applications for GPGPU. Multiple levels of threads, memory, and synchronization provide fine-grained data parallelism and thread parallelism, nested within coarse-grained data parallelism and task parallelism. Thus gradient based mini-batch or even iterative optimization techniques such as SGD may be efficiently run in parallel on the GPU. Regarding flexibility and capabilities GPGPU is positioned between high level parallel programming lnguages such as OpenMP and classical shader programming (see Table 1).

To illustrate the potential of GPGPU programming for machine learning we experimented with a Boltzman machine for solving TSPs [7]. They belong to the class of auto-associative networks that have one layer of neurons. They are completely connected, meaning that changes in activity of a single neuron propagate iteratively across the whole network. Boltzmann Machines do not support direct feedback, i.e., a neuron is not connected to itself. Thus, in principal

auto-associative networks are no neural networks. A Boltzmann Machine is inherently parallel and thus we obtained a 487-fold speedup for 30 towns. While
the application scales almost linearly on the GPU, it scales exponentially on the
CPU. For more than 120 consumption exceeds the limits of the grapics device.

We encapsulate data fields that needs to be copied between CPU and GPU to
minimize the number of data transfers and to store the data in the order in which
it is accessed by the threads. Size and indices of data fields are encapsulated and
data fields are buffered since older GPU architectures only support 32-bit words.
The indices are stored in 1-dimensional texture memory, since this contains a
cache even in older GPU architectures and every thread frequently accesses the
indices. Besides, this reduces memory complexity because data is conglomerated
in a buffer and thus data transfers are handled in one single transaction. If
required it is also possible to just copy single data fields of arbitrary size.

Concerning the infrastructure, the running time is evaluated with functions
from the NVIDIA CUDA Event API. It guarantees precise measurements even if
the program execution is handed to the GPU for several seconds for synchronous
calls in the worst case. The GPU (GeForce GTX 470) of the experiments has
been overclocked by Zotac. It contains 14 streaming processors. Since the warp
size is currently 32, there will be at most $30 \cdot 14 \cdot 32 = 13440$ concurrent threads
at a time on the chip that will be executed with a shader clock frequency of
1215 MHz. The memory size (1280 MB) is sufficient for all data sets that are
used in this work. As opposed to older GPUs its shared memory size is 64 KB
(older architectures normally have 16 kilobyte of shared memory) and supports
atomic floating point arithmetic. The CPU (i5-7502) from Intel has 2.66GHz
clock frequency and 8192 KB Cache. The operating system was Ubuntu 11.04
32 bit. Dependent on the algorithm and its input data it was necessary to close
the X-server before running the program. We used Valgrind as a profiling tool
to identify the parts of the application with a high arithmetic complexity.

3   Stochastic Gradient Descent and Parallelization

SGD approximates the true gradient for each new training example by $\theta =
\theta - \eta \sum_{i=1}^{N} \nabla L(\theta_i)$, where θ is a weight vector, η is the (adaptive) learning rate
and L is some loss function. SGD is inherently sequential and tends to converge
to local minima for non-convex problems. As a compromise θ may be updated
by mini-batches, consisting of the sum of several training examples. The idea of
mini-batches complements the semi-parallel CUDA programming paradigma

SGD converges to a good global solution, while the parallel computation of
the gradients is likely to produce poor results because the parallel processing
of the input data has the negative side effect that threads do not profit from
and even more do not consider the changes in the objective that other threads
are performing at the same time. A hybrid approach is to use the non-optimal
parallel solution to rapidly converge to some adequate solution and than further
improve this solution by using the CPU-based solution. This approach combines
the shorter execution time for one training iteration on the GPU with the better

precision on the CPU. The time for data transfer alone often exceeds the complete CPU-based training time. Therefore, it is necessary to also implement the validation on the GPU. Although the validation only requires reading access, we adopted the memory access pattern from the training procedure.

Bottou [1] states that SGD is well suited for SVMs because the problem is based on a simple convex objective function. This also applies well for CF. Even for SVMs we found that almost 70% of the CPU instructions are used for vector addition and scalar products, an indicator that the application might benefit from GPGPU. But since the vector length is most often limited to a few dozen elements, standard functions such as those from the CUBLAS-library are practically inapplicable. The input data is already provided as support vectors, which are used to fix θ in each episode. Since the vectors lengths vary greatly, they cannot be simply partitioned on thread blocks with a fixed number of threads. Additionally each training episode requires numerous memory accesses to θ that do not exhibit spatial locality which could be efficiently exploited by the VRAM-controller. As a solution to this problem, θ might be loaded into shared memory. Considering the limited shared memory size of only 64KB the training data has to be loaded piecewise and a hash function has to be defined so that every thread may infer its input data from its thread ID. In other words the hash function allows a block of threads to load exactly those elements of θ into shared memory which are needed for the training data that has been assigned to this block.

4   Application: Collaborative Filtering

Matrix Factorization for CF is based on the idea that any matrix $\mathbb{R} \in \mathbb{R}^{N \times M}$ with ratings can be approximated by a matrix $P \in \mathbb{R}^{N \times K}$ of user IDs and a matrix $Q \in \mathbb{R}^{K \times M}$ with article IDs: $R \approx PQ$. Here N is the number of users, M is the number of articles and K is the number of parameters, that are used to characterize those. The bigger one chooses K the more precisely R can be approximated. This approach holds the advantage to generalize to non-existent ratings based on two low-dimensional matrices. Takács et al. [11] calculate the prediction error by

$$e_{ui} = \frac{1}{2}((r_{ui} - \hat{r}_{ui})^2 + \lambda \mathbf{p}_u^T \mathbf{p}_u + \lambda \mathbf{q}_i^T \mathbf{q}_i), \tag{1}$$

where r_{ui} is the actual rating, $\hat{r}_{ui}$ the prediction and λ is a regularization factor.

Thus the gradient may be calculated by $\quad \dfrac{\partial}{\partial p_{uk}} e'_{ui} = -e_{ui} \cdot q_{ki} + \lambda \cdot p_{uk} \quad (2)$

$$\frac{\partial}{\partial q_{ki}} e'_{ui} = -e_{ui} \cdot p_{uk} + \lambda \cdot q_{ki} \tag{3}$$

and therefore the SGD update rule in each step for user p_{uk} and movie q_{ki} is:

$$p'_{uk} = p_{uk} + \eta^p(u, i, k) \cdot (e_{ui} \cdot q_{ki} - \lambda^p(u, i, k) \cdot p_{uk}) \tag{4}$$

$$q'_{ki} = q_{ki} + \eta^q(u, i, k) \cdot (e_{ui} \cdot p_{uk} - \lambda^q(u, i, k) \cdot q_{ki}). \tag{5}$$

To compare the SGD to a batch optimization we also implemented an Alternating Least Squares optimization on the GPU where the update step is basically $\mathbf{p}_u = \mathbf{W}_u \mathbf{d}_u$, where d_u denotes the input-output covariance vector and W_u is the updated inverted covariance matrix of input.

Although solving this least squares problem normally involves matrix inversion, Koren et al. [6] developed an update rule that is based on the Sherman–Morrison formula and only shows quadratic complexity.

The idea is to adjust the inverted covariance matrix in each step to the new training example rather than completely recalculate it.

$$\mathbf{W}_u = \mathbf{W}_u - \frac{(\mathbf{W}_u \mathbf{q}_i) \otimes (\mathbf{q}_i^T \mathbf{W}_u)}{1 + \mathbf{q}_i^T \mathbf{W}_u \mathbf{q}_i} \tag{6}$$

$$\mathbf{d}_u = \mathbf{d}_u + \mathbf{q}_i \cdot r_{ui} \tag{7}$$

This technique is also based on matrix factorization but yields the advantage that P and Q are alternately being updated so that either P or Q can be treated as in- or output and be written in parallel.

Fig. 4 shows that first of all P and Q are being compressed to the required dimensions. Afterwards a hash function ϕ is being created that maps every user to the movies he has rated. Thus multiple threads can simultaneously process the

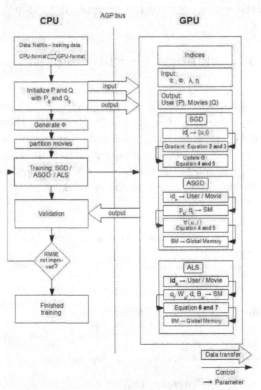

Fig. 1. Control flow in Collaborative Filtering

ratings by one user in a shared memory. Next the training data is transferred to the GPU and the optimization is being performed. Batch (ALS) and mini-batch (ASGD) optimization need an extra step to load the data into shared memory.

As application we choose the Netflix-competition that was finished in 2009 and awarded the winners with one million US-Dollar. First of all, Netflix provided with over hundred million user ratings the biggest real data set for collaborative filtering so far. Secondly, during the competition many interesting machine learning techniques have been developed. Two of them, both based on matrix factorization, will be accelerated by the GPU in this work. Netflix is an online DVD rental agency, which uses an AI-based system to recommend movies to users based on their previous purchases. The system that Netflix used until the conclusion of the competition on September 21st in 2009 had a root mean squared error (RMSE) of 0.95256. The RMSE is defined as follows (τ denotes the training set):

$$RMSE = \sqrt{SSE/\mid\tau\mid} \text{ with } SSE = \sum_{(u,i)\in\tau} e_{ui}^2 = \sum_{(u,i)\in\tau} \left(r_{ui} - \sum_{k=1}^{K} p_{uk}q_{ki} \right)^2$$

Töscher et al. [12] won the competition with a final RMSE of 0.8554. They used (amongst others) an estimator called *Biased Regularized Incremental Simultaneous Matrix Factorization* (BRISMF). It has been introduced in 2008 in the context of a progress report for the Netflix competition. It also uses SGD. We re-implemented BRISMF for the GPU, Fig. 2 shows the profile of time vs. accuracy for our implementation of BRISMF using the netflix data.

Before measuring the RMSE for the first time we train the model once with the complete training data set which is why the RMSE *only* improves by about 10 percent afterwards. This first training episode is also the reason why the curves do not start at time zero. We see that the naive parallelization gives good results. The error (0.9101) is slightly bigger than the original one (0.9068), on

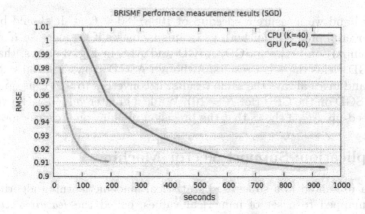

Fig. 2. BRISMF time-accuracy trade-off for $K = 40$

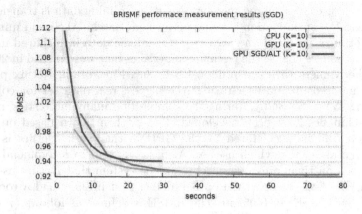

Fig. 3. SGD and ASGD for $K = 10$

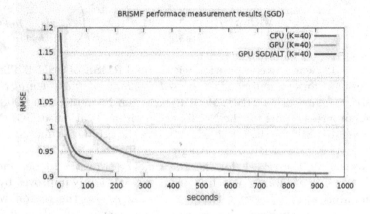

Fig. 4. SGD and ASGD for $K = 40$

the other hand we measure a speedup of $1088/180 = 6.04$. It should be noted that the overall precision for both programs increases if we increase K.

The comparison between SGD, ASGD and ALS in Fig. 3 shows, that alternating SGD yields the worst results. Although ASGD shows a $80/30 \approx 2.66$-fold speedup and gives always the same results, it converges to 0.941, as opposed to 0.922 for SGD on the CPU (for $K = 10$). While a greater value for K gives up to 9-fold speed-up, Fig. 4 shows that the precision remains on a clearly lower level.

5   Application: Support Vector Machine

Raw data presented to a supervised statistical machine learning algorithm [10] is often mapped to a set of numerical values, called the *feature vector*. The classification problem deals with the prediction of the labels l of previously unknown feature vectors $\mathbf{x} \in \mathbb{R}^d$ that constitute the test data. During training,

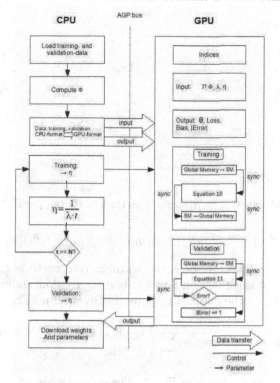

Fig. 5. Control flow in SVM training

a partitioning of the feature space $\mathbb{R}^d$ is learned, where each partition is assigned a label based on a set of training samples with known label. The challenge is to approximate the unknown distribution without overfitting the training data.

Support Vector Machines [13] achieve this task by learning coefficients for a kernel mapping to a high-dimensional space, where a linear class border is spanned up by a number of support vectors that outline the data.

We keep the presentation brief as there are text books on SVMs and related kernel methods [4,9]. Theoretically, it should be sufficient to determine the class border by just three support vectors. However, it is not known in advance if any of the known kernels realises a suitable mapping. The use of generic kernels instead leads to a much larger number of support vectors (which critically influence classification time). In the worst case finding a separating hyperplane takes quadratic time in the number of data points.

Leon Bottou [1] uses a SVM to classify text documents. He applies stochastic gradient decent for training and classifying wrt. a linear SVM. This state-of-the-art already gives good results after a very short time (order-of-magnitudes speedup) compared to other libraries, like SVMLight or SVMPerf[2]. The gradient update rule for an observation x and corresponding classification y is given by

---

[2] http://leon.bottou.org/projects/sgd

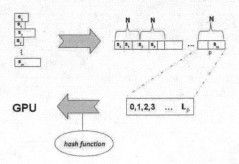

Fig. 6. A hash function to map input to threads during parallel execution

$$\theta_{t+1} = \theta_t - \eta_t \nabla \ell(x_{i(t)}, y_{i(t)}; \theta_t) - \eta_t \cdot \nabla r(\theta_t), \qquad (8)$$

where θ is the weight vector, η_t is the learning rate at time t, ∇ is the first derivative, ℓ is some loss function and $i(t)$ is some random index. The error on the validation data can be checked by summing over all misclassifications:

$$\text{Number of errors} = \sum_i \begin{cases} 1, & \text{if} \quad y_i(\theta \cdot x_i - b) < 0 \\ 0, & \text{else.} \end{cases} \qquad (9)$$

The control of flow is shown in Fig. 5. The compression of the input vectors in Fig. 6 is implemented with an STL-vector and has been accelerated with OpenMP. While the support vectors vary in length and are scattered across θ, the hash function sorts the input data so that every block of threads processes an equal amount of spatially correlated input data. The hash is like a register that enables each thread to map its input to the global weight vector. This is significantly more efficient on the GPU than transferring the indices itself for each thread, because this would double the size of input data. Creating the hash and resorting the input data is implemented with arrays since dynamic data structures like lists are too slow and would over-compensate the speedup from the following calculation of ϕ.

```
int n = 0;
for (id = min; id < max; ++id) {
    weight = input[id];
    if (hash[weight].map >= |θ|)
        hash[weight].map = n++;
    output[id] = hash[weight].map; }
```

To speed up the data transfer, floating point numbers are compressed to 16-bit integers on the CPU via the OpenEXR[3]-library and extracted on the GPU via `half2float`, which is very accurate especially for input values near zero

---

[3] http://www.openexr.com

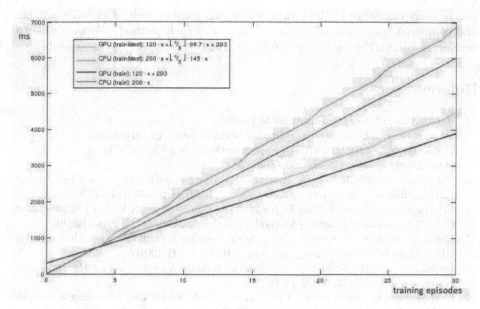

Fig. 7. SVM episodes on GPU/CPU with and without validation

and does not affect the overall precision. Threads collaborate block-wise during training. At first all of the weights, which are required by the threads, are loaded into shared memory. Then comes a thread barrier. Finally each of the thread processes adds the delta to the shared memory. The mapping of shared memory into global memory is implemented by the hash function. Afterwards there is another thread barrier before the threads collaboratively write the delta from the shared memory to the global memory, i.e. add it to θ. Loading the data works analogous for the validation. Each thread checks for the correct classification and adds one to the global error counter in case its wrong. The training data size is substantial ($\approx$ 350MB). Since training takes only about 1.4 seconds and the training data must be first of all uploaded to the GPU, the best possible speed-up is limited. The results with/without cross validation are shown in Fig. 7. It shows that training on the CPU is faster for up to four training episodes because of the initial computational overhead for creating a hash function and transferring data to the GPU. After five episodes the combined training and validation is faster on the GPU.

6   Concluding Remarks

In this paper we showed, that GPUs are already suited to accelerate machine learning techniques with gradient decent. We used different optimization techniques to minimize the memory requirements on the GPU and were able to process hundreds of megabytes on the GPU efficiently. Momentarily, parameters have to be adjusted sometimes to the specific GPU architecture, although this is likely to change in the future. We tested local as well as global gradients and compared speed, precision and scalability of each method. We were able to accelerate BRISMF by a factor of 6 while SVMs showed a 1.66-fold speedup.

References

1. Bottou, L.: Stochastic gradient SVM (2010), http://leon.bottou.org/projects/sgd#stochastic_gradient_svm
2. Carpenter, A.: cuSVM: a CUDA implementation of SVM (2009), http://patternsonascreen.net/cuSVMDesc.pdf
3. Catanzaro, B., Sundaram, N., Keutzer, K.: Fast support vector machine training and classification on graphics processors. In: ICML, pp. 104–111 (2008)
4. Cristianini, N., Shawe-Taylor, J.: An Introduction to Support Vector Machines and Other Kernel-based Learning Methods. Cambridge University Press (2000)
5. Kato, K., Hosino, T.: Singular value decomposition for collaborative filtering on a GPU. Materials Science and Engineering 10(1), 12–17 (2010)
6. Koren, Y., Bell, R., Volinsky, C.: Matrix factorization techniques for recommender systems. Computer 42, 30–37 (2009)
7. L-Applegate, D., Bixby, R.E., Chvatal, V., Cook, W.J.: The Travelling Salesman Problem. Princeton University Press (2006)
8. Platt, J.C.: Sequential minimal optimization: A fast algorithm for training support vector machines (1998), http://research.microsoft.com/pubs/69644/tr-98-14.pdf
9. Schoelkopf, B., Smola, A.J.: Learning with Kernels. MIT Press (2001)
10. Summa, M.G., Bottou, L., Goldfarb, B., Murtagh, F., Pardoux, C., Touati, M. (eds.): Statistical Learning and Data Science. Chapman & Hall (2011)
11. Takács, G., Pilászy, I., Németh, B., Tikk, D.: Matrix factorization and neighbor based algorithms for the Netflix Prize problem. In: ACM Conf. on Recommendation Systems, pp. 267–274 (2008)
12. Toescher, A., Jahrer, M., Bell, R.M.: The bigchaos solution to the Netflix Grand Prize (2009)
13. Vapnik, V.N., Chervonenkis, A.Y.: Theory of Pattern Recognition. Nauka, USSR (1974) (in Russian)
14. Zastrau, D.: Beschleunigte Maschinelle Lernverfahren auf der GPU (2011), http://anonstorage.net/PStorage/74.diplomarbeit-david-zastrau.pdf

Improved Query Suggestion by Query Search

Xiaomin Zhang[1], Sandra Zilles[2], and Robert C. Holte[3]

[1] Amazon.com
xiaominz@amazon.com
[2] University of Regina
zilles@cs.uregina.ca
[3] University of Alberta
holte@cs.ualberta.ca

Abstract. At the Web Intelligence conference in 2009, Jiang, Zilles, and Holte introduced a novel approach to query suggestion based on query search (QSQS), as well as a system-centered evaluation method. For each potentially relevant document, QSQS creates a complex query—called a lexical alias for the document—that ranks the document in its top 20. A technique called Query Search then builds query suggestions by simplifying the lexical alias.

The present paper improves the state of the art by proposing two new query suggestion systems, IQSQS and GQSQS. Both replace the generation of lexical aliases by a simpler and more effective term selection process. They differ in their control structure: IQSQS builds query suggestions separately for each potentially relevant document, GQSQS builds them for a set of documents at once.

Both our new systems substantially outperform QSQS in the measures introduced by Jiang *et al.* to evaluate QSQS; we achieve improvements of up to 30 percent in these measures for short user queries and up to 100 percent for long user queries. We show empirically that query expansion, which forces the user's query to be included in each suggested query, is significantly superior to allowing the system the freedom to include or exclude terms from the user's query at its discretion.

1 Introduction

It is well known that users of search engines such as Google are unlikely to view documents beyond the top 20 returned by a query [15,6,5]. A query is therefore only effective in satisfying a user's information needs if relevant documents are returned in its top 20. If a user's initial query is not effective, it is necessary to issue subsequent queries until an effective one is found. Query suggestion systems assist the user in this process by suggesting a small number of alternative queries that are likely to be effective.

In this paper we follow the approach to query suggestion pioneered by Jiang *et al.* [9,7] and present two query suggestion systems, called IQSQS and GQSQS, that are substantially superior to Jiang *et al.*'s system according to their own evaluation measures (called MCC and MEC) and methodology. These systems are our paper's main contributions. An additional contribution is strong experimental evidence that query suggestion systems aiming to score well according to MCC and MEC should do query "expansion", *i.e.*, they should add terms to the user's query rather than creating queries that do not contain the user's query.

B. Glimm and A. Krüger (Eds.): KI 2012, LNCS 7526, pp. 205–216, 2012.
© Springer-Verlag Berlin Heidelberg 2012

2 Query Suggestion by Query Search (QSQS)

Following Jiang *et al.*, we say that a query "covers" a document if the document is among the top 20 documents returned by the search engine when the query is issued. Jiang *et al.*'s approach to query suggestion is based on their observation [8] that the probability of a document being relevant to the user's initial query is inversely proportional to the rank of the document in the initial query's results list. A query suggestion that covers documents that the initial query ranks high (but not in its top 20, since the user has already seen and rejected those) is therefore more likely to be effective than a query suggestion that covers documents that the initial query ranks low. They called the documents returned in positions 21–120 by the initial query "reference documents" and designed their query suggestion system to find queries that cover these documents.

2.1 Objective and Evaluation

Jiang *et al.* [9] evaluated a set of query suggestions by the number of reference documents the set covers, either collectively ("MCC") or on average individually ("MEC").[1]

For example, if the set of query suggestions contains 10 queries that collectively cover a total of 75 reference documents, MCC for this set of suggestions would be 75. If each of the suggested queries, considered individually, covered 8 reference documents, MEC would be 8.0. In general, MCC can be no larger than 100, the number of reference documents. The maximum possible value for MEC is 20, the largest number of reference documents a single query can potentially cover. For a given MEC value, the maximum possible value for MCC when 10 queries are suggested is 10*MEC. This happens only if no reference document is covered by two different suggested queries. The difference between MCC and this maximum value is an indication of the overlap in the set of reference documents covered by different suggested queries. In the extreme case, when exactly the same set of reference documents is covered by each of the suggested queries, MCC will equal MEC.

MCC and MEC relate to the standard Recall measure in the following way. Recall is the ratio of the number of retrieved relevant documents over the number of all relevant documents. In our context, all and only the reference documents are considered relevant. Since their number is always 100, it can be ignored. Retrieving a document by a query in our context means covering it, *i.e.*, returning it among the top 20 results. Hence MCC measures the collective Recall of the set of query suggestions a system returns, whereas MEC measures the expected Recall of a single query suggestion, averaged over all query suggestions returned for one initial query.

In a similar way, it would be possible to compute Precision values for Jiang *et al.*'s system and our new systems. High Precision values are not what we strive for though, for the following reason. Achieving high Precision means that the query suggestions made by the system cover as few non-reference documents as possible. As opposed to that, one of our declared goals is to have a substantial number of non-reference documents among the results covered by a query suggestion, in order to allow for a more

---

[1] This is the simpler pair of measures Jiang *et al.* proposed. The other measures take into account the exact ranks of the reference documents covered. "MCC" is an abbreviation for "Measure of Cumulative Coverage", "MEC" means "Measure of Expected Coverage".

diverse set of documents to be displayed to the user and to take into account the fact that the assumption that *only* the reference documents are relevant is not realistic. We hence restrict the evaluation of our systems to the MCC and MEC measures.

The aim of the system developed by Jiang *et al.* [9], which we call Query Suggestion by Query Search (QSQS), is to find a set of 10 suggested queries that maximizes MCC and, as a secondary criterion, also maximizes MEC.

2.2   The QSQS System Architecture

The design of the QSQS system closely follows the design of Martin and Holte's system for finding content-based addresses for web documents [12] and makes heavy use of their "Query Search" method. Query Search is a generic method for finding a query that covers a document by forming queries from various subsets of a given set of search terms and testing if the document is covered by issuing those queries to the search engine and examining their top 20 results.

Pseudocode describing the key steps in the QSQS system is given in Algorithm 1. The first processing stage (lines 1 to 4), called "Lexical Alias Search", constructs, for each reference document, a query, called the document's lexical alias, that covers the document. The second processing stage (lines 5 to 10), called "Query Suggestion Candidate Search", uses the lexical aliases to construct a set of queries from which the final query suggestions will be drawn. The third processing stage (lines 11 to 16) uses a greedy method to select the final set of K queries to suggest to the user.

Algorithm 1. Query Suggestion by Query Search (QSQS)

Input: a set *RefDocs* of reference documents and a number K
Output: a set QS containing K query suggestions
  1: // **Lexical Alias Search**
  2: **for all** $d \in RefDocs$ **do**
  3:     use Query Search to find a lexical alias for d, LA_d, based on d's title terms and most frequent terms
  4: **end for**
  5: // **Query Suggestion Candidate Search**
  6: initialize QSC, the set of query suggestion candidates, to be empty.
  7: **for all** $d \in RefDocs$ **do**
  8:     use Query Search to find the set, QSC_d, of minimal subqueries of LA_d that cover d
  9:     $QSC = QSC \cup QSC_d$
 10: **end for**
 11: // **Greedy Selection of final Query Suggestions**
 12: initialize QS to be empty.
 13: **for** $i = 1$ to K **do**
 14:     add to QS the query $qs \in QSC$ that most increases MCC (break ties to maximally increase MEC)
 15:     remove qs from QSC
 16: **end for**
 17: **return** QS

---

3   Improvements to QSQS

In this section we describe a system, IQSQS, that follows the same general pattern of processing as QSQS. The key difference is that lexical aliases are not used in IQSQS. The primary role of lexical aliases in QSQS is to supply a sequence of search terms that will be combined in various ways to create candidate query suggestions. Instead of finding a lexical alias for each document d, ISQS constructs an ordered set of search terms drawn from document d. These are chosen and ordered based on their ability to cover any of the reference documents, not just the document from which they are drawn. By focusing, from the outset, on overall coverage rather than the coverage of a single document, it is hoped that the set of candidate queries constructed from these terms will be much better than the candidate queries constructed from the lexical aliases.

Algorithm 2. Improved Query Selection by Query Search (IQSQS)

Input: the user's query, Q_0, the set *RefDocs* of reference documents for Q_0, a number $N \leq 20$, and a number K

Output: a set QS containing K query suggestions

 1: // **Term Selection**
 2: **for all** $d \in RefDocs$ **do**
 3:     quickly find a set, F_d, of up to 20 terms in d that are likely to be useful in constructing queries with high coverage
 4:     score each term in F_d according to its coverage when combined with Q_0 to form a query
 5:     sort F_d (highest scoring term first) and delete all but the first N terms
 6: **end for**
 7: // **Query Suggestion Candidate Generation**
 8: initialize QSC, the set of query suggestion candidates, to be empty.
 9: **for all** $d \in RefDocs$ **do**
10:     generate a set, QSC_d, of queries built from terms in F_d
11:     $QSC = QSC \cup QSC_d$
12: **end for**
13: // **Greedy Selection of final Query Suggestions**
14: initialize QS to be empty.
15: **for** $i = 1$ to K **do**
16:     add to QS the query $qs \in QSC$ that most increases MCC (break ties to maximally increase MEC)
17:     remove qs from QSC
18: **end for**
19: **return** QS

Pseudocode for IQSQS is shown in Algorithm 2. The first processing stage (lines 1 to 6), "Term Selection", replaces the "Lexical Alias Search" stage in QSQS. The second processing stage (lines 7 to 12) serves exactly the same purpose as the "Query Suggestion Candidate Search" and is similar in many of its details. The third processing stage (lines 13 to 18) is identical to QSQS's. We will now describe the first two stages of IQSQS in detail.

3.1   Term Selection

For each reference document d, the Term Selection stage has two steps: pre-selection (line 3 in Algorithm 2) and final selection (lines 4 and 5).

The input to the pre-selection step is the entire set of terms in the reference document, which may number in the thousands. Pre-selection reduces this number to around 20, a manageable number for the somewhat expensive scoring function used in the final selection step. Most term selection methods can be applied here, we examined two. The "Frequency" method selects the 20 terms that occur most frequently in the document; the "Snippet" method uses the terms in the fragment of text extracted from the document that Google returns to indicate the connection between the document and the user's initial query. An experimental comparison (not reported here, see [22] for details) showed that IQSQS's MCC and MEC scores with either of these methods were virtually the same. In the remainder of our experiments we used snippets for term pre-selection.

The final selection of terms involves scoring each term t individually by appending it to the user's initial query Q_0 and issuing the resulting query, which we will refer to as "$Q_0 + t$", to the Google API so that its coverage can be assessed. Our coverage score takes into account two factors, OC (Overall Coverage score) and LA (Lexical Alias score). For term t in the set F_d of terms for document d, the OC score is the number of reference documents that $Q_0 + t$ covers, and the LA score is 1 if $Q_0 + t$ covers d and 0 otherwise. These two scores are multiplied by weights and summed up to get the term's final score. In our experiments the weight for LA was three times the weight for OC.

3.2   Query Suggestion Candidate Generation

For each reference document, a small set of terms have now been selected and ordered according to the OC and LA scores. The next processing stage creates queries from these terms that will be the candidates for suggesting to the user. A set of candidates is created for each reference document using the selected terms for that document.

Although there are only a small number of terms to consider at a time, the number of possible queries that can be created from even as small a number of terms as 10 is astronomical. Every different subset is a different query, as is every different ordering of the terms. As we will see below, repeating a term in a query changes the results returned in the top 20 and therefore provides yet another way of defining queries from terms. Terms could also be combined into phrases (a sequence of terms surrounded by double quotes), or adorned with special directives (such as "+"), and so on. It is certainly possible to generate queries using the full range of options available, but in IQSQS, like QSQS, we have taken a very simple approach, only generating queries by taking subsets of the terms that have been selected for each reference document. In addition, we severely restrict the size of these subsets. The order of the terms in a query is always the order in which they occur in F_d.

We considered two ways of generating candidate queries from a given set F_d of terms. The first, AC, sets N, the number of selected terms, to 10, and generates all subsets (with no repetitions) of sizes 1 to 3, thus generating 820 (10+10*9+10*9*8) query suggestion candidates per reference document. The second method, BS, uses beam search to enable N to be larger; all pre-selected terms are considered instead of just 10.

Table 1. Comparison of Query Suggestion Candidate Generation methods on short user queries

	MCC	MEC
AC	56.66	7.26
BS	53.90	6.69
Q_0AC	70.88	8.99
Q_0BS	70.82	9.15

BS first ranks all the pre-selected terms by their OC scores, using each individually as a length 1 query. Then, all length 2 queries that can be created by expanding one of the B top-scoring length 1 queries are ranked with respect to their OC score. B is called the "beam width"; it was 15 in our experiments. Finally, BS generates all the length 3 queries that can be created by expanding one of the B top-scoring length 2 queries. All queries of lengths 1–3 thus generated are considered as query suggestion candidates.

We are interested in whether there is any benefit for query suggestions to include the user's initial query Q_0 as part of the query suggestion; we therefore considered variations of AC and BS called Q_0AC and Q_0BS. The query suggestion candidates for Q_0AC are computed by taking each query suggestion candidate created by AC and appending it to Q_0. For Q_0BS the beam search generates potential query suggestions exactly as described above but it evaluates a query q via the OC score of $Q_0 + q$.

3.3 Experiment Comparing AC, BS, Q_0AC and Q_0BS

We compare the MCC and MEC scores of the query suggestions produced by AC, BS, Q_0AC and Q_0BS on 50 short user queries (length 2 or less) drawn at random from the 250 short queries used in Jiang et al.'s experiments [9,7]. The average MCC and MEC scores over the 50 queries are shown in Table 1.

The most obvious conclusion from Table 1 is that including Q_0 in a query suggestion is of enormous benefit, increasing both MCC and MEC by approximately 25% regardless of whether AC or BS is used to generate query suggestion candidates. In all our results, the statistical significance of the difference in the scores (MCC or MEC) of two systems was determined using a sign test. Each of the 50 queries used in an experiment was considered an independent Bernoulli trial, with the null hypothesis being that it was equally likely, in any given trial, for either system to outperform the other. A difference was considered significant if the p-value computed in this way was less than 0.01 ($p =$ the probability of the observed difference occurring by chance). The scores (MCC or MEC) of the system (AC or BS) with Q_0 used in the query are significantly better than the scores of the same system without Q_0 used in the query.

The difference in scores (MCC or MEC) between the system using AC and the system using BS are fairly small but statistically significant; AC outperforms BS on both measures. The MCC and MEC differences between Q_0AC and Q_0BS are not statistically significant. As a final comparison we ran these two systems on 50 long user queries (length 3 or more) drawn at random from the 250 long queries used in Jiang et al.'s experiments [9,7]; the average MCC and MEC scores are shown in Table 2. The MCC and MEC differences between the two methods are statistically significant ($p < 0.001$).

Table 2. Comparison of Q_0AC and Q_0BS on long queries

	MCC	MEC
Q_0AC	73.83	9.70
Q_0BS	78.05	10.66

We conclude that Q_0BS is the best of the Query Suggestion Candidate Generation methods we explored and use it in subsequent experiments involving IQSQS.

4   Greedy Query Suggestion by Query Search (GQSQS)

QSQS and IQSQS process each reference document individually to accumulate a set of query suggestion candidates and, at the very end, select K of them as query suggestions. In a second variant on Jiang *et al.*'s system, we change the control structure. Instead of generating query suggestion candidates for each reference document separately, we generate one query suggestion at a time from terms extracted from all reference documents, each time aiming for the largest possible MCC increase. The pseudocode of this system, Greedy Query Suggestion by Query Search (GQSQS), is shown in Algorithm 3.

GQSQS first identifies a set F of promising search terms in the same way IQSQS generates terms (line 3). The system then proceeds in K rounds, where K is the number of query suggestions to be produced. In each round, one query suggestion is generated in the following way. The first processing stage (lines 8 to 11), "Term Selection", selects terms from F in a way that is similar to IQSQS, except for a change in the coverage score measure, which takes into account the whole set of remaining (not yet covered) reference documents. Query suggestion candidates are generated (line 13) on the selected terms as in IQSQS, with Q_0BS. In each round the query that most increases MCC is chosen (breaking ties by selecting a query that also most increases MEC) and added to the set of final query suggestions (line 14). At the end of each round, we update the set of not yet covered reference documents (line 16) and, for each search term, update the set of covered documents accordingly (line 18).

The modified coverage score of a term t, used by GQSQS in the term selection stage, results from adding together the two following scores:

- the OC (Overall Coverage) score of t, as used in the term selection stage by IQSQS,
- the EOC (Extra Overall Coverage) score, for the current round index i, which equals the number of reference documents covered by $Q_0 + t$ but not yet covered by the query suggestions added to the set QS in rounds prior to round i.

Terms achieving the highest modified coverage score are ranked highest.

5   Comparison of QSQS, IQSQS, and GQSQS

To compare QSQS to our two new systems, we ran experiments using the same sets of 50 short queries and 50 long queries as used for the experiments reported in Section 3. In these experiments, we used the Q_0BS method for generating query suggestion candidates in IQSQS and GQSQS.

Algorithm 3. Greedy Query Suggestion by Query Search (GQSQS)

Input: the user's query, Q_0, the set *RefDocs* of reference documents for Q_0, a number $N \leq 20$, and a number K
Output: a set QS containing K query suggestions
1: initialize QS, the set of query suggestions, to be empty
2: initialize *DocsToCover*, the set of not yet covered reference documents, to equal *RefDocs*
3: quickly find a set, F, of terms occurring in documents in *RefDocs* that are likely to be useful in constructing queries with high coverage score wrt *RefDocs*
4: **for** each $t \in F$ **do**
5:     $Covered(t)$ = set of documents in *RefDocs* that are covered by the query $Q_0 + t$
6: **end for**
7: **for** $i = 1$ to K **do**
8:     // **Term Selection**
9:     using the size of $Covered(t)$, score each term in F according to its modified coverage score wrt *DocsToCover* when combined with Q_0 to form a query
10:    sort F (highest scoring term first)
11:    F_i = the set of the first N terms in F
12:    // **Query Suggestion Generation**
13:    generate a set, QSC_i, of queries built from terms in F_i
14:    add to QS the query $qs_i \in QSC_i$ that most increases MCC (break ties to maximally increase MEC)
15:    // **Update Set of Documents to be Covered**
16:    remove the reference documents covered by qs_i from *DocsToCover*
17:    **for** each $t \in F$ do **do**
18:        $Covered(t) = Covered(t) \cap DocsToCover$
19:    **end for**
20: **end for**
21: **return** QS

The resulting average MCC and MEC scores for QSQS, IQSQS, and GQSQS are reported in Table 3. Our results show IQSQS and GQSQS superior to QSQS on both short queries and long queries. Sign tests (see Section 3) show the performance differences between IQSQS and QSQS (and between GQSQS and QSQS) to be highly significant ($p < 10^{-5}$ in every case). Hence we consider our new systems a substantial improvement over the state of the art. The MCC and MEC values achieved are noteworthy in their own right, not just in comparison with QSQS's. An MCC value over 67 means that over two-thirds of the reference documents are covered by one or more of the queries our systems suggest. An MEC value over 9 means that, on average, more than 9 of the top 20 documents retrieved by the each of the queries our systems suggest are reference documents, *i.e.*, highly likely to be relevant to the user's needs.

Most of the documents that our suggested queries retrieve that are not reference documents are novel documents, *i.e.*, not documents covered by the user's initial query. For IQSQS on the short queries, for example, of the 20 documents covered by one of our query suggestion, approximately 9 are reference documents (MEC=9.15, see Table 3), 2 are documents covered by the user's original query, and the remaining 9 were ranked beyond position 120 by the initial query. Our suggested queries are therefore achieving

Table 3. Comparison of QSQA, IQSQS, and GQSQS, on short and long queries

	Short Query		Long Query	
System	MCC	MEC	MCC	MEC
QSQS	54.80	6.89	42.86	5.34
IQSQS	70.82	9.15	78.05	10.66
GQSQS	63.88	9.73	68.82	11.08

a good balance between retrieving reference documents (very likely to be relevant given that the initial query's top 20 are not relevant), reminding the user of documents covered by the initial query, and injecting novelty into the set of results.

The observations that IQSQS outperforms GQSQS in terms of MCC, and that the opposite is true for MEC, are both highly significant statistically ($p < 0.005$ in both cases). In conclusion, both systems offer excellent performance in terms of both MCC and MEC. Applications that place greater emphasis on MCC should use IQSQS, and those that place greater emphasis on MEC should use GQSQS.

6 Query Suggestion Examples

Table 4 shows the queries suggested by Google, by QSQS, and by our methods IQSQS and GQSQS, for the queries "volcanos in italy", "herbs" and "ibm thinkpad 760c".

The most striking feature of Google's query suggestions are how "understandable" they are. It is very easy to imagine the subtopics they are intended to retrieve. However as the MCC and MEC scores show, these query suggestions are extremely poor at retrieving reference documents. Exactly the opposite is true of the queries suggested by our systems. They have relatively high MCC and MEC values, but in many cases it is not at all clear what subtopics they represent. We believe this is not a failing of our systems, or something that could be easily fixed by adding to our scoring criteria some measure of "understandability". We believe that the ranking functions used by Google, and undoubtedly other modern search engines too, have become sufficiently sophisticated and unintuitive that understandable query suggestions will often not be effective in satisfying a user's information needs.

A particular example of this phenomenon is the effect of repeating a term more than once; see Table 4. The effect on the documents returned in the top 20, like the effect of ordering the terms (which we observed in our work but did not systematically study), is substantial and largely unintuitive. Consider, for example, the query suggestion "herbs herbs" generated by IQSQS for the initial query "herbs". Here the reference document term "herbs" was appended to the initial query. IQSQS selects "herbs herbs" because this query covers more reference documents than other query suggestion candidates. In particular, the top 20 results for "herbs" are substantially different from those for "herbs herbs". Many documents covered by "herbs herbs" contain the term "herbs" twice in key positions such as the title. For instance, the titles of some top results for "herbs herbs" from Google (Nov. 24th, 2010) are "Herbs To Herbs", "Herbs Herbals herb and herbal remedies – HerbsHerbals.com", "Herb's Herbs & Such", "Medicinal herbs – Affordable herbs", etc. These are not among the top results for the query "herbs".

Table 4. The query suggestions for the queries "volcanos in italy", "herbs" and "ibm thinkpad 760c" by Google, QSQS, and our methods, as of Nov. 24, 2010

Google	QSQS	IQSQS	GQSQS
major volcanoes in italy	italy volcanoes	volcanos in italy studies volcano volcanoes	volcanos in italy volcanos
famous volcanoes in italy	volcanoes worldwide	volcanos in italy italy	volcanos in italy italy org
many volcanoes italy	volcano etna italy	volcanos in italy volcano erupted volcanoes	volcanos in italy pacific volcanos growing
three volcanoes italy	volcanoes italy active	volcanos in italy cams active east	volcanos in italy japan
	volcano diagram photo	volcanos in italy volcano feb 7	volcanos in italy lands
	italian volcanos	volcanos in italy tv etna	volcanos in italy 3350
	volcanoes forces nature mount	volcanos in italy moderate eruptions	volcanos in italy brief pacific world
	volcano information encyclopedia com	volcanos in italy explore eruption	volcanos in italy uploaded
	online volcano information volcanoes	volcanos in italy volcanos specifically	volcanos in italy deal
	amazon com volcano adventure guide	volcanos in italy pacific	volcanos in italy diagram
MCC=5 MEC=1.5	MCC=35 MEC=3.7	MCC=60 MEC=7.2	MCC=49 MEC=6.3
list of herbs	herbs herbal	herbs com herbs	herbs herbs learn herb
types of herbs	herbs website	herbs company herbs site	herbs herbs co
cooking herbs	herbs com	herbs herbal provides	herbs herbs com website
growing herbs	herbs herb gardens gardening	herbs herbs gardens	herbs information
culinary herbs	information herbs	herbs information	herbs medical herb site
pictures of herbs	herbs organic	herbs com vitamins	herbs herbs
medicinal herbs	herb store herbs herbal	herbs drying seeds method	herbs gardens
herbal medicine	medicinal herbs	herbs herbs chinese herbal	herbs herbs information database
	herbs home	herbs herbology 1	herbs remedies
	site herb growing herb herbal	herbs herbs education programs	herbs seeds
MCC=15 MEC=1.9	MCC=47 MEC=6.1	MCC=54 MEC=5.7	MCC=52 MEC=6.8
	thinkpad 760c replacement	ibm thinkpad 760c 755 760 ibm	ibm thinkpad 760c wholesale 760
	thinkpad 760c	ibm thinkpad 760c 365 760 ibm	ibm thinkpad 760c 560 365
	760c 9547	ibm thinkpad 760c 760 dont mailing	ibm thinkpad 760c car
	ibm centre thinkpad 755cv	ibm thinkpad 760c lcd 24	ibm thinkpad 760c 355
	memory ibm thinkpad 760c	ibm thinkpad 760c 9546 page laptop	ibm thinkpad 760c repair
	760c 760cd	ibm thinkpad 760c fix	ibm thinkpad 760c 29
	760c 9546 product	ibm thinkpad 760c 1995	ibm thinkpad 760c 370 shopping
	ibm thinkpad 760 reviews	ibm thinkpad 760c replacement 760ld	ibm thinkpad 760c shop
	thinkpad 760c win	ibm thinkpad 760c vista 760 ibm	ibm thinkpad 760c wholesale 755cd
	ibm 760c battery	ibm thinkpad 760c 760 image com	ibm thinkpad 760c 560e 755 380
MCC=0 MEC=0.0	MCC=60 MEC=8.2	MCC=80 MEC=11.0	MCC=63 MEC=11.4

If nowadays effective query suggestions necessarily border on being incomprehensible in terms of which subtopics they represent, research on query suggestion must pursue two goals. The first, represented by this paper, is to find ever better ways to create effective query suggestions without requiring that the queries be comprehensible. The second aim is to find comprehensible summaries of document sets, e.g., by cluster labelling methods [11,16,3,2,4,17] or multi-document text summarization [10,14].

7 Related Work

The approach to query suggestion introduced by Jiang *et al.* [9] of using Query Search to create query suggestions, is fundamentally different than other approaches because it evaluates the queries it creates by issuing them to the search engine and observing the documents returned in the top 20, rather than using a surrogate evaluation measure such as the similarity of the terms in the suggested query to those in the user's query [11,1,18,19,21]. Most similar to our approach is the *pseudo-relevance feedback* approach (also called blind-relevance feedback) [13,20]. This assumes that the top T documents in the results of the user's query are relevant (including the top 20, unlike our approach) and extracts terms from these documents that best discriminate them from the documents not in the top T. These terms are used to construct query suggestions, but, unlike our approach, these suggestions are not evaluated by observing the results they return.

8 Conclusion

We proposed two new query suggestion systems using query search, based on Jiang *et al.*'s QSQS system [9]. The changes to QSQS consist mainly of replacing the construction of lexical aliases by a more elegant and more effective process of term selection. Query suggestion candidates are no longer generated by simplifying a complex query (a lexical alias) top-down, but by forming queries from promising search terms bottom-up. The two systems we present both use this method but vary in their control structure.

Both new systems substantially outperform QSQS in the measures that were proposed by Jiang *et al.* and that were explicitly used as objective functions in the design of QSQS. IQSQS improves QSQS by about 30% (both MCC and MEC) on short queries, and on long queries by about 80% (MCC) and 100% (MEC); GQSQS is even more effective in terms of MEC on long queries. Part of this improvement is due to forcing our systems to return queries that *expand* the initial query, as we verified empirically. This suggests that including the initial query in a query suggestion is generally advisable.

Acknowledgements. We thank Google's University Research Program for providing access to the Google API[2] and Shen Jiang for his help in early stages of this work. We gratefully acknowledge financial support by Google, the Alberta Innovates Centre for Machine Learning (AICML), and Canada's Natural Sciences and Engineering Research Council (NSERC).

---

[2] See http://research.google.com/university/search/docs.html for documentation.

References

1. Carpineto, C., Mori, R., Romano, G., Bigi, B.: An information-theoretic approach to automatic query expansion. ACM Transactions on Information Systems (TOIS) 19, 1–27 (2001)
2. Chen, J., Zaïane, O.R., Goebel, R.: An unsupervised approach to cluster web search results based on word sense communities. In: WI 2008, pp. 725–729 (2008)
3. Cutting, D., Karger, D., Pederson, J., Tukey, J.: Scatter/gather: a cluster-based approach to browsing large document collections. In: ACM SIGIR 1992, pp. 318–329 (1992)
4. Geraci, F., Pellegrini, M., Maggini, M., Sebastiani, F.: Cluster generation and labeling for web snippets: A fast, accurate hierarchical solution. Internet Mathematics 3, 413–443 (2006)
5. Jansen, B., Spink, A.: How are we searching the world wide web?: a comparison of nine search engine transaction logs. Inf. Process. Manage. 42(1), 248–263 (2006)
6. Jansen, B., Spink, A., Saracevic, T.: Real life, real users, and real needs: a study and analysis of user queries on the web. Inf. Process. Manage. 36(2), 207–227 (2000)
7. Jiang, S.: Searching for queries to improve document retrieval in web search. Master's thesis, University of Alberta (2009)
8. Jiang, S., Zilles, S., Holte, R.: Empirical analysis of the rank distribution of relevant documents in web search. In: WI 2008, pp. 208–213 (2008)
9. Jiang, S., Zilles, S., Holte, R.: Query suggestion by query search: a new approach to user support in web search. In: WI 2009, pp. 679–684 (2009)
10. Lin, C.-Y., Hovy, E.: From single to multi-document summarization. In: ACL, pp. 457–464 (2002)
11. Manning, C., Raghavan, P., Schutze, H.: Introduction to Information Retrieval. Cambridge University Press (2008)
12. Martin, J., Holte, R.: Searching for content-based addresses on the world-wide web. In: Proceedings of the 3rd ACM Conference on Digital Libraries, pp. 299–300 (1998)
13. Mitra, M., Singhal, A., Buckley, C.: Improving automatic query expansion. In: ACM SIGIR 1998, pp. 206–214 (1998)
14. Radev, D., Jing, H., Sty, M., Tam, D.: Centroid-based summarization of multiple documents. Inf. Process. Manage. 40(6), 919–938 (2004)
15. Silverstein, C., Rauch Henzinger, M., Marais, H., Moricz, M.: Analysis of a very large web search engine query log. SIGIR Forum 33(1), 6–12 (1999)
16. Stein, B., Zu Eissen, S.M.: Topic identification: framework and application. In: Proceedings of the International Conference on Knowledge Management, pp. 522–531 (2004)
17. Treeratpituk, P., Callan, J.: Automatically labeling hierarchical clusters. In: Proceedings of the 2006 International Conference on Digital Government Research, pp. 167–176 (2006)
18. Voorhees, E.M.: Query expansion using lexical-semantic relations. In: ACM SIGIR 1994, pp. 61–69 (1994)
19. Wang, X., Zhai, C.: Mining term association patterns from search logs for effective query reformulation. In: Proceedings of the 17th ACM Conference on Information and Knowledge Management, pp. 479–488 (2008)
20. White, R., Clarke, C., Cucerzan, S.: Comparing query logs and pseudo-relevance feedback for web-search query refinement. In: ACM SIGIR 2007, pp. 831–832 (2007)
21. Xu, J., Croft, W.: Query expansion using local and global document analysis. In: ACM SIGIR 1996, pp. 4–11 (1996)
22. Zhang, X.: Search term selection and document clustering for query suggestion. Master's thesis, University of Alberta (2010)

Knowledge-Base Revision
Using Implications as Hypotheses

Özgür Lütfü Özçep

Institute for Software Systems (STS)
Hamburg University of Technology
Hamburg, Germany
oezguer.oezcep@tu-harburg.de

Abstract. In semantic integration scenarios, the integration of an assertion from some sender into the knowledge base (KB) of a receiver may be hindered by inconsistencies due to ambiguous use of symbols; hence a revision of the KB is needed to preserve its consistency. This paper analyses the new family of implication based revision operators, which exploit the idea of revising hypotheses on the semantic relatedness of the receiver's and sender's symbols. In order to capture the specific inconsistency resolution strategy of these operators, the novel concept of uniform sets, which are based on prime implicates, is elaborated. According to two main results of this paper these operators lend themselves to practical use in systems for semantic integration: First, the operators are finitely representable. Second, the non-sceptical versions of these operators can be axiomatically characterised by postulates, which provide a full specification of the operators' effects.

Keywords: belief revision, semantic integration, postulate, prime implicate.

1 Introduction

Belief revision [1] deals with the problem of integrating an assertion stemming from an agent (sender) into a knowledge base (KB) of another agent (receiver). If the receiver trusts the incoming information—and classical belief revision assumes he does—the integration may trigger a revision of the KB because the trigger may be incompatible with the KB; hence some of its formulas have to be eliminated. Belief revision explains the incompatibility with false information in the KB. Therefore, the elimination of formulas in the KB is an adequate means.

But if the diagnosis for the incompatibility is not false information but ambiguous use of symbols, a different strategy seems more appropriate. For example, suppose an agent (the receiver) uses the terminus "article" to denote a publication either in proceedings or in journals while the sender agent uses it to mean publications in journals only. The receiver has different sentences in his KB in which he uses "article" in this sense. So, a trigger sentence stemming from the sender may lead to inconsistencies with the receiver's KB. In order to resolve

B. Glimm and A. Krüger (Eds.): KI 2012, LNCS 7526, pp. 217–228, 2012.
© Springer-Verlag Berlin Heidelberg 2012

the inconsistencies, it would not be a good idea to eliminate only one sentence of the KB that contains "article" and that is involved in the conflict; because the next time the receiver integrates a (different) trigger from the sender, the other interpretation of "article" may again lead to inconsistencies.

An appropriate means to deal with conflicts caused by ambiguous use of symbols between different agents is first to state hypotheses on the semantical relatedness of symbols from different agents and second to eliminate some of the hypotheses that are involved in the conflict. This is the general approach of semantic integration based on semantic mappings (or bridging axioms) for heterogeneous knowledge bases [4,17,21]. Every KB is assigned a unique name space, and semantic mappings associate symbols of different name spaces. In the case of the example above this means distinguishing between the use of "article" in the receiver's name space and in the sender's name space and initially hypothesising that the uses are equivalent. If the integration of a trigger containing "article" into the receiver's KB leads to inconsistency, a proper strategy for resolving the conflict is eliminating the equivalence hypothesis and possibly replacing it by a weaker hypothesis compatible with the trigger (e.g., by hypothesising that the sender's use is narrower (wider) than the receiver's use).

Based on this strategy for inconsistency resolution, this paper investigates a new class of operators for revising propositional KBs with propositional triggers. The hypotheses used in these operators are implications of the form $p' \to p$ or $p \to p'$ where p' stands for the p in the name space of the receiver, and p is the p of the sender. These operators generalise the revision operators of [6] which considers biimplications of the form $p \leftrightarrow p'$ only. Using implications rather than biimplications allows for a more fine-grained analysis of what caused the conflict between the sender's trigger and the receiver's KB.

Though the technical definitions of the revision operators of this paper and of [6] are similar, the theory developed in this paper deviates considerably from that in [6]. On of its main innovative features is a formal specification and analysis of the uniformity property which distinguishes the implication (and biimplication) based operators from classical belief-revision operators. The main idea of the analysis is first to equivalently represent the KB by its most atomic components (prime implicates) and then describe the effect of the implication based operators on the prime implicates by uniform closure conditions.

The implication based revision operators provide a useful abstract implementation model for semantic integration scenarios in which conflicts caused by ambiguous use of symbol between heterogeneous KBs have to be resolved. Though the definitions of the operators are based on infinite sets, they can be described equivalently by finite operators that are appropriate for implementation means (see Th. 2). This is the first main result of this paper. Moreover, anyone implementing the non-sceptical versions of these operators gets a declarative specification of their properties (including uniformity): as a second main result (Th. 4) this paper describes a set of axiomatic postulates which are fulfilled by the operators and which characterise them in the sense that all other operators fulfilling them are representable as implication based choice revision operators.

The paper is structured as follows: The second section provides background on propositional logic and belief revision. The third section discusses the revision operators of J. Delgrande and T. Schaub [6]. The following section introduces the implication based revision operators and shows that these are indeed different from the operators of Delgrande and Schaub. Moreover, the finite representability by a partial polarity flipping operator is proved. The last section before the section on related work and the conclusion gives an axiomatic characterisation of non-sceptical implication based revision operators by postulates.

Proofs of all results in this paper can be found in the technical report [18].

2 Logical Preliminaries

This section introduces notation and concepts from propositional logic and belief revision that are used in the paper. I take for granted the syntax and semantics (interpretation, entailment etc.) of propositional logic, the notion of (sub)clause and the notion of the conjunctive (disjunctive) normal form, CNF (DNF).

Let $\mathcal{P}$ be a set of propositional symbols; form$(\mathcal{P})$ denotes the set of propositional logical formulas over $\mathcal{P}$, which are denoted by lowercase greek letters $\alpha, \beta \ldots$. Finite sets of formulas are called *knowledge bases* or *belief bases* and are denoted by B as well as primed and indexed variants of B (e.g. B_1, B', $\bar{B}$). symb(B) is the set of propositional symbols in B. Int$(\mathcal{P})$ denotes the set of *interpretations (assignments)* $\mathcal{I}$ with domain $\mathcal{P}$. $\mathcal{I} \models B$ for a set B is a short notation for $\mathcal{I} \models \bigwedge B$. The set of *consequences* of B over the set of propositional symbols S is $\mathrm{Cn}^S(B) = \{\alpha \in \mathrm{form}(S) \mid B \models \alpha\}$. If the index is left out in some context, then the consequences have to be understood with respect to the maximal set of propositional symbols discussed in the context. If two sets B_1 and B_2 have the same sets of consequences of formulas in form(S), write $B_1 \equiv_S B_2$. For $\alpha \in \mathrm{form}(\mathcal{P})$ and $S \subseteq \mathcal{P}$, the *clausal closure* of α w.r.t. S is the set clauseCl$^S(\alpha)$ of clauses that have only symbols from S and that follow from α.

Let Θ_S denote an operator that, given a formula α and a set S of symbols $S \subseteq \mathcal{P}$, computes a formula representing all consequences of α that do not contain symbols in S. (Compare the general framework of forgetting in [14].) This operator will be used as a technical aid for calculating belief-revision results based on hypotheses. For $\mathcal{I} \in \mathrm{Int}(S)$ let $\alpha_{\mathcal{I}}$ be defined as follows: Substitute all occurrences of $p \in S$ in α where $p^{\mathcal{I}} = \mathcal{I}(p) = 1$ by $\top$, else $\bot$ is substituted for p. Now let $\Theta_S : \alpha \mapsto \bigvee_{\mathcal{I} \in \mathrm{Int}(S)} \alpha_{\mathcal{I}}$. For arbitrary $S \subseteq \mathcal{P}$ let $\Theta_S(\alpha) = \Theta_{\mathrm{symb}(\alpha) \cap S}(\alpha)$. For example, let $\alpha = (p \wedge q) \vee (r \wedge s)$ and $S = \{p, r\}$. Then $\Theta_S = ((\bot \wedge q) \vee (\bot \wedge s)) \vee ((\bot \wedge q) \vee (\top \wedge s)) \vee ((\top \wedge q) \vee (\bot \wedge s)) \vee ((\top \wedge q) \vee (\top \wedge s))$. This is equivalent to the formula $s \vee q$. The following facts concerning Θ_S for $S \subseteq \mathcal{P}$ can be proved easily. For all $\alpha \in \mathrm{form}(\mathcal{P})$: $\alpha \models \Theta_S(\alpha)$ and $\mathrm{Cn}^{\mathcal{P} \setminus S}(\alpha) = \mathrm{Cn}^{\overline{\mathcal{P} \setminus S}}(\Theta_S(\alpha))$. Note, that $\Theta_S(\alpha)$ can be described as the quantified boolean formula $\exists S.\alpha$.

The new operators defined in this paper are based on the concept of *dual remainder sets*, a concept similar to the concept of remainder sets [2] used in the classical paper of Alchourrón, Gärdenfors and Makinson (AGM) [1] for the construction of partial-meet revision functions. Let $B \top \alpha$, *the dual remainder sets modulo* α, denote the set of inclusion maximal subsets X of B that are consistent with α, i.e., $X \in B \top \alpha$ iff $X \subseteq B$, $X \cup \{\alpha\}$ is consistent and for all $\bar{X} \subseteq B$ with $X \subset \bar{X}$ the set $\bar{X} \cup \{\alpha\}$ is not consistent. The notion of dual remainders is extended to arbitrary belief bases B_1 as second argument by defining $B \top B_1$ as $B \top \bigwedge B_1$.

An analysis of belief-revision functions involves the investigation of postulates they fulfil. Some postulates for belief-base revision operators $*$ that I will refer to are given below. (In contrast to belief-sets [1] belief bases [10] do not have to be logically closed.)

(BR1) $B * \alpha \not\models \bot$ if $\alpha \not\models \bot$.
(BR2) $\alpha \in B * \alpha$.
(BR3) $B * \alpha \subseteq B \cup \{\alpha\}$.
(BR4) For all $\beta \in B$ either $B * \alpha \models \beta$ or $B * \alpha \models \neg\beta$.
(BR5) If for all $\bar{B} \subseteq B$: $\bar{B} \cup \{\alpha\} \models \bot$ iff $\bar{B} \cup \{\beta\} \models \bot$, then $(B * \alpha) \cap B = (B * \beta) \cap B$.

Postulate (BR1) is the *consistency postulate* [1]; it says that the revision result has to be consistent in case the trigger α is consistent. Postulate (BR2) is the *success postulate* [8]; the revision must be successful in so far as α has to be in the revision result. (BR3) is called the *inclusion postulate* for belief-base revision [12, p. 200]. The revision result of operators fulfilling it are bounded from above. Postulate (BR4) is the *tenacity postulate* [9]; it states that the revision result is complete with respect to all formulas of B. Postulate (BR5) is the *logical uniformity postulate* for belief-base operators [11]. It says that the revision outcomes are determined by the subsets (in)consistent with the trigger.

3   Revision Based on Hypotheses

One example for belief-revision operators that are based on hypotheses are the operators of Delgrande and Schaub [6]. The general idea is to internalize the symbols of the receiver's KB thereby dissociating the name spaces of the receiver, who holds the KB, and the sender, who is the holder of another KB from which the trigger stems. Both name spaces are related by one special form of formula (bridging axiom), namely the biimplication. Holding to a biimplication $p \leftrightarrow p'$ means believing that the propositional symbol p of the receiver (holder of B) has the same meaning as the propositional symbol p of the sender. In order to resolve inconsistencies the internalized KB stays untouched, but some subset of the biimplications are eliminated. If $p \leftrightarrow p'$ is eliminated during the revision process, this can be interpreted as diagnosing the inter-ambiguity of p between the sender and the agent as the culprit for the inconsistency. After the elimination the name space dissociation is abandoned by retaining only those formulas of the old vocabulary. I recapitulate the definitions of the operators and their properties because the revision operator I will introduce is an extension, which uses implications $p' \to p$ and $p \to p'$ as hypotheses.

For a given set of propositional symbols $\mathcal{P}$ let $\mathcal{P}'$ denote the set $\{p' \mid p \in \mathcal{P}\}$ of *internal* or *internalized* propositional symbols. Similarly B' denotes the pendant of B where all symbols p are substituted by the corresponding internalized variant p'. I use the following space saving abbreviations (for $p \in \mathcal{P}$): $\overleftrightarrow{p} = p \leftrightarrow p'$, $\overrightarrow{p} = p \rightarrow p'$ and $\overleftarrow{p} = p' \rightarrow p$. A *belief-change scenario* $\langle B_1, B_2, B_3 \rangle$ consists of three sets B_i ($i \in \{1, 2, 3\}$) of formulas over the set of propositional symbols $\mathcal{P}$. B_1 is the initial KB of the receiver, B_2 is a KB that must be contained in the change result and B_3 is a KB that is not allowed to be in the change result. Classical revision of B with α is modelled by the belief-change scenario $\langle B, \{\alpha\}, \emptyset \rangle$; classical contraction of B with α is modelled by the belief-change scenario $\langle B, \emptyset, \{\alpha\} \rangle$. A *belief-change extension* [6, p. 9] (*bc extension* for short) of the belief change scenario $\langle B_1, B_2, B_3 \rangle$ is a set of the form $\mathrm{Cn}^{\mathcal{P}}(B_1' \cup B_2 \cup EQ_i)$, where $EQ_i \subseteq EQ = \{\overleftrightarrow{p} \mid p \in \mathcal{P}\}$ is an inclusion maximal set of biimplications fulfilling the following integrity condition: $\mathrm{Cn}(B_1' \cup B_2 \cup EQ_i) \cap (B_3 \cup \{\bot\}) = \emptyset$. If no such EQ_i exists, then let form$(\mathcal{P})$ be the only bc extension.

In case of classical belief revision—represented by $\langle B, \{\alpha\}, \emptyset \rangle$—the set of bc extensions E_i have the form $E_i = \mathrm{Cn}^{\mathcal{P}}(B' \cup EQ_i \cup \{\alpha\})$, where $\bot \notin \mathrm{Cn}(B' \cup \{\alpha\} \cup EQ_i)$. Let $(E_i)_{i \in I}$ be the family of all bc extensions in the belief-change scenario $\langle B, \{\alpha\}, \emptyset \rangle$. A selection function c over the index set I selects exactly one index $c(I) \in I$. With these notions, the operators of *choice revision* $\dotplus_c$ based on a selection function c and *sceptical revision* $\dotplus$ are defined as follows.

Definition 1. *[6, p. 11]* $B \dotplus_c \alpha = E_k$ *(for $c(I) = k$) and* $B \dotplus \alpha = \bigcap_{i \in I} E_i$.

Though the revision results under both operators $\dotplus_c, \dotplus$ are not finite, Delgrande and Schaub can show that these operators are finitely representable. That is more formally, for an operator $\circ \in \{\dotplus_c, \dotplus\}$ one can define an operator $\circ^{fin}$ such that it operates on a finite KB B as left argument, a formula α as right argument and outputs a finite KB $B \circ^{fin} \alpha$ such that $\mathrm{Cn}(B) \circ \alpha = \mathrm{Cn}(B \circ^{fin} \alpha)$. The corresponding finite operators are based on substituting propositional symbols by their negation, thereby flipping the polarity of the symbols. Let $\mathcal{B} = \langle B, \{\alpha\}, \emptyset \rangle$ be a bc scenario and EQ_i a set of biimplications. The formula $\lceil \alpha \rceil_i$ results from α by substituting all occurrences of propositional symbols $p \in \mathcal{P} \setminus \mathrm{symb}(EQ_i)$ with their negation $\neg p$. Let $(E_i)_{i \in I}$ be the family of bc extensions over $\mathcal{B}$ and c a selection function with $c(I) = k$. Then Delgrande and Schaub define the flipping operators by $\lceil \mathcal{B} \rceil = \bigvee_{i \in I} \bigwedge_{\beta \in B} \lceil \beta \rceil_i$ and $\lceil \mathcal{B} \rceil_c = \bigwedge_{\beta \in B} \lceil \beta \rceil_k$ and finite revision operators by:

$$B \dotplus_c^{fin} \alpha = \lceil (B, \{\alpha\}, \emptyset) \rceil_c \wedge \alpha \text{ and } B \dotplus^{fin} \alpha = \lceil (B, \{\alpha\}, \emptyset) \rceil \wedge \alpha$$

The finite representability is stated in Theorem 1.

Theorem 1. *[6, p. 17]* $B \dotplus_c \alpha \equiv B \dotplus_c^{fin} \alpha$ *and* $B \dotplus \alpha \equiv B \dotplus^{fin} \alpha$.

This theorem evokes a new perspective on what has caused the inconsistency between the KB and the trigger: a flip in the polarity of a propositional symbol. By re-flipping the propositional symbols that caused the inconsistency the result becomes consistent. A remarkable point here is that the flip of a propositional symbol concerns all its occurrences in the formula, it is a kind of uniform flipping. This uniformity can be interpreted as a systematic use of the proposition in just the opposite sense. Referring to the example of the introduction, the receiver would have to substitute all occurrences of "article" by its negation.

4   Using Implications as Hypotheses

By using the set of implications $Impl = \{\overrightarrow{p}, \overleftarrow{p} \mid p \in \mathcal{P}\}$ as set of hypotheses instead of the set of biimplications $EQ = \{\overleftrightarrow{p} \mid p \in \mathcal{P}\}$ new classes of revision operators result. This generalisation from biimplications to implications as hypotheses allows for a more fine-grained diagnosis of the properties of the symbol p that are responsible for the inconsistency. While in the case of Delgrande's and Schaub's operators the diagnosis is a rough "The sender's and the receiver's p have different meanings and so an inconsistency is caused", the implication based operators account for the "direction" in which the inconsistency was caused. If the hypothesis $p' \to p$ is eliminated, but $p \to p'$ is kept in the revision result, then the diagnosis for the inconsistency is the following: the hypothesis that the meaning of the receiver's p is narrower than (or equal to) the sender's meaning of p leads to an inconsistency. But still we can hold on to the hypothesis that the meaning of the sender's p is narrower than the receiver's meaning of p.

The notion of belief extension for biimplication based revision is easily adapted to the case of implications; a set $\mathrm{Cn}^{\mathcal{P}}(B \cup \{\alpha\} \cup X)$ is an *implication based belief extension* iff $X \in Impl\top(B' \cup \{\alpha\})$. (Remember that $\top$ denotes the operator for dual remainder sets defined in Section 2). Let $(Impl_i)_{i \in I}$ be the set of all implication based consistent belief set extensions of $\langle B, \{\alpha\}, \emptyset \rangle$ and c be a selection function for I with $c(I) = k$. The new operators are defined as follows:

Definition 2. *The* implication based choice revision $\dotplus_c^{Impl}$ *and the* implication based sceptical revision $\dotplus^{Impl}$ *are defined by :*

$$B \dotplus_c^{Impl} \alpha = Impl_k \ (\text{for } c(I) = k) \ \text{and} \ B \dotplus^{Impl} \alpha = \bigcap_{i \in I} Impl_i$$

As in the case of the Delgrande/Schaub revision operators, one can finitely represent the results by an operation on the KB. The finite representation uses the notion of positive and negative occurrences of propositional symbols. For convenience, I assume that only the connectors $\land$, $\lor$ and $\neg$ are allowed in the formulas; this is no real restriction as this set of connectors is functionally complete. An occurrence of a propositional symbol is *syntactically positive* iff it occurs in the scope of an even number of negation symbols, otherwise it is *syntactically negative*. I also speak of the *(positive, negative) polarity* of a propositional symbol's occurrence. In contrast to the polarity switching of [6], the operator of partial flipping does not change the polarity of all occurrences of a symbol p but only of those of a particular polarity—depending on which implication $\overrightarrow{p}$ or $\overleftarrow{p}$ is missing in the given set of implications.

Definition 3. *Let* $(Impl_i)_{i \in I}$ *be the family of belief extensions for a belief-change scenario* $\mathcal{B} = (B, \{\alpha\}, \emptyset)$ *and let* $Impl_k$ *be an implication based belief extension chosen by the selection function,* $c(I) = k$. *Then define the operator of* partial flipping $\lceil \mathcal{B} \rceil_k^{Impl} = \lceil \mathcal{B} \rceil_c^{Impl}$ *in the following way: If* $p \to p' \notin Impl_k$, *then switch the polarity of the negative occurrences of p in $\bigwedge B$ (by adding $\neg$ in front of these occurrences). If* $p' \to p \notin Impl_k$, *then switch the polarity of the positive occurrences of p in $\bigwedge B$. Let* $\lceil \mathcal{B} \rceil^{Impl} = \bigvee_{i \in I} \lceil \mathcal{B} \rceil_i^{Impl}$.

With this definition at hand, the following representation theorem follows:

Theorem 2. *The following equivalences hold:*
$$B \dotplus_c^{Impl} \alpha \equiv \lceil (B, \{\alpha\}, \emptyset) \rceil_c^{Impl} \wedge \alpha \text{ and } B \dotplus^{Impl} \alpha \equiv \lceil (B, \{\alpha\}, \emptyset) \rceil^{Impl} \wedge \alpha$$

A simple example shows that $\dotplus_c^{Impl}$ is different from the operators $\dotplus_c, \dotplus$.

Example 1. Let be given $\mathcal{P} = \{p, q\}$, $B = \{p \leftrightarrow q\}$, and $\alpha = \neg(p \leftrightarrow q)$. Writing B in CNF (as $(p \vee \neg q) \wedge (\neg p \vee q)$), one can see that it has a positive and a negative occurrence of p, q, respectively. But these different polarities are not dealt with by the biimplication based hypotheses. The two inclusion maximal sets of biimplications are $EQ_1 = \{\overleftrightarrow{p}\}$ and $EQ_2 = \{\overleftrightarrow{q}\}$. Let $I = \{1, 2\}$ and $c_1(I) = 1$, $c_2(I) = 2$. Using $\Theta_{\{p', q'\}}$ or the representation theorem we can calculate the outcomes: $B \dotplus_{c_1} \alpha = B \dotplus_{c_2} \alpha = B \dotplus \alpha = \mathrm{Cn}^{\mathcal{P}}(p \leftrightarrow \neg q)$.

On the other hand, the implication based revision operator recognizes the polarities of the propositional symbols; hence, more possibilities to resolve the conflict result. Here, there are four possibilities given by the following four inclusion maximal sets of implications: $Impl_1 = \mathrm{Cn}^{\mathcal{P}}(\{\overrightarrow{q}, \overrightarrow{p}\})$, $Impl_2 = \mathrm{Cn}^{\mathcal{P}}(\{\overrightarrow{q}, \overleftarrow{p}\})$, $Impl_3 = \mathrm{Cn}^{\mathcal{P}}(\{\overleftarrow{q}, \overrightarrow{p}\})$, and $Impl_4 = \mathrm{Cn}^{\mathcal{P}}(\{\overleftarrow{q}, \overleftarrow{p}\})$. These lead to four different choice revisions. Let $I = \{1, 2, 3, 4\}$ and $c(I) = i$. The corresponding revision results are: $B \dotplus_{c_1}^{Impl} \{\alpha\} = B \dotplus_{c_4}^{Impl} \{\alpha\} = \mathrm{Cn}^{\mathcal{P}}(\neg p \wedge q)$ and $B \dotplus_{c_2}^{Impl} \{\alpha\} = B \dotplus_{c_3}^{Impl} \{\alpha\} = \mathrm{Cn}^{\mathcal{P}}(p \wedge \neg q)$. For illustration, the calculation of the equation $B_1 := B \dotplus_{c_1}^{Impl} \{\alpha\} = \mathrm{Cn}^{\mathcal{P}}(\neg p \wedge q)$ is given below.

$$
\begin{aligned}
B_1 &= \mathrm{Cn}^{\mathcal{P}}(\{p' \leftrightarrow q', \neg(p \leftrightarrow q), \overrightarrow{q}, \overrightarrow{p}\}) \\
&= \mathrm{Cn}^{\mathcal{P}}(\Theta_{\{p', q'\}}((p' \leftrightarrow q') \wedge \neg(p \leftrightarrow q) \wedge \overrightarrow{q} \wedge \overrightarrow{p})) \\
&= \mathrm{Cn}^{\mathcal{P}}((\neg(p \leftrightarrow q) \wedge q) \vee (\neg(p \leftrightarrow q) \wedge \neg q \wedge \neg p)) \\
&= \mathrm{Cn}^{\mathcal{P}}((\neg(p \leftrightarrow q) \wedge q)) = \mathrm{Cn}^{\mathcal{P}}(q \wedge \neg p)
\end{aligned}
$$

In particular, $\dotplus_{c_1}^{Impl}$ gives results different from those of $\dotplus_{c_1}, \dotplus_{c_2}$ and $\dotplus$.

The example above does not exclude the possibility that the sceptical versions of the biimplication based revision operators and the sceptical versions of the implication based revision operators are the same; it could be the case that the effects of a fine-grained conflict resolving strategy by distinct maximal sets of implications nullify each other. But again, we can show with an example that the use of implications as (enhanced) set of hypotheses has different affects on sceptical revision than the use of biimplications.

Example 2. Let be given $B = (\neg p \wedge q \wedge r \wedge \neg t) \vee (p \wedge \neg q \wedge r \wedge t)$ and $\alpha = (p \wedge \neg q \wedge r \wedge \neg t) \vee (\neg p \wedge q \wedge \neg r \wedge t)$. The maximal sets of biimplications are $EQ_1 = \{\overleftrightarrow{r}, \overleftrightarrow{t}\}$ and $EQ_2 = \{\overleftrightarrow{r}, \overleftrightarrow{p}, \overleftrightarrow{q}\}$. For neither of these sets the model corresponding to $\mathcal{I} := \neg p \wedge q \wedge \neg r \wedge t$ is implied. More concretely, using Theorem 1, one calculates: $B \dotplus \alpha = (\lceil B \rceil_1 \vee \lceil B \rceil_2) \wedge \alpha = ((p \wedge \neg q \wedge r \wedge \neg t) \vee (\neg p \wedge q \wedge r \wedge t) \vee (\neg p \wedge q \wedge r \wedge t) \vee (p \wedge \neg q \wedge r \wedge \neg t)) \wedge \alpha \equiv (p \wedge \neg q \wedge r \wedge \neg t)$. In contrast to this, there is a maximal set of implications $Impl_1$ that together with $B' \cup \{\alpha\}$

implies $\mathcal{I}$, namely $Impl_1 = \{\overleftrightarrow{t}, \overrightarrow{p}, \overleftarrow{q}, \overrightarrow{r}\}$. So one can calculate:

$$B \,\dot{+}_1^{Impl}\, \alpha = ((\neg p \wedge q \wedge \neg r \wedge \neg t) \vee (\neg p \wedge q \wedge \neg r \wedge t)) \wedge \alpha \equiv \neg p \wedge q \wedge \neg r \wedge t$$

Now, $B \,\dot{+}_1^{Impl}\, \alpha \models B \,\dot{+}^{Impl}\, \alpha$; hence $\mathcal{I} \models B \,\dot{+}^{Impl}\, \alpha$ but $\mathcal{I} \not\models B \,\dot{+}\, \alpha$.

5   A Representation Theorem

Following the usual approach in classical belief revision [1], I will characterise the non-sceptical implication based revision operators $\dot{+}_c^{Impl}$ by postulates. According to the terminology used in the belief revision literature (cf. [12]), the main theorem of this section (Theorem 4) can be described as a *representation* result: there is a set of postulates such that the class of revision operators $\dot{+}_c^{Impl}$ represents (modulo equivalence) all revision operators fulfilling that set of postulates. Using postulates is a well established methodology in belief revision for declaratively specifying the properties (or the interface) of revision operators that one wants to construct or has constructed. In addition to an implementation-independent specification of revision operators, postulates offer a logical means to compare different revision operators.

The main distinctive feature of Delgrande's and Schaub's operators $\dot{+}_c, \dot{+}$ as well as of $\dot{+}_c^{Impl}, \dot{+}^{Impl}$ is that these operate on a finite set B of formulas as left argument, but do not depend on the specific representation of B. So in contrast to belief-base revision operators they are operators on the knowledge level [16] and thus should be termed *knowledge-base revision operators* [7]. In order to adapt the postulates for belief-base revision one has to replace all references to the set B and its subsets by syntax insensitive concepts.

The key for the adaptation is the use of prime implicates entailed by the KB B. Roughly, prime implicates are the most atomic clauses implied by B. Let be given a set of propositional symbols $\mathcal{P}$ and a subset $S \subseteq \mathcal{P}$ thereof. Let $\alpha \in \text{form}(\mathcal{P})$. Let α be a non-tautological formula. The set $\text{prime}^S(\alpha)$ of prime implicates of α over S is defined in the following way.

$$\text{prime}^S(\alpha) = \{\beta \in \text{clauseCl}^S(\alpha) \mid \emptyset \not\models \beta \text{ and } \beta \text{ has no}$$
$$\text{proper subclause in } \text{clauseCl}^S(\alpha)\}$$

For tautological formulas α let $\text{prime}^S(\alpha) = \{p \vee \neg p\}$, where p is the first propositional symbol occurring in α with respect to a fixed order of $\mathcal{P}$. For example, let $\alpha = (p \vee q) \wedge (\neg q \vee r)$ and $S = \{p, q, r\}$. Then $\text{prime}^{\{p,q,r\}}(\alpha) = \{p \vee q, \neg q \vee r, p \vee r\}$. For knowledge bases let $\text{prime}^S(B) = \text{prime}^S(\bigwedge B)$.

A well known but fundamental fact is that the set of prime implicates of a KB B is equivalent to B itself: $\text{prime}(B) \equiv B$. An additional relevant fact is that if $B_1 \equiv B_2$, then $\text{prime}(B_1) = \text{prime}(B_2)$. These facts justify the perspective on the set of prime implicates as a canonical representation for the knowledge contained in the KB. Moreover, these facts are a useful means for understanding the syntax-insensitive conflict resolution strategy of knowledge-base revision operators.

A second adaptation of the belief-base postulates concerns the uniformity of the operators $+_c, +$ as well of $+_c^{Impl}, +^{Impl}$. The conflicts between B and the trigger α are handled on the level of symbols and not on the level of formulas. Therefore, in order to mirror this effect on the prime implicates one has to impose a uniformity condition. If, e.g., the hypothesis $p' \rightarrow p$ is eliminated in the conflict resolution process, then formulas of the knowledge base B, in which p occurs positively, are not preserved in the revision result. In general, if a set of implication based hypotheses Im is given, then $B' \cup Im$ preserves a subset of prime implicates of B which fulfils some closure condition concerning the polarities of symbols. These sets of prime implicates can be characterised as uniform sets according to the following definition.

Definition 4. *Let $B \subseteq \mathrm{form}(\mathcal{P})$ be a KB. A set $X \subseteq \mathrm{prime}(B)$ is called* uniform *w.r.t. to B and implications, $X \in U^{Impl}(B)$ for short, iff the following closure condition holds: If $pr \in \mathrm{prime}(B)$ is such that (a) $\mathrm{symb}(pr) \subseteq \mathrm{symb}(X)$ and (b) for all symbols p in pr there is a $pr_p \in X$ that contains p in the same polarity, then pr is contained in X, i.e., $pr \in X$.*

Example 3. Let $B = \{p \vee q, p \vee r \vee s, r \vee t, s \vee u\}$. Then $\mathrm{prime}(B) = B$. Now, among all subsets $X \subseteq \mathrm{prime}(B)$ only the set $X := \{p \vee q, r \vee t, s \vee u\}$ is not uniform as it would have to contain $p \vee r \vee s$, too. Formally, $U^{Impl}(B) = \mathrm{Pow}(\mathrm{prime}(B)) \setminus \{\{p \vee q, r \vee t, s \vee u\}\}$. ($\mathrm{Pow}(X)$ denotes the power set of X, i.e. the set of all subsets of X.)

A proper justification for Definition 4—in the sense that it really captures the intended concept—is Theorem 3 below. It shows that for all B, Im one can find a uniform set X that is equivalent to $B' \cup Im$. The set X exactly describes the collection of logical atoms (prime implicates) of the receiver's KB B that are preserved after dissociating the name spaces of the sender and receiver (step from B to B') and adding hypotheses on the semantical relatedness in Im.

Theorem 3. *Let $\mathcal{P}$ and $\mathcal{P}'$ be disjoint sets of propositional symbols. Let B be a KB and σ be a injective substitution for some subset $S = \{p_1, \ldots, p_n\} \subseteq \mathcal{P}$ such that $\sigma(S) = \{p'_1, \ldots, p'_n\} \subseteq \mathcal{P}'$ and let Im be a set of implication based hypotheses containing at most primed symbols of $\sigma(S)$. Then there is a uniform set $X \in U^{Impl}(B)$ such that: $B' \cup Im \equiv_{\mathcal{P}} X$.*

Now, we give postulates for revision operators $*$ that characterise the implication based choice revision operators. They are variants of the postulates mentioned in the section on logical preliminaries.

(R1) $B * \alpha \not\models \bot$ if $B \not\models \bot$ and $\alpha \not\models \bot$.

(R2) $B * \alpha \models \alpha$.

(R3) There is a set $H \subseteq U^{Impl}(B)$ s.t. $B * \alpha \equiv \bigwedge \bigcup H \wedge \alpha$ or $B * \alpha \equiv \bigwedge \bigcup H$.

(R4) For all $X \in U^{Impl}(B)$ either $B * \alpha \models X$ or $B * \alpha \models \neg \bigwedge X$.

(R5) For all $Y \subseteq U^{Impl}(B)$: If $\bigcup Y \cup \{\alpha\} \models \bot$ iff $\bigcup Y \cup \{\beta\} \models \bot$, then $\{X \in U^{Impl}(B) \mid B * \alpha \models X\} = \{X \in U^{Impl}(B) \mid B * \beta \models X\}$.

Postulate (R1) can be termed the postulate of weak consistency; it says that the revision result has to be consistent (satisfiable) in case both the trigger α and the KB B are consistent. The consistency postulate for AGM belief revision and belief base revision (BR1) is stronger as it demands the consistency also in the case where only α is consistent. Postulate (R2) is a weak success postulate; the revision must be successful in so far as the result has to imply α. It is weaker than the postulate (BR2) for belief bases. (R3) is an adapted version of the inclusion postulate for belief base revision (BR3), which can be rewritten as: There is a $\bar{B} \subseteq B$ such that $B * \alpha = \bar{B} \cup \{\alpha\}$ or $B * \alpha = \bar{B}$. In (R3) B is replaced by the set of uniform sets w.r.t. B, and set identity is shifted to equivalence. Postulate (R4) can be called uniform tenacity. It is a very strong postulate, which states that all uniform sets w.r.t. to B either follow from the result or are falsified. This postulate captures the maximality of the operator $+_c^{Impl}$. Postulate (R5) is an adaptation of the logical uniformity postulate for belief-base operators (BR5). It says that the revision outcomes w.r.t. to the revision operator $*$ are determined by the uniform sets implied by the revision result.

Postulates (R1)–(R5) are sufficient to represent the class of implication based choice revision operators modulo equivalence.

Theorem 4. *A revision operator $*$ fulfils the postulates (R1)–(R5) iff it can be equivalently described as $+_c^{Impl}$ for some selection function c.*

6 Related Work

The work described in this paper follows in general the belief-revision tradition as initiated by the pioneering work of AGM [1], but has main differences due to a different explanation of the inconsistencies. Moreover, classical belief-revision functions à la AGM operate on a logically closed (and hence infinite) set called *belief set* and a formula which triggers the revision of the belief set into a new belief set. In belief-base revision [10] the revised KB is allowed to be an arbitrary not necessarily closed (finite) set of sentences called *belief base*. The negative property of belief-base revision of being syntax sensitive is remedied in the case of *knowledge-base revision operators* which are exemplified by the revision operators of this paper as well as those of [6] and [5].

The revision operators of this paper are based on the elimination of hypotheses that have the role of semantic mappings [17]. The idea of using belief revision techniques to revise semantic mappings has already been worked in the literature [15], [21]. But these approaches consider the set of semantic mappings as the object of revision, while the approach of this paper considers the semantic mappings as revision aids that are deleted after the revision.

The notion of a prime implicate is used in the approaches of [20], [22], [3]. In contrast to the approach of this paper, these do not use prime implicates in the formulation of the postulates; they (only) define new belief-revision operators based on prime implicates and show that they fulfil some classical postulates.

The implication based revision operators exhibit a symbol-oriented rather than a sentence-oriented strategy for inconsistency resolution. A different symbol-oriented approach is described by Lang and Marquis [13]. Their revision operators do not use hypotheses but the well-known concept of forgetting [14].

7 Conclusion and Outlook

I have presented a new type of revision operator, which resulted as a generalisation of Delgrande's and Schaub's operators [6] by considering implications rather than biimplications as hypotheses. Similar to a result of [6], it can be shown that the operators are finitely representable and hence suitable for implementation.

But we have seen (cf. beginning of Section 4) that the generalisation from biimplications to implications adds the value of having a more fine-grained diagnosis of what exactly leads to the ambiguity. Moreover, I described postulates that integrate the uniformity property in order to characterise the implication based operators. Delgrande and Schaub [6] show which (classical) postulates their operators fulfil but do not give a representation theorem. In this paper, I could at least show that the implication based choice revision can be characterised by a set of postulates (Theorem 4). A slightly different notion of uniform set leads to a representation theorem for biimplication based choice revision.

I motivated the perspective to consider the sets of biimplications and implications as hypotheses on the semantical relatedness of symbols belonging to different name spaces. This perspective leads naturally to the question what other initial sets of hypotheses on the semantical relatedness could be used as a basis for new revision operators. In fact, one could consider bridging axioms like $p' \leftrightarrow q$, which relate symbols hypothesised to be synonyms. Using a set H of such creative hypotheses may induce operators that are quite different from classical revision operators as the former may not be conservative: $B' \cup H$ may imply formulas $\beta \in \text{form}(\mathcal{P})$ that do not already follow from B. Such creative behaviour does not occur for $H = Im_i$ or $H = EQ_i$.

There already exist approaches in the area of ontology alignment where more expressive semantic mappings are handled (e.g., [4]). We note that the framework of this paper is extendable to more expressive KR formalisms like first order logic [19] by using a more syntactical notion of prime implicate.

References

1. Alchourrón, C.E., Gärdenfors, P., Makinson, D.: On the logic of theory change: partial meet contraction and revision functions. Journal of Symbolic Logic 50, 510–530 (1985)
2. Alchourrón, C.E., Makinson, D.: Hierarchies of regulations and their logic. In: Hilpinen, R. (ed.) New Studies in Deontic Logic, pp. 125–148. D. Reidel Publishing (1981)
3. Bienvenu, M., Herzig, A., Qi, G.: Prime implicate-based belief revision operators. In: Ghallab, M., Spyropoulos, C.D., Fakotakis, N., Avouris, N.M. (eds.) ECAI, vol. 178, pp. 741–742. IOS Press (2008)

4. Bouquet, P., Giunchiglia, F., van Harmelen, F., Serafini, L., Stuckenschmidt, H.: Contextualizing ontologies. Web Semantics: Science, Services and Agents on the World Wide Web 1(4), 325–343 (2004)
5. Dalal, M.: Investigations into a theory of knowledge base revision: preliminary report. In: Proceedings of the 7th National Conference on Artificial Intelligence (AAAI 1988), pp. 475–479. AAAI Press, St. Paul (1988)
6. Delgrande, J.P., Schaub, T.: A consistency-based approach for belief change. Artificial Intelligence 151(1-2), 1–41 (2003)
7. Eschenbach, C., Özçep, Ö.L.: Ontology revision based on reinterpretation. Logic Journal of the IGPL 18(4), 579–616 (2010) (first published online August 12, 2009)
8. Gärdenfors, P.: Rules for rational changes of belief. In: Pauli, T. (ed.) Philosophical Essays Dedicated to Lennart Aquist on his Fiftieth Birthday, pp. 88–101. Philosophical Society and Department of Philosophy, Uppsala University (1982)
9. Gärdenfors, P.: Knowledge in Flux: Modeling the Dynamics of Epistemic States. The MIT Press, Bradford Books, Cambridge, MA (1988)
10. Hansson, S.O.: Belief Base Dynamics. Ph.D. thesis, Uppsala University (1991)
11. Hansson, S.O.: Reversing the Levi identity. J. of Phil. Logic 22, 637–669 (1993)
12. Hansson, S.O.: A Textbook of Belief Dynamics. Kluwer Academic Publishers (1999)
13. Lang, J., Marquis, P.: Reasoning under inconsistency: A forgetting-based approach. Artificial Intelligence 174(12-13), 799–823 (2010)
14. Lin, F., Reiter, R.: Forget it! In: Proceedings of the AAAI Fall Symposium on Relevance, pp. 154–159 (1994)
15. Meilicke, C., Stuckenschmidt, H.: Reasoning support for mapping revision. Journal of Logic and Computation (2009)
16. Newell, A.: The knowledge level. Artificial Intelligence 18, 87–127 (1982)
17. Noy, N.F.: Semantic integration: a survey of ontology-based approaches. SIGMOD Record 33(4), 65–70 (2004)
18. Özçep, O.L.: Knowledge-base revision using implications as hypotheses (extended version). Technical report, Institute for Softwaresystems (STS), Hamburg University of Technology (2012), http://www.sts.tu-harburg.de/tech-reports/papers.html or http://dl.dropbox.com/u/65078815/oezcep12KnowledgeTRExtended.pdf
19. Özçep, O.L.: Minimality postulates for semantic integration. Accepted for Publication in the Proceedings of BNC@ECAI 2012 (2012)
20. Pagnucco, M.: Knowledge Compilation for Belief Change. In: Sattar, A., Kang, B.-H. (eds.) AI 2006. LNCS (LNAI), vol. 4304, pp. 90–99. Springer, Heidelberg (2006)
21. Qi, G., Ji, Q., Haase, P.: A conflict-based operator for mapping revision. In: Grau, B.C., Horrocks, J., Motik, B., Sattler, U. (eds.) Proceedings of the 22nd International Workshop on Description Logics (DL 2009). CEUR Workshop Proceedings, vol. 477 (2009)
22. Zhuang, Z.Q., Pagnucco, M., Meyer, T.: Implementing Iterated Belief Change Via Prime Implicates. In: Orgun, M.A., Thornton, J. (eds.) AI 2007. LNCS (LNAI), vol. 4830, pp. 507–518. Springer, Heidelberg (2007)

Improving Confidence of Dual Averaging Stochastic Online Learning via Aggregation

Sangkyun Lee

Fakultät für Informatik, LS VIII
Technische Universität Dortmund
44221 Dortmund, Germany
sangkyun.lee@tu-dortmund.de

Abstract. Stochastic online learning algorithms typically exhibit slow convergence speed, but their solutions of moderate accuracy often suffice in practice. Since the outcomes of these algorithms are random variables, not only their accuracy but also their probability of achieving a certain accuracy, called confidence, is important. We show that a rather simple aggregation of outcomes from parallel dual averaging runs can provide a solution with improved confidence, and it can be controlled by the number of runs, independently of the length of learning processes.

1 Introduction

In stochastic online learning, we search for the solutions of the convex optimization problem

$$w^* \in \operatorname*{arg\,min}_{w \in \mathbb{R}^n} \quad \phi(w) := \mathcal{R}(w) + \Psi(w). \tag{1}$$

Here $\mathcal{R}(w)$ is the *risk* of a predictor $f_w : \mathcal{X} \to \mathcal{Y}$, parametrized linearly by $w \in \mathbb{R}^n$, for some input and output spaces $\mathcal{X}$ and $\mathcal{Y}$. For a convex loss function $\ell : \mathcal{Y} \times \mathcal{Y} \to \mathbb{R}_+$, we define the risk as the expected loss against an (unknown) probability distribution $\mathbb{P}(X,Y)$, that is, $\mathcal{R}(w) := \mathbb{E}[\ell(f_w(X), Y)] = \int_{\mathcal{X},\mathcal{Y}} \ell(f_w(X), Y) d\mathbb{P}(X, Y)$. Then $\mathcal{R}(w)$ is also a convex function.

The second term $\Psi(w)$ in (1) is a convex *regularizer* such that $\Psi : \mathbb{R}^n \to \mathbb{R} \cup \{-\infty, +\infty\}$, which is closed (every level set of Ψ is closed) and proper (dom $\Psi := \{w \mid \Psi(w) < +\infty\} \neq \emptyset$ and $\{w \mid \Psi(w) = -\infty\} = \emptyset$). We also assume that dom Ψ is a closed set. Regularizers promote certain structures in w^*, such as sparsity ($\Psi(w) = \|w\|_1$) or group sparsity ($\Psi(w) = \sum_{g=1}^{G} \|w_g\|_2$, w_g is a subvector of w).

1.1 Regularized Dual Averaging

We consider the regularized dual averaging (RDA) [5] for finding a solution of (1). RDA is an extension of the primal-dual averaging method [3], and works better on finding solution structures since it identifies the optimal manifold [2]. The RDA algorithm is shown in Algorithm 1.

The convergence of RDA can be described as follows.

B. Glimm and A. Krüger (Eds.): KI 2012, LNCS 7526, pp. 229–232, 2012.
© Springer-Verlag Berlin Heidelberg 2012

Algorithm 1. The RDA Algorithm.

Initialize: set $w_1 = \mathbf{0}$, $\bar{w}_1 = \mathbf{0}$, and $\bar{g}_0 = \mathbf{0}$. $\theta > 0$ is given.
for $t = 1, 2, \ldots, T$ **do**
> Sample ξ_t from Ξ and compute a subgradient $g_t \in \partial\ell(f_{w_t}(X_{\xi_t}), Y_{\xi_t})$;
> Update the dual average: $\bar{g}_t = \frac{t-1}{t}\bar{g}_{t-1} + \frac{1}{t}g_t$;
> Compute the next iterate:
>
> $$w_{t+1} = \arg\min_{w:\|w-w_t\|\leq D}\left\{\langle \bar{g}_t, w\rangle + \Psi(w) + \frac{\theta}{\sqrt{t}}\|w\|^2\right\};$$
>
> Update the primal average, $\bar{w}_{t+1} = \frac{t}{t+1}\bar{w}_{t-1} + \frac{1}{t+1}w_{t+1}$;

end

Proposition 1 (A Single RDA). *For the iterates $w_1, w_2, \ldots, w_T$ generated by the RDA algorithm with $\theta = \frac{2G}{D}$, an average of the iterates $\bar{w}_T := \frac{1}{T}\sum_{t=1}^{T} w_t$ satisfies that for a given error level $\epsilon > 0$,*

$$\mathbb{P}\left(\phi(\bar{w}_T) - \phi(w^*) \leq \epsilon\right) \geq \beta, \quad \beta = 1 - e^{-\frac{1}{8}\left(\frac{\epsilon\sqrt{T}}{DG}-1\right)^2},$$

when $T = \left\lceil \frac{(DG)^2}{\epsilon^2}\left(1 + 2\sqrt{2}\sqrt{\ln\frac{1}{1-\beta}}\right)^2 \right\rceil$, where $D := \sup_{w,w'\in\mathrm{dom}\,\Psi}\|w - w'\|$ and $G := \sup_{w\in\mathrm{dom}\,\Psi,\xi_t\in\Xi}\|g_t\|$ with $g_t \in \partial\ell(f_w(X_{\xi_t}), Y_{\xi_t})$. We call $\beta \in (0, 1)$ the confidence of achieving the error level ϵ.

Proof. Under the given conditions, Theorem 5 of [5] implies that

$$\mathbb{P}\left(\phi(\bar{w}_T) - \phi(w^*) \geq \frac{DG}{\sqrt{T}} + \frac{2\sqrt{2}DG\sqrt{\ln(1/\delta)}}{\sqrt{T}}\right) \leq \delta, \quad \forall T \geq 1, \delta \in (0, 1).$$

Replacing $\epsilon = \frac{1+2\sqrt{2}\sqrt{\ln(1/\delta)}}{\sqrt{T}}DG$ and $\delta = 1 - \beta$ leads to the claim. □

2 Aggregated Regularized Dual Averaging

We propose a simple approach based on an aggregated outcomes from *independent* runs of RDA, to obtain solutions with improved confidence.

Theorem 1 (Aggregated RDA). *Suppose that we have K independent RDA runs of the same length T, all using $\theta = 2G/D$, to obtain the iterates $w_1^k, w_2^k, \ldots, w_T^k$ and their averages $\bar{w}_T^k = \frac{1}{T}\sum_{t=1}^{T} w_t^k$ for $k = 1, 2, \ldots, K$. For an error level $\epsilon > 0$ and confidence $\beta \in (0, 1)$, the aggregated average $\bar{\bar{w}}_{T,K} = \frac{1}{K}\sum_{k=1}^{K}\bar{w}_T^k$ satisfies*

$$\mathbb{P}\left(\phi(\bar{\bar{w}}_{T,K}) - \phi(w^*) \leq \epsilon\right) \geq \beta, \quad \beta = 1 - e^{-\frac{K\epsilon^2}{8(DG)^2}},$$

when

$$T = \left\lceil \frac{4(DG)^2}{\epsilon^2} \right\rceil, \quad K = \left\lceil \frac{8(DG)^2}{\epsilon^2}\ln\left(\frac{1}{1-\beta}\right)\right\rceil.$$

Proof. Let us define the gap sequence $\delta_{T,k}$ for the iterates of each RDA run by

$$\delta_{T,k} := \max_{w:\|w-w_t^k\|\leq D} \left\{ \sum_{t=1}^{T} \left(\langle g_t^k, w_t^k - w \rangle + \Psi(w_t^k) - T\Psi(w) \right) \right\}, \quad k = 1, 2, \ldots, K,$$

where $g_t^k \in \partial \ell(f_{w_t^k}(X_{\xi_t^k}), Y_{\xi_t^k})$. If we also define $\hat{g}_t^k := \mathbb{E}[g_t^k \mid \xi_1^k, \xi_2^k, \ldots, \xi_{t-1}^k]$, which is a subgradient of $\mathcal{R}(w_t^k)$ due to [4], then together with the convexity of $\mathcal{R}(\cdot)$, we obtain

$$\delta_{T,k} \geq \sum_{t=1}^{T} \left(\langle g_t^k, w_t^k - w^* \rangle + \Psi(w_t^k) - \Psi(w^*) \right)$$

$$= \sum_{t=1}^{T} \left(\langle \hat{g}_t^k, w_t^k - w^* \rangle + \Psi(w_t^k) - \Psi(w^*) \right) - \sum_{t=1}^{T} \langle \hat{g}_t^k - g_t^k, w_t^k - w^* \rangle$$

$$\geq \sum_{t=1}^{T} \left(\mathcal{R}(w_t^k) - \mathcal{R}(w^*) + \Psi(w_t^k) - \Psi(w^*) \right) - \sum_{t=1}^{T} \langle \hat{g}_t^k - g_t^k, w_t^k - w^* \rangle$$

$$\geq T \left(\phi(\bar{w}_T^k) - \phi(w^*) \right) - \sum_{t=1}^{T} z_t^k.$$

Here we have defined $z_t^k := \langle \hat{g}_t^k - g_t^k, w^* - w_t^k \rangle$. Using the fact that $\delta_{T,k} \leq DG\sqrt{T}$ for each k [5, Corollary 2(a) and Appendix B.2], summing up the above inequality for $k = 1, 2, \ldots, K$, and using the convexity of ϕ, we get

$$\sum_{t=1}^{T} \sum_{k=1}^{K} z_t^k \geq T \sum_{k=1}^{K} \left(\phi(\bar{w}_T^k) - \phi(w^*) \right) - \sum_{k=1}^{K} \delta_{T,k} \tag{2}$$

$$\geq TK \left(\phi(\bar{\bar{w}}_{T,K}) - \phi(w^*) \right) - DGK\sqrt{T}.$$

The random variables $\bar{z}_T^k := \frac{1}{T} \sum_{t=1}^{T} z_t^k$ for $k = 1, 2, \ldots, K$ are independent by definition, and

$$|\bar{z}_T^k| \leq \frac{1}{T} \sum_{t=1}^{T} \|g_t^k - \hat{g}_t^k\| \|w^* - w_t^k\| \leq 2DG,$$

$$\mathbb{E}[\bar{z}_T^k] = \frac{1}{T} \sum_{t=1}^{T} \mathbb{E}\left[\langle \mathbb{E}[g_t^k \mid \xi_1^k, \xi_2^k, \ldots, \xi_{t-1}^k] - \hat{g}_t^k, w^* - w_t^k \rangle \right] = 0.$$

From the Hoeffding's inequality [1] on $\frac{1}{K} \sum_{k=1}^{K} \bar{z}_T^k$, we obtain for any $\eta > 0$ that

$$\mathbb{P}\left(\phi(\bar{\bar{w}}_{T,K}) - \phi(w^*) \geq \frac{DG}{\sqrt{T}} + \eta \right) \overset{(2)}{\leq} \mathbb{P}\left(\frac{1}{K} \sum_{k=1}^{K} \bar{z}_T^k \geq \eta \right) \leq e^{-\frac{K\eta^2}{2(DG)^2}},$$

Then our claim follows when we replace $\epsilon/2 := \frac{DG}{\sqrt{T}}$ and $\eta := \epsilon/2$. $\qquad\square$

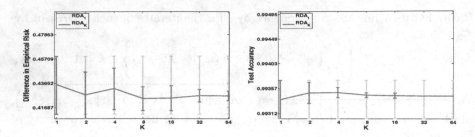

Fig. 1. (Left) Difference in empirical risk $\hat{\mathcal{R}}(\bar{\bar{w}}_{T,K}) - \hat{\mathcal{R}}(\hat{w}^*)$. (Right) Test set accuracy. Mean and standard deviation over 30 trials are shown. All axes are in logarithmic scale.

3   Experiments

We consider logistic regression with ℓ_1-regularization ($\Psi(\cdot) = 0.01\|\cdot\|_1$) on the MNIST data set (http://yann.lecun.com/exdb/mnist/), classifying the digits 6 and 7. The entire set is randomly split into a training set ($m = 12183$ examples) and a test set (1986 examples), where $n = 780$. We fix $T = 10m$ for all runs. We simulate a possibly infinite streaming data source by creating new examples adding Gaussian noise to the original m training examples.

The results are shown in Figure 1. On the left, we present the accuracy of $\bar{\bar{w}}_{T,K}$ in terms of $\hat{\mathcal{R}}(\bar{\bar{w}}_{T,K}) - \hat{\mathcal{R}}(\hat{w}^*)$, where $\hat{\mathcal{R}}(\cdot)$ is an empirical risk on the m examples. For the fixed T, the accuracy of RDA$_K$ was better than that of RDA$_1$. Rapid decrease in the deviation of solutions from RDA$_K$ supports our improving confidence argument. The plot on the right shows test prediction performance. Although our analysis does not directly extend to this type of performance measure, the plot shows that the uncertainty diminishes as K increases for RDA$_K$.

Acknowledgements. This work was supported by Deutsche Forschungsgemeinschaft (DFG) in the Collaborative Research Center SFB 876 "Providing Information by Resource-Constrained Analysis", project C1.

References

1. Hoeffding, W.: Probability inequalities for sums of bounded random variables. Journal of the American Statistical Association 58(301), 13–30 (1963)
2. Lee, S., Wright, S.: Manifold identification of dual averaging methods for regularized stochastic online learning. In: Proceedings of the 28th International Conference on Machine Learning, pp. 1121–1128 (2011)
3. Nesterov, Y.: Primal-dual subgradient methods for convex problems. Mathematical Programming 120, 221–259 (2009)
4. Rockafellar, R.T., Wets, R.J.B.: On the interchange of subdifferentiation and conditional expectation for convex functionals. Stochastics 7(3), 173–182 (1982)
5. Xiao, L.: Dual averaging methods for regularized stochastic learning and online optimization. Journal of Machine Learning Research 11, 2543–2596 (2010)

Supporting Fuzzy Metric Temporal Logic Based Situation Recognition by Mean Shift Clustering

David Münch, Eckart Michaelsen, and Michael Arens

Fraunhofer IOSB, Gutleuthausstraße 1, 76275 Ettlingen, Germany
{david.muench,eckart.michaelsen,michael.arens}@iosb.fraunhofer.de

Abstract. This contribution aims at assisting video surveillance operators with automatic understanding of situations in videos. The situations
comprise many different agents interacting in groups. To this end we extended an existing situation recognition framework based on Situation
Graph Trees and Fuzzy Metric Temporal Logic. Non-parametric mean-
shift clustering is utilized to support the logic-based inference process for
such group-based situations, namely to improve efficiency. Additionally,
the underlying knowledge base was augmented to also handle multiagent queries and the situation inference was adapted to also handle
inference for group-based situations. For evaluation the publicly available BEHAVE video dataset was used consisting of partially annotated
real video data of persons. The results show that the proposed system
is capable of correctly and efficiently understanding such group-based
situations.

Keywords: Situation Recognition, Situation Graph Trees (SGT), Fuzzy
Metric Temporal Logic (FMTL), Mean-Shift Clustering.

1 Introduction

Automatic video understanding is an important and challenging task. Frequent
queries in surveillance for security issues consider not primarily the actions of
individuals but instead situations where a couple of humans act as a group.
A knowledge-based logic understanding approach can handle such reasoning by
introducing a group concept. This will be instantiated from data containing
individuals based on predicates such as proximity. However, such concept may
cause considerable computational effort. In such situations logical systems –
in their emphasis of soundness – tend to lead to deep exponentially branching
search. Here, benign predicates such as proximity – not only in space, but also in
time or intention etc. – allow the utilization of machine learning methods to aid
the search. In this work we propose an automatic video understanding system
for assisting human operators in surveillance applications.

Situation recognition using Fuzzy Metric Temporal Logic and Situation Graph
Trees in the domain of traffic is presented by [1]; in the domain of human behavior in [3], and in the domain of video surveillance in [5]. [4] presents a way
to include a kind of Hough-transform into a knowledge-based representation.

B. Glimm and A. Krüger (Eds.): KI 2012, LNCS 7526, pp. 233–236, 2012.
© Springer-Verlag Berlin Heidelberg 2012

Fig. 1. Two snapshots from the BEHAVE video dataset [2]. The proposed SGT/FMTL framework recognizes the situations *InGroup* (yellow, thick) and concurrently *Approach* (red, thin) of a person (left). Mean-shift clustering results of frame 5370 (right).

This approach demonstrates how the combinatorial limitations of rule-based systems can be supported by prominent non-declarative methods such as clustering. The declarative aspect remains; moreover the declarative approaches become productive systems in real applications.

2   Methods

The SGT/FMTL framework was originally used within the cognitive vision system architecture described in [6]. The framework is extended in [5] to recognize multiple concurrent situations with each situation having an independent Degree of Validity. Basic knowledge is encoded in FMTL rules. On the one hand, basic knowledge is canonical knowledge such as relations like *Distance_is(agent,patient,distance)*, on the other hand these FMTL rules are concepts on a lower level with minor complexity such as *Have_distance(agent2, agent6,small)* which means that the distance of *agent2* and *agent6* is *small*. The knowledge about the expected situations in the domain of video surveillance is encoded in an SGT.

We assume a calibrated camera and a given transformation from the real observed scene to the image plane. The mean-shift clustering is performed in the provided ground plane of the observed scene. The density to be considered is the spatial and temporal proximity of persons. Figure 1 (right) depicts the mean-shift clustering result for an example image sequence where five persons are present. Two groups of two persons each are walking together and one single person is passing by one group. The applied clustering performs well without merging the single person with the group.

When there occur more agents the number of binary and n-ary relations to be examined by the inference process exponentially rises. We overcome this severe limitation and introduce list-based rules in the SGT/FMTL framework. Other languages such as Prolog support list-based computations. Motivated by its pure functionality we extended the knowledge base and inference process of FMTL by so called filters which apply predicates on a whole list, see Equation (1). Internally the *call/N* predicate is called recursively on the whole input list. In [7] the use of *call/N* is discouraged. Thus, we introduce and apply *call/3* throughout this work. In Equation (1) the proposed *Truefilter* is shown. It is implemented as FMTL rule. The □ operator is the temporal *always* operator, all the other syntax is standard logic syntax. When trying to satisfy Equation (1), Equation (2) is recursively called until end recursion terminating. The variables of *Truefilter* are defined as follows: *res* contains all elements of *in* with *Fun(agent, elem, parameter)* true.

$$\Box\{\textbf{\textit{Truefilter}}(in, Fun, agent, parameter, res) \leftarrow \qquad (1)$$
$$Truefilter\_(in, Fun, agent, parameter, res) \wedge res <> []\}$$

$$\Box\{\textbf{\textit{Truefilter}}\_([elem|in], Fun, agent, parameter, res) \leftarrow \qquad (2)$$
$$functor = ..[Fun, agent, elem, parameter]$$
$$\wedge [(call(functor) \wedge res = [elem|new] \wedge !) \vee res = new]$$
$$\wedge Truefilter\_(in, Fun, agent, parameter, new)\}$$

Thus, the introduction of list-based rules in the SGT/FMTL framework allows easily recognizing situations where more than two agents are involved. However this combinatorial explosion of satisfying instances leads to a decreasing runtime of the FMTL inference engine.

3   Evaluation

The proposed methods were evaluated on the BEHAVE video dataset [2]. Not for every frame but for some parts of the video there exists annotated ground-truth. The situations of interest are: *InGroup, Approach, WalkTogether, Meet, Split, Ignore, Chase, Fight, RunTogether, and Following*. It has to be said that *Meet* occurs only once in the ground-truth and *Ignore* twice. Thus, both situations cannot be evaluated properly.

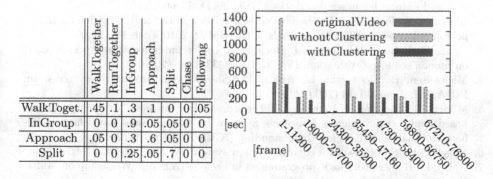

	WalkTogether	RunTogether	InGroup	Approach	Split	Chase	Following
WalkToget.	.45	.1	.3	.1	0	0	.05
InGroup	0	0	.9	.05	.05	0	0
Approach	.05	0	.3	.6	.05	0	0
Split	0	0	.25	.05	.7	0	0

Fig. 2. The confusion matrix of situation recognition applied to frames 18000 − 23700 (left). On the left the actual situation; above the recognized situation. The duration of the original video file and the runtime with and without the clustering (right).

Table 2 (left) depicts the confusion matrix of frames 18000 – 23700 of the BEHAVE video dataset. The true positive rate of the seven situations to be recognized is almost 1 when using an interval based measure as e.g. proposed in [8]. Thus, practically no situation is missed. But there do arise some false positives. The confusion matrix gives a short overview of these. In Figure 2 (right) the runtime of the presented approach without and with the mean-shift clustering from Section 2 is shown. It can be seen that applying mean-shift clustering on the whole BEHAVE video dataset reduces the runtime of the situation recognition significantly. Thus, in this case real-time processing is reached.

4 Conclusion

In this article the SGT/FMTL situation recognition framework was extended by the concept "group". Thus, situations in which groups of individuals interact can be described more naturally. In order to do so we made use of certain higher-order logic programming mechanisms processing logical queries on possibly large data bases. Thus, the declarative SGT model describing the interaction of groups of people on surveillance videos turns out to be tractable in real-time on contemporary standard hardware. For verification we used the publicly available BEHAVE video dataset as representative example.

The introduced clustering concept needs further comparative evaluation on larger datasets. As real-time performance is achieved with this improvement the next steps are the integration into a multi-camera network. We have shown that the clustering performs well on basic "group" concepts; therefore we will investigate in how far such methods can be applied on higher levels such as how the same behavior of agents leads to groups.

References

1. Arens, M., Gerber, R., Nagel, H.H.: Conceptual representations between video signals and natural language descriptions. IVC 26(1), 53–66 (2008)
2. Blunsden, S., Fisher, R.: The behave video dataset: ground truthed video for multi-person behavior classification. Annals of the BMVA 2010(4), 1–12 (2010)
3. González, J., Rowe, D., Varona, J., Roca, F.X.: Understanding dynamic scenes based on human sequence evaluation. IVC 27(10), 1433–1444 (2009)
4. Michaelsen, E., Doktorski, L., Arens, M.: Shortcuts in production-systems. In: PRIA, vol. 2, pp. 30–38 (2008)
5. Münch, D., Jüngling, K., Arens, M.: Towards a Multi-purpose Monocular Vision-based High-Level Situation Awareness System. In: International Workshop on Behaviour Analysis and Video Understanding (ICVS 2011), p. 10 (2011)
6. Nagel, H.H.: Steps toward a cognitive vision system. AI Mag. 25(2), 31–50 (2004)
7. Naish, L.: Higher-order logic programming in prolog. Tech. rep. Workshop on Multi-Paradigm Logic Programming (1996)
8. Oh, S., et al.: A large-scale benchmark dataset for event recognition in surveillance video. In: CVPR, pp. 3153–3160 (2011)

Ontology-Based Information Extraction for French Newspaper Articles

LATL, Department of linguistics
University of Geneva
Switzerland
kamel.nebhi@unige.ch

Abstract. In this paper, we describe a rule-based approach to perform
automated semantic annotation of named entities in a corpus of newspaper articles. The originality of our system is in the fact that it establishes a connection between the French named entity, the DBpedia
ontology and the DBpedia databank. We present our system, discuss its
architecture and report the first evaluation results.

Keywords: Ontology-based Information Extraction, Semantic Web,
Linked Data.

1 Introduction

The goal of the Semantic Web, as described by Tim Berners-Lee [1], is to bring
meaning to the Web, creating an environment where software agents can readily
carry out sophisticated tasks of users. Thus, the realization of this Web of data on
a large scale implies the widespread annotation of Web documents with ontology-
base knowledge markup.

In this paper, we present an Ontology-based Information Extraction (OBIE)
system for French newspaper articles using a rule-based approach. Our system
establishes relation between named entities in a text, the ontological standard-
ized semantic content of the DBpedia ontology and the DBpedia databank.

This article is structured as follows : section 2 defines Ontology-based Information Extraction; section 3 describes the proposed system architecture. In
section 4, we present the first evaluation results. We conclude and give some
perspectives in section 5.

2 OBIE

Information Extraction (IE) is a key NLP technology to introduce supplementary information and knowledge into a document. The term "Ontology-based
Information Extraction" has been conceived only a few years ago and has recently emerged as a subfield of IE. OBIE is different from traditional IE because
it finds type of extracted entity by linking it to its semantic description in the

B. Glimm and A. Krüger (Eds.): KI 2012, LNCS 7526, pp. 237–240, 2012.
© Springer-Verlag Berlin Heidelberg 2012

formal ontology. The task of OBIE has received a specific attention in the last few years [9] with many publications that describe systems. Several of these systems have not been integrated in the general schema of Semantic Web and are essentially developed for English documents. To solve this problem, we propose an OBIE system for French that uses *Linked Data* such as DBpedia databank.

3   System Description

Our OBIE system is built on GATE [3] to annotate entities in text and relate them to the DBpedia ontology[1] where appropriate. The DBpedia ontology is a shallow, cross-domain ontology, which has been manually created based on the Wikipedia projects. The ontology organizes the knowledge according to a hierarchy of 320 classes and 1650 different properties.

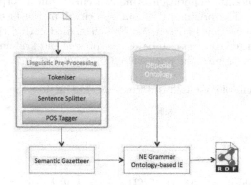

Fig. 1. Ontology-based Information Extraction Architecture

Figure 1 describes the architecture of our OBIE system. The source data is a set of newspaper articles from *LeMonde.fr*. Semantic annotation is performed by GATE with respect to the DBpedia ontology. The GATE application consists of a set of processing resources executed in a pipeline over a corpus of documents. The pipeline consists of 4 parts :

- Linguistic pre-processing
- Gazetteer (used to identify entities directly via look-up)
- Rule-based semantic annotation
- Final output creation

The linguistic pre-processing phase contains GATE components such as tokenisation and sentence splitter. It also contains specific tools like TreeTagger for French part-of-speech tagging. The gazetteer lookup phase comprises combination of default gazetteer lists from ANNIE[2] and some newly gazetteer lists

---

[1] http://wiki.dbpedia.org/Ontology

[2] GATE is distributed with an IE system called ANNIE (A Nearly-New IE system). It comprises a set of core processing like tokeniser, sentence splitter, POS tagger, Gazetteers, JAPE transducer, etc.

extract from Wikipedia and DBpedia. The grammar rules for creating semantic annotation are written in a language called JAPE [4] which is a finite state
transducer. The rules are based on pattern-matching using several informations
taken from the gazetteer or the part-of-speech tags. In total, the application
contains approximately 100 grammar rules.

For example, the rule of the Figure 2 is used to identify a city directly via look-
up in gazetteer. So the string "Liverpool" found in the text might be annotated
with the features :

```
class : http://dbpedia.org/ontology/City
inst. : http://dbpedia.org/ontology/#Liverpool
linked-data : http://dbpedia.org/data/Liverpool
```

```
Rule: CityLookup
({Lookup.minorType == city}):cityLabel
-->
:cityLabel {
    String city = stringFor(doc, cityLabelAnnots);
    String baseUri = "http://dbpedia.org/"
    newFeatures.put("class", baseUri + "ontology/City");
    newFeatures.put("inst", baseUri + "ontology/#" + city);
    newFeatures.put("linked-data", baseUri + "data/" + city)
        ;
}
```

Fig. 2. An example of a JAPE rule

4 Experience

Traditional IE systems are evaluated using Precision, Recall and F-Measure.
These measures are inadequate when dealing with ontologies. In order to take
ontological similarity into account our OBIE system was evaluated using the
Balanced Distance Metric [6]. To evaluate the performance of the system we applied the processing resources on the evaluation corpora of 40 newspaper articles

Table 1. Results

	F_1	BDM_F_1
Location	0.92	0.94
Organization	0.91	0.95
Person	0.90	0.94
Total	0.91	0.94

240   K. Nebhi

of *LeMonde.fr*. We manually annotated these documents with the concepts of the DBpedia ontology. Then, we compare the system with the gold standard. For the evaluation, we only use Person, Organization and Location named entity categories. In table 1, the system achieved a traditional F-Measure of 91% and an augmented F-Measure of 94%.

5   Conclusion - Further Work

In this paper we have presented an Ontology-based Information Extraction system for French newspaper articles. We have successfully integrated the system in the general schema of Semantic Web using *Linked Data*. As our evaluation shows, performance measured through BDM look promising.

In future work, we intend to provide deeper linguistic processing with the Fips analyzer [8]. We also try to integrate the application into a ReSTful Web service [7].

References

1. Berners-Lee, T., Fischetti, M.: Weaving the web: The original design and ultimate destiny of the World Wide Web by its Inventors. Harper, San Francisco (1999)
2. Brewster, C.: Natural Language Processing as a Foundation of the Semantic Web. Now Publishers Inc., Delft (2009)
3. Cunningham, H., et al.: Text Processing with GATE (Version 6). University of Sheffield (2011)
4. Cunningham, H., Maynard, D., Tablan, V.: JAPE: a Java Annotation Patterns Engine. Technical report, University of Sheffield (2000)
5. Handschuh, S., Staab, S.: Annotation for the Semantic Web. IOS Press, Amsterdam (2003)
6. Maynard, D., Peters, W., Li, Y.: Evaluating Evaluation Metrics for Ontology-Based Applications: Infinite Reflection. In: Proc. of 6th International Conference on Language Resources and Evaluation (LREC), Marrakech (2008)
7. Richardson, L., Ruby, S.: RESTful Web Services. O'Reilly (2007)
8. Wehrli, E.: Fips, a deep linguistic multilingual parser. In: ACL 2007 Workshop on Deep Linguistic Processing, Prague, Czech Republic (2007)
9. Wimalasuriya, D.C., Dou, D.: Ontology-Based Information Extraction: An Introduction and a Survey of Current Approaches. Journal Inf. Science (2010)

Semantic Approach to Identity in Coreference Resolution Task*

Maciej Ogrodniczuk[1] and Magdalena Zawisławska[2]

[1] Institute of Computer Science, Polish Academy of Sciences
[2] Institute of Polish Language, Warsaw University

Abstract. It has been recently discussed in linguistics that the notion of identity in the task of coreference resolution is of continuous nature, ranging from "complete" identity to non-identity. The current paper confronts this idea with experimental data for Polish, resulting in a new approach to the notion of identity. It extends the definition of coreference with speaker/recipient relation, believed to be valid for all languages, and explains the near-identity with lexical and conceptual means. The theory is supported with Polish-English examples presenting difficulties in coreference interpretation.

1 Introduction

Two recent works on the nature of identity-of-reference relation in coreference resolution by Recasens et al. [1,2] discuss the situation when "two references denote *almost* the same thing". Such need is said to arise when e.g. metonymy is used to refer to objects non-identical in strict sense, but carrying the common reference due to traditional reading (such as *the White House* denoting *the US president*). To express this phenomenon, a concept of *near-identity* is introduced in line with "complete" identity and non-identity and the typology of coreferential relations is presented with four main types (name metonymy, meronymy, class and spatio-temporal function) and 15 subtypes, based on the nature of difference between coreferent objects and degree of their similarity. This concept is further extended by referring to mental space and conceptual blending theories [3] and introducing dual operations of refocusing and neutralization.

The above-mentioned ideas are currently being tested in a *Computer-based methods for coreference resolution in Polish texts* project financed by the Polish National Science Centre and targeted at implementation of coreference resolution tools for Polish. One of its subtasks is preparation of the manually annotated corpus containing identity-of-reference direct nominal coreference (the Polish Coreference Corpus, PCC), 15% complete (wrt. target size) at the moment of paper submission. The results of this first annotation phase encourage us to dispute the concept of near-identity and redefine the notion of coreference by inclusion of the speaker in the process of signalling coreference.

* The work reported here was carried out within the *Computer-based methods for coreference resolution in Polish texts (CORE)* project financed by the Polish National Science Centre (contract number 6505/B/T02/2011/40).

B. Glimm and A. Krüger (Eds.): KI 2012, LNCS 7526, pp. 241–244, 2012.
© Springer-Verlag Berlin Heidelberg 2012

242 M. Ogrodniczuk and M. Zawisławska

2   Verification of the Typology of Identity

The first stage of the annotation resulted in an interesting observation. First
of all, the annotators were quite confident with distinguishing the "complete
identity" relation from the near-identity. The latter was selected not as rarely as
expected, making 13% of the total links (calculating the number of identity links
as identity cluster size minus one). However, a closer adjudicator examination
indicated that the quasi-identity links were mostly used to represent semantic
relations between lexical items such as mero-/holonymy (part-whole, element-
set), sometimes hyperonymy, or other relations, e.g:

(1)   PL: impreza ⟷ balanga
      EN: a party ⟷ the bash

(2)   PL: trzy córki ⟷ najmłodsza, 12-letnia
      EN: three daughters ⟷ the youngest, 12-years-old one

(3)   PL: (zniszczyć) pszczoły ⟷ barć
      EN: (to destroy) bees ⟷ a hollow in a tree where bees live

Taking into account only the "true" quasi-identical links following assumptions
resulting from the classification of Recasens et al., they appeared considerably
less frequently (3.4% of the total number of links, using the method of calculation described above). This disparity poses a fundamental question about the
character of identity, its relation to quasi-identity and the way it is perceived by
recipients of the textual message (here: the annotators). To answer it, we have
to rethink the nature of quasi-identity and probably supplement the definition
of coreference.

3   From Pragmatics to Speaker-Recipient Relation

Recasens et al. define coreference as "a scalar relation holding between two (or
more) linguistic expressions that refer to DEs [discourse entities] considered to be
at the same granularity level relevant to the linguistic and pragmatic context".

   This example definition, corresponding to the common understanding of coreference, takes into account only the recipient's point of view in the process of
decoding the textual content. The term is itself fuzzy — it is not clear whether
coreference is primarily linguistic or conceptual phenomenon. While most NLP
researchers stop at the border of discourse-world entities, the conceptual level
should be also taken into consideration: the knowledge, experience and beliefs
about the world common (or individual) to the speaker and the recipient due
to differences in environment, culture, education etc. Then come two additional
layers influencing the process: the language — the imperfect tool we describe the
world with, and pragmatics, making the message intelligible. All these means are
used by the speaker to intentionally "establish the coreference" which in turn
the recipient "decodes".

4   Does Near-Identity Really Exist?

Following this argumentation we can confront the sheer idea of near-identity as a "continuum, ranging from full identity to non-identity" ([2], p. 1139). Such vagueness of identity does not appear to be the property of objects, but a matter of interpretation, safe from blurring their identity. A popular quasi-identical example of spatio-temporal pseudo-splitting of an object into its multiple layers does not really seem to split the object at all — a person aged 3 and 40 is still the same person (as far as identity is concerned). On the contrary, sharing a set of features is not enough to make two objects identical — they are at most similar, which does not require invocation of the new term of near-identity. All relations described as such by [1] are in principle either semantic relations between expressions in the text or similarity relations between the discourse-world objects. What makes this interpretation possible is referring to the role of the speaker who triggers the impression that the recipient should perceive one object as two different entities.

5   Linguistic and Conceptual Reasons of Difficulties in Coreference Interpretation

A closer look at the experimental data shows that it is our conceptual system and language which may make the interpretation of coreference difficult for the recipient. Below we present an initial classification of situations which correspond to this problem based on experimental data from PCC and several external sources. In our opinion these cases can be explained without referring to the notion of near-identity, but appear as a result of disturbance of the interpretation of the text by the recipient (due to numerous reasons):

- violation of the linguistic system or poor stylistics:

   (4)   *PL: parówki dla dzieci, które mają dużo mięsa*
         EN: sausages for children, which contain lots of meat

- limitations of the linguistic system; for example, Polish does not use articles for signalling the (in)definite character of objects, which sometimes makes it unclear whether the text refers to "an entity" or "the particular entity",
- lexical reasons; the speaker can use different tools to indicate coreference, such as anaphora, synonymy, hyperonymy. Very often phrases can carry contradictory semantic features and at the same time stay coreferent in a particular text:

   (5)   *PL: Anna: Co to za okropne zielsko?*
         Jan: Ładna roślinka, ale Ø parzy!
         Piotr: To pokrzywa — zioło, które obniża poziom cukru we krwi.
         EN: Ann: What is this horrible weed?
         John: Nice plantlet, but it stings!
         Peter: It's a nettle — a herb which reduces blood sugar level.

- different perspectives of discussing the same object (particularly specific to dialogues):

(6)   PL: *Podobało mi się to przedstawienie — powiedział Jan. ØUśmiechnął się do Marii. — A mnie nie! Nie rozumiem, coś ty zobaczył w tym kiczu! — skrzywiła się Maria.*
    EN: *I liked the show — said John. He smiled to Mary. — And I hated it. I can't understand what you saw in this kitsch! — grimaced Mary.*

- syntactic reasons (e.g. hidden predicative usage of nominal phrases or simple ellipsis, easily mistaken for near-identity):

(7)   *Have you read "Gone with the Wind"? No, but I've seen [the film based on] it (the book).*

- differences between the speaker and recipient's conceptual systems:

(8)   *The Einstein-Rosen-bridge is a hypothetical topological feature of space-time. (...) However, there is no observational evidence for the wormhole.*

- redefinition of the object or category contrary to their real features:

(9)   PL: *ØJestem teraz bardziej doświadczony, ale Øbrakuje mi starego mnie, gdy Øbyłem bardziej spontaniczny.*
    EN: *I am now more experienced, but I miss my old self, when I was more spontaneous.*

6   Conclusions

Our annotation experiments with identity vs. quasi-identity show that the common definition of coreference should be enhanced with the speaker/recipient relation, being the factor that makes the reference resolvable. Although the theory of refocusing and neutralization can help with the most straightforward cases of quasi-identity relations (such as name metonymy or instantiation of the discourse entity in different temporal or physical locations), the conceptual background seems better explanation of the underlying phenomena of the ostensible identity change.

References

1. Recasens, M., Hovy, E., Marti, M.A.: A Typology of Near-Identity Relations for Coreference (NIDENT). In: Calzolari, N., Choukri, K., Maegaard, B., Mariani, J., Odijk, J., Piperidis, S., Rosner, M., Tapias, D. (eds.) Proceedings of the Seventh International Conference on Language Resources and Evaluation, LREC 2010, Valletta, Malta. European Language Resources Association, ELRA (2010)
2. Recasens, M., Hovy, E., Marti, M.A.: Identity, non-identity, and near-identity: Addressing the complexity of coreference. Lingua 121(6), 1138–1152 (2011)
3. Fauconnier, G., Turner, M.: The Way We Think: Conceptual Blending and the Mind's Hidden Complexities. Basic Books (2002)

Matching Points of Interest
from Different Social Networking Sites

Tatjana Scheffler[1], Rafael Schirru[1,2], and Paul Lehmann[3]

[1] DFKI GmbH, Alt-Moabit 91c, 10559 Berlin, Germany
{tatjana.scheffler,rafael.schirru}@dfki.de
[2] University of Kaiserslautern, Gottlieb-Daimler-Strasse,
67663 Kaiserslautern, Germany
[3] Brandenburg University of Applied Sciences, Magdeburger Str. 50,
14770 Brandenburg an der Havel, Germany

Abstract. Valuable user-generated information about locations (points of interest, POIs) is stored in various online social media platforms. Merging the data associated with one POI is hard because the platforms lack common identifiers. In addition, user-generated data is commonly faulty or contradictory. Here we present an approach matching POIs from Qype and Facebook Places to their counterparts in OpenStreetMap. The algorithm uses different similarity measures taking the geographic distance of POIs into account as well as the string similarity of selected metadata fields, showing good results.

Keywords: Data Integration, Social Networks, User-Generated Content, Points of Interest.

1 Introduction

In recent years, users have contributed valuable information about locations (points of interest, POIs) in community projects such as OpenStreetMap[1] (OSM) as well as in commercial social networks like Yelp or its German variant, Qype.[2] These platforms often provide different types of information for the same objects, for example ratings (Qype), check-ins (Facebook Places[3]), descriptions, categories, etc. For researchers and application developers it is often necessary to merge these distinct representations of POIs in order to obtain rich and complete information about the associated locations. Unfortunately the records representing the POIs do not share a common identifier across platforms thus making their matching a difficult task. In this paper we present an approach matching POIs from Qype and Facebook Places to their counterparts in OSM. The algorithm uses different similarity measures taking the geographic distance of POIs into account as well as the string similarity of selected metadata fields.

---

[1] http://www.openstreetmap.org/
[2] http://www.qype.com/
[3] http://www.facebook.com/facebookplaces

B. Glimm and A. Krüger (Eds.): KI 2012, LNCS 7526, pp. 245–248, 2012.
© Springer-Verlag Berlin Heidelberg 2012

2   Related Work

Elmagarmid et al. survey methods proposed in the literature tackling the issue of lexical heterogeneity, i. e., records have fields that are identically structured across databases, but different representations of the data are used to refer to the same real-word objects (e. g., *44 West Fourth Street* vs. *44 W. 4th St.*) [3]. A data integration approach used for similarity joins in data bases is presented by Cohen [1]. Dozier et al. present Concord, a generic tool for constructing record resolution systems [2]. The tool streamlines the matching task into several steps, including finding a correspondence between fields in the two data bases, defining similarity functions between the fields, and setting up a machine learner to train and use a model for distinguishing good and bad matches. To our knowledge, all of these previous approaches do not specifically deal with POI data.

3   Approach

Our approach integrating POIs from different social platforms is a three staged process. First we apply a geo filter restricting the search space to a smaller number of candidate POIs. For the POIs in the candidate list we apply string preprocessing on their titles and then conduct a two phase matching process.

We use the geographic coordinates (latitude and longitude) of the POIs to localize the search space and reduce the number of comparisons that are required to find the counterpart of a query POI in the OSM data base. For that purpose we determine a bounding box of configurable size d ($d = 0.01°$ in our experiments) around the query POI and add all POIs from OSM that lie within the borders of the bounding box to a list of matching candidates. This list is used as the basis for further processing.

In order to match POI title strings the titles are normalized by removing non-alphanumeric characters, lowercasing and filtering stop words. The string matching phase is itself divided into a two phase process. In the first phase we check whether the title of a candidate POI is within a 10% edit distance of the title of the query POI, i. e., the number of required edit operations is less or equal than 10% of the length of the title of the query POI. The edit distance between two titles of POIs s_1 and s_2 is the minimum number of required edit operations (insertion, deletion, substitution) to transform s_1 into s_2. The measure is often also referred to as Levenshtein distance (e.g., [4] p. 58). If this condition is met, the candidate POI is counted as a match.

In case that no match can be found in phase one, our approach calculates the cosine similarity between the TF-IDF weighted term vectors representing the query POI and the candidates. TF-IDF is a term weighting measure that is widely used in the field of information retrieval [5]. It assigns a higher weight to terms that are supposed to be more discriminative, i. e., terms that appear frequently in one document but rarely in the whole document corpus. In our system the titles of the matching candidates and query POI constitute the corpus for the TF-IDF measure. We represent each document as a bag of words.

The document representations are mapped to a vector space where each axis represents a term and the respective value is its weight as determined by TF-IDF. The similarity between the query document and a matching candidate is then obtained by calculating their cosine similarity (cf. [4], pp. 120-123). In order to count a match, we require a minimum cosine similarity between the vectors of two POIs of 0.5. If candidate POIs exceeding this threshold are available, the most similar candidate is selected as a match. Otherwise no match has been detected.

4   Evaluation

To evaluate our algorithm, we manually chose 50 random POIs in the area of Berlin from Facebook Places and 50 POIs from Qype respectively. Then we obtained the detailed metadata of the POIs from the platforms. From Qype only the metadata of 49 POIs could be obtained. When developing the algorithm, we split the data in training (34 instances FB Places, 33 instances Qype) and test data (16 instances). However, as the amount of data is rather small, we chose to present the results based on the complete data set for each platform. To determine the accuracy of our approach, we add the number of correct matches and the number of POIs for which it has been correctly detected that an OSM match does not exist.

We compare the results of our approach (geo filter combined with string pre-processing and a vector space model, GSV) with two baseline algorithms:

Nearest Point of Interest (NP): The first baseline is selection of the nearest POI, within a threshold radius of 0.001°. This baseline only takes the geographic location of a POI into account without considering other metadata. We calculate the Euclidean distance between the query POI and the candidate POIs from the OSM data base, disregarding the curvature of the earth. However as all POIs in

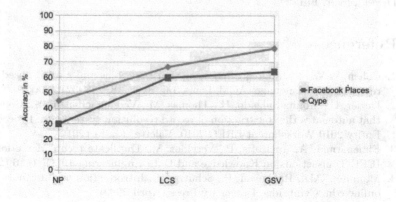

Fig. 1. Accuracy of the baseline approaches nearest POI (NP), longest common substring (LCS) and our method (GSV) for the platforms Qype and FB Places

our data base are restricted to the area of Berlin/Germany this measurement is
precise enough for our purposes.

Longest Common Substring (LCS): The second baseline selects the candidate whose title shares the longest common substring with the target POI,
independent of location. If several candidates have a LCS of equal length, we
select the one with the highest ratio of the length of the LCS to the length of
the candidate's title. Minimum ratio of candidate to target POI title is 40%.

In general it can be observed that the geographic information on its own
(method NP) does not lead to satisfactory results when integrating POIs from
different platforms. Comparing the titles of the POIs (method LCS) results in
a higher accuracy. However the best results are obtained when geo data is combined with string similarities in the matching process. Figure 1 shows the overall
accuracy of the approaches. For Qype our approach achieves an overall accuracy
of 79% compared to 45% for NP and 67% for LCS. For FB Places the accuracy
of our method is 64% against 30% for NP and 60% for LCS.

5 Conclusion and Future Work

In this paper we presented an approach matching the representations of POIs
from different platforms to obtain rich descriptions about locations. The method
combines geographic information with string similarities thus achieving a higher
accuracy in the matching process than two baseline approaches that either rely
on geographic information or string similarity respectively. In our future work we
have to consider further metadata that is often annotated for POIs. For instance,
category information is often available which can help to distinguish POIs that
lie close around a famous place (e.g., a square) and carry the name of the place.

Acknowledgements. This research has been funded by the Investitionsbank
Berlin in the project "Voice2Social", and co-financed by the European Regional
Development Fund.

References

1. Cohen, W.W.: Data integration using similarity joins and a word-based information
   representation language. ACM Trans. Inf. Syst. 18, 288–321 (2000)
2. Dozier, C., Molina-Salgado, H., Thomas, M., Veeramachaneni, S.: Concord - a tool
   that automates the construction of record resolution systems. In: Proceedings of the
   Entity 2010 Workshop at LREC 2010, Valetta, Malta (2010)
3. Elmagarmid, A., Ipeirotis, P., Verykios, V.: Duplicate record detection: A survey.
   IEEE Transactions on Knowledge and Data Engineering 19(1), 1–16 (2007)
4. Manning, C.D., Raghavan, P., Schütze, H.: Introduction to Information Retrieval,
   online edn. Cambridge University Press (April 2009)
5. Sparck Jones, K.: A statistical interpretation of term specificity and its application
   in retrieval. Journal of Documentation 28(1), 11–21 (1972)

Semi-analytic Natural Number Series Induction

Michael Siebers and Ute Schmid

Cognitive Systems Group
Faculty Information Systems and Applied Computer Science
University of Bamberg
{michael.siebers,ute.schmid}@uni-bamberg.de

Abstract. The induction of natural number series is a prototypical intelligence test task. We present a system which solves this task semi-analytically. As first step the term structure defining a given number series is guessed. Then the semi-instantiated formula is used to abduct new number series examples which can be solved more easily.

Keywords: natural number series, example abduction.

1 Introduction

In cognitive science research inductive reasoning is considered as basic mechanism for knowledge expansion by exploiting previous experience (Tenenbaum et al., 2006). Induction problems such as number series or geometric matrix series address general, analytical intelligence. That is, one can assume that persons with a high skill in such tasks will also show high performance in more complex induction problems such as identifying operator sequences in problem solving domains such as Tower of Hanoi (Schmid and Kitzelmann, 2011). To our knowledge, there are only two approaches concerned with solving number series problems: Burghardt (2005) applied anti-unification modulo equation theory to solve typical intelligence test problems; Ragni and Klein (2011) investigated how well number series of the On-Line Encyclopedia of Integer Sequences (OEIS) can be predicted with a neural network approach. Both of these approaches are not intended as cognitive models.

In the following, we will present an algorithm which tries to realize a more human-like strategy when dealing with number series problems. In this approach enumeration and search are much stronger restricted as in the previous approaches and hypothesis formation is guided by an analytical strategy. In section 3 we will evaluate our new algorithm. We will conclude with further research questions.

2 Inducing Natural Number Series Definitions

A natural number series is a sequence of natural numbers such that each element is defined algorithmically. For example, the number of days per month

B. Glimm and A. Krüger (Eds.): KI 2012, LNCS 7526, pp. 249–252, 2012.
© Springer-Verlag Berlin Heidelberg 2012

starting in January 2000 $(31, 29, 31, \dots)$, or the natural numbers starting from *two* $(2, 3, 4, \dots)$. The later series can be defined more formally as $b_0 = 2$; $b_n = b_{n-1} + 1$.

A number series may depend on an auxiliary series. The series $a : 1, 3, 6, 10, \dots$ can be defined using the series b from above as $a_0 = 1$; $a_n = a_{n-1} + b_{n-1}$.

In this paper we will focus on finding formulas for number series. Other types of regularities, e.g. numbers being prime or being sorting alphabetically, will not be covered. Every natural number series formula can be expressed by m constants $c_0, \dots, c_{m-1}$ (the initial elements), and r terms $t_0, \dots, t_{r-1}$, which are applied sequentially alternating to calculate the consecutive elements:

$$a_n = \begin{cases} c_n & \text{for } 0 \leq n < m \\ t_{(n-m) \bmod r} & \text{for } n \geq m \end{cases}$$

Here a *term* is either a *constant number*, the value of some *predecessor* a_{n-i}, the *position* number n of the current element, or some value of an *auxiliary number series* $b(n+j)$, where $0 < i \leq m$ and $j \geq -m$. Additionally terms are recursively defined: If t_1 and t_2 are terms then $(t_1 \odot t_2)$ with $\odot \in \{+, -, \times, \div, \hat{}\}$ is also a term. These are all terms.

A *term structure* is an abstract representation of a term holding only term types instead of terms, e.g., $(\langle\text{Predecessor}\rangle + \langle\text{Constant}\rangle)$, instead of $(a_{n-2} + 5)$.

Finding a formula for a given series of natural numbers $x_0, \dots, x_{s-1}$ is a search problem. Find $m, c_0, \dots, c_{m-1}, r$ and $t_0, \dots, t_{r-1}$ such that $a_n = x_n$. We propose a combination of heuristic search and analytical simplification: Given a number series tupels of $m, c_0, \dots, c_{m-1}, r$ and r *term structures* are enumerated heuristically. For each tupel instantiations for the term structures are semi-analytically searched that correctly predict the number series. The first found instantiation is returned.

2.1 Term Structure Enumeration

The enumeration heuristic can be summarized as follows: (a) Assume that no initial constants are needed ($m = 0$), increase m if necessary; (b) Begin with easy term structures, increase complexity if necessary; (c) Allow auxiliary series only if process fails otherwise.

Complexity of term structures is defined as an ordering: constants < predecessor < positions value < auxilary series. For compound terms $(t_1 \odot t_2)$ prefer structure trees with lower height. Within each height order trees according to the used operator ($+ < - < \times < \div < \hat{}$).

Since this is a first implementation we restricted the induction process to one term ($r = 1$) and used no terms with a height above 3.

Additionally to the heuristic we can make certain simplifications: (1) Terms using division hardly ever define a natural number series, so do not induce the division operator; (2) As multiplication with negative numbers is allowed, do not induce the subtraction operator; (3) Terms which could be expressed more naturally (e.g., $\langle\text{Position}\rangle + \langle\text{Position}\rangle$) are omitted as far as possible; (4) Each

Input: A number series $x_1, \ldots, x_{s-1}$

for $m \in \{0, \ldots, \lfloor \frac{s}{3} \rfloor\}$ **do**

    $\forall i \in \{0, \ldots, m-1\}\ c_i = x_i$;

    foreach *term structure ts in increasing complexity excluding aux. series* **do**

        $t \leftarrow$ induce term for ts, x, m;

        if $t \neq$ error **then**

           | **return** *Definition* with $c_0, \ldots, c_{m-1}$, t;

        end

    end

end

repeat above loop allowing auxiliary series;

Algorithm 1. Main loop of semi-analytic number series induction.

inducible regularity patterns must occure at least twice in a series, first to build a hypothesis and then to test this hypothesis. As regularities depend on the initial constants at most one third of the series should consist of constants: $m \leq \lfloor \frac{s}{3} \rfloor$.

2.2 Semi-analytical Search

A term is searched that calculates every number of the number series not already covered by the initial constants: A $\langle$Constant$\rangle$ can be instantiated iff all numbers are equal; for $\langle$Predecessor$\rangle$ all allowed predecessors from a_{n-1} to a_{n-m} are tried; a $\langle$Position$\rangle$ succeeds iff $x_n = n$; for $\langle$Aux. Series$\rangle$ the main induction is applied on the numbers to predict[1].

For $(ts_1 \odot ts_2)$ the search branches. If the search is to succeed the following equation must hold: $t_2(n) = a_n \odot^{-1} t_1(n)$. Consequently terms for ts_1 are enumerated and the desired output of t_2 is calculated. The semi-analytic search is then applied to the new calculated series and ts_2. If $\odot$ is not commutative the same is conducted again exchanging the roles of ts_1 and ts_2.

3 Evaluation

Though the OEIS contains a lot of series, most of them are to complex to be induced by human observers despite beeing tagged as *easy* (e.g. the Catalan numbers $C_n = \frac{(2n)!}{n!(n+1)!}$). Consequently, since we take a cognitive view on number series induction, we did not test our approach on the OEIS as Ragni and Klein (2011) did. Instead we compiled our own collection of number series[2]. The collection consists of 25.000 randomly created number series using addition, subtraction, division, multiplication and exponentiation. Up to 4 initial constants and 4 interleaving terms were used.

---

[1] The recursive application of the main induction is only sensible in a recursed application of the semi-analytic search.

[2] The number series collection is available for download at
www.uni-bamberg.de/kogsys/services/forschung/projects/numberseries.

We induced the number series definitions using 12 numbers and evaluated on 3 numbers. The evaluation result was considered *correct* iff all three numbers were predicted correctly.

Our system induced 93.2 % of the definitions correct. This high accuracy is surprising, as our system cannot induce definitions with interleaving terms. Nevertheless, many interleaved series were predicted correctly. For example the series $0, 7, 8, 21, 16, 35, 24, \ldots$, created by the formula $a_{2n} = 8n$; $a_{2n+1} = 14n + 7$ is correct predicted by $a_0 = 0$; $a_1 = 7$; $a_2 = 8$; $a_3 = 21$; $a_n = 2a_{n-2} - a_{n-4}$.

4   Conclusion

The first prototype of our system is already able to induce a wide range on natural number series. In a next step it will be extended to allow for induction of interleaving definitions. Although many interleaving definitions can be represented alternatively, humans usually grasp interleaved definitions more easily.

For our approach we used term structure complexity as search heuristic, and thus as difficulty measure. In the context of intelligence tests, the difficulty of number series problems is usually characterized by the percentage of subjects in a representative study which solved a given problem. However, from a perspective of cognitive oriented AI, it is of interest to analyse difficulty on the level of the complexity of mental operations involved in detecting the regularity which underlies as series. Such a cognitive analysis was up to now only presented for another classical test of inductive intelligence – the Raven Progressive Matrix Test (Lovett et al., 2010).

Furthermore, to make our approach more cognitively plausible, not only the term structure and the operator difficulty, but also the starting number of a series should be taken into account, since it is to be expected that regularities in larger numbers are harder to detect for humans than in smaller numbers. A further aspect is to identify series characteristics which trigger search for auxiliary series in human problem solvers.

References

Burghardt, J.: E-generalization using grammars. Artificial Intelligence 165, 1–35 (2005)

Lovett, A., Forbus, K., Usher, J.: A structure-mapping model of Raven's Progressive Matrices. In: Proceedings of CogSci 2010 (2010)

Ragni, M., Klein, A.: Predicting Numbers: An AI Approach to Solving Number Series. In: Bach, J., Edelkamp, S. (eds.) KI 2011. LNCS, vol. 7006, pp. 255–259. Springer, Heidelberg (2011)

Schmid, U., Kitzelmann, E.: Inductive rule learning on the knowledge level. Cognitive Systems Research 12(3), 237–248 (2011)

Tenenbaum, J., Griffiths, T., Kemp, C.: Theory-based Bayesian models of inductive learning and reasoning. Trends in Cognitive Sciences 10(7), 309–318 (2006)

The Online Encyclopedia of Integer Sequences (2012), http://oeis.org/

Dependency Parsing with Efficient Feature Extraction

Alexander Volokh and Günter Neumann

DFKI, Stuhlsatzenhausweg 3, 66123 Saarbrücken, Germany
{alexander.volokh,neumann}@dfki.de

Abstract. The fastest parsers currently can parse an average sentence in up to 2.5ms, a considerable improvement, since most of the older accuracy-oriented parsers parse only few sentences per second. It is generally accepted that the complexity of a parsing algorithm is decisive for the performance of a parser. However, we show that the most time consuming part of processing is feature extraction and therefore an algorithm which allows efficient feature extraction can outperform a less complex algorithm which does not. Our system based on quadratic Covington's parsing strategy with efficient feature extraction is able to parse an average English sentence in only 0.8ms without any parallelisation.

1   Introduction

Dependency parsers have recently become very popular and beneficial for many natural language processing (NLP) tasks, because of their ability to reliably capture useful information within a sentence. However, the quality of the result is not the only requirement. Many applications, especially those which work with huge amounts of data or applications where processing has to be done online within milliseconds, require parsing to be particularly fast in order to be eligible for use.

In the 2000s, the very popular CoNLL-X [2] shared tasks in dependency parsing brought a lot of progress to the field. However, the evaluation highly preferred accuracy and efficiency was neglected. Some of the most widely used parsers from that time, e.g. MaltParser_SVM [7], Stanford Parser [5] or MST Parser [6], have great accuracies but can only parse around 3 sentences per second. The more recent works: e.g. MaltParser_Liblinear, Ensemble [8], mate-tools [1] or ClearParser [3] have better efficiencies. MaltParser trained with linear classifiers can parse up to 1 sentence in 2.5ms, Ensemble in 10 ms, Bohnet's parser - 77ms and ClearParser - 2.29 ms.

All dependency parsers can be split into two approaches: transition-based and graph-based. Whereas the accuracies of these systems are quite similar, the numbers above clearly demonstrate that transition-based systems are more efficient (mate-tools is the only graph-based). We will restrict ourselves to the transition-based.

Transition-based systems start at some initial configuration and perform a sequence of transitions to some final configuration, such that the desired dependency graph is derived in the process. There are plenty of parsing strategies with different sets of possible transitions, which are capable of solving this task. It is usually considered that the number of configurations is the most important property for the efficiency of the algorithm. E.g. Nivre's arc-standard (AS) and arc-eager (AE) algorithms [7] require $O(n)$ transitions, whereas Covington's parsing strategy [4] requires $O(n^2)$ in the

B. Glimm and A. Krüger (Eds.): KI 2012, LNCS 7526, pp. 253–256, 2012.
© Springer-Verlag Berlin Heidelberg 2012

worst-case. Therefore there are a lot different variations of Nivre's algorithm (including all of the above parsers), whereas Covington's strategy is much less popular.

However, the number of configurations is not the only important property of an algorithm. It is rather important how long it takes to perform a transition from one configuration to another. We have used profiling technology in order to determine which parts of code amount for which percentage of execution time and found out that most of the running time is spent for extracting features (also reported by [1] for their graph-based system), which are used to predict the most probable transition. Even though less complex algorithms require feature extraction less often, we will show that feature extraction costs vary considerably across different strategies.

In this paper we show that Covington's parsing strategy is particularly suitable for efficient feature extraction. Despite the fact that its theoretical complexity is quadratic in the length of the sentence, in practice the worst-case never occurs and thus it can easily outperform linear strategies without efficient feature extraction. In our experiments we could achieve parsing speed of 0.8 ms per sentence.

2   Complexity in Theory

Given a sentence s, consisting out of words w_1 to w_n the objective of a transition-based parsing strategy is to find all dependencies (w_i, l, w_j), i.e. pairs of words w_i and w_j, which stand in a syntactic relation l. The most naive strategy to do that is to examine every possible pair of words and link them if necessary. Covington's strategy proposes an intelligent refinement to this. First, when searching for potential links for a word j it works backward. This way heads and dependents are found earlier, because they are more likely to be near than far away. Second, many pairs are discarded because they violate permissibility, i.e. well-formedness constraints of a dependency tree. Examples of such constrains are that words can have only one head, the whole structure can have only one root, there can be no cycle and if necessary that there are no crossing branches (projectivity). The worst-case complexity remains $O(n^2)$.

Nivre's AE or AS algorithms propose a further restriction of the search space. They use two stacks and allow only top elements from these stacks to be linked, which guarantees that no invalid dependency structure comes into being. Additionally, already processed words are removed from the stacks, such that they are no longer eligible for other words to come. This way the algorithms have $O(n)$ complexity.

3   Complexity in Practice

Let us consider the sentence $Economic_1$ $news_2$ had_3 $little_4$ $effect_5$ on_6 $financial_7$ $markets_{8.9}$. We have used MaltParser, which has all algorithms implemented, with option "-m testdata" in order to analyse how many transitions are necessary to parse the data. With Nivre's arc-eager strategy it took 16 transitions to parse the example sentence, for Nivre's arc-standard 17 transitions were necessary and for Covington's algorithm 33 word pairs are examined, however, 17 of them are not permissible and thus there are only 16 real configurations. By real configurations we mean those for which feature vectors actually have to be constructed and the correct transition has to be predicted. For non-permissible states it is not necessary and they therefore hardly influence the overall performance. Thus the theoretically more complex Covington's strategy in practice does not re-quire more real configurations than Nivre's linear algorithms. We have performed similar experiments for the whole CoNLL English development data and found out that for these 1337 sentences 63916 real configurations are required with Covington's algorithm, 64137 with AE and 65148 with AS.

4   Feature Extraction

In order to predict what transition should be performed in which parser state, the parser state is trans-formed into a feature vector and according to the previously learned model the best transition is selected. The algorithms presented in this paper require a similar number of feature templates in order to achieve similarly competitive performance. In MaltParser arc-standard default algorithm runs with 21 different templates, arc-eager with 22 and Covington's algorithm also uses 22 feature templates.

In his PhD [7] Nivre differentiates between static and dynamic feature templates. Static templates always return the same value for the same input, e.g POS tags of the words never change. Dynamic feature templates might change their output in course of processing, e.g. the dependency label of a word is null in the beginning and changes to some non-null value as soon as the word gets a head.

The decisive difference between the algorithms is that many other features, which actually are also static can only be reused in Covington's and not in Nivre's algorithms, where the reusability of features is limited, because one never knows what the stacks will look like and it would be too memory intensive to keep all possibilities in memory until it is clear which one of them is correct. The reusability of static features considerably improves the performance of an algorithm, since it is no longer necessary to look up the value of a feature and then its index in a global alphabet (mapping of strings to unique integers constructed during the training of the model; might contain tens of thousands of different values and thus is not so fast) so often. Instead, we consult the global mapping only once for all features which are used many times and store those in a different local (i.e. valid only within the current sentence) data structure from where they can be retrieved much faster.

Additionally, in order to compensate for the lack of a kernel, which creates conjoined features implicitly, one has to add artificial feature combinations manually. In MaltParser's feature models for Liblinear around 40% are feature combinations, which are concatenations of basic features.

String is an immutable basic type in Java, each time you append something a new String is created, the old value is stored the new value is added, and the old String is thrown away. The longer the strings the longer the concatenations take, but even for typical feature lengths of ~10 characters it takes around 0.25 µs. For 780,000 feature combinations (the amount required for 65000 configurations) it would mean around 0.2 seconds, i.e. around 20% of the whole time if one aims to parse a sentence in less than 1ms. Therefore it is even more important that feature combinations are reused whenever possible, since they contain costly string operations.

Even though String operations are expensive in Java, there are no alternatives. Tricks like translating features to integers and substituting concatenation by multiplication do not work better, since they require a mapping from the String values to ints and the look up in such large collections is even more expensive than concatenation.

5   Results and Conclusion

We have implemented a system which is based on Covington's parsing strategy and reuses static features whenever possible. We could achieve a parsing speed of 0.8 ms/sentence for an average English sentence (24.41 words). Despite the worse theoretical complexity, we have shown that in practice other properties are more important. In particular, that most of the execution time is spent on feature extraction and thus the suitability of an algorithm for efficient feature extraction is decisive.

For space reasons we could not discuss the accuracies of different algorithms and models. However, running MaltParser with default models has shown that the accuracy of Covington's algorithm for English is better than the accuracy with Nivre's algorithms. Both the default MaltParser's model and a model where the feature conjunctions are replaced by static ones have very similar accuracies.

The tests were performed on a 2.4 GHz CPU with only one core used.

Acknowledgements. The work presented here was partially supported by a research grant from the German Federal Ministry of Education and Research (BMBF) to the DFKI project Deependance (FKZ. 01IW11003).

References

1. Bohnet, B.: Top Accuracy and Fast Dependency Parsing is not a Contradiction. In: COLING 2010, Beijing, China (2010)
2. Buchholz, S., Marsi, E.: CoNLL-X shared task on multilingual dependency parsing. In: Proceedings of CONLL-X, New York, pp. 149–164 (2006)
3. Choi, J.D., Palmer, M.: Getting the Most out of Transition-based Dependency Parsing. In: ACL: HLT 2011, Portland, Oregon, USA, pp. 687–692 (2011)
4. Covington, M.A.: A Fundamental Algorithm for Dependency Parsing. In: Proceedings of the 39th Annual ACM Southeast Conference (2000)
5. Klein, D., Manning, C.D.: Accurate Unlexicalized Parsing. In: ACL 2003, pp. 423–430 (2003)
6. McDonald, R., Pereira, F., Ribarov, K., Hajič, J.: Non-Projective Dependency Parsing using Spanning Tree Algorithms. In: HLT 2005 (2005)
7. Nivre, J.: Inductive Dependency Parsing (Text, Speech and Language Technology). Springer-Verlag New York, Inc., Secaucus (2006)
8. Surdeanu, M., Manning, C.D.: Ensemble Models for Dependency Parsing: Cheap and Good? In: NAACL 2010 (2010)

Strategies for Modelling Human Behaviour for Activity Recognition with Precondition-Effect Rules

Kristina Yordanova, Frank Krüger, and Thomas Kirste

University of Rostock, Institute of Computer Science, MMIS Group, Germany
{kristina.yordanova,frank.krueger2,thomas.kirste}@uni-rostock.de
http://mmis.informatik.uni-rostock.de

Abstract. The manner in which the human behaviour and the environment are modelled greatly influences the activity recognition performance in context-aware systems and an inappropriate choice of modelling mechanism could lead to unwanted or unexpected model behaviour. In this work we present an approach for modelling human behaviour based on precondition-effect rules, and discuss in detail different modelling strategies. As a result, the paper provides useful guidelines for modelling human behaviour for activity recognition, including best practices and pitfalls that should be avoided for one to build a successful model.

Keywords: human behaviour modelling, activity recognition, causal models

1 Introduction and Background

In a world where intelligent devices and environments are becoming part of our everyday life, activity recognition plays a central role. There are two main directions to activity recognition – using training data and using prior knowledge. In the first case, a model is trained on a specific dataset and later it is able to classify new observations as belonging to a specific situation or activity. Although powerful, if it is applied to new settings or situation, the model performance usually drops significantly and is not able to correctly recognise the activity resulting in expensive collection of new sensor data. To solve this problem, the second type of approaches for activity recognition could be used. These approaches do not use training data, but rather take their knowledge from context information. This information is encoded in human behaviour models that describe the user actions, the environment, and the interactions between them [4,5]. One such approach is to define a catalogue of abstract actions that can later be parameterised with problem-specific details. Such actions are based on causal links ensuring the action execution only if a specific state of the world is true. Later, the model is mapped to a probabilistic inference machine that allows probabilistic reasoning about the current user state and her intentions. The current state is estimated based on observations, while to infer the intention, the likelihood of all possible execution paths is calculated and the one with the highest likelihood is selected [6].

This paper discusses such approach where the user actions are described as Computational Causal Behaviour Models (CCBM) [2]. The aim of the paper is not to discuss the activity recognition process, as we already presented it in previous work [6,3]. Rather, its aim is to discuss our modelling experiences and to present useful modelling strategies that greatly influence the model performance during activity recognition.

B. Glimm and A. Krüger (Eds.): KI 2012, LNCS 7526, pp. 257–261, 2012.
© Springer-Verlag Berlin Heidelberg 2012

2 Modelling Paradigm

CCBM describes user actions in terms of operators with preconditions and effects, and given an initial world state, a goal, and an observation model, they are compiled into a probabilistic model such as HMM or particle filter with which state estimation and intention inference can be done [1]. In CCBM the actions are modelled as abstract operators in extended PDDL-like notation which can later be parameterised with problem-specific values, allowing the reusability of the model for different settings. Given a set of predicates $P= \{p_1, p_2, ..., p_n\}$, states s and s', and an action $a = (V, P_{pre}, P_{eff-}, P_{eff+})$, where V is a set of parameters, $P_{pre} \subset P$ is a set of preconditions, $P_{eff-} \subset P$ is a set of negative effects, and $P_{eff+} \subset P$ is a set of positive effects, an action a can be specified as a mapping from state s to s' with $s = P_{pre}$ being the state of the world before a is executed, and $s' = (s - P_{eff-} + P_{eff+})$ being the state of the world after a takes place. Additionally, the notation provides parallel actions execution when more than one agents are specifies. Furthermore, the durations definition was extended to support probability distributions. Apart from the action definition, the notation specifies observations which link the domain specification with the observation model $p(y|x)$ needed for performing probabilistic inference.

3 Strategies for Modelling Human Behaviour

Every modelling formalism has its specific mechanisms for building a good model. CCBM for activity recognition is not an exception. Below are some mechanisms that provide good recognition performance.

Durative Actions: Our notation is able to define duration probability density functions. However, additional mechanism is needed to ensure that the effects taking place at the beginning of the action will not affect the world after the action is over. To avoid this problem, a start-end action pair can be defined. Such pair is a **macro structure** that collapsed would represent a non-durative action with preconditions, those of the *start-action*, and effects – the effects of *start-action* and *end-action*. To ensure that the parameter-specific information is carried from the begin-action to the end-action, or that no other actions take place during the macro execution, **lock flags** are used.

Effects that Influence Multiple Agents: When multiple users influence each other's actions, the modelling could become complicated. To ensure that a single user action changes the state of the world of all present agents, the clause **forall** can be used. It ensures that the effects of the action will be true for all agents. Similarly, the **when** clause ensures that only when specific state of the world holds, the effect can take place.

Multiple Agents that Influence One Action: In situations where the execution of a given action depends on multiple agents, to ensure that the preconditions for this action are satisfied by all agents, a **forall** clause could be used in the action precondition.

Parallel and Interleaving Actions: The notation allows multiple agents to execute their actions in parallel, but it is rather an agent's personal choice to execute a given action. To ensure that actions will be executed in parallel, **forall** clause can be used in the action's preconditions. Similarly, **interleaving actions** can be modelled either implicitly, by removing **lock flags** which allows for other actions to take place in between start-end action pair; or they could be modelled explicitly, by defining the action's preconditions and effects so that the preconditions are satisfied only after the start-action has taken place, and whose effects are needed for the end-action to be executed.

Repeating Behaviour, Forgetfulness and Pauses: Although there is no explicit mechanism to model **repeating behaviour**, one way of achieving it, is to introduce counter objects and a predicate that makes use of the counters and that is set to true every time an action is executed. Similarly, **forgetful behaviour** could be modelled by introducing an action that allows for one to retreat her steps and repeat the action. In a similar manner, **pauses** could be modelled by introducing an action, with preconditions satisfied by the begin part of the action to be paused, and effect satisfying the preconditions of the end part of the action.

Object Type Hierarchy: In CCBM every parameter is of the default type *object*, if no other type is assigned to it, or it could belong to one of the types or subtypes, introduced by the model designer. The usefulness of types and subtypes comes from the fact that one could define a complex type hierarchy, allowing the limitation of parameters the predicates use, and reducing the resulting state-space.

Reusable Actions: The action abstraction is useful for defining operators that could be reused in different settings, provided that they are later parameterised with the suitable problem-specific parameters. However, this abstraction also has its drawbacks – the more reusable an action is, the more grounded predicates it produces, which results is a huge state-space. Although in previous work we showed that our mechanism can still perform activity recognition with a state-space of more than 600 000 states [6], it hinders the model performance. Thus one should be extremely careful when defining abstract actions and to find the middle ground between reusability and performance.

4   Real World Example

To show the importance of using appropriate strategies, we built a new model for the 3-Person meeting scenario described in [3] and tested it on the same dataset. We estimated the state of the separate users, and their team behaviour by mapping the model to a particle filter that 49 times performed forward filtering with different random seeds on 20 3min long meeting. The runs are due to the fact that the particle filter performs an approximate inference and we want to reduce the influence a given seed could produce and to bring it nearer to exact inference. Thus, the estimated state was calculated by majority vote. The MSE for for the agent behaviour was 0.0565, and for the team behaviour – 0.0885, which stands to show that the model is able to recognise the user activities with more than 90% accuracy. The incorrectly recognised states are due to the transition states, where the filter estimated earlier or later the start and end of the activities.

5   Discussion and Conclusion

In our work we showed that by choosing appropriate modelling strategies for CCBM, our tool is able to recognise the multiagent behaviour with 94% accuracy and team one with accuracy of about 91%. Compared to our results in [3] where a simple CCBM was used to recognise the users' states from the same dataset with accuracy of 62%, the current results imply that the modelling mechanisms and strategies influence the model performance. The process of finding successful modelling strategies was one of trials and errors and led us to the following lessons learned. To build a successful model (1) one should use locks to enforce specific behaviour and limit the possible actions; (2) use preconditions with *forall* clauses to track multiagent behaviour; (3) use effects that influence multiple agents to force the agents to follow a common goal; (4) if one is able to model an action with a simple mechanism, one should not use complex structures that will make the model difficult to understand and will probably increase the state space; (5) use type hierarchy to reduce the state-space; (6) use normal durations for long lasting activities; (7) use exponential or normal durations for short activities; (8) insert actions for forgetfulness and pauses to make the model more flexible; and (9) use macros to represent durative actions especially when multiagent behaviour is estimated. On the other hand we learned some strategies that one should not use when trying to achieve good model performance. Namely, (1) do not use locks that create block states which do not lead to the goal; (2) do not use models for team behaviour to track parallel actions execution; (3) carefully use *when* clauses as they could increase the state-space exponentially; (4) do not use exponential durations for long lasting activities; and (5) carefully use too abstract actions as they increase the state space immensely.

In the future, we intend to continue our work in the field of activity recognition with Computational Causal Behaviour Models and to gather more modelling examples and experience. Furthermore, we intend to extend our work toward defining abstract action templates that could be reused in different settings without the need of the model designer to remodel them every time they are used.

Acknowledgements. This work is supported by the German Research Foundation (DFG) as part of the graduate school MuSAMA (grant no. GRK 1424/1).

References

1. Kirste, T.: Making use of intentions. Technical Report CS-01-11, Institut für Informatik, Universität Rostock, Rostock, Germany (March 2011) ISSN 944-5900
2. Kirste, T., Krüger, F.: CCBM-A tool for activity recognition using Computational Causal Behavior Models. Technical Report CS-01-12, Institut für Informatik, Universität Rostock (May 2012) ISSN 0944-5900
3. Krüger, F., Yordanova, K., Burghardt, C., Kirste, T.: Towards creating assistive software by employing human behavior models. Journal of Ambient Intelligence and Smart Environments 4(3), 209–226 (2012)
4. Wurdel, M., Burghardt, C., Forbrig, P.: Supporting ambient environments by extended task models. In: Proceedings of AMI 2007 Workshop on Model Driven Software Engineering for Ambient Intelligence Application, Darmstadt, Germany (November 2007)

5. Roy, P.C., Giroux, S., Bouchard, B., Bouzouane, A., Phua, C., Tolstikov, A., Biswas, J.: A Possibilistic Approach for Activity Recognition in Smart Homes for Cognitive Assistance to Alzheimer's Patients. In: Chen, L., Nugent, C.D., Biswas, J., Hoey, J., Khalil, I. (eds.) Activity Recognition in Pervasive Intelligent Environments. Atlantis Ambient and Pervasive Intelligence, vol. 4. Atlantis Press (April 2011)
6. Yordanova, K., Krüger, F., Kirste, T.: Context aware approach for activity recognition based on precondition-effect rules. In: Proceedings of the Workshop COMOREA at PerCom 2012, Lugano, Switzerland (March 2012)

Gated Boosting:
Efficient Classifier Boosting and Combining

Mohammad Reza Yousefi and Thomas M. Breuel

Image Understanding and Pattern Recognition Group,
Department of Computer Science, TU Kaiserslautern, Germany
{yousefi,tmb}@iupr.com

Abstract. We study boosting by using a gating mechanism, *Gated Boosting*, to perform resampling instead of the weighting mechanism used in Adaboost. In our method, gating networks determine the distribution of the samples for training a consecutive base classifier, considering the predictions of the prior base classifiers. Using gating networks prevents the training instances from being repeatedly included in different subsets used for training base classifiers, being a key goal in achieving diversity. Furthermore, these are the gating networks that determine which classifiers' output to be pooled for producing the final output. The performance of the proposed method is demonstrated and compared to Adaboost on four benchmarks from the UCI repository, and MNIST dataset.

1 Introduction

AdaBoost is one of the most popular combining methods among those that adaptively change the training set distribution [2]. Initially, AdaBoost generates a base classifier from a uniform distribution of training samples. According to the first classifier error, a new distribution over the training set is calculated, such that the weights of the misclassified samples are increased, and the weights of those correctly classified are decreased. Consecutive classifiers are trained with new distributions formed in a similar way, and therefore they are more focused on the difficult samples that were misclassified by their previous classifiers. The final output for a given input sample is determined by weighted averaging of the base classifiers' outputs.

In this paper, we propose a novel method for boosting base classifiers by an efficient resampling step, as well as a simple, yet effective, way of combining the base classifiers' outputs. In our proposed method, called *Gated Boosting*, a sequence of base classifiers, similar to AdaBoost, are trained with different distributions of the training set; however, the training set distribution for each base classifier, is determined by *gating networks* which are trained to point out to parts of the input space that the previous base classifiers made errors in. The gating networks also determine which of the base classifiers can contribute to form the ensemble output for a given input sample. Our proposed method is distinguished from the previously mentioned boosting methods, by introducing the novel resampling and combining method carried out by the gating networks.

B. Glimm and A. Krüger (Eds.): KI 2012, LNCS 7526, pp. 262–265, 2012.
© Springer-Verlag Berlin Heidelberg 2012

2 Gated Boosting

Given an integer L as the number of base classifiers, Gated Boosting trains L base classifiers (C_l) along with L corresponding gating networks (M_l). For training a base classifier C_l, the training set S_l is generated from $\mathcal{T}$ according to the weights of each training sample that is being updated by the gating network M_{l-1}. A gating network updates a training sample's weights based on its distance to the prototype of the correct and incorrect classifications of its corresponding base classifier.

The prototype estimation, performed by the gating networks, is done similar to the *local mean-based* method introduced in [4]. Succinctly stated, the gating network M_l, for each training sample, calculates the distance to the prototype of the K-nearest neighbours in *each* of the two classes of correct and incorrect classifications of the base classifier C_l. And if the distance of the ith sample to the prototype of correct classifications of C_l, $d_c^l(i)$, is smaller than its distance to the prototype of its incorrect classifications, $d_w^l(i)$, its weight remains unchanged, whereas if $d_w^l(i)$ is smaller than $d_c^l(i)$, relative to the value of $d_w^l(i)$, the sample's weight $(W_l(i))$ is increased (the samples' weights are normalized using a normalizing constant, Q_l, to ensure that $W_l(i)$ represents a true distribution).

Gated boosting algorithm is described in Algorithm 1 in more detail. In forming $C^*(\mathbf{x})$, the gating network's output, $M_l(\mathbf{x})$ is either 0 or 1, in correspondence to the cases where a base classifier's output is stopped or allowed for being considered in the final output, respectively. Ultimately, the average votes of those classifiers that are *gated* through, produce the final ensemble output.

Algorithm 1. The Gated Boosting Algorithm

---

   input : Training set $\mathcal{T}$, classifier C, integer L
   output: Classifier C^*

1 For the n training samples in $\mathcal{T}$, initialize $W_1(i) = 0, i = 1, \ldots, n$;
2 Initialize by training C_1 on $\mathcal{T}$, and form gating M_1;
3 **for** $l \leftarrow 2$ **to** L **do**

4     $W_l(i) \leftarrow \dfrac{W_{l-1}(i) + \begin{cases} 0 & \text{if } M_{l-1}(i) = 1 \text{ (when } d_c^{l-1}(i) < d_w^{l-1}(i)) \\ d_w^{l-1}(i) & \text{if } M_{l-1}(i) = 0 \text{ (when } d_c^{l-1}(i) \geq d_w^{l-1}(i)) \end{cases}}{Q_l}$;

5   train classifier C_l using S_l, sampled from $\mathcal{T}$ according to $W_l(i)$, and form gating M_l;

6 **end**
7 **return** $C^*(\mathbf{x}) = \dfrac{\sum_{l=1}^{L} M_l(\mathbf{x}) \times C_l(\mathbf{x})}{\sum_{l=1}^{L} M_l(\mathbf{x})}$;

In order to classify a sample x, the following steps are performed:

- $d_c^l(x)$ and $d_w^l(x)$ are obtained by each gating network l

- $M_l(x) = \begin{cases} 1 \text{ if } d_c^l(x) < d_w^l(x) \\ 0 \text{ if } d_c^l(x) \geq d_w^l(x) \end{cases}$

- Return $C^*(x)$ as the classification, according to step 7 in Algorithm 1.

The main advantage of Gated Boosting lies in its robust resampling scheme. Using the distance-based weighting scheme, not only the misclassified samples, but also a set of neighbouring samples which are prone to be misclassified by the previous base classifies, are resampled as the training set for a consecutive base classifier. Furthermore, gating networks provide information on whether their corresponding base classifiers can perform a correct classification on a given input, or not. This information can be effectively utilized for producing the final output by combining the output of base classifiers, which justifies the operation in forming $C^*(\mathbf{x})$.

3   Experiments and Results

We conducted a set of experiments on four benchmarks (Satimage, Parkinson Telemonitoring, Statlog, and Letter) from the UCI repository[1] and MNIST [2] dataset, in order to compare the performance of Gated Boosting with Adaboost in classification tasks.

Table 1. Test error rates of Gated Boosting and AdaBoost algorithms on different datasets. The base MLP parameters are represented as $n@m$, in which n and m refer to the number of hidden nodes and iterations for each network, respectively.

Dataset	Method	# Base MLPs	Base MLP Parameters	Gating Parameters	Error Rate (%)
MNIST	Gated Boosting	10	18@40	$K = 5$	2.81
	AdaBoost	10	18@40	−	3.29
Letter	Gated Boosting	10	20@60	$K = 5$	6.33
	AdaBoost	10	20@60	−	9.96
Satimage	Gated Boosting	10	35@50	$K = 5$	16.94
	AdaBoost	10	35@50	−	24.66
Parkinson	Gated Boosting	20	70@85	$K = 2$	48.41
	AdaBoost	20	70@85	−	72.33
Statlog	Gated Boosting	10	50@70	$K = 2$	7.22
	AdaBoost	10	50@70	−	11.24

In our experiments, the base classifiers in both boosting methods are Multi-layer Perceptron (MLP) neural networks [3]. In our implementations, we used boosting by resampling [6]. The distance calculations in the gating networks are performed using the fast approximate nearest neighbour library [5]. Choice of the value K (the number of neighbours the gating networks used for prototype estimation) depends on the dataset; however, choosing an excessively large value

---

[1] UC Irvine Machine Learning Repository. http://archive.ics.uci.edu/ml

[2] The MNIST Databse of Handwritten Digits. http://yann.lecun.com/exdb/mnist

for K slightly deteriorates the performance. In our experiments, $K = 2$, for smaller datasets like Statlog and Parkinson, and $K = 5$ for larger ones like MNIST, turned out to yield the lowest classification error.

As shown in Table 1 Gated Boosting, overall, gave better results that outperformed AdaBoost by reducing the error rate between 36.45%, for the Letter dataset, to 14.59% for the MNIST dataset. The error rates are the average of 20 times running each algorithm. Each MLP base classifier in this experiment is the one with the smallest training error picked out of five times running with different initial weights.

4   Conclusion

This paper has described a boosting algorithm that provides improved classification performance, compared to the similar Adaboost method, by taking advantage of gating networks, which effectively update the distribution of each base classifier training instances based on the predictions of all the prior base classifiers. Furthermore, gating networks provide a more reliable way of combining the outputs of the base classifiers, by knowing which base classifier(s) are good at classifying a given instance.

Observing the behaviour of Adaboost and Gated Boosting in the resampling phase, in case of a simple binary classification task (not shown here for brevity) can provide insights on the advantages of a gating mechanism in the *adaptive* boosting process, which is probably the more effective step in forming robust boosting classifiers [1]. The proposed method was demonstrated on a set of benchmarks from UCI repository and the MNIST dataset, showing the superior performance of Gated Boosting to AdaBoost.

Future work includes extending the algorithm towards a more scalable and parallelizable method. Also, comprehensive experiments and comparisons with different variants of Adaboost can be performed on a variety of small- and large-scale datasets to examine the pros and cons of each boosting method in different contexts.

References

1. Breiman, L.: Bias, variance, and arcing classifiers. Tech. Rep. 2 (1996)
2. Freund, Y., Schapire, R.E.: A Decision-Theoretic Generalization of On-Line Learning and an Application to Boosting. Journal of Computer and System Sciences 55(1), 119–139 (1997)
3. Haykin, S.: Neural networks: a comprehensive foundation. Prentice Hall (1999)
4. Mitani, Y., Hamamoto, Y.: A local mean-based nonparametric classifier. Pattern Recognition Letters 27(10), 1151–1159 (2006)
5. Muja, M., Lowe, D.G.: Fast approximate nearest neighbors with automatic algorithm configuration. In: International Conference on Computer Vision Theory and Application, VISSAPP 2009, pp. 331–340. INSTICC Press (2009)
6. Seiffert, C., Khoshgoftaar, T.M., Hulse, J.V., Napolitano, A.: Resampling or Reweighting: A Comparison of Boosting Implementations. In: 2008 20th IEEE International Conference on Tools with Artificial Intelligence, pp. 445–451 (2008)

Author Index